from front flap)

. white r~   ⌐atives, whos⌐
were ·   ⌐firmed by
⊃.

COMMISSION POLITICS

COMMISSION POLITICS

THE PROCESSING
OF RACIAL CRISIS
IN AMERICA

Michael Lipsky
and David J. Olson

Transaction Books

New Brunswick, New Jersey

Library of Congress Catalog Number: 74-20192.

ISBN: 0-87855-078-X (cloth).

Printed in the United States of America.

HV.
6477
.L56
1977

Library of Congress Cataloguing in Publication Data.

Lipsky, Michael.
    Commission politics.

    Includes index.
    1. Riots—United States.   2. Governmental
investigations—United States.   I. Olson, David J.,
joint author.   II. Title.
HV6477.L56   364.1'43   74-20192
ISBN 0-87855-078-X

For

Hannah and Eleazar Lipsky

and

Alice and Lloyd Olson

Contents

Preface

What we need to question is whether systems can be shown to have devised typical ways for aborting. . .possible stress before it arises or alleviating its consequences if it seems imminent.

> David Easton
> *A Framework for Political Analysis*

Perceptions of phenomena by those who act are a critical facet of the transaction to be explained.

> Murray Edelman
> *Politics as Symbolic Action*

I read that report. . .of the 1919 riot in Chicago, and it is as if I were reading the report of the investigating committee on the Harlem riot of '35, the report of the investigating committee on the Harlem riot of '43, the report of the McCone Commission on the Watts riot.

I must again in candor say to you members of this Commission—it is a kind of Alice in Wonderland—with the same moving picture reshown over and over again, the same analysis, the same recommendations, and the same inaction.

> Kenneth B. Clark,
> in testimony before the National Advisory Commission on Civil Disorders, quoted by the Commission in its *Report*

We began work on this book in the summer of 1967, when the fate of the nation seemed to wait upon the resolution of racial crisis. The drumroll had started in 1964 with uprisings in New York City, Philadelphia, and Rochester, New York. It had escalated in 1965 with the Watts rebellion in Los Angeles, and had built on riots in Chicago, San Francisco, Dayton, and Cleveland during the next summer. In the summer of 1967, substantial numbers of people in over 150 cities, including almost all the great cities of the country, rioted and rebelled.

The riots meant mayhem. People were killed by the scores, injured by the hundreds, and arrested by the thousands. Looting prevailed in the land of opportunity. Curfews and police cordons suspended normal civic life. The military patrolled the streets of major cities. Fires destroyed block after block of housing. Stores were smashed by both the forces of disorder and the guardians of order. Daily intercourse in the ghettos of America was suspended as participants and observers alike adjusted to the wasting of neighborhoods and uneasily anticipated future actions and possible reprisals. Some families mourned the death of children; others mourned their early maturation to a world of violence and politics. The residual anger of black Americans had found a medium.

The riots permeated the lives of Americans living outside the ghetto as well. White Americans watched the smoke rise over their cities, listened to far-off sirens wail, turned to their television sets to gain a measure of information and some sense of the direction of events. They were not easily reassured. They worried about the extension of the riots to white neighborhoods and downtown business districts. They listened to white politicians desperately trying to steer a path of leadership both stern yet at the same time suggesting the possibility of reconciliation. They listened to others who would brook no possibility of sympathy while lawlessness reigned. They listened to black spokesmen trying to explain the roots of civil disorder to a skeptical and frightened audience.

Easily alarmed by rumors and fantasy that amplified the terrifying reality even further, they went out and bought ammunition and sidearms in unprecedented amounts and numbers. They went to church. They stayed indoors and waited to understand.

The summer of 1967 represented to many observers the greatest internal crisis experienced by the United States since the Civil War. While earlier riots could be dismissed as the pathology of individual cities, virtually no one in the summer of 1967 underplayed their significance for the society as a whole or disagreed with the view that a crisis of profound importance was at hand. They might disagree over whether the situation called for suppression or amelioration, intervention by the Army and police or by social welfare agencies. But they did not disagree over the portentousness of the riots.

By the early 1970s, when we completed research for this book, concern for race relations and the welfare of blacks in American cities had largely evaporated. Certainly such concern no longer occupied a place of high priority on the national political agenda. Today it is rather common to question what happened to the violence and protest politics of the 1960s, characterized by street confrontations, protest demonstrations, and major episodes of group violence.

One answer often provided is that the race and urban crises have been replaced by successive crises focused on Vietnam, ecology, inflation, official corruption, and energy scarcity. This argument is enhanced by a study of race relations throughout this century, revealing the fluctuating cycle of concern for racial issues, with peak interest concentrated in years when racial violence has created attention for an otherwise neglected subject. The succession of crisis upon crisis without doubt diverted attention away from race and urban questions and reduced their positions of priority on political agendas.

Another view of the diminished interest in black welfare is that it was entirely predictable that the plight of a distinct minority would not long preoccupy the majority. This perspective focuses on the long-standing neglect and suppression of black demands, and disinterest in the needs of blacks so long as civil order prevails.

Neither of these views are adequate, however. The United States is a country in certain respects ideologically pledged and committed in law to liberty, equality, and domestic tranquility, if not fraternity. Moreover, these concerns are shared by some relatively powerful people and groups, and they regularly find expression in political debate. It is too simplistic to understand the drift away from civil rights and black welfare as automatic and inevitable, although it may often seem to be so. Studied disinterest and suppression at least are outcomes that need to be explained.

In the decade following the riots of 1967 we have observed an elaborate *processing of racial crisis*. This process has (with some differences) operated consistently in the past. And (again with differences) it may be expected to operate in the future if and when a high degree of political mobilization around racial issues again occurs.

Our study attempts to account for the structural arrangements and political processes that develop in the management of racial crisis. We identify the political and institutional resources, and the strategies and tactics employed by political elites in transforming racial crisis into politics-as-usual. We focus on those features of American politics that apparently tend to minimize the potential impact of severe conflict and reinforce the status quo so successfully in the short run.

This outcome of riots stands in stark contrast to the forecasts of commentators who incorrectly expected the riots to signal at long last a significant change in relations between the races, and the relationship of blacks to the state. Yet it was entirely the outcome desired and explicitly sought by political leaders. This was the case both with the Johnson administration, confronted with the immediate problem of responding to the riots, and the Nixon administration, which inherited the management of the long-term implications and effects of the riots. In an essay reviewing domestic policy in the Nixon administration, Daniel P. Moynihan acknowledged that the riots confronted the government "with a perceived crisis of serious proportions" in response to which policymakers designed measures to "bring to a close a particular period of disorder: nothing more."* Moynihan celebrated the capacity of government to reduce the level of violence. In doing so he supports one of our primary general propositions: that racial conflict can be and is managed by governmental intervention and elite actions are primarily aimed at reducing the levels and the persistence of racial violence. Coping with the urban and race crises by ending the violence that gave them visibility is only one standard for proclaiming an achievement worthy of celebration, and a rather narrow and managerial-based one at that. Our study inquires beyond the reduction in levels of violence to consider the terms on which the levels of conflict were reduced, the processes elites employed in that task, and the implications of these outcomes for future conflict.

When we undertook this study our primary concern was to inquire into the relatively direct political impact of the riots. We sought to chart and then understand the character, direction, and intensity of the political system's responses. We designed research to investigate the ways in which elites at the national and local level responded to the riots, both in words and in deeds. In this we were motivated by the observation, a starting point for us but elusive to many, that political

*Daniel P. Moynihan, *Coping: On the Practice of Government* (New York: Random House, 1973), p. 49.

events are interactive, that to understand the meaning of political actions one must inquire simultaneously into the ways in which they are perceived and responded to. In particular we sought to answer a question of wide interest during and immediately after the riots: were the riots political? (Or, as some would have it, were they mere nonpolitical, pathological episodes or criminal sprees?) Our discussion of this issue is reported in chapter 1.

We surveyed responses to riots in the past in order to see the current period in historical perspective. In this research we found that *the appointment of riot commissions*, or their near equivalents, has been *the typical political response to racial disorders in this century*. Support for this proposition is provided in chapter 2, with attention to the common features of past riot commissions. Chapter 3 provides a general discussion of the nature of riot commissions and the political functions they serve.

The next seven chapters (chapters 4 through 10) examine the political, organizational behavior of riot commissions, to which the public looked for answers to questions concerning riots; and the development of public policy in response to riot events. Part 2 treats these matters at the national level, where the National Commission on Civil Disorder (Kerner Commission) dominated public affairs. Part 3 develops these matters at the municipal level, focusing on Newark, Detroit, and Milwaukee, the three cities experiencing the most severe disorders in 1967. In a final chapter we analyze the liberal suppression of minority demands and discuss the implications of the processing of racial crisis for American politics.

Research for this study was conducted during periods of high political tension and controversy, and initially we experienced corresponding difficulties in obtaining access to information. We are thus particularly indebted to the dozens of thoughtful people working with the Kerner Commission; the (New Jersey) Governor's Commission on Civil Disorder; the New Detroit Committee; the (Detroit) Mayor's Development Team; and the Office of Mayor in Milwaukee whose assistance and cooperation under difficult circumstances made this study possible. We deeply appreciate the support and advice of Kenneth M. Dolbeare, Murray Edelman, Margaret Levi, Duane Lockard, Paul E. Peterson, and Thomas Wolanin, who provided thoughtful comments on the manuscript, and of Walter Dean Burnham, Robert Fogelson, Allen D. Grimshaw, Ira Katznelson, Bernard Klien, and Martin Rein, who gave helpful and timely comments on individual chapters. The several revisions of this book were aided by the invaluable research assistance of Robert Goehlert, Wanda Ellert, and Richard Rich, and the tolerance of Marion Lovelace and Marianne Platt, who assisted in preparing the manuscript.

Particular appreciation is due Irving Louis Horowitz, who first provided encouragement for this project, and has since provided useful criticism and sustained interest in and support for our work. In various phases of our research we have received financial support from *Transaction* magazine (now *Society*), the Institute for Research on Poverty of the University of Wisconsin, the Massachusetts Institute of Technology-Harvard Joint Center for Urban Studies, and the Brookings Institution.

COMMISSION POLITICS

I
AMERICAN RIOTS AND RIOT COMMISSIONS: AN INTRODUCTION

1

The Question of Civil Disorder: An Introduction

Race-related violence has been a persistent theme in American society. Equally persistent has been the recurring process of minimizing the political origins and implications of mass racial violence. The process begins with attempts to discredit the political demands of subordinate minorities. It continues with the development of mediating institutions to "process" remaining demands. It ends with the failure to implement officially approved responses to the crisis events.

This book is about the process of reducing the political significance of racial crisis in America. We attempt to show how an unsettling and threatening racial crisis is converted into "politics as usual," where "normal" patterns of influence supportive of the status quo prevail. We focus on the official responses to race riots which have been typical throughout American history, the appointment (and subsequent action) of riot commissions or their equivalents, and the post-riot impact of these commissions' policies. We do not claim that riot commissions are the only official or elite response to racial violence. But we do argue that an understanding of riot commission politics is critical to understanding the nature and degree of response to black political demands in this century.

Central to the analysis of civil disorders[1] in the 1960s is the question: to what extent were the riots "political?" Should the riots be viewed as expressive of political demands and indicative of black community attitudes? Did they represent an attempt to contribute to a political process by which black goals could be secured? Or were the riots, aside from their obvious threat to domestic order, essentially apolitical?

In one sense these questions are fatuous. It can be easily demonstrated that the state forcefully intervened to stop the riots; that political leaders styled their public images around fears generated by riots; that legislatures passed laws seeking to control riotous behavior; that politicians responded to the disorders with rhetoric and proclamations of varying content. In short, like oil spills, mining accidents and natural disasters, civil disorders engaged political institutions and evoked responses from them. In this respect, any event that has more than minimal impact on society is politically significant.

In another sense, however, the questions are more complicated and their implications more significant. Public officials in whose jurisdictions riots occurred said again and again that the riots were meaningless acts engaged in by unrepresentative members of the community. They repeatedly proclaimed that riotous behavior would not be tolerated or rewarded. If the riots were, as many officials argued, meaningless outbursts against the law, conducted in a carnival spirit and unrelated to black community interests, then once they had been suppressed, public officials could, in effect, ignore them.

However, from a contrary perspective, the riots cannot be so easily dismissed. If in some sense they were rebellions against ghetto conditions and were engaged in or supported by a substantial portion of the black community, then they demand serious consideration for reasons of social justice and domestic tranquility.

We may therefore put the question somewhat differently: Were the disorders explicit and implicit demands for changes in the ways values are allocated in society?[2] Or were they unrelated to the distribution of power and resources? Answers to these questions are fundamental to understanding the content and structure of recent civil disorders and their meaning for the American political process.

How can we assess the political content and meaning of recent civil disorders, particularly in light of the controversy suggested above? As usually posed, the issue cannot be resolved, except superficially, because conventional approaches fail to consider the *entire* political process in which civil disorders occur and are transformed. The way society interprets the events is as much a problem as determining rioters' motivations. Perhaps the American *response* to riots minimizes their political content. Like the tree falling unheard in the forest (to use a familiar metaphor), the political meaning of events may depend as much on the reception as on the generation of demands. Having reviewed the evidence concerning the political characteristics of riots, Robert Fogelson agrees with this approach. "The blacks delivered a protest," he concludes, "but most whites did not receive it."[3]

"Demands" in a political system need not be neatly packaged and labeled. They may be concisely or diffusely articulated, addressed to specific or general audiences. David Easton defines demands as "articulated statements, directed toward the authorities, proposing that some kind of authoritative allocation ought to be undertaken." But he also observes that people "may be quite unaccustomed to imposing such demands, except perhaps in times of great crises."[4] Writing about the functions and structures of political systems, Gabriel Almond notes that "anomic interest groups" play important roles in the articulation of interests. "By anomic interest groups we mean more or less spontaneous breakthroughs into the political system from the society, such as riots and demonstrations." Almond gives the following example of the process by which diffuse statements and attitudes can become demands:

> The murmurs and complaints in the bazaar in Baghdad are not in the political system until they break out, for example, in an act of violence—an anomic act of interest articulation—or when Haroun-el-Rashid, disguised as a water bearer, overhears the murmurs and translates them into political claims. As the diffuse and inarticulate murmur is translated into a claim on the use of "public authority," it passes the boundary and enters the political system as an act of "interest articulation."[5]

Not only are demands sometimes diffuse and poorly articulated, as in this example, but the *channels* of communication are also important. Easton makes this point when he observes: "To reach their destination—in this case the authorities—messages must be able to flow along channels, whether they be by word of mouth, through mass media, correspondence, or the like."[6] We go somewhat further, in this volume, by suggesting that the notion of demands is inextricably linked to that of channels—no channels, no demands.

Equally important is how demands are received. In Almond's example, diffuse murmurs are most likely to become claims on public authority when public officials become interested in what the peasants are saying, or otherwise develop a concern for the political content of mass opinion. So, too, when the bells of racial violence toll, public officials may send for information of a political or nonpolitical nature.

Recent riots in the United States have threatened widely shared social values of order, security and property, and have been engaged in by members of groups with long-standing grievances. In response, public officials have tried to reduce the likelihood that rioting will recur and the perception of threat generated by riots. The effort to achieve these ends has taken three forms: (1) increasing the costs of rioting to participants beyond tolerable limits; (2) reducing the extent to which mass publics perceive riots as related to real grievances and to strategies designed to achieve redress; and (3) reducing blacks' sense of grievance over inequities or the processes by which inequities are maintained.

The first method involves suppressing rioters, guarding against future recurrence of rioting and maintaining an official posture that indicates riotous behavior will be neither condoned nor rewarded. Some aspects of this approach have clearly been evident in the reactions of American elites to civil disorders. Since the race riots of 1917, as discussed in the next chapter, the highest public officials have indicated that riots would not be rewarded and persistent riotous behavior would not be tolerated.[7]

However, continuous surveillance and repression of aggrieved groups involves great costs to the entire society. It implies a denial of civil liberties to some citizens, indiscriminate treatment of members of an aggrieved group, considerable expense and a reduction in liberty for society as a whole. Furthermore, there is no guarantee it would be effective. For these and other reasons, this course has generally been rejected in recent years.[8]

Official reactions to recent civil disorders have been characterized by the initiation of processes related to the second and third types of response. Public officials consistently maintained that racial violence was of no political significance and that only a small and unrepresentative fraction of the community engaged in riots.[9] Further, while they have rarely acknowledged the legitimacy of rioters' grievances, almost without exception public officials have responded to civil disorders by appointing a commission or somewhat similar body (task force, review team, study group) to explain the episodes, study the issues and make recommendations for future official action.[10]

These bodies have had license to confer legitimacy on the complaints of rioters and to make authoritative recommendations for ameliorating the conditions associated with grievances. Thus rioters have been rewarded in the limited sense that the events they precipitated have been submitted to study, with at least the possibility that favorable findings and recommendations will be made and adopted as policy.

We do not emphasize riot commissions because they represent the only way elites have responded to civil disorders, but because they are the typical official response. Indeed, virtually every significant racial disorder in this century has been quickly followed by the appointment of a commission or study group to investigate the incident.[11]

Most recent riot commissions have condemned violence as a political tactic and those who condone its use. Yet they have also concluded that blacks have legitimate grievances; that riots were approved by a wide segment of the black community; and that major changes in public policy are called for, involving some alteration of priorities and redistribution of resources. This creates something of a paradox. If riots can plausibly be considered expressive of political demands and if public bodies are created which often legitimate those demands and are generally sympathetic to black claims,[12] how do we account for the prevalent view that recent riots were not political and the continued failure of the political system to act positively on those demands? As suggested earlier, the answer may lie in the structure of responses to riots rather than in the content or intentions of the rioters themselves.

Allan Silver has compared the traditional response to mob action in Western society—typified by mobs in preindustrial, eighteenth-century Europe—to that in the United States. He argues that American society has never viewed mob action as expressive of political demands. Whereas European elites understood that the preindustrial mobs rioted for redress of grievances, and with rioters "jointly define[d] the meaning of riotous acts,"[13] in the United States the tendency to understand riots in this way is rare or nonexistent. In the United States and elsewhere, expectations of public order have generally increased and police forces have been introduced to protect property and the personal security of the expanding middle classes. These developments, Silver argues, have resulted in the tendency to define behavior directed against property or against privileges of the middle and upper classes as antipolice; such behavior is "criminal," hence, nonpolitical. The mythology that riots are caused by the "riffraff" is consistent with such developments. Silver's essay attempts to provide theoretical linkages between one form of collective violence and failure to perceive and respond to its political content. In this study we are similarly concerned with identifying and analyzing *the prevailing process by which racial crisis is reduced in America.*[14]

The Contemporary Study of Civil Disorders

While comparatively little attention has been given the impact of civil disorders on public policy, an extensive literature has developed around describing and explaining the causes of riots, ascertaining the background of participants and discussing the extent to which riot behavior was deliberate. Immediately after civil disorders occur, interpretations are presented which tend to structure public understanding of the events. These interpretations in part function as myths to simplify the events, make them understandable and reduce anxiety over what in reality are deeply complex social phenomena. These myths complement the needs of elites and mass alike. Political leaders ask for simple explanations which make it easier for them to appear to act as leaders. And mass publics, anxious and searching for ways to understand the complex events, are reassured and "quieted" by answers which seem clear, simple and suggest that the problem in question can easily be solved.[15] Such myths thus make a critical contribution to the interpretation of civil disorders.

The social context in which problems are perceived contributes to the character and quality of policy resolution. The notion that riots were fomented by outside agitators moving from city to city, for example, encourages congressmen to make it a federal offense to cross state lines for the purposes of riot agitation. The myth that snipers played a significant role in riots leads legislators to provide funds for local police riot control. Moreover, a shift in the relative priority of one issue affects the priority of others. Thus the character of riot mythology has a number of policy implications.

In the rest of this introductory chapter we seek to trace selectively the careers of certain ideological assumptions which have had a profound influence upon attitudes about recent civil disorders. These assumptions are likely to have a greater effect on elite opinion, since elites are more likely than average citizens to be attentive to scholarly pronouncements. Mass attitudes are probably less affected by academic analyses, although they may be influenced by elite opinion in the long run.

Many scholars studying recent civil disorders have attempted to question and sometimes invalidate popular interpretations and widely held beliefs. On an intellectual level, many such efforts appear to have been successful. However, the influence of myths probably diminished as the perception of threat declined. Public and elite willingness to consider alternative explanations for the causes of, participation in, and the meaning of riots may be due as much to diminishing fear of racial violence as to the influence of scholars' efforts at myth-puncturing. Mythic thinking may increase considerably if the threat of mass urban violence reemerges.16

Causes of Disorder

The initial reaction of most public officials whose jurisdictions have been torn by racial violence is incredulity that "it could happen here." The belief that local officials, and local jurisdictions, are somehow responsible lingers even after the fact of racial turmoil has been accepted. Mayors, governors and presidents solemnly urge self-examination to discover the roots of local responsibility. They search for reasons why some cities experience civil disorders and others are spared. Of the 17 questions President Lyndon B. Johnson posed to his National Advisory Commission on Civil Disorders, the first was: "Why [do] riots occur in some cities and do not occur in others?" Underlying this inquiry was the belief, widely held at the time, that black violence was the product of characteristics peculiar to some cities, characteristics which could be isolated.

The National Advisory Commission on Civil Disorders failed to confirm this assumption:

> We have been unable to identify constant patterns in all aspects of civil disorders. We have found that they are unusual, irregular, complex and, in the present state of knowledge, unpredictable social processes. Like most human events, they do not unfold in orderly sequences.17

Other studies have yielded similar results. The Lemberg Center for the Study of Violence compared three cities which experienced civil disorders in the summer of 1966 to three cities which had not and sought to determine the environmental, structural and attitudinal characteristics that accounted for rioting. Underlying the Center's objective was the assumption, reflecting popular belief, that characteristics indigenous to some cities but not others account for the eruption of civil disorders. It found, however, that no single factor or combination of factors was responsible: "Comparisons of the data obtained in the riot and non-riot cities do not reveal any simple explanation as to why the three *did* riot and the other three did *not.*"[18] Studies which have used a larger sample have similarly failed to identify any causal city characteristics. An analysis of 72 riots over a 50-year time span, for example, yielded no association between the occurrence of racial violence and such factors as increases in black population, housing conditions, employment levels or store ownership.[19]

The futility of attempting to explain the causes of riots by reference to indigenous community characteristics is further suggested in Table 1.1 which updates experiences in the Lemberg Center's six cities. The three nonriot or control cities proved, in fact, to be no control at all. Pittsburgh and Boston experienced civil disorders in each of the two years after the Center designated them "nonriot." Akron, the other "nonriot" city, did not have a riot until 1968. Each of the 1966 disorder cities also experienced subsequent racial violence.

The progressive escalation of racial conflict and violence in American cities during the 1960s poses severe limitation on studies that compare riot cities with nonriot cities (see Table 1.2). The proliferation of civil disorders in the 1960s left virtually no large American city with a sizable black population untouched by racial violence. Events themselves have invalidated theories of riot causation focusing on city characteristics.

This line of inquiry feeds the myth that civil disorders are the product of isolated malfunctioning institutions and unfortunate characteristics of certain cities.[20] It also tends to obscure the extent to which the responsibility for causes of civil disorders are distributed over the entire political system, not just a few deviant cities. As T. M. Tomlinson observes:

> Clearly what produces riots is not related to the political or economic differences between cities. What produces riots is the shared agreement by most Negro Americans that their lot in life is unacceptable, coupled with the view by a significant minority that riots are a legitimate and productive mode or protest. What is unacceptable about Negro life does not vary much from city to city, and the differences in Negro life from city to city are irrelevant. The unifying feature is the consensus that Negroes have been misused by whites, and this perception exists in every city in America.[21]

8

TABLE 1.1

Incidence of Civil Disorders in Lemberg Center's Six Cities

Riot City	Riot Date(s)	Non-Riot Pair	Riot Date(s)
CLEVELAND	1966, 1967[a]	PITTSBURGH	1967[a], 1968[b]
DAYTON	1966, 1967[a], 1968[b]	AKRON	1968[c]
SAN FRANCISCO	1966, 1967[a]	BOSTON	1967[a], 1968[b]

Sources: a. National Advisory Commission on Civil Disorders, *Report*, pp. 158-59.
           b. New York *Times*, 14 April 1968, p. 2E.
           c. Akron Commission on Civil Disorders, *Report*.

TABLE 1.2

Incidence of Serious Racial Conflict:
1 January 1964 through 18 August 1967

Year	Number of Racial Incidents Involving Violence
1964 — — — — — — — — — — —	14
1965 — — — — — — — — — — —	15
1966 — — — — — — — — — — —	53
1967 — — — — — — — — — — —	139
1968 — — — — — — — — — — —	125
TOTAL	345

Sources: U.S. Commission on Civil Rights,
            "Serious Incidents of Racial Conflict;
            1 January 1964 Through 18 August
            1967," reported in National Advisory
            Commission on Civil Disorders,
            Report, p. 114; and New York *Times*,
            14 April 1968, p. 25.

Disorder Participants

The second prominent myth promoted by public officials and some riot commissions focuses on the number and characteristics of disorder participants. According to the "riffraff theory,"[22] black participants in civil disorders are few in number, unrepresentative of the larger black community, and of generally marginal social status:

> The violence of this summer raised up a new and serious threat to local law enforcement. It spawned a group of men whose interest lay in provoking—in provoking—others to destruction, while they fled its consequences. These wretched, vulgar men, these poisonous propagandists, posed as spokesmen for the underprivileged and capitalized on the real grievances of suffering people.[23]
> —*Lyndon B. Johnson*

> The criminal participants in the riots in Newark—the ambushers of firemen, the killers of children, the mass looters—amount to approximately 1% of the Negro population of that city.[24]
> —*Richard J. Hughes*

Don't let anyone tell you this terrible thing is the result of the lack of social planning. This was done by the criminal element.[25]
    —*George Romney*
We cannot and shall not condone the wanton acts of a criminal few such as our city experienced during the night. There will be no coddling of criminals no excusing the criminal acts.[26]
    —*Henry W. Maier*

The "official" collective portrait of riot participants shows some sorry people indeed: black transients from the ranks of the unemployed, the uneducated, the ill-housed—a small and repudiated minority of their community.

If public officials initially created the riffraff theory, some riot commissions have periodically reinforced it. The Governor's Commission on the Los Angeles Riots (McCone Commission), for example, said those involved in the 1965 Los Angeles disorder represented only 2 percent of the black community and were uprooted Southern transplants lacking sound education, stable, well-paying jobs and adequate housing.[27] Mayor Richard J. Daley's Chicago Riot Study Committee, investigating the disorder after the assassination of Dr. Martin Luther King in 1968, reaffirmed the riffraff interpretation by concluding that "participation in the riots and disorders was limited to a small fraction of the city's total population, to a small fraction of the city's black population and to a small minority of the residents of the immediately affected areas."[28]

Like the "city characteristics" explanation, the riffraff theory does not challenge the status quo, which may help explain why public officials find it attractive. If people believe that only a small fraction of the black community participated in civil disorders, then contemporary black violence can be ended by suppressing the deviant few and, thus, the violence need not pose a severe threat to social relations. The riffraff theory has obvious policy implications. If it can be shown that the participants are "riffraff," then only minor efforts to uplift or suppress the black lower class will terminate the violence and prevent its recurrence. The theory also permits liberal whites to condemn riot excesses while supporting black aspirations expressed through conventional political channels.

The riffraff theory has recently found some support among academics. Edward C. Banfield views contemporary civil disorders as the innate expression of restlessness, lawlessness and brawling instincts among the black lower class that has historical precedent in similar behavior by the white lower class of earlier generations. The lower class is naturally attracted to violent behavior, Banfield argues, because of characteristics inherent in its position in society:

> It would appear, then, that what requires explanation is not so much rebellion by Negroes (whether against the whites, the slum, their "own masochism," the police, or something else) as it is outbreaks of animal spirits and of stealing by slum dwellers, mostly boys and young men and mostly Negro.[29]

Drawing entirely on secondary sources, Banfield develops a more generalized (although questionable) interpretation of lower-class black life that undergirds and supports the riffraff theory.

Some empirical evidence has been developed that purports to confirm the riffraff interpretation. After surveying 239 disorders, Bryan Downes concludes that disorder participants are noteworthy because they constitute a distinct minority:

> About 150,000 persons actively participated in the 239 outbursts, although this figure could go as high as 250,000. This still represents a small percentage of the 21.5 million Negroes in the United States in 1968 and only about 10 percent of the 15 million who reside in our metropolitan areas. The news media, particularly television, have been largely responsible for creating the impression that greater numbers of Negroes participate in hostile outbursts, for they tend to devote most of their coverage to only the most violent outbursts. We did, however, find that the number of participants varied considerably from incident to incident, with the greatest number generally participating in more violent outbursts.[30]

Downes's observations suffer from numerous limitations and reveal how apparently systematic analysis can be supportive of riot mythology.

To observe that more rioters participate in the more violent disorders is merely saying the obvious: the most significant measure of the severity of a riot is the number of participants. To criticize the press for inflating the number of disorder participants is inappropriate because Downes bases his data on newspaper estimates of how many blacks engaged in violence. Downes's estimate that 150,000 blacks took part in the 239 disorders is inaccurately described as "only about 10 percent of the 15 million who reside in our metropolitan areas" when it is actually 1 percent. But this same 150,000 figure is difficult to reconcile with the report that 49,607 rioters were arrested in the same outbursts.[31] If both figures are correct, the police arrested an incredible one-third of all participants in the 239 civil disorders.

Finally, even if the estimate of 150,000 participants is accepted as correct, an additional limitation involves Downes's comparison of this figure with the 21.5 million blacks in the United States or with the 15 million blacks who live in metropolitan areas. A more appropriate base on which to compute riot participation is "potential rioters."[32] Excluding all children under 12 and adults over 60 from the black population in the riot area would considerably alter the participation proportions.

Empirical research has challenged the riffraff theory on the number of disorder participants and their socioeconomic characteristics. The Los Angeles Riot Study team, for example, took issue with the McCone Commission's assertion that only 2 percent of the black residents in Watts took part in the 1965 Los Angeles disorder. It found, instead, that participation far exceeded initial estimates:

Up to 15 percent of the Negro adult population, or about 22,000 persons, were active at some point during the rioting, and in more than a "spectator" role. An additional 35 to 40 percent of the Negro adult population, or at least an additional 51,000 persons, were active spectators to the disturbance.[33]

These findings have been replicated for other cities. The University of Michigan's Survey Research Center found a participation rate of 11.2 percent among blacks 15 years of age and over in the 1967 Detroit disorder and an impressively high 45.4 percent among black males between ages 15 and 35 in the 1967 Newark civil disorder.[34] In an important study of riot participation in six cities, Robert Fogelson and Robert Hill found riot participation ranged from a low of 4 percent in Cincinnati to a high of 35 percent in New Haven.[35]

The degree of support riot participants attract from the larger black population also belies the riffraff theory. A survey of more than 5,000 blacks in fifteen cities revealed that rioters enjoyed widespread support from other blacks (see Table 1.3). Less than one-fourth of the black respondents reacted unsympathetically to rioters while over half

TABLE 1.3

Support for Riot Participants from Nonparticipants

	Men	Negroes Women (In percent)	Total
Sympathetic	50	57	54
Unsympathetic	23	26	24
(Inapplicable: willing to join in)	11	6	8
Other, don't know, not ascertained	16	11	14
	100	100	100

Question: "Even if you didn't join in (a riot) would you feel in sympathy with Negroes who did choose to join, or would you feel unsympathetic toward them?"

Source: Angus Campbell and Howard Schumann, "Racial Attitudes in *Supplemental Studies for the National Advisory Commission on Civil Disorders* (Washington, D.C.: U.S. Government Printing Office, 1968), Table V-s, p. 55.

offered supportive responses. David Sears and John McConahay also contend that a relatively low rate of active participation in a disorder does not necessarily indicate a low level of support. When psychologically supportive attitudes are included, they note of the Watts riot: "The picture portrayed by these data is one of widespread community involvement in the riot. . .a majority of the area's inhabitants were involved in the incidents, at one level or another."36

The assertion that only a tiny fraction of the black community took part in civil disorders is only half of the riffraff theory. The other has to do with the social and economic characteristics of participants. The riffraff theory contends that rioters lack education, employment, income and have a low attachment to community institutions (partially related to their status as recent migrants from the South to urban centers in the North).

14

This view is challenged by examining arrest records of blacks involved in the 1965 Los Angeles disorder. In fact, the records show that compared to characteristics of average residents of the riot neighborhood, those blacks arrested had lived longer in Watts and had more stable and higher status employment histories.[37] Subsequent investigations further disputed the riffraff interpretation:

> Support for the riot was as great among relatively well educated and economically advantaged persons as among the poorly educated and economically disadvantaged. Support for the riot was as great among the long-time residents of South Central Los Angeles as it was among the more recent migrants from the South.[38]

Disorder participants in Watts appear to have come from a representative cross section of the adult black community, except for the elderly.

The profile of the typical rioter developed by the National Advisory Commission on Civil Disorders also repudiates the myth that disorder participants are unemployed, uneducated, transients, hoodlums or habitual criminals. The commission found the Detroit and Newark rioter to be significantly better educated that nonparticipants. It also found the Newark rioter could not be distinguished from nonrioters in his employment patterns but was more likely to have participated in discussions about Negro rights and the activities of civil rights groups and to have knowledge about political issues and public officials.[39] Fogelson and Hill's discussion of rioters' social traits in ten cities shows that participants are overwhelmingly adults and less likely than nonparticipants to be Southern born. They are equally likely to be employed and to hold skilled jobs.[40]

The riffraff interpretation of who takes part in civil disorders has been discredited. Investigators have consistently found that blacks involved in civil disorders are either much like other people in their communities or better educated, more knowledgeable about political issues and have lived longer and with greater involvement in the community. One analyst has recently gone so far as to argue that rioters are "the cream of urban Negro youth in particular and urban Negro citizens in general."[41]

The Meaning of Disorders

Competing views of the causes of riots and uncertainty over the social backgrounds and numbers of participants contribute to the broader difficulty of interpreting the disorders and determining their significance. In this area, as well as those treated above, simplified interpretations of civil disorders that serve essentially symbolic functions have dominated public discussion.

As suggested earlier, public officials and riot commissions often view civil disorders as meaningless outbursts devoid of logic, rationality or justification. The McCone Commission again provided the initial impetus for this interpretation. The commission described the Watts violence as a "spasm" and the rioters as "marauding bands" who "seemed to have been caught up in an insensate rage of destruction." Moreover, "What happened was an explosion—a formless, quite senseless, all but hopeless violent protest—engaged in by a few but bringing distress to all."[42] If recent civil disorders can be viewed as anomic outbursts by a socially deviant group lacking any following in the larger black population, their relevance for changes in public policy can be minimized.

Perhaps the most prominent advocate of the view that recent riots were politically meaningless is, again, Banfield. In his essay, "Rioting Mainly For Fun and Profit," Banfield goes to considerable lengths to try to document his assertion that the civil disorders of the sixties were pure and simple rampages by street gangs out to steal liquor, foodstuffs, cigarettes, drugs, clothing, television sets, appliances and furniture.[43] He denies that the riots had any political content, and dismisses the possibility that the disorders expressed black grievances. For supportive evidence, Banfield relies upon the informed judgment of J. Edgar Hoover: "[civil disorders] were, he said, 'purposeless attacks' in which youths were responsible for most of the violence, and he classed them with the college-boy riots that occurred about the same time." He denies even that blacks were angry about police misconduct:

> It was somewhat more plausible to claim that they were angry about mistreatment by the police, but even this view did not fit the facts entirely, for the rioters had shown themselves more interested in burning and looting than in fighting the police.[44]

This reasoning not only ignores the fact that targets of anger can be displaced, but also that the police were heavily armed and willing to defend themselves. The rioters, on the other hand, were unarmed but aware that the police could not prevent them from looting white-owned retail stores.

Central to Banfield's thesis is his assertion that those who claim recent civil disorders had political meaning are really offering a *post hoc* explanation, and therefore a justification, for the violence. This is illustrated clearly in Banfield's analysis of the Kerner Commission report:

> In March 1968, the process of explanation and, by implication, justification reached its apogee with the publication of the report of the National Advisory Commission on Civil Disorders (the Kerner Commission), which found that "white racism," poverty, and powerlessness were mainly responsible for the riots. The next month there were riots in several cities following the assassination of the Reverend Martin Luther King, Jr. These riots followed the familiar pattern of looting, burning, and vandalism, and it was apparent that despite all that had been done to give a political character to these events, most rioters were not there in order to protest. "It wasn't vengeance," a Chicago poverty worker said, "just material gain."[45]

At another point Banfield similarly argues:

> But what probably did most to make rioting seem legitimate was acceptance of the claim that the Watts riot was a "revolt" and that the rioting everywhere had some political purpose. . .explanations that find the cause of rioting in the rioters' environment are bound to be taken as justifications, or at any rate extenuations, of their behavior and therefore tend to reinforce the irresponsibility that is characteristic of the age and class culture from which rioters are largely drawn.[46]

Thus it seems Banfield's real objection to the suggestion that disorders are endowed with political content is aimed at those who make the suggestion after the fact. This objection, however, provides a weak basis for demonstrating that such reasoning is either illogical or wrong.

Banfield is particularly critical of *post hoc* arguments by blacks: "Negro spokesmen at once [after the Watts disorder] proclaimed that it was politically motivated. . . .No one gave a very clear or convincing account of what the rioters were revolting against, however."[47] Banfield, of course, would be the first to admit that his reasoning, too, is *post hoc* and independent of confirming evidence concerning motivation.

Since Banfield mobilizes very little evidence and ignores findings contradictory to his argument, one must evaluate his treatment of riots in terms of its "reasonableness"—the extent to which it "fits" with available information. It is necessary to draw attention to aspects of the picture which Banfield neglects: the meaning of civil disorders to participants, as best we can discover it, and the impact blacks expected disorders to have on the political system.

His assumption that recent disorders are politically meaningless is partially challenged simply by the sheer number of participants and their background characteristics, as we have described.[48] Survey research provides more direct information on the political meaning blacks saw in the riots. In a post-riot survey of Watts residents, 62 percent of the black residents perceived the 1965 Los Angeles disorders as a form of black protest, while 56 percent thought the violence had some political purpose. Among the goals of the violence identified by respondents were: "(a) to call attention to Negro problems; (b) to express Negro hostility to whites; or (c) to serve an instrumental purpose of improving conditions, ending discrimination, or communicating with the 'power structure'."[49] Blacks in Detroit, Newark, Milwaukee and other cities regularly explained the disorders as protest concerning housing, jobs, police and community institutions.[50] Angus Campbell and Howard Schuman's 15-city survey includes a question that probes black and white perceptions on the meaning of civil disorders. The question is phrased to elicit responses structured around a "political protest" or a Banfield-like "looting" interpretation. The survey results are reproduced in Table 1.4.

It is not surprising that a majority of black respondents saw the disorders mainly in terms of protest. What may be surprising is that most white respondents perceived the recent racial violence as political protest when asked to choose among the alternative explanations. While many white men tended to agree that the "looting" interpretation had merit, even a significant proportion of this group saw the disorders primarily as political protest.

Some may question the validity of sample surveys in this context. Banfield objects that blacks are really only rationalizing and justifying their behavior in political terms after the fact. In any event, he argues, surveys cannot capture past motivations by *post hoc* questioning.

Granting Banfield's undeniable epistemological point, this argument is no more or less valid than any other criticism of attitudinal surveys. Over the past two decades considerable experience and expertise have been developed in American survey research. Banfield himself has used

TABLE 1.4

Perception of Civil Disorders' Meaning

	Black		White	
	Men	Women	Men	Women
		(in percent)		
Mainly protest — — — — — —	56	59	38	48
Mainly looting — — — — — —	9	10	33	24
50/50 mixture — — — — — —	30	25	25	25
Don't know — — — — — — —	5	6	4	4
Total	100	100	100	100

Question: "Some people say these disturbances are mainly a protest by Negroes against unfair conditions. Others say they are mainly a way of looting and things like that. Which of these seems more correct to you?"

Source: Campbell and Schumann, *Supplemental Studies*, p. 47 (Table V-a).

survey techniques in his research, undoubtedly because as a *tool* for determining public attitudes over time and testing some hypotheses, survey research is unparalleled.[51] *Post hoc* reconstruction of events by respondents operates as much in survey research on voting behavior as it does in black attitudes toward riots. Thus to challenge the surveys reporting black attitudes toward riots but not other uses of surveys is to propose a curious double standard of validity for social research.

Murray Edelman's more compelling suggestion is that, in explaining violent actions, people tend to justify behavior in terms of perceived manifest deprivations.[52] Deprivations may exist beforehand; the violence facilitates giving expression to the grievances.

Even if one rejects *post hoc* evidence of human motivation, we can still argue that the way people reconstruct events may be as important as their attitudes during the events themselves. The strong tendency among blacks to see recent civil disorders as a form of political protest may be more important than the more ambiguous reports by observers of what actually took place during the events. Like other students of mass political behavior, we argue that people caught up in complex and confusing events search for meaning to reduce attendant ambiguity and anxiety.53 An event is likely to "become" what people later rationalize it to be. To deny the importance of political meanings of events attached after the fact would be to reduce political life to an antiseptic caricature, in which only statements clearly labeled as "demands" and composed in fully rational and instrumental fashion are permitted to engage our attention. To dismiss strongly expressed black views of civil disorders as political protest is to ignore a critical reality which does not depend upon what blacks were thinking when they stoned policemen, burned liquor stores, or observed their neighbors looting.

If most blacks consider civil disorders a form of political protest, what kinds of responses did they expect the political system to make? In condemning civil disorders, most public officials and some riot commissions insist that racial violence will only bring about deprivations. The logic of the condemnation usually runs something like this: when blacks loot they impair businesses serving them, when they burn buildings in their neighborhood they only destroy black residences. Most important, when blacks engage in civil disorders, the more powerful white society will inevitably respond with repressive force.

In contrast, many black Americans tended to perceive civil disorders as a means for redress of continuing grievances. In October 1964, when few civil disorders had occurred, 39 to 63 percent of blacks in selected cities rejected the notion that "no good can come from riots." Dividing black respondents into three categories—"Black Nationalist Sympathizers," "Militants," and "Conservative"—Gary Marx reports that 72 percent of the first group agreed that "riots do some good, while almost half of the respondents in *both* other groups concurred."54 Subsequent studies tend to confirm this pattern. They indicate that significant proportions of blacks think the riots brought about long-delayed policies favorable to blacks, particularly in housing and employment,55 and they expected favorable results from the disorders.56

The view that riots may be understood as expressive of political demands has thus been advanced by a plurality of black people, by black leaders and by various scholars. This view is at least *plausible.* It is based upon evidence that rioters were a large and representative minority of the young adults in the ghetto; that during some of the riots and after most, blacks often stated explicitly that they were rioting to arouse white concern; that during the riots clear patterns were observable in their targets—stores which charged excessive prices or sold shoddy merchandise, and the police—while in some cities stores displaying "soul brother" signs were spared; and, perhaps most important, that an extremely large plurality of blacks, when interviewed subsequently, considered the riots to be at least partly a protest against their condition. Perhaps needless to say, motivation for such behavior and attitudes may be found in their history in America.[57]

At the very least, the evidence casts grave doubts on the view that the civil disorders in the 1960s represented aberrant and pathological behavior engaged in and supported by a small minority of the black community. Most blacks tended to perceive civil disorders as a means to achieve redress of grievances and a substantial proportion of the black community entertained expectations that racial violence would evoke important changes in their social, economic and political status. *At the very least, we must conclude that civil disorders were somehow connected to black consciousness of exploitation, grief and neglect in white America, and to a communal sensibility that disruption might succeed where other avenues of redress had failed.* The putative demands expressed by blacks in civil disorders failed, in part because they were perceived as anomic expressions unassociated with group goals. *And they failed as well because they were mediated through a complex political process in which they were deprived of their instrumental content and in which the demands they represented were washed away in the undertow of conventional politics.*

This study will describe and analyze how riots are "processed" in American politics. Initially, we focus on the internal and external politics of riot commissions, since these bodies so clearly dominated the inital responses to riots by public officials. We then turn to the implementation of commission recommendations and their impact at the national and especially the city level.

In addition to describing the response to riots of critical local, state and national institutions, we also touch on several significant empirical and theoretical questions for students of American politics. What has happened in American cities, particularly in public policy in the aftermath of racial violence? Curiously, virtually no systematic attention has been paid to this essential question.[58] How does the American political system respond to severe internal crisis? Most studies of American politics tend to focus on "politics as usual," when severe conflicts are minimal. The occurrence of racial disorders on the scale seen in the 1960s poses fundamental challenges to the paradigmatic works on American politics.[59]

Such works have continued to use consensual models of the political system that stress harmony, brokerage politics and cooperative interaction. They portray conflict among various interests as a process of negotiation, bargaining and eventual compromise. They emphasize a relatively high degree of stability conducive to the study of system persistence, but not to research on rapid social and political change or "dissensus" politics.[60] Until very recently few American political scientists even studied civil violence.[61]

Related to the preference for consensual and equilibrium models has been the tendency to equate stable democracy with successful democracy and, correspondingly, to consider severe conflict and violence as pathological.[62] This is especially true in pluralist theory, which maintains that violence has been minimized in the American context because, it is asserted, groups representing competing interests have arisen and successfully engaged the political process, wielding a measure of influence and power resulting in shared governmental goods and services. Dahl, for example, concludes that "the normal American political system. . .appears to be a relatively efficient system for reinforcing agreement, encouraging moderation, and maintaining social peace. . . ."[63] The genius of American democracy, according to the pluralists, rests on its efficiency in promoting harmony, instilling consensus and preventing conflict and violence. A widespread distribution of power among diverse groups, each lacking sovereignty, contributes to political stability: "power itself will be tamed, civilized, controlled, and limited to decent human purposes, while coercion, the most evil form of power, will be reduced to a minimum."[64]

The emphasis on stability in paradigms of American politics is arguable on at least three important grounds. First, it is not at all clear that severe conflict and violence are transient phenomena in the United States. The President's Commission on the Causes and Prevention of Violence recently concluded, for example: "In total magnitude of civil strife plus the total duration of strife, the United States ranks first among the 17 Western democracies."[65]

Second, stability may not be equally desired by all groups in the population. As in the case of American race relations prior to 1960, stability may be accompanied by grossly inequitable distributions of resources and status. Although not without risk, subordinate groups may come to challenge the distribution of values and thus the prevailing social stability. Subordinate groups may well ask: "stability for whom?"

Third, stability may persist simply because conflict has been suppressed or potentially dissenting groups have been coopted. The violent outbursts of the 1960s cast retrospective doubt on the perceptions of those who observed stability in American race relations in the past. These considerations are further raised in our examination of the eventual outcomes of conflict and opposition to the status quo inherent in recent riots. In the processing of the claims presented in civil disorders, we see denial, bargaining, suppression, cooptation, minimalist amelioration and other modes of conflict regulation that fall short of meaningful accommodation.[66]

Pluralist theory, while severely challenged by events of the 1960s, continues to dominate conceptions of the political system in the absence of alternative paradigms that would better accommodate the degree of violence, dissent and alienation that has been characteristic in recent years. Although it is often assumed that intense conflict and violence are dysfunctional, the nature of the dysfunctions are rarely specified. The possible positive functions of civil conflict also remain unexplored and are usually either dismissed as too isolated to merit attention or interpreted as pathological for the political system. This perspective may largely account for the general failure to examine the impact of conflict and violence on the political system.

A Note on Method and the Plan of the Book

In the first nine months of 1967, civil disorders erupted in more than 100 American cities.[67] In an atmosphere of uncertainty and confusion about the causes of these riots and the potential for more riots in the future, we began this study primarily interested in understanding whether collective violence furthers the interests of the group engaged in disorders. We particularly wanted to answer a series of questions of special significance during the months immediately after the rioting: Did the riots do any good? Were they in any way productive, as many black spokesmen claim? Were they uniformly detrimental to black interests, as white public officials insisted?

We decided to examine two related phenomena: (1) elite responses to the disorders; and (2) observable changes (if any) in public policy toward blacks that might be attributed to the disorders. Concretely, we focused on the political and organizational behavior of riot commissions, the appointment and activity of which may be considered the modal American response to civil disorders and on public policy developments which might hypothetically be related to riot events. We did not approach the riot commissions and their recommendations as the total response of the political system. But we assumed that they were sufficiently representative of the political system's response to merit our attention.[68]

In addition to studying the National Advisory Commission on Civil Disorders (Kerner Commission), we chose three cities for intensive analysis: Detroit, Michigan; Milwaukee, Wisconsin; and Newark, New Jersey. The choice of these three cities was prompted by three reasons. First, they experienced the most severe civil disorders among the cities affected by racial violence in 1967.[69] Second, public officials immediately responded to the disorders by creating investigatory or recommendatory bodies in each of the three cities. Third, the three cities exhibit important differences in political behavior and political culture and, relatedly, in the proportion of the city's population represented by blacks. Thus, to the extent possible in a three-case study, these cities would permit us to develop and tentatively test hypotheses concerning the influence of the proportionate size of the black population on a city's post-riot response.

Field research began in late 1967 and continued through mid-1970. Several research trips were made to each of the three cities and to Washington, D.C., where personnel associated with the Kerner Commission were interviewed. A minimum of six weeks was spent conducting field research in each of these cities. Prior to this, we engaged in a detailed review of historical accounts of collective racial violence in the United States, particularly in the twentieth century. We also drew upon accounts of other riots and riot commissions prior to conducting our field research.

Our information on the politics of riot commissions was obtained through a variety of methods. The official documents of the commissions were analyzed in detail. These consisted of the formal reports of the commissions, minutes, transcripts and tape recordings of meetings, testimony at hearings, task force reports, consultants' papers, staff papers and reports, internal memoranda and documents submitted to the commissions by interested groups and individuals. Newspaper coverage of the commissions' activities was also followed. Focused interviews were conducted with commissioners, commission staff personnel, consultants and leaders of groups whose interests were affected by the commissions' deliberations and reports. This same procedure was followed in obtaining information from participants in what we call, in chapter 8, "competing riot commissions."

Information on the degree to which riot commission recommendations were implemented in the cities was also obtained through a variety of methods. Interviews were conducted with those public officials and city agency staff personnel most directly affected by the recommendations for change proposed by riot commissions, people who would be most directly responsible for implementing them. Agency clienteles and other groups whose interests were affected by commission recommendations were similarly surveyed. Public reports of city agencies and the files of agencies provided crucial information in determining the degree of compliance with proposed changes. Additionally, during field research we attended a number of meetings which dealt with the formulation and implementation of changes. Newspaper accounts of events in the three cities enabled us to follow developments when we were not conducting field research.

The research procedures outlined above were conducted in a somewhat ordered sequence. Initial field research trips consisted of preliminary investigations. Documents were then collected, newspaper accounts examined, city agency reports and records compiled and interviews with informants but not key participants were conducted. During subsequent visits to the three cities, interviews were conducted with key participants and remaining materials were collected.[70] Because our research was conducted while changes were still taking place in the cities, city agencies agreed to provide us information and status reports on the outcome of proposals recommended by the riot commissions.

The Plan

In the next chapter we survey the American experience in responding to racial disorders, focusing on the widespread use of riot commissions and the ways in which public officials have responded to racial violence. The second part of this book traces the development and operations of the National Advisory Commission on Civil Disorders. We are concerned with the commission as it appeared to the public and attempted to develop a public image; with the pressures and problems associated with the commission's attempt to provide answers to questions of concern; and with the ways the commission attempted to resolve the critical contradictions inherent in the commission as a governmental entity. In the third part, the analysis of riot commissions is extended to these and somewhat similar bodies as they operated at the city level. Additionally, we assess the extent to which recommendations were implemented in Newark, Milwaukee and Detroit, so as to be able to comment on the role of the commission in the political process. We also report on other aspects of post-riot politics in the cities. In conclusion, we explore some of the implications of our analysis for understanding the meaning of riots, the role of riot commissions and the response to severe stress in the American political process.

NOTES, CHAPTER 1

1. Throughout this volume we shall use the terms *civil disorders, disorders* and *riots* interchangeably. We do so principally for readability, although we are mindful of the implications attached to the different terminology by different audiences. Black leaders who insist the *disorders* were politically motivated, for example, prefer to call these events *rebellions* or *revolts*. For those who deny these implications, *riots* is usually the preferred term. We are also mindful of the analytic implications of the different terms. *Civil disorder* implies the prior existence of a state of "civil order" and *race riot* conventionally applies only to direct violent clashes between racial groups. At the start of ch. 2 we distinguish between *race riots* and *civil disorders* for the purpose of historical analysis, but otherwise we use the various terms interchangeably.

2. Here we paraphrase two widely accepted uses of the term *political*. See David Easton, *A Framework For Political Analysis* (Englewood Cliffs, N.J.: Prentice-Hall, 1965), p. 50; and Harold Lasswell, *Politics: Who Gets What, When, How* (New York: McGraw-Hill, 1936). To Easton, *political* refers to the *authoritative* allocation of values; an allocation is authoritative when people "consider that they are bound by it." Among the reasons people might feel bound are: the use of force by government, tradition, and social opprobrium. Clearly, challenges to racial status involve attempts to alter or manipulate the mechanisms by which values are allocated.

3. Robert Fogelson, *Violence As Protest* (New York: Doubleday, 1971), p. 16.

4. Easton, *Framework for Political Analysis*, p. 120.

5. Gabriel Almond, "Introduction: A Functional Approach to Comparative Politics," in *The Politics of the Developing Areas*, ed. Gabriel Almond and James Coleman (Princeton, N.J.: Princeton University Press, 1960), pp. 8, 34.

6. Easton, *Framework for Political Analysis*, p. 121. Easton perhaps supplies the appropriate epigraph for this volume when he writes: "[W]hat we need to question is whether systems can be shown to have devised typical ways for aborting. . .possible stress before it arises or alleviating its consequences if it seems imminent."

7. While it is generally true that public officials express intolerance toward this form of behavior, a conspicuous and important exception is the part played by law enforcement personnel during race riots from 1917 through 1943. Police officers and national guardsmen often proved lax in suppressing the violence when rioting featured white mobs attacking black people. In fact, law enforcement officers periodically joined with white mobs in the attacks against blacks. See Allen D. Grimshaw, "Actions of Police and the Military in American Race Riots," in *Racial Violence in the United States*, ed. Allen D. Grimshaw (Chicago: Aldine, 1969), pp. 269-87.

8. See H. L. Nieburg, *Political Violence: The Behavioral Approach* (New York: St. Martin's Press, 1969), p. 135. Illustrative of the fact that many people at least feared that this alternative might prevail was the statement of Kerner Commission social scientists on "The Garrison State," in their unpublished document, "The Harvest of American Racism." See ch. 5.

9. See Allan Silver, "The Demand for Order in Civil Society: A Review of Some Themes in the History of Urban Crime, Police and Riot," in *The Police: Six Sociological Essays*, ed. David Bordua (New York: John Wiley, 1966), pp. 1-24.

Platt surveys the extensive use by public officials of the "riffraff" stereotype to explain racial violence. He concludes:

These kinds of inference serve to dramatize the criminal character of riots, to undermine their political implications, and to uphold the argument that social change is only possible through lawful and peaceful means. If riots can be partly explained as the work of a few agitators or hoodlums, it is then much easier to engage wide support in repudiating violent methods of social protest. Official investigations generally publicize the fact that normal, ordinary, law-abiding persons do not instigate riots.

(Anthony M. Platt, *The Politics of Riot Commissions* [New York: Collier, 1971,] p. 34).

10. See ch. 2 for the continuity of commission creation in response to racial violence throughout the twentieth century.

11. The appointment of the Kerner Commission in the summer of 1967 raised the problem of racial violence to the level of a national issue and thereby preempted, in important ways, the creation of riot commissions in local areas experiencing racial violence. With the appointment of the Kerner Commission, local bodies considered themselves released from the obligation to treat certain issues. Thus while our generalization holds for racial disorders up to 1967, there have been several important exceptions to this pattern since the Kerner Commission was formed.

12. See Allan Silver, "Official Interpretations of Racial Riots," in *Urban Riots: Violence and Social Change, Proceedings of the Academy of Political Science*, ed. Robert Connery, vol. 24, no. 1 (1968): 150-51. Platt suggests that recent identification of riot commissions with black claims results from commissions' needs to account for extensive participation in and support for riots by blacks while continuing to deny the legitimacy of this form of political behavior.

> While commissions generally deplore the violence of "rioters" (but minimize or ignore the the significance of official violence) and attribute rioting to the "riffraff" element, they are still faced with the problem of explaining why riots are participated in by a cross section of the ghetto communities, and given wide support by those communities. Given these facts, few serious official treatments of riots now attempt to explain the resulting violence purely in terms of a "riffraff" theory. . . .Most commissions resolve this dilemma by arguing that riots are invariably aggravated or instigated by the criminal activities of a small group of provocateurs who take advantage of human weakness and transform basically nonviolent individuals into an irrational mob. Thus, riots are widely characterized as outlets for pent-up frustrations and grievances sparked by a few.

See Platt, *The Politics of Riot Commissions*, pp. 36-37.

13. See Silver, "The Demand for Order in Civil Society," p. 23 and passim.

14. Hugh Graham and Ted Gurr note: "For riots and local uprisings we often know nothing of their aftermaths even a year later. . . .What has happened in the black ghettos wracked by riots between 1965 and 1968?" See Hugh Davis Graham and Ted Robert Gurr, "Conclusion," in *The History of Violence in America*, ed. Graham and Gurr (New York: Bantam, 1969), p. 820. Lipsky has previously suggested the need for similar research: "Future research should continue assessment of

the relationship between riots and the conditions under which access to the political system has been limited." Michael Lipsky, "Protest as a Political Resource," *American Political Science Review* 62, no. 4 (December 1968): 1,158.

The virtual absence of research on the political response to racial violence is confirmed in reviewing the literature that addresses these events. For a ten-page bibliography listing studies on domestic racial violence, see John R. Krause, Jr., "Ghetto Revolts and City Politics," in *Riots and Rebellion: Civil Violence in the Urban Community*, ed. Louis H. Masotti and Don R. Bowen (Beverly Hills, Calif.: Sage, 1968), pp. 441-51. See also Stanley E. Gunterman, "A Bibliography on Violence and Social Change," in Connery, *Urban Riots: Violence and Social Change*, pp. 183-90.

15. For a discussion of the functions performed by such political myths, see Murray Edelman, "Myths, Metaphors, and Political Conformity," *Psychiatry* 30, no. 3 (August 1967): 217-28. Also see Edelman, *The Symbolic Uses of Politics* (Urbana, Ill.: University of Illinois Press, 1964), especially pp. 30-31.

16. See Murray Edelman, *Politics as Symbolic Action: Mass Arousal and Quiescence* (Chicago: Markham, 1971), pp. 60-63.

17. National Advisory Commission on Civil Disorders, *Report* (New York: Bantam, 1968), pp. 109-110, 536. Hereafter, this reference is abbreviated as *Report*. For the convenience of most readers, references throughout are to the widely distributed paperback edition published by Bantam. The official printed version is *Report* (Washington, D.C.: Government Printing Office, 1968). A commercial edition in hardcover is *Report* (New York: E. P. Dutton, 1968).

18. "Six-City Study: A Survey of Racial Attitudes in Six Northern Cities, Preliminary Findings" (Lemberg Center for the Study of Violence, Brandeis University, June 1967, mimeo), p. 6. The report nevertheless does not refrain from speculating on causes of civil disorders indigenous to the riot communities. See pp. 22-23.

19. This same study did find, however, that, "Riot cities not only employ fewer Negro policemen, but they are also communities whose electoral systems tend to be less sensitive to the demands of the electorate." See Stanley Leiberson and Arnold R. Silverman, "The Precipitants and Underlying Conditions of Race Riots," *American Sociological Review* 30, no. 6 (December 1965): 887-98. Bloombaum's reanalysis of the Lieberson and Silverman data also found no single factor discriminating between riot and control cities. See Milton Bloombaum, "The Conditions Underlying Race Riots as Portrayed by Multidimensional Scalogram Analysis: A Re-Analysis of Lieberson and

Silverman's Data," *American Sociological Review* 33, no. 1 (February 1968): 76-91.

Longitudinal analysis, represented by the two works above, may be doomed for a theoretical reason discussed in ch. 2: they do not take into account the qualitative differences in race-related riots during the twentieth century. Thus associations that might obtain for traditional forms of "race riots" may be washed out statistically when applied to racial violence in the form of "civil disorders" like the 1935 and 1943 Harlem eruptions.

20. Ziblatt makes much the same point: "An attempt to contrast riot and nonriot cities on the basis of their socioeconomic or administrative characteristics now appears fruitless from both a practical and theoretical point of view. What produces riots is only vaguely related to intercity differences." See David Ziblatt, "Urban Violence: Research Questions and Images of Political Change" (paper delivered at the Midwest Political Science Association Meetings, 2-4 May 1968, Chicago, Ill.), p. 2. However, to the extent that these studies are read and appreciated, their lack of positive findings may contribute to rejection of this perspective.

21. T. M. Tomlinson, "The Development of a Riot Ideology Among Urban Negroes," *American Behavioral Scientist* 11, no. 4 (March-April 1968): 29.

22. The phrase *riffraff theory* appears in the work of Robert M. Fogelson who finds its origin in remarks by Paul Screvane, acting mayor of New York City, and Nelson Rockefeller, governor of New York, explaining the Harlem, Bedford-Stuyvesant, and Rochester riots of 1964. See Fogelson, "White on Black: A Critique of the McCone Commission Report on the Los Angeles Riots," *Political Science Quarterly* 82, no. 3 (September 1967): 342.

23. Remarks of Lyndon B. Johnson on 14 September 1967 before the International Association of Chiefs of Police. See *Public Papers of the Presidents of the United States, Lyndon B. Johnson, Containing the Public Messages, Speeches, and Statements of the President, 1967, Book II, July 1 to December 31, 1967* (Washington, D.C.: U.S. Government Printing Office, 1968), p. 835.

24. Speech by Governor Richard J. Hughes of New Jersey before the 75th Anniversary Convention of the International Longshoremen's Association, Hotel Di Lido, Miami Beach, Fla., 20 July 1967, p. 2.

25. Remarks of Governor George Romney of Michigan. Quoted in the Detroit *News*, 26 July 1967.

26. Remarks of Mayor Henry W. Maier of Milwaukee. Quoted in the Milwaukee *Journal*, 1 August 1967.

27. Governor's Commission on the Los Angeles Riots, *Violence in*

the *City—An End or a Beginning?* (Los Angeles, Calif: State of California, 2 December 1965), pp. 1-9, and passim.

28. Chicago Riot Study Committee, *Report* (Chicago, Ill.: State of Illinois, 1 August 1968), p. 3. The report continues: "A relatively small number of so-called natural leaders among the young blacks of high school age were generally the catalysts and leaders of the April disorders in Chicago....As in any community, white or black, the black communities in Chicago include a few citizens, young and old, with vested interests in violence. To some extent simple delinquency and a desire for troublemaking and larceny played their parts."

29. Edward C. Banfield, *The Unheavenly City* (Boston: Little, Brown, 1970), pp. 197-98. For an assessment of this work see *The Unheavenly City Revisited,* ed. Harry C. Bredemeier (in manuscript; forthcoming).

30. Bryan T. Downes, "Social and Political Characteristics of Riot Cities: A Comparative Study," *Social Science Quarterly* 49, no. 3 (December 1968): 507. Downes also observes that the 15 percent participation found by other scholars is a "relatively small proportion of the Negro population." But, relative to what? As noted in the text, other scholars contend that the 15 percent participation figure is large relative to other categories of participation and constitutes a significant minority of the black community.

31. Downes's arrest figures appear on p. 509 in ibid.

32. See Robert M. Fogelson and Robert B. Hill, "Who Riots?: A Study of Participation in the 1967 Riots," in *Supplemental Studies for the National Advisory Commission on Civil Disorders* (Washington, D.C.: U.S. Government Printing Office, 1968), pp. 229-31.

33. Nathan E. Cohen, "Los Angeles Riot Study: Summary and Implications for Policy" (Los Angeles, Calif.: Institute of Government and Public Affairs, University of California, 1967, mimeo), p. 3.

34. *Report,* n. 112, p. 172.

35. See Fogelson and Hill, "Who Riots?," p. 231, Table 2.

36. David O. Sears and John B. McConahay, "Los Angeles Riot Study: Riot Participation" (Los Angeles, Calif.: Institute of Government and Public Affairs, University of California, 1967), p. 21. For similar evidence see David O. Sears and T. M. Tomlinson, "Riot Ideology in Los Angeles: A Study of Negro Attitudes," *Social Science Quarterly* 49, no. 3 (December 1968): 488.

37. Fogelson, "White on Black," p. 346.

38. Cohen, "Los Angeles Riot Study: Summary and Implications for Policy," p. 4.

39. *Report,* pp. 111, 127-35; 174 n. 126; the Newark rioter was also more likely to distrust city hall than the nonrioter. See pp. 139-41, n. 127; 175, 177, 178.

40. Fogelson and Hill, "Who Riots?," pp. 233-38.

41. Tomlinson, "The Development of a Riot Ideology Among Urban Negroes," p. 28.

42. Governor's Commission on the Los Angeles Riots, *Violence in the City—An End or a Beginning?*, pp. 1, 4, 5.

43. Banfield, *The Unheavenly City*, p. 197. Banfield does not discuss the selective pattern of looting and burning that occurred in most cities and the implications for ghetto violence that targets were selectively chosen.

44. Ibid., p. 194, 196. The adequacy of the data utilized by Banfield in constructing the "meaningless" view of recent riots is assessed in David J. Olson, "Did Banfield Run Riot In Writing 'Rioting Mainly For Fun and Profit'?" in Bredemeier, *The Unheavenly City Revisited.*

45. Banfield, *The Unheavenly City*, pp. 301-302, n. 44. Banfield's criticism of the Kerner Commission's report for attempting to give a political character to disorder events represents a serious misreading of that document. While the commission included a sizable amount of data and extensive discussion on participants in civil disorders, including nine pages of text and eight pages of footnotes with 33 tables, its report contains virtually no data or discussion of what the civil disorders meant to the black community.

46. Ibid., pp. 200-201.

47. Ibid., p. 196.

48. The data on rioters reviewed above are particularly damning of Banfield's assumptions about recent black riots as lower-class phenomena, since riot participants did not display the background characteristics Banfield associates with the lower class.

49. Tomlinson, "The Development of a Riot Ideology Among Urban Negroes," p. 28.

50. See Detroit Urban League, "A Survey of Attitudes of Detroit Negroes after the Riot of 1967" (Detroit, 1967); Opinion Research Corporation, "Negro and White Attitudes Toward Problems and Progress in Race Relations: A Study among Residents of Newark and Adjacent Communities" (Governor's Select Commission to Study Civil Disorders, January 1968, mimeo); Jonathan A. Slesinger, "Study of Community Opinions Concerning the Summer 1967 Civil Disturbance in Milwaukee" (The University of Wisconsin-Milwaukee, 1 April 1968); Lemberg Center for the Study of Violence, "A Survey of Racial Attitudes in Six Northern Cities: Preliminary Findings."

51. See James Q. Wilson and Edward C. Banfield, "Political Ethos Revisited," *American Political Science Review* 65, no. 4 (December 1971): 1,048-62. In this study, Wilson and Banfield rely upon survey

evidence to determine how respondents would "vote" on various public expenditure issues. While post-hoc reconstruction of events is not involved here, an equally if not more complex problem of validity arises because respondents are asked to "vote" on hypothetical expenditure issues as if they actually confronted them when, in reality, they have not. On the limits of the uses of survey research evidence, see Edelman's discussion in *Politics as Symbolic Action*, pp. 4-6.

52. Edelman, *Politics as Symbolic Action*, p. 108.

53. Ibid.

54. Gary Marx, *Protest and Prejudice* (New York: Harper and Row, 1967), pp. 32, 115.

55. Lemberg Center for the Study of Violence, "Six City Study," p. 18. Also see Slesinger, "Study of Community Opinions," p. 33.

56. See Tomlinson, "The Development of a Riot Ideology among Urban Negroes," p. 28; Opinion Research Corporation, "Negro and White Attitudes," p. 41; and Table V-e in Campbell and Schuman, *Supplemental Studies*, p. 49.

57. For a discussion of this evidence see Fogelson, *Violence as Protest*, ch. 1. It may be of some interest in the context of this chapter that the social scientists on the staff of the Kerner Commission concluded in a report, never fully incorporated into the final *Report*, that at least one of the major disturbances of 1967 was a "political rebellion." See ch. 5 of this book; also David Boesel, Louis Goldberg, and Gary Marx, "Rebellion in Plainfield," in *Cities Under Siege: An Anatomy of the Ghetto Riots, 1964-1968*, ed. David Boesel and Peter Rossi (New York: Basic Books, 1971), pp. 67-82.

58. See footnote 14 above. For discussions of the importance of studying the actual impact of public policies, see, for example, Austin Ranney, *Political Science and Public Policy* (Chicago: Markham, 1968); Herbert Jacob and Michael Lipsky, "Outputs, Structure, and Power," *Journal of Politics* 30, no. 2 (May 1968): 510-38; James Q. Wilson, *City Politics and Public Policy* (New York: John Wiley, 1968).

59. The evolution of Easton's position on the proper paradigm for research on American politics illustrates the nature of the challenge posed by racial violence for current political research. In 1959 Easton attacked A. R. Radcliffe-Brown's emphasis on force, coercion, conflict and violence because he "overemphasizes the role of coercive sanctions, especially force," in the political process. Easton noted that Brown's position "is an approach that research in American political science has all but abandoned, although it still has enough vitality to raise its head from time to time." See David Easton, "Political Anthropology," in *Biennial Review of Anthropology: 1959*, ed. Bernard J. Siegel (Stanford, Calif.: Stanford University Press, 1959), pp. 213-19. But note the

change in Easton's emphasis in his presidential address to the American Political Science Association:

> Today the hazards of neglecting our normative presuppositions are all too apparent. There can be little doubt that political science as an enterprise has failed to anticipate the crises that are upon us. One index of this is perhaps that in the decade from 1958 to 1968 this [American Political Science] Review published only 3 articles on the urban crises; 4 on racial conflicts; 1 on poverty; 2 on civil disobedience; and 2 on violence in the United States. . . .How can we account for our neglect of the way in which the distribution of power within the system prevents measures from being taken in sufficient degree and time to escape the resort to violence in the expression of demands, a condition that threatens to bring about the deepest crisis of political authority that the United States has ever suffered?

See David Easton, "The New Revolution in Political Science," *American Political Science Review* 63, no. 4 (December 1969): 1,057.

60. One elaborate consensual model is that developed by Easton in *A Systems Analysis of Political Life* (New York: John Wiley, 1965). Easton conceptualizes change processes in terms of the political system's ability to cope with stress on two essential variables: value allocation by decision makers, and compliance with the allocations by members. The dynamic, adaptive process of change in the political system is located in the generation of outputs in response to stress on the two essential variables whereby political systems are allowed to "transform their internal structures," p. 19. But this conception of change directs attention to outputs in response to stress for purposes of explaining equilibrium maintenance between the political system and its environment, rather than drawing attention to characteristics indigenous to the political system that stimulate impulses toward change. Easton's model is singled out here only because of its pervasive influence on other political scientists. Similar criticism can equally be applied to variations on this consensual model provided in the work of Truman, Downs, Almond, and others who adopt the influential formal model of how political systems persist. See David B. Truman, *The Governmental Process* (New York: Alfred A. Knopf, 1951); Anthony Downs, *An Economic Theory of Democracy* (New York: Harper and Row, 1957); and Gabriel Almond and Sidney Verba, *The Civic Culture* (Princeton, N.J.: Princeton University Press, 1963).

61. Walker notes, for example, that:

American political scientists have not been sufficiently concerned with the role of violence in the governmental process. Among all the articles published in *The American Political Science Review* between 1906 and 1963, there was only one whose title contained the word "violence," only one with the word "coercive". . .and none with the word "force."

Jack L. Walker, "A Critique of the Elitist Theory of Democracy," *American Political Science Review* 60, no. 2 (June 1966): 894.

62. See Almond and Verba, *The Civic Culture*, p. 473; and Seymour Martin Lipset, *Political Man* (New York: Doubleday-Anchor Books, 1963), p. 71.

63. Robert A. Dahl, *A Preface to Democratic Theory* (Chicago: University of Chicago Press, 1956), p. 151.

64. Robert A. Dahl, *Democracy in the United States: Promise and Performance*, 2nd ed. (Chicago: Rand McNally, 1972), p. 24. At another point Dahl notes: "Yet to say that severe political conflict is undesirable is not to say that all political conflict is undesirable. . . .This is therefore the dilemma: In a democracy moderate political conflict is both inevitable and desirable. Yet severe political conflict is undesirable, for it endangers any political system, and not least a polyarchy," pp. 302-303.

65. National Commission on the Causes and Prevention of Violence, *Progress Report to President Lyndon B. Johnson* (Washington, D.C.: U.S. Government Printing Office, 9 January 1969), p. A-6. The commission also reported: "In total magnitude of strife, the United States ranks 24th among the 114 larger nations and colonies of the world. In magnitude of turmoil alone it ranks sixth," p. A-7. For a review of literature on labor, ethnic, and interracial violence in America's past see David J. Olson, "Perspectives on Political Violence," *Dialog* 8, no. 4 (Winter 1969): 9-17. For a treatment of severe conflict in American politics historically, see Dahl, *Democracy in the United States*, ch. 23.

66. See William A. Gamson, *Power and Discontent* (Homewood, Ill.: Dorsey Press, 1968).

67. According to the National Advisory Commission on Civil Disorders, they occurred in 128 cities during this period. See *Report*, p. 114.

68. Although we declined to treat it, we recognized the importance of still another general phenomenon possibly resulting from the disorders. A comprehensive study of the results and impact of the riots of 1967 would also have to treat the mass and elite attitudinal changes resulting from the disorders.

69. The civil disorders in Detroit and Newark were respectively, and

without question, the most severe disorders during the summer of 1967. See *Report*, "Charts," pp. 611-59. Some have questioned whether Milwaukee experienced a severe civil disorder in 1967. The National Advisory Commission on Civil Disorders, however, termed the disturbance in Milwaukee a "major disorder." The category of "major disorder" applied to only eight (or five percent) of the 164 disorders identified by the commission during the first nine months of 1967 in 128 cities. The category "major disorder" indicated civil disorders of greatest severity and duration, p. 113. In terms of number of deaths, number of injuries, type and duration of law enforcement mobilization and duration of the civil disorders, the Milwaukee civil disorder ranks third, behind only Detroit and Newark: p. 163 (for deaths and injuries); pp. 611-59 (for type and duration of civil disorders). The issue of whether Milwaukee experienced a major civil disorder was debated in the *Supplemental Studies* of the commission. It was resolved by including Milwaukee among cities of "high severity." See National Advisory Commission on Civil Disorders, *Supplemental Studies*, p. 78.

70. Conducting interviews with public officials about recent and current events has the advantage of obtaining the respondent's reconstruction of events while still fresh and allows the observer to compare the statements made with subsequent behavior. The disadvantage of such interview timing is that some public officials may be reluctant to discuss their political strategy concerning pending events.

II
THE KERNER COMMISSION

2

Race Riots: Official Interpretations and Political Responses, A Historical Survey

There is nothing new or uniquely contemporary about racial violence in America. For those with historical perspective, the riots in Watts in 1965, Cleveland in 1966, Detroit and Newark in 1967 and Washington, D.C. in 1968 only refreshed the memory of similar severe rioting in East St. Louis in 1917, Chicago and Washington, D.C. in 1919, Detroit in 1925 and 1943 and Harlem in 1935 and 1943.

Important differences do exist, however, between the "race riots" of the first half of the twentieth century and the "civil disorders" of the 1960s. The earlier "race riots" were characterized by violent interracial clashes between blacks and whites, usually initiated by whites.[1] The later "civil disorders," on the other hand, featured clashes between blacks and law enforcement officials.[2] The target of aggression in race riots has been people (for reasons of racial identity), while in civil disorders it has been primarily property (usually white-owned property) and secondarily symbols of authority (such as the police). Nonetheless, race-related collective violence is a recurrent, periodic theme in American history.

A common official response to racial violence in the twentieth century has been to create riot commissions.[3] While the locale of the riots, the participants, racial climate and political orientations of the elites have varied, the appointment of a commission to study the outburst has been the usual, almost reflexive, American response. From 1917 through 1943, at least 21 commissions were appointed to make recommendations to prevent the recurrence of riots. At least 13 riot commissions were appointed between 1964 and 1968 with similar mandates (exclusive of those we treat more extensively later in the study), and the figure would undoubtedly have been much higher if the 1967 Kerner Commission had not preempted the field for many locales. So routine has been the creation of riot commissions following mass race-related violence that we may characterize the politics surrounding riot commissions and their reports as the typical elite response to racial violence in the United States.

In this chapter we shall examine the 34 riot commissions indicated above to discover their common characteristics and the extent to which they can be called the prevailing mode of political response to racial disorders.[4] Several themes emerge. Representatives of established interests are consistently appointed as commission members while representatives of subordinate groups are systematically ignored. Riot commissions tend to rely upon explanations of racial violence that reflect the interests of these same dominant economic and political groups. Organizationally, riot commissions are confronted with unresolvable conflicts between the tasks they are assigned to perform and the resources with which they are supposed to accomplish them. Partially as a result of these limits, they make few reform proposals that address the underlying causes of racial violence. Even fewer reform proposals are implemented.

This chapter will focus on five aspects of riot commissions: (1) the circumstances of their creation: (2) their composition; (3) how they conduct their internal affairs; (4) their interpretations of racial violence; and (5) their proposals for preventing future racial violence. Because race-related riots in American history cluster around periods of foreign wars—World War I, World War II, and the Vietnam War—we have organized our analysis around these time periods.[5]

Race Riots of the World War I Era

The 1917 East St. Louis Riot

At least 48 persons, including 39 blacks and 9 whites, died in the earliest and most severe race riot of the World War I period, which occurred in East St. Louis, Illinois in 1917.[6] Mobs composed mainly of unskilled white laborers violently attacked blacks who had recently migrated to East St. Louis from the deep South, lured by employers' promises of stable and well-paying employment. In the riot's aftermath, no fewer than four official commissions were created and variously charged with the responsibility to investigate the causes of the riot, describe the events, determine who participated and develop recommendations to prevent future racial violence. Each commission included representatives from some, but not all, interests in the city and issued reports which reflected favorably upon the interests of groups represented on the commissions.

The first investigation of the East St. Louis race riot was conducted by a labor subcommittee of the Illinois State Council of Defense, later known as the Walker Committee after one of its members. As acting president of the Illinois Federation of Labor, John H. Walker had participated in a public forum immediately preceding the violence at which labor leaders harangued a crowd of white workers with inflammatory speeches. Organized labor was hostile to blacks because they were imported from the South by employers as strike breakers. Lower-class whites also resented the job competition from blacks, who were a source of cheap labor.

After the initial outbreak of white violence against the recently arrived blacks, prolabor Mayor Fred Mollman of East St. Louis and leaders of the Central Trades and Labor Union appealed to the Illinois State Council of Defense to investigate the riot's causes. The three-member Walker Committee held hearings in East St. Louis and subsequently issued its report. Predictably, this commission concluded that the riot resulted from employers' practices of importing black laborers. The committee neither investigated nor discussed violence by white workers. The inflammatory conduct of Walker preceding the riot also went unreported. Elliot Rudwick summarizes the content of the final report:

> The Walker Committee, with the support of East St. Louis labor organizers, blamed the riots on a deliberate conspiracy of employers to import "an excessive and abnormal number" of Negroes to East St. Louis. The Walker group condemned employers but made no attempt to discover the identity of the rioters or recommend the prosecution of mob members. These actions, in seeming to condone the riot, hardly discouraged those who took the law into their own hands.[7]

Thus the Walker Committee gave sympathetic public expression to the labor interests represented on the investigating commission and blamed employers, who were not represented, for causing the riot.

Less than one week after the exoneration of the white laborers' behavior and their leaders' inflammatory rhetoric, racial violence again erupted in the city, this time with heightened severity. The high number of deaths and the duration of this violence raised numerous critical questions about the military's role in suppressing the riot. Mayor Mollman, prominent businessmen, and the press charged that the indifference of the police and the National Guard toward the violence amounted to gross neglect of duty. They also charged the military with official misconduct because the police and national guardsmen allegedly encouraged and sometimes aided mob attacks on black residents. In response to this criticism, Illinois Governor Frank Lowden appointed his equivalent of a riot commission, a Military Board of Inquiry, to investigate the militia's behavior during the riot.[8]

The Military Board of Inquiry heard scores of witnesses during three days of open hearings. Although it submitted a report to the Adjutant General of the Illinois National Guard, the document was not released to the public, "despite the impatience and consuming curiosity of newspapers." Rudwick reports:

> State officials decided that publication of the report would be far more politically damaging than its suppression, probably because the findings deviated so sharply from the testimony of most non-military witnesses.

Civilian testimony, particularly by businessmen, repeatedly emphasized that national guardsmen ignored white mob attacks on blacks and sometimes even aided the mobs. However, the Military Board of Inquiry chose to base its findings "essentially on testimony of militia company officers. This testimony differed so markedly from statements of most non-military witnesses, that it is difficult to believe both accounts concerned the same riot." By paying attention only to the military witnesses, the board avoided jeopardizing its members' military careers and, de facto, solved the problem of conflicting testimony.

The Military Board of Inquiry compounded its selective approach to available information by rationalizing guardsmen's ineffective and inappropriate conduct. Rudwick explains the board's rationalization: "Faced with overwhelming evidence that Negroes were killed in the presence of guardsmen, the Board concluded that the soldiers were so greatly outnumbered by mobs that the victims' lives could not have been saved." In turn, the board used this rationalization to argue for additional personnel and Guard training: "The Military Board of Inquiry, unwilling to suggest cowardice or fraternization, emphasized not only insufficient numbers but also the inexperience of militiamen."[9] The board thus transformed the widely condemned performance of the National Guard into a justification for advancing the Guard's organizational objectives.

The favorable interpretations of the role of labor organizers and national guardsmen did not go uncontested. Disturbed by the exoneration of labor and the failure to censure guardsmen, East St. Louis business leaders appealed for a federal investigation. Businessmen hoped that a thorough federal riot investigation might ease racial tensions and restore a climate favorable to commercial activity. They also feared that a rapid exodus of harassed blacks from East St. Louis might deprive them of an important labor surplus.

Business concern about the flight of black laborers from East St. Louis seems to have been well-founded. In one account of the consequences of racial tensions following the riot it was noted:

For months after the July riot, interstate commerce was interfered with and hindered, not, however, by open acts of violence, but by a subtle and effective intimidation of colored men who had been employed by the railroads to handle freight consigned from one state to another. So many of these men were driven out of East St. Louis as the result of the July riot that the railroads could not secure necessary help. After the worst effects of the riot had passed, this class of labor remained so frightened and intimidated that it would not live in East St. Louis.[10]

The petition for a federal investigation was ignored by the Southern-oriented Wilson administration, but Congress acted favorably upon the request.

Three months after the Walker Committee and the Military Board of Inquiry concluded their deliberations, a five-member special committee of the U.S. House of Representatives convened to investigate the riot. The Congressional Committee took 5,000 pages of testimony during one month of hearings in the city and released its report on the violent events and their causes on July 15, 1918. Its findings dramatically diverged from those of the two prior investigations.

The Congressional Committee dismissed the findings of the Walker Committee as invalid and maintained that the initial hostilities were, in fact, provoked at the labor union rally. Of one speaker at this union-sponsored meeting the committee said:

> His inflammatory speech caused many of his hearers to rush into the streets and to resort to acts of violence. . . .He was in full sympathy with the action of the mob. They followed his advice and the scenes of murder and arson that ensued were the logical result of his utterances.[11]

The Congressional Committee's report similarly called the investigation of the Military Board of Inquiry a "trifling inquiry." It censured the guardsmen's commanding officer, Colonel S. O. Tripp, charging him with blundering ineffectiveness and strongly condemned the behavior of individual guardsmen:

> The conduct of the soldiers who were sent to East St. Louis to protect life and property puts a blot on that part of the Illinois militia that served under Colonel Tripp. They were scattered over the city, many of them being without officers to direct or control them. In only a few cases did they do their duty. They seemed moved by the same spirit of indifference or cowardice that marked the conduct of the police force. As a rule they fraternized with the mob, joked with them and made no serious effort to restrain them.[12]

These initial findings prompted the committee to request authorization from Governor Lowden for an additional investigation of the military's role in the riot. The Governor refused to act on the recommendation.

In addition to challenging the interpretations of the earlier commissions, the Congressional Committee singled out what it considered malfunctioning political structures in East St. Louis, exposed corrupt public officials and blamed both employers and labor organizers for creating conditions eventually leading to the race riot. Although the committee's final report included several allegations of official misconduct by military personnel, no court-martial proceedings resulted. Similarly, while the committee made numerous recommendations for improving race relations in East St. Louis, virtually no effort was made to implement the measures.[13]

42

The investigations of the East St. Louis race riot helped to restore the economic and political relationships existing before the violence.[14] The labor, military and business groups that either directly participated in the violence or had a stake in the assignment of responsibility used the investigations to maintain their respective preriot standings. The investigation of the riot events by representatives of dominant groups in a manner reflecting favorably upon them proved conducive to their interest in maintaining the status quo ante. Interests represented on the riot commissions were absolved of blame for the violence while unrepresented, often competing, groups were judged guilty. Also, recommendations for change consistently reflected the economic and political interests of the groups forming the riot commission and had little relevance to preventing future race warfare. To the extent that they helped to restore preriot relations, the commissions tended to preserve dominant economic and political relationships.[15]

The Summer of 1919 and the Chicago Commission on Race Relations

Twenty-six American cities experienced race riots during the "red summer" of 1919.[16] So extensive was the violence that contemporaries began to regard race riots as endemic to the postwar period, and afterwards, official commissions convened in nearly all cities to investigate the riots.[17] The violence reached its apex with a race riot in Chicago which lasted five days; it took at least 38 lives, resulted in over 500 injuries, destroyed the homes of over 1,000 persons and resulted in a quarter-million dollars worth of property damage.[18] The duration and severity of the 1919 Chicago riot made it the single most important case of racial violence during the post-World War I era.

Various groups probed the cause of the riot and issued recommendations,[19] but the Chicago Commission on Race Relations was the main investigative body. Indeed, the commission ranks as the most important of its kind during the first half of the twentieth century because of its thoroughness, the wide scope of its recommendations and its extensive resources. Analysis of how it functioned and its impact on race relations in Chicago is of significance in itself, but we are particularly interested in highlighting its similarities to contemporary riot commissions.

During the racial violence in Chicago, two quite different groups petitioned Governor Frank Lowden for an investigatory commission. The first petition came from the NAACP's national offices and called

43

for a commission "to study troubles and formulate definite programme [sic] of race relations for state."[20] A second appeal to the governor arrived simultaneously from an amalgam of Chicago's social and economic elite.[21] Three weeks later the governor appointed the Chicago Commission on Race Relations. Its prestigious membership included six whites and six blacks. Its staff numbered 37, 22 whites and 15 blacks. The commission heard 175 witnesses over 18 months. In 1922 the University of Chicago Press published a 672-page hardback edition of the final commission report.

Governor Lowden appointed the six white members. Julius Rosenwald, of Sears, Roebuck and Company and a white member of the commission, recruited the six black members. The primary criteria for selecting commission members proved to be persons "prominent and powerful in the white and Negro communities who had also in some way concerned themselves with race relations."[22] The prominence of commission members is reflected in their occupations: five lawyers, two editors, two real estate dealers, one minister, one merchant and a physician.

The commission faced a series of problems immediately after being appointed, including financial obstacles:

> The Commission was seriously handicapped at the outset by a complete lack of funds. The legislative session of 1919 had ended before the riot, and the next regular session was not to convene until January, 1921. The Commission felt that it could not with propriety seek to raise funds on its own appeal. To meet this situation a group of citizens offered to serve as a co-operating committee to finance the Commission's inquiry and the preparation and publication of its report.[23]

The problem of securing funds plagued the commission throughout its existence. Although initially promised enough money to conduct its business, the commission repeatedly had to divert staff time and resources to raise money.[24]

A second immediate problem was recruiting staff personnel. Four commissioners canvassed possible candidates for high-level staff positions in the period between the commission's appointment on August 20 and its first meeting on October 9. Differences regarding staff organization began to surface among commissioners. Some preferred a single staff director responsible for all personnel, but this raised the

44

issue of whether he would be white or black. Other commissioners argued for two staff directors, one white and one black; eventually a white was named executive secretary and a black became associate executive secretary. Unforseen difficulties involving these appointments and the recruitment of other staff personnel delayed initial staff work until December 7, 1919—three and one-half months after the commission's creation.

Shortly after commencing staff research, the two staff directors proposed an outline that substantially set the commission's agenda. The outline carried the imprint of the noted sociologist Robert E. Park who heavily influenced the work of the commission; Waskow indicates that the commission's final report "is clearly the direct offspring of" the outline.[25] Adoption of an outline to guide commission deliberations was related to a third problem that confronted the commission.

In its initial deliberations the commission had to decide what its role should be in the aftermath of the Chicago violence. It faced two alternatives. It could establish its legitimacy by thoroughly and impartially investigating the race riot. This orientation was suggested when Governor Lowden asked the commission to search for riot causes and to recommend programs to prevent a recurrence of violence. Alternatively, it could conduct its investigation in a manner compatible with powerful interests in Chicago and to phrase its report in politically acceptable terms. This orientation derived from the commission's dependence upon such interests for funding and for implementing its recommendations. For the commission to have an impact on future race relations in Chicago, hard political realities had to be taken into account. Waskow describes the commission's options:

> The two simplest possible roles were that of a political body which could mediate, manage, and "accommodate" new racial disputes as they rose; and that of a purely scholarly body which could study, analyze, and explain the one historical event of the 1919 Chicago riot.[26]

The Chicago Commission chose the scholarly path. It followed the most sophisticated social science research procedures of its day and, in fact, developed new social research techniques that strongly influenced later students of race relations.[27] But in choosing a thorough, social scientific approach to its work, the political acceptability of its recommendations was impaired.

45

In Waskow's terms, the commission decided "between being a politics-oriented organization, resolving racial tensions, or a research-oriented organization, studying only the past" through a series of steps. In accepting the outline as an agenda and in recruiting social scientists as staff personnel, the commission indicated that it preferred to study the riot events rather than to try to heal racial tensions by directly intervening between whites and blacks. Financial limitations also precluded the commission's continuing involvement in Chicago politics to ease racial frictions. Direct intervention between the lower-class white and black antagonists was additionally of limited feasibility due to the elite status of commission members. But the Chicago commission possessed the tools appropriate to the study and analysis of the riot and it became a staff-oriented commission, except for the final review of the report.[28]

Other internal problems arose. Social scientists competent in designing study procedures and information-gathering techniques were not as competent in presenting their information to commissioners and writing the final report.[29] The problem of executive intervention arose when final proofs of the report were being discussed. Governor Lowden objected to the commission's argument against "prevailing misconceptions" that "Negroes have inferior mentality," because Negroes were, he said, still inferior to "the race which furnished. . .[the world] with Aristotle more than 2000 years ago."[30] The commission also faced the prospect of a dissenting opinion. One black commissioner, Edward Morris, refused to sign the preliminary report to Governor Lowden. In the final report, his signature is not affixed and it is recorded that he "does not concur in" the report, summary or recommendations,[31] although no explanation of his specific objections is given.

This extensive investigative effort was constrained from the beginning by internal organizational difficulties and the intrinsic contradictions of charging an *ad hoc* commission with simultaneous responsibility for explaining the nature of the disorders and obtaining support from political elites. What resulted from this massive intellectual effort? Governor Lowden was hopeful, but guarded. As he wrote in his foreword to the commission's report: "The report contains recommendations, which, if acted upon, will make impossible, in my opinion, a repetition of the appalling tragedy which brought disgrace to Chicago in July of 1919."[32]

The commission's report, however, went unheeded outside scholarly circles, and had only a minimal impact on future race relations in

Chicago. Two leading chronicles of blacks in Chicago record only marginal changes in race relations following the report's release.[33] In 1935 Gosnell described Chicago's response to the commission's report:

> Thirteen years have now gone by since the Commission on Race Relations made its recommendations to the police, the city council and administrative boards, the park boards, the civic organizations, and the white and colored public. While the bombing of Negro homes has greatly decreased and there have been no race riots, the Negro politicians have been unable or unwilling to prevent police brutality, to check crime conditions in the Negro community, to insist upon adequate recreational and educational facilities, to provide the best possible health services, and to secure sufficient housing at reasonable rentals. . . .Over the entire period complaints were common regarding vice and crime in the "Black Belt," discrimination against Negroes in the parks and the public schools, and the failure of the government to protect the health, the safety, and the security of the Negro minority.[34]

Waskow maintains that the commission's decision to orient its work along social scientific lines and "its unwillingness to give its recommendations a political cast and political relevance was probably the major factor in preventing its work from having a social effect." But did the Chicago Commission really have the option of gaining both social scientific and political bases of legitimacy? Or did it face an either-or choice? Waskow argues that the commission could have been politically effective and that the two tasks were not incompatible: "There was a third possibility, less obvious and more difficult: to unite the functions of scholarship and politics, by applying an analysis of past racial clashes like the Chicago riot to the control of continuing racial conflict."[35] However, it may be that features endemic to riot commissions prevent them from combining the quests for scientific truth and political viability.

Other Race Riots Following World War I

Racial violence in 1919 extended beyond urban areas when white vigilante groups in Phillips County, Arkansas attacked alleged black "insurrectionists." Afterwards, Governor Charles Brough appointed the Committee of Seven to investigate riot events. In reality the Committee of Seven "had grown out of the earlier secret committee of Phillips County whites to investigate rumors of an uprising."[36] This investigative committee employed torture and other forms of duress to extract testimony from blacks to substantiate its view that conspiratorial insurrectionists caused the Phillips County race riot. The committee also officially ruled upon cases of blacks indicted for insurrection by a local grand jury. Individuals and groups rejecting the committee's interpretation called upon Congress for a federal investigation, but without immediate success.

The national office of the NAACP eventually entered the post-riot intrigues in Arkansas with an investigation of its own. The NAACP riot study team conducted its inquiry and released a report which directly contradicted the conspiracy and insurrection interpretation offered by the Committee of Seven. It contended that unprovoked whites had attacked blacks in the riot and it accused the Committee of Seven of denying this basic fact about the rioting because the plantation-owner members of the committee profited by obscuring the real causes. The NAACP gave national visibility to its findings as a means for appealing to Congress and the Department of Justice for further investigation into the riot events. Both the Senate and the House eventually received testimony on the Phillips County riot which discredited the Committee of Seven's conclusions. Thus, by creating its own riot investigation, the NAACP was able to appeal to a national audience, receive a favorable hearing and challenge the official interpretation.

Another community's response to its 1919 race riot differed dramatically from the local investigation in the Phillips County case. After rioting subsided in Charleston, South Carolina, a local coroner's jury blamed white sailors for attacking blacks and precipitating violence. Waskow reports that:

> The city of Charleston thus demonstrated throughout its system of police, law enforcement, and government and from the very beginning of the riot, a degree of neutrality between the races that was unique in the seven major riots of 1919.[37]

This atypical behavior may have resulted from the fact that the sailors were "outsiders"; thus Charleston authorities did not have to decide between the claims of competing local groups. Later the Navy Department convened a board of inquiry to investigate the Charleston riot. It charged a number of white sailors with causing the riot and indicted them accordingly. They were convicted on charges of manslaughter.

The final race riot of the World War I era occurred in Detroit in 1925 following the purchase of a home in an all-white neighborhood by a black family. A commission appointed by the mayor investigated the violence and subsequently issued a report which "arrived at many specific recommendations involving official policy and governmental action" intended to alleviate racial tensions. But the commission's recommendations were never implemented:

> Even though this committee urged "a permanent race commission" and many effective measures, Detroit persisted in its "business as usual" psychology through large and small riots and other disorders climaxed by the riots at the Sojourner Truth Houses in 1942, the strikes at the Packard Plant, and then the riots throughout a large area of the city on Bloody Monday in 1943.[38]

Like the Chicago Commission, the Detroit Commission developed ameliorative program proposals but was unable to put them into effect.

Race Riots of the World War II Era

Responses to racial violence early in this century commonly included the appointment of an official investigative commission to determine responsibility and to recommend steps to prevent recurrence. The appointment to these bodies of individuals representative of established interests is consistent with their development of recommendations supportive of such interests. The Chicago Commission on Race Relations appears to be something of an exception. This remarkably "modern" commission made an unprecendented effort to study riot causes in objective, scholarly fashion. As crude, overt antiblack attitudes diminished in intensity and as the social sciences achieved greater respectability, the Chicago Commission became less of an exception. But in the more contemporary period, new factors develop to parallel the problems of earlier commissions.

Racial violence during the World War I era uniformly conformed to patterns of "race riots" wherein whites attacked blacks. Racial violence during the World War II era included traditional race riots and some civil disorders similar to contemporary attacks by blacks against white property and symbols of white authority. Disorders of the latter variety occurred in New York City's Harlem in 1935 and again in 1943.

The 1935 Civil Disorder In Harlem

The 1935 Harlem civil disorder broke the prior pattern of race riots. After the arrest of a 16-year-old black youth for a minor theft, rumors spread through Harlem that the youth had been killed by police in the basement of a department store. In the spontaneous rioting that followed, blacks looted white-owned stores and police officers exhibited restraint to a degree unmatched in earlier race riots.[39] The rioting lasted only one day—March 19, 1935—and resulted in under 100 arrests and two deaths.

Mayor Fiorello H. LaGuardia appointed an official riot commission the day after the violence ended. In creating The Mayor's Commission on Conditions in Harlem, LaGuardia sought a thorough investigation into the violent events of March 19, their causes and advice on appropriate measures to resolve racial tensions in Harlem. The Mayor's Commission delivered at least two reports to LaGuardia, but he suppressed both, apparently because they identified causes and recommended changes too far reaching, even for the liberal reformer LaGuardia.

The Mayor's Commission initially consisted of ten members, six of whom were blacks (including its chairman, Charles H. Roberts). In addition to being the only official riot commission in this century on which blacks constituted a majority, the commissioners were uniformly liberal toward race relations.[40] The commission assigned different areas of study to six subcommittees composed of members of the full commission. One subcommittee developed the first report of the Mayor's Commission just two months later and submitted its findings and recommendations to LaGuardia signed by all ten members of the full commission.

The subcommittee which developed the first report consisted of three blacks and two whites and was chaired by Arthur Garfield Hays, a white lawyer and civil libertarian. Hays led the subcommittee in conducting 21 public and four closed hearings. The first report did not equivocate in specifying what conditions in Harlem gave rise to the rioting:

This sudden breach of the public order was the result of a highly emotional situation among the colored people of Harlem due in large part to the nervous strain of years of unemployment and insecurity. To this must be added their deep sense of wrong through discrimination against their employment in stores which live chiefly

50

upon their purchases, discrimination against them in the school system and by the police, and all the evils due to dreadful overcrowding, unfair rentals and inadequate institutional care. It is probable that their justifiable pent-up feeling, that they were and are the victims of gross injustice and prejudice, would sooner or later have brought about an explosion.

This first report was additionally remarkable for its political orientation, its rejection of then current theories of a conspiracy by Communist instigators, and its forthright statements about police behavior despite the unprecedented restraint shown by police.[41]

Considerable attention was given to documenting discriminatory practices by the police department. The report attempted to convey attitudes of Harlem residents to the mayor and other public officials:

We regret that we find much to criticize in the conduct of the police. Nothing more alarming has been developed in the hearings held by this committee than the intensity of the feeling against the police. It is a grave state of affairs when the inhabitants of a large section of the city have come to look upon the men in police uniforms as lawless oppressors who stop at no brutality or at the taking of human life. . . .(The) existence of intense hostility on the part of the law-abiding element among the colored people toward the police is proof positive that there is something seriously wrong in the attitudes of the officers toward the people whom they are there to serve and to aid and not to browbeat or abuse. . . .(We) believe that a simple recital of the facts brought out before us will prove that there is solid ground for the bitter resentment of the people of Harlem.[42]

Beyond conveying what it considered justified antipolice sentiments of Harlem residents, the first report also dealt critically with the conduct of police officers during the disorder. It raised objections to police arrests of persons attempting to hold a public rally:

The speakers were arrested before they had an opportunity to say anything. Worse than that, the evidence shows that two of the speakers were taken to jail, were denied the opportunity to communicate with their attorneys, were beaten by the police and left without food for almost twenty-four hours. The barbarity with which at least one of them was treated is shocking and there has been no denial of his statement that the police made derogatory and threatening remarks suggesting a definitely prejudiced attitude toward Negroes.[43]

The report recommended the creation of a civilian review board to pass judgment on police conduct. It urged that the reveiw board have from five to seven representatives from Harlem who "should include in their number one or more men who are dissenters from established institutions and also men who are likely to have contact with victims of injustice." With similar emphasis, it condemned violence by police officers: "It is too readily assumed that an officer who kills or gravely injures a citizen is acting in the line of duty and must be upheld at any cost lest the authority of the police and their power be weakened." The report concluded by recommending changes in other policies within the city:

> It is futile to condemn the propagandists or to denounce them for fishing in troubled waters. The only answer is to eliminate the evils upon which they base their arguments. The blame belongs to a society that tolerates inadequate and often wretched housing, inadequate and inefficient schools and other public facilities, unemployment, unduly high rents, the lack of recreation grounds, discrimination in industry and public utilities against colored people, brutality and lack of courtesy of the police. As long as these conditions remain, the public order cannot and will not be safe.[44]

Few riot commissions in the twentieth century have spoken so bluntly about police behavior or placed the cause of racial violence so unequivocally on social and economic inequality in the black community, inequality resulting in part from institutional racism practiced by municipal agencies.

This first report was submitted directly to LaGuardia. It appealed to his demonstrated liberal credentials as the basis for optimism about the implementation of recommendations:

> You, Mr. Mayor, have long been a leader among liberals, and have often expressed your devotion to the ideals of civil liberty. You, as well as the police Commissioner, have received a heritage of wrong police psychology and a resulting resentment by people who have suffered injustice for many years. . . .The responsibility for a system and psychology which has developed in the course of years, cannot be placed on any individual. The opportunity however to correct present conditions is to a large extent in your hands, and we feel confident that you and [Police] Commissioner Valentine will seize that opportunity eagerly.[45]

The recommendations of this initial report held out the promise of fundamental changes in race relations in New York City. But support failed to materialize. LaGuardia failed to "seize the opportunity" envisioned by the authors and the report received no official action or response.

After submitting its initial report, the Mayor's Commission continued to study the causes of the 1935 civil disorder and to formulate additional recommendations. The commission's work proceeded through investigations by five subcommittees: health and hospitalization; housing; crime and delinquency and police; schools; and social services and relief agencies. The commission hired as director of research E. Franklin Frazier, a black professor of sociology at Howard University and author of *The Negro Family*. He assembled the subcommittees' work into a second report which was submitted to LaGuardia almost one year after the 1935 civil disorder. In the ten months between the filing of the first and second reports, Mayor LaGuardia appointed three new members to the commission—two whites and one black—but the new members did not temper the harsh criticism in the commission's findings.

The second report elaborated on discriminatory practices and racist structures in areas other than police performance and concluded with 26 recommendations for change.[46] A contemporary observer noted the report's far-reaching findings and reform proposals and indicated the likelihood of a favorable response from the city administration:

> The public awaits the full and official publication of what is, without doubt, an important document on the present state of Harlem. When published, the findings will shock the general public and all but the few social experts already familiar with the grave economic need and social adjustment in Harlem and the inadequacies of short-sighted provisions in basic civic facilities of schools, hospitals, health centers, housing control and the like—a legacy of neglect from the venal, happy-go-lucky days of Tammany-controlled city government. Now with a socially minded city and national government the prospects of Negro Harlem—and for that matter all handicapped sections—are infinitely brighter.[47]

This second report fared no better than the first. LaGuardia and other city officials suppressed it because of its forthright condemnation of racist institutions and its comprehensive proposals for change. The document has never been fully released to the public, although parts appeared in the *New York Amsterdam News.* 48

Civil Disorders: 1943

Eight years later, Harlem again erupted in a massive civil disorder. As New York City contemplated possible responses to the 1943 disorder, the executive director of the NAACP's national office declared:

> New York had another riot in 1935. Mayor LaGuardia appointed a bi-racial commission which held hearings and submitted a report which included recommendations that might have prevented, or at least made less likely and less destructive, the riot of August 1, 1943. But unfortunately, the report was never made public and most of its recommendations were unheeded. It is to be hoped that this mistake will not be made again.49

Harlem experienced its most severe civil disorder in 1943 when rioting claimed the lives of 5 blacks, injured 565 persons, resulted in over 500 arrests and caused an estimated $5 million worth of property damage.50 As in 1935, the older pattern of race rioting does not accurately portray the 1943 Harlem violence because "clashes among white and Negroes were only incidental to the disorders, which consisted mainly of looting."51 The classic form of race rioting did reassert itself, however, in other cities in 1943. One account lists 13 cities where whites attacked blacks in a manner similar to racial violence during the World War I era.52 Following these race riots, public officials again turned to commissions to investigate the violence and to formulate preventive recommendations. After the "zoot-suit" riots against blacks and Mexican-Americans in Los Angeles, for example, California Governor Earl Warren appointed an investigative commission, as did the attorney general of California.53

The 1943 Detroit Riot

The most severe violence during the summer months of 1943 erupted in Detroit. It resulted in the arrest of 1,893 persons, the death of 25 blacks and 9 whites and the injury of 675 others, destroyed about $2 million worth of property and was not suppressed until federal troops were summoned.54 It also resulted in an "impulse to investigate" by several public officials and private groups, all of whom had an immediate stake in fixing blame for the rioting and in taking steps to prevent its continuation or recurrence.

54

Three days after "Bloody Monday," as the day of the most intense rioting was called, at least four different inquiries into the racial violence were proposed. Congressman Martin Dies, chairman of the House Committee on Un-American Activities, threatened to bring the committee to Detroit to conduct hearings on the causes of the rioting. Dies eventually withdrew his proposal because of active opposition from Detroit civic leaders, newspapers and labor union officials. The Reverend Gerald L. K. Smith, a nationally prominent spokesman for right-wing and antiblack groups, was one of Dies's few supporters. A second inquiry was announced by Dr. Lowell S. Selling, head of the Recorder's Court Psychiatric Clinic of Detroit, who proposed to study the mental condition of 1,000 rioters. Third, the Detroit Council of Churches convened to seek reasons for the rioting and to urge corrective measures upon public officials. The final, and most important, investigation was revealed by Governor Harry F. Kelly of Michigan when he appointed an official commission to thoroughly investigate riot deaths and to inquire into the underlying causes of racial turmoil in Detroit.

The appointment of an official riot commission by the governor was a response, at least in part, to widespread charges of inappropriate conduct by Detroit police officers, the Michigan State Police and the National Guard. As in the 1917 East St. Louis riot, law enforcement officers were accused of having ignored white mobs and actually joined with them in attacks against blacks.[55] The official commission was also created because of the widely held belief that the rioting resulted from the recent in-migration of large numbers of black and white laborers from the South who lacked adequate housing and recreational facilities and educational opportunities. As city officials would later, Governor Kelly initially supported the view that riots represented flaws in otherwise healthy systems: "(The) whole thing is sociological and we've got to establish by scientific investigation what sort of maladjustments bring about such a situation."

To provide a scientifically based profile of participants, Governor Kelly directed the Michigan State Department of Social Welfare to prepare a set of questionnaires to be used in interviewing jailed rioters. Interviews were conducted with 340 rioters and the results contradicted the apparently always-prevalent "riffraff" theory: "(Few) [rioters] were recent migrants to Detroit, and most had steady jobs and were eager to get back to work."[56] The governor's riot commission had at its disposal considerable data on the characteristics of arrested riot participants. This information, combined with the governor's request for a "scientific investigation," held out the promise of a thorough and objective appraisal.

The impulse to investigate the 1943 Detroit race riot was not confined to the four preceding groups. One day after the governor appointed the official state riot commission, Detroit Mayor Edward J. Jeffries appointed the biracial Mayor's Committee on Inter-Racial Relations consisting of six blacks and six whites. Although initially charted as an investigative body, at its first meeting three days later the committee chose to concentrate its activities on easing race tensions rather than determining the causes of the riot. This decision coincided with the release of a "white paper" by Detroit police commissioner John H. Witherspoon, also a member of the governor's official riot commission, in which law enforcement personnel were absolved of any wrongdoing prior to, during and after the riot. Responsibility for starting the riot was assigned instead to Detroit's black population. The Mayor's Committee continued to function after this time, but it deferred to the governor's riot commission on questions of riot causality and recommendations for change.

Commissioner Witherspoon's "white paper" failed to reassure all city officials that the deaths during the riot and riot causes would be thoroughly investigated. Detroit city councilman George C. Edwards proposed a six-point program for responding to the riot, including a call upon the governor to empanel a grand jury specifically charged to inquire into the unsolved murders during the riot. The City Council refused to endorse Edwards's request for a grand jury, but it did create a City Council committee charged with formulating programs to upgrade the status of black citizens.

Two additional investigations were conducted and made public before release of the official report from the Governor's Commission. First, the Reverend Horace White, a black member of the Detroit Housing Commission, made public a report—conducted by Sheridan A. Bruseaux, a private investigator from Chicago—on the rioting. The report attributed the riots to inadequate facilities in housing and recreation. A second report was authored by United States Attorney General Francis Biddle and was submitted to President Roosevelt. This report denied that a conspiracy caused the riot; assigned the causes of the riot to in-migration of blacks, inadequate housing, insufficient recreation opportunities and inadequate manpower in the Detroit

Police Department; and concluded with six recommendations including prohibiting further migration of blacks to Detroit.[57]

After deliberating less than two months, the official Governor's Commission produced an 8,500-word report. The commission's report, entitled "Factual Report of the Committee to Investigate the Riot Occurring in Detroit on June 21, 1943," was far from "factual." The document consistently neglected information available to the commission, blamed the riot on black leaders and black news media and "whitewashed the activities of law enforcement agencies and government officials."[58]

Discrepancies between the promised scientific investigation and the end product may be explained by the composition of the Governor's Commission. The commission consisted of four members, all prominent law enforcement officers and all involved in one way or another with the riot. These included: Police Commissioner Witherspoon; Wayne County Prosecutor W. E. Dowling; State Police Commissioner Oscar Olander; and Michigan Attorney General H. J. Rushton. Because its members uniformly represented law enforcement interests, the Governor's Commission (following the pattern suggested earlier) became an official instrument for exonerating questionable behavior of police officers and public officials.

The Governor's Commission primarily blamed black leaders for the Detroit riot. Its final report equated demands for justice by black leaders with exhortations to violence:

> Perhaps most significant in precipitating the racial tension existing in Detroit is the positive exhortation by many so-called Negro leaders to be "militant" in the struggle for racial equality. A. Philip Randolph's statement appearing in the January 2, 1943 issue of the *Detroit Tribune* charging that: "Justice is never granted, it is extracted. It is written in the stars that the darker races will never be free until they make themselves free. This is the task of the coming year" clearly constitutes an appeal to extract "justice" by violence.[59]

Newspapers serving the black community in Detroit also came under sharp attack for urging their readers to become more militant in pursuing racial equality. The *Michigan Chronicle* received the commission's harshest indictment. Indicative of the emotional content of the commission's final report were a series of rhetorical questions aimed at the black news media:

Who has exhorted them [blacks] to overthrow established social order to obtain "racial equality"? Who exaggerates and parades before these same elements sordid stories of sensational crime, giving an antisocial complexion to these incidents readily absorbed by the audience? Who constantly beats the drums of "racial prejudice, inequality, intolerance, discrimination" and challenges these hoodlum elements "militantly" to rise against this alleged oppression? Who charges by their news stories and their editorials that all law enforcement agencies are anti-Negro, brutal, and vicious in the handling of Negroes, and bent upon their persecution?60

In each instance the Governor's Commission answered its rhetorical questions by blaming the black-controlled news media.

The Governor's Commission strongly defended law enforcement agencies in Detroit. It rejected demands by Black groups that the racial identity of law violators not be made public. It argued: "This committee feels that the fact that the Negroes in Detroit, who constitute less than 10 percent of the population, commit more than 71 percent of the major crimes is one the public should know."61 Detroit Police Commissioner Witherspoon provided his fellow riot commission members with questionable police department statistics to support such allegations. Upon release of the report, the *Detroit Free Press* charged a "whitewash" that was "largely drawn up by Police Commissioner Witherspoon. . . .With Commissioner Witherspoon furnishing most of the evidence, it is hardly conceivable that he would suggest an investigation of himself and his Department."62

Although it was the official state riot commission and had successfully preempted several proposed inquiries, the Governor's Commission did not have the field to itself. Shortly after Governor Kelly announced his appointments to the official commission, a separate investigation of riot events was undertaken by Thurgood Marshall, chief counsel of the NAACP. Marshall began by intensively interviewing blacks about the riot, then collecting affidavits from blacks who charged instances of brutality by police officers and, finally, hiring two private investigators to follow up leads in the affidavits. The final report of the Marshall investigation was published in full in a 1943 issue of *Crisis.* 63

The Marshall report challenged the validity of the official investigation, particularly concerning police conduct. Entitled "The Gestapo in Detroit," the report was blunt about official violence by police officers:

"Much of the blood spilled in the Detroit riot is on the hands of the Detroit police department. In the past the Detroit police have been guilty of both inefficiency and an attitude of prejudice against Negroes." It continued:

> In the June riots of this year, the police ran true to form. The trouble reached riot proportions because the police once again enforced the law with an unequal hand. They used "persuasion" rather than firm action with white rioters, while against Negroes they used the ultimate in force: night sticks, revolvers, riot guns, sub-machine guns, and deer guns. As a result, 25 of the 34 persons killed were Negroes. Of the latter, 17 were killed by police. . . .All these crimes are matters of record; many were committed in the presence of police officers, several on the pavement around City Hall. Yet the record remains: Negroes killed by police—17, white persons killed by police—none. The entire record, both of the riot killings and the previous disturbances, reads like the story of the Nazi Gestapo.[64]

The report concluded by urging a study of the treatment of blacks by the Detroit Police Department, the background characteristics of police personnel and Commissioner Witherspoon's plans for coping with possible future rioting.

The Marshall investigation was strongly opposed by city officials. Mayor Jeffries and Police Commissioner Witherspoon defended the police department from the moment Marshall announced his inquiry. Mayor Jeffries told the Detroit Common Council: "The Police Department role in the riot needs no defense. . . .On the whole it was splendid and at times magnificent." The mayor, at this early date, denied charges of police brutality and attacked black leaders of the Marshall investigation:

> I am rapidly losing my patience with those Negro leaders who insist that their people do not and will not trust policemen and the Police Department. After what happened, I am certain that some of these leaders are more vocal in their caustic criticism of the Police Department than they are in educating their own people to their responsibilities as citizens.[65]

The Detroit chapter of the NAACP denounced the mayor's statements and asserted that the Marshall investigative group was the proper forum for discussing the riot. The president of the Detroit NAACP chapter told the mayor:

> In 1941, you appointed a Mayor's Committee after the Northwest- ern High School Riot. The committee...studied the conflict situation. Its recommendations were laid upon your desk where they lie, today, unheeded. ....Today we have a new committee. Its report can be written now. The question is whether you will do anything about it. ....

Jeffries eventually supported one demand of the Marshall study group by proposing a one-man grand jury investigation into riot deaths, but he did so because of the positive "psychological reaction" such an inquiry would produce.[66]

The competitive nature of relations between alternative study groups was dramatically illustrated by several exchanges between members of the Governor's Commission and sponsors of the Marshall investigation. At one point in its deliberations the Marshall group called for a grand jury "not only to probe the causes of the riot but also to find the killers of the riot victims."[67] After denying repeated requests to convene a grand jury, Wayne County Prosecutor Dowling, one of four members of the Governor's Commission, turned his attack against the Detroit chapter of the NAACP—the sponsoring group for the Marshall investigation—for withholding information from law enforcement authorities. Dowling characterized the NAACP as a "troublemaking organization" for collecting information on riot deaths and refusing to release that information to the Governor's Commission. Of one NAACP informant, Dowling commented:

> Rev. Baber told me (the Detroit *News* quoted Prosecutor Dowling as saying) that there were a lot of facts that he could not disclose to me, that would justify a grand jury. I asked him what these facts were. He said that he was pledged to secrecy about them, but that he had turned them over to the NAACP.

The Reverend Baber provided a different version of this exchange in a sworn affidavit:

> I...stated that I knew persons who had information that they would present only to a Grand Jury. Mr. Dowling wanted to know what the Negroes were doing with their information. I stated that many were

turning their information over to the National Association for the Advancement of Colored People to the end that proper protective measures might be pursued. Whereupon, Mr. Dowling pounded the table and jumped to his feet, saying, "Why do you turn your information over to the National Association for the Advancement of Colored People? They were the biggest instigators of the recent race riot. If a Grand Jury were called, they would be the first indicted." Continuing in the same vein, he charged, "You people have no confidence in the law enforcement agents but turn your information over to a troublemaking organization like that."[68]

Police Commissioner Witherspoon supported Dowling by questioning the validity of the information gathered by both the NAACP and the Marshall investigation. Finally, the commission advised Governor Kelly that it saw no justification for a grand jury and the governor did not appoint one.

The Governor's Commission made public its final report while the Marshall investigation continued. The date of the release coincided with a meeting of the national convention of chiefs of police in Detroit. A renewed petition for a grand jury investigation nevertheless received the endorsement of the *Detroit Free Press*, the United Automobile Workers Union, and Common Councilman Edwards. As demands for a grand jury persisted, release of the Governor's Commission's report had the following effect:

For all official purposes, the controversy ended August 11 when the Governor's Committee concluded that "the ordinary law enforcement and judicial agencies have thus far adequately and properly dealt with the law violators." These agencies, of course, were headed by the committee members themselves—Witherspoon, Dowling, State Police Commissioner Olander, and Attorney General Rushton.[69]

The repeatedly requested grand jury investigation never materialized.

This review of official reactions to race riots in the first half of the twentieth century reveals several important continuities. After the violence ended, political executives commonly appointed official commissions to investigate the causes of race riots and to make recommendations to prevent them from recurring. In almost all cases the official riot commission members viewed riot causality in terms favorable to the political executive who appointed them and invariably in a manner compatible with the economic or political interests that they themselves represented. Similarly, the final reports appear to have advanced the economic and political interests of groups represented on the commissions. In response, groups not represented on the official commissions tended to create alternative or "competitive" investigative bodies to challenge the validity of official interpretations and recommendations. These competing commissions used procedures similar to those employed by the official riot commissions to maximize their own legitimacy, undermine the legitimacy of official interpretations and impair as much as possible the implementation of official recommendations.

The politics of post-riot response in early twentieth-century riots thus appear to consist of continued competition among dominant groups in the larger political system, with few important changes resulting from the crisis generated by the race riots.

Riots during the Vietnam War: An Introduction to the Current Era

The 1964 Rochester Disorder

The most recent era of civil disorders began in 1964 when blacks rioted in New York City, Philadelphia and in Rochester, New York. The Rochester disorder began on July 24, 1964, after police arrested a black youth at a street dance. Three days later, an emergency session of the Rochester City Council requested an investigation into the disorder by Rochester's City Manager. After nine months of study, the City Manager submitted a 22-page report to the City Council. Although the City Manager's investigation was not formally conducted by a riot commission, in many respects it served similar purposes.

White residents of Rochester reacted to the disorder with disbelief and "many blamed it on outside agitators, local extremists, or Negro criminals."[70] The City Manager's report took issue with these popular beliefs. It contended that "the riots were not planned or organized."[71] Using data from arrest records, the report analyzed rioters' backgrounds to support the argument that most riot participants lived in Rochester, were employed and were between 20 and 40 years of age. Many white residents also criticized law enforcement officers for treating riot participants too leniently. The City Manager's report similarly tried to contest these sentiments:

The claim that firearms should have been used by policemen is without justification. Their use probably would have led to a blood bath. The use of firearms directed at or over the heads of rioters is not recommended by responsible police officials. . . .The charge that policemen were ineffective on these critical nights because of the presence of a civilian Police Advisory Board is without foundation. It also is an unjust criticism of policemen who conducted themselves with distinction, with courage, with common sense and with restraint.

The City Manager's report was, however, defensive about the city administration's record. The administration, in a sense, was the only interest formally represented in the investigation and the report's conclusions reflect this:

I believe, after thorough examination of the records of this and prior City administrations and after long conversations with a variety of sources, that nothing the City government could have accomplished in the past few years would have so dramatically changed conditions for the Negro in the riot areas that his frustrations and anger would have been eliminated. . . .Many of the things the Negro wants are beyond the power of the City government to give.[72]

Rochester's alleged inability to prevent racial violence did not deter the report's author from praising measures taken to meet grievances of black residents. Such praise was, of course, self-praise. The report claims: "No place in the country has made greater efforts to marshal all its resources or established more agencies to deal with racial discrimination and related problems than have New York State and its localities—particularly Rochester."[73] After praising city agencies and administrators, the report found fault with community leaders for inaccurately reading ghetto sentiments. In reaction to charges that city officials were unprepared for a civil disorder, the report contends:

Conversations with supposed leaders and persons regarded as being aware of situations indicated. . .expressions of considerable satisfaction with the City's public housing efforts, the City School District's program to eliminate racial imbalance in the schools and Rochester employers' moves to provide broader opportunities for employment. It certainly would be inaccurate to claim there was total satisfaction. It is factual to say that there was a feeling of satisfaction that things were moving in the right direction.

The report urged the adoption of measures more likely to augment power in the Office of City Manager than to address the grievances of black residents. The report notes that the City Manager "in the proposed 1965-66 budget, recommended establishment of a Community Service Office, working in the field, as a component of the City Manager's Office. That recommendation is reiterated." A second recommendation proposed expanding the jurisdiction of the Rochester Housing Authority so that "acres of vacant and relatively inexpensive land in the Towns surrounding Rochester [could] be zoned for low-income apartment use." In effect the report argued that if Rochester could do little to alleviate the hardships of its black residents, then maybe suburban areas could.

Because this investigation was conducted by a public official, it is not surprising that the report emphasized two positive steps taken after the civil disorder. The first dealt with reassuring anxious whites that sufficient police personnel and detailed plans existed to prevent a repetition of the disturbances.[74] Additionally, the report described attempts to reassure black citizens that their demands had been heard and were being acted upon.[75] Blacks were also told that new housing initiatives had been undertaken that would virtually "eliminate ghetto conditions."[76]

A year after Rochester's civil disorder, Harper concluded that, "[b]y and large, nothing," constructive had been accomplished in Rochester since the riots. He evaluated the report's claims that positive steps had been taken:

> Some people claim that more has been done since the riots. They cite such things as the expansion of social work programs, the creation of biracial committees, and the pronouncements and programs of existing groups. These kinds of activities will no doubt continue and they will probably give some small relief to the symptoms of Rochester's racial problems. But they offer little hope for the solution of those problems.[77]

The 1965 Watts Disorder

The 1965 civil disorder in the Watts section of Los Angeles proved to be the most severe instance of racial violence since the 1943 Detroit riot. It continued for six days, with over $40 million in property destroyed, over 1,000 injuries recorded, nearly 4,000 arrests made and 34 persons killed.[78] One week after the restoration of order, Governor

Edmund G. Brown of California created an official commission to investigate the violence. Eight commissioners were appointed and John A. McCone was named chairman.

Although considered a liberal, Governor Brown recruited relatively conservative commissioners. He may have hoped their interpretation of the Los Angeles disorder would help insulate him from the expected opposition of moderate Democrats in the impending primary election. Moreover, Brown apparently reasoned that meaningful change could be evoked from established groups only if the commission represented those groups. This consideration weighed heavily in the selection of McCone as chairman. He was a California businessman who had once been head of the Central Intelligence Agency.[79]

McCone was hardly a passive chairman. Initially, he exercised a veto over the Governor's choices for membership on the commission. McCone also drafted a memorandum that eventually became Brown's charge to the commission and which in turn set the agenda. McCone chaired the executive committee which made all important decisions about hiring staff, conducting investigations and holding hearings. Moreover, he dominated the critical stage of writing the report.[80] Because of his activist role, the "Governor's Commission" became the "McCone Commission" not only in the rhetoric of the media but also within the commission.

The McCone Commission encountered several operational problems. Governor Brown imposed a three-month deadline for the issuance of the report.[81] Given 100 days to complete its work, the commission had to recruit staff from competent persons who were readily available. Potential staff members meeting these two primary qualifications proved to be lawyers, not social scientists; lawyers were thus hired as full-time staff personnel and social scientists as consultants.[82]

The shortage of time affected the commission's incorporation of social science findings and new research into the body of its report. The requirement for social science studies was embodied in Governor Brown's charge to "probe deeply the immediate and underlying causes of the riots."[83] But the commission did not, except in one instance, use social science data to explain riot causes.[84] The report's education section was the exception. Professor Kenneth A. Martyn's commissioned research was incorporated into the final document, which may account for the fact that the education section has been the least criticized portion of the report. Lack of time further limited the staff in conducting hearings. Conot reports that "in fact, even as the final report was in preparation, witnesses were still being interrogated by staff investigators."[85]

Financial resources were also limited. Governor Brown allocated $100,000 from his emergency funds at the beginning, but this money soon ran out and additional funds had to be sought elsewhere. The Ford Foundation eventually gave $150,000 to the commission.[86]

Internal conflicts plagued the McCone Commission. Division of staff work into two general areas produced initial conflict between the two groups. This, coupled with the realignment of staff officials, led to the resignation of two high-level staff members. Conflict also occurred between the professional staff and commission members. Chairman McCone decided early that the staff would be limited to generating "facts." In most instances, however, members did not look with favor upon staff reports, and in some cases they rejected them. Thus, the report often is not supported by staff papers and staff reports and sometimes is directly contradicted by them.[87]

Another internal conflict concerned the members' inability to arrive at a consensus. One dissent from the commission report is appended to the document and is labeled "comments from the Rev. James Edward Jones." Reverend Jones, one of two blacks on the commission, argued forcefully against two conclusions in the report. To the report's conclusion that California welfare programs encouraged migration of Southern blacks to Los Angeles he declared: "I have been unable to find statistics to justify this statement and violently disagree with this unjustifiable projection." He was also disturbed by the report's statement on various forms of political activity and gave an eloquent defense of black political protest.[88] This dissenting opinion thwarted the McCone Commission's desire for a unanimous report. One account indicates that "great pressure" was applied in an unsuccessful attempt to persuade Reverend Jones to withdraw his two objections.[89]

Like most riot commissions, the McCone Commission had to choose between a scientifically defensible report or a politically acceptable interpretation of the disorder. Students of the commission uniformly agree that it chose the latter. The scarcity of time and money may have helped orient the report toward being politically acceptable rather than scientifically based. More likely, the conservative members viewed the available evidence selectively and, in so doing, allowed certain perspectives to prevail despite evidence to the contrary.[90] The commission concluded that the disorder was formless, meaningless and senseless and that participants represented only a small minority from the poorest sector of the black community. The conduct of Los Angeles public officials and police officers received, at best, only token evaluation. Political protest against acknowledged grievances was condemned and ultimate blame for the disorders was placed squarely on the black community. Recommendations to prevent a recurrence of violence consisted of minimal programs hardly designed to challenge existing power relations.[91]

Concurrent with the appointment of the McCone Commission, a White House task force headed by Attorney General Ramsey Clark was formed to investigate the disorder and issue a report. Chairman McCone, seeing the task force as a competitor, contacted the White House and suggested that "it might be appropriate to wait until we came out with a report and recommendations before any White House pronouncement was made on what should be done in our city."[92] The White House task force yielded to McCone's expressed wish and no report was ever issued.

The McCone Commission preempted other potential study groups in California in a similar manner. Immediately after the August disorder the Southern California Advisory Committee to the United States Commission on Civil Rights was established as a subcommittee of the statewide California Advisory Committee. Composed of members of the statewide committee residing in southern California, it contemplated conducting an investigation into the Los Angeles disorder, but the McCone Commission gave assurances that all areas would be investigated in a thorough manner.[93] The committee then temporarily left the field of investigation to the McCone Commission, but only temporarily.

One month after release of the McCone Commission's report, the Southern California Advisory Committee issued a report which severely criticized the McCone Commission:

We are sorely disappointed by the McCone Commission Report. . . .It prescribes aspirin where surgery is required. The report is elementary, superficial, unoriginal and unimaginative. It offers little, if anything, in the way of a study of economic and sociological conditions not previously available in published reports of public agencies.

The committee charged that the McCone Commission attempted to stifle political protest, misconstrued the impact of an open housing referendum on the black community and exonerated misconduct by public officials and police officers. Los Angeles Mayor Sam Yorty was singled out for condemnation for "attitudes and actions" which "prior to and during the riot contributed substantially to its existence and duration." The committee argued that the McCone Commission whitewashed the improper administration of the Police Department under Chief William H. Parker. What particularly incensed the committee was the McCone Commission's failure to fulfill its promise of a thorough investigation:

> We were assured by the McCone Commission that it considered the Muslim Temple episode of substantial significance and that it would treat it fully. Nevertheless, the report of the McCone Commission fails to contain a single word concerning the Muslim Temple incident. This, we do not understand.[94]

The committee not only criticized the McCone Commission for exonerating official misconduct, it also defended the role of Glenn M. Anderson, the only public official attacked in the commission report.[95] The report concluded with seven full pages of recommendations, developed, it said, because of inadequacies in the McCone proposals.

This six-member competing commission experienced consensus problems much like those confronting the McCone Commission. One member, who had recently been appointed to the civilian Police Commission of Los Angeles, issued a dissenting opinion applauding the McCone report as an "intensive study and evaluation of facts by a Blue Ribbon cross section of devoted public-minded individuals." He took strong exception to the committee's comments on the conduct of law enforcement officers during the civil disorder: he claimed that the committee's specific purpose was to erroneously place:

> all the blame for the rioting, looting, killing and arson on the Law Enforcement agencies in general, and the Los Angeles Police Department in particular. Chief William H. Parker, a national symbol of Police honesty, discipline and integrity has been made the principal target of senseless tirades. His surrender to the forces of evil and civil disobedience, under any pretense, is impossible.[96]

The committee's report was thus undercut by one of its own members.[97]

The McCone Commission emphasized the importance of implementing the report's recommendations to reduce racial animosities in Los Angeles and to upgrade the status of blacks. As an *ad hoc* organization the commission technically ceased to exist after presenting its report, but concern for seeing its proposals adopted prompted its members to extend the organization's life. The commission decided to "reconvene periodically to review actions taken to implement the recommendations in our report."[98] Although originally intended to involve all commission members, the periodic reviews consisted solely of conferences between the chairman and vice-chairman. These conferences yielded two "status reports" ostensibly charting the degree to which commission recommendations had been adopted.[99] In reality the periodic reviews were to defend "itself [the commission] against some of the attacks which have been made upon it" and served as a public relations device.[100]

The McCone Commission's impact on post-riot politics in Los Angeles has been uneven. Where the recommendations appear to be in harmony with values dominant in the city, they have been implemented to a limited extent. Thus Fogelson notes: "As the official version of the Los Angeles riots, moreover, 'Violence in the City' has shaped public policy—witness the federal subsidy to the Transit District—and also guided popular opinion."[101] But where recommendations are more controversial, implementation of proposals has been minimal. Conot reviews point by point the fate of the McCone Commission's recommendations.[102] Some programs affecting police practices were initially adopted but subsequently declared to be "not in operation." Over 250 employers banded together to provide jobs for those who previously had been declared unemployable. Ninety employers alone hired nearly 5,000 unemployed black laborers. Despite these efforts, employment problems continued in Los Angeles as the public relief rolls increased 20 percent during the first 18 months after the disorder. The McCone recommendations on education were based on thorough analysis, but were not carried out. Conot concludes that most of the commission's recommendations were not implemented because "the report failed to present the hard and often harsh facts and figures on which the recommendations were based."[103]

The Watts disorders, as distinct from the activities of the McCone Commission, apparently had a mixed impact on Los Angeles. Some analysts maintain that the disorder stimulated the inflow of federal funds. Greenstone and Peterson, for example, show that poverty program funds rose from $25 per low-income family in Los Angeles before the disorder to $158 immediately afterward. They attribute the increase solely to the 1965 disorder.[104] The Los Angeles Riot Study group's analysis, however, concludes:

> Since the Los Angeles riot, white political and civic leaders have apparently become more responsive to Negro demands. To this point, such responsiveness is more verbal and visible than it is substantive: the degree of policy change that can be observed is minimal. . . .The McCone Commission Report recommendations represent a maximum program to most whites, including most white leaders, but only a minimum and largely symbolic program not only to the Negro leadership but followership alike. The very nature of the political structure is producing barriers to the accomplishment of even these "minimal" recommendations.[105]

Civil Disorders, 1966-1968

Civil disorders occurred in Chicago, Cleveland, San Francisco and Dayton, Ohio during the summer months of 1966. None approached the severity of the 1965 Los Angeles violence; but in the summer of 1967 race-related disorders escalated to an unprecedented degree. One hundred twenty-eight American cities experienced racial violence in that year. Several governors and numerous mayors created official riot commissions to investigate the violence that had transpired in their jurisdictions, and President Johnson appointed a national commission to conduct a similar inquiry (see chapters 4-6). Curiously, the appointment of a national commission did not ease the "impulse to commission."

In the single month of April 1968, following the assassination of Dr. Martin Luther King, Jr., 125 cities exploded in racial violence more intense than even the prior summer's disorders. A month later, in what was beginning to seem like a ritual response, President Johnson created the National Commission on the Causes and Prevention of Violence. This immediately followed the assassination of Senator Robert F. Kennedy, but included a directive to investigate civil disorders. Governors and mayors emulated the national response by appointing numerous riot commissions to inquire into racial violence affecting their jurisdictions. Commissions created in Pittsburgh, Chicago and Akron are selected for discussion here.

The 1968 Pittsburgh Disorder

A civil disorder began in Pittsburgh on April 5, 1968 and continued for seven days. Not since the 1877 railroad riots had Pittsburgh experienced comparable violence. Afterwards Mayor Joseph M. Barr appointed a seven-member "task force" to investigate the disorder, examine city programs designed to aid affected neighborhoods and formulate recommendations. The investigative group described itself as an "internal task force" because all seven of its members were city officials. They included two city councilmen, the city solicitor, director of city planning, urban renewal director, director of public safety, and executive assistant to the mayor who served as chairman of the group. Staff personnel for the task force were similarly drawn from city agency employees, with four of the seven permanent staff members coming from Pittsburgh's police and fire departments. The Pittsburgh investigation was thus a city hall interpretation of the disorder and what should be done about it.

After two months, the task force submitted an interim report to Mayor Barr and the city council. The report cited the toll taken by the disorder: one dead, over 500 fires, over 900 arrests and over half a million dollars in damage. It rejected a conspiratorial interpretation of the causes, described selective patterns of looting and burning aimed at merchants charging high prices for inferior goods and "recognized that there are legitimate social and economic grievances in these [disorder] areas and much reason for despair." Conduct by policemen and firemen received commendation and the interim report noted the absence of sniping by ghetto residents.

The mayor's task force made a series of recommendations aimed at upgrading conditions for residents of Pittsburgh's three primarily black neighborhoods. These included proposals affecting housing and employment conditions, educational reform and police procedures. The task force recommendations were deliberately written to produce quick and visible action.[106] One week after release of the report, Mayor Barr appeared before the Pittsburgh City Council and embraced the report's findings and recommendations, calling for immediate implementation of two reforms suggested in the report. The first consisted of increasing the police force by 10 percent at an annual cost of over $1 million and the second included the transfer of $1 million in state redevelopment funds for immediate improvements in the black "Hill district."[107]

The 1968 Chicago Disorder

After the assassination of Dr. King, Chicago experienced three days of disorder, during which nine deaths were recorded and over 3,000 arrests were made. Federal troops had to be summoned to quell the violence. In response, Mayor Richard J. Daley appointed an 11-member "Chicago Riot Study Committee" and charged it with the task of conducting "a complete and detailed factual investigation into the events immediately preceding, on and subsequent to April 4, 1968, in Chicago in order to determine precisely what, why and how" the disorder of April 5-7 occurred.[108] Mayor Daley specifically asked the Chicago Committee not to repeat or duplicate studies released during the same year by the National Advisory Commission on Civil Disorders and a local citizens' committee on police-community relations.

Membership on the Chicago Committee consisted of three lawyers, two businessmen, two judges, two city officials, one university administrator and one state official.[109] The committee relied entirely upon a volunteer staff composed of 60 lawyers and operated without a budget under severe time pressure. Even so, the committee was able to conduct ten days of hearings, hear 47 witnesses and collect 1,900 pages of testimony. The volunteer staff also interviewed more than 900 citizens of Chicago and distributed questionnaires to nearly 500 Chicago police officers.

The Chicago Committee explicitly disavowed suggestions that a conspiracy by outside agitators caused the 1968 civil disorder. It did contend, however, that "a relatively small number of so-called natural leaders among the young blacks of high school age were generally the catalysts and leaders of the April disorders in Chicago." The committee report failed to give so much as passing reference to the assassination of Dr. King as the single most important triggering event leading to the disorder. Instead it attributed the cause of the disorder to "a few citizens, young and old, with vested interests in violence. To some extent simple delinquency and a desire for troublemaking and larceny played their part."[110] The committee held that only a small minority of Chicago's black residents participated, and that they lacked support from other blacks.

The report gives a chronology of events during the disorder and lists services provided for the black community in Chicago by public agencies and private groups, implying that substantial programs already existed to meet social and economic problems. The committee emphasized measures designed to prevent the recurrence of violence through tighter security measures rather than substantial changes in services to Chicago's black community. Its report hedged on controversial issues. Nowhere, for example, is Mayor Daley's post-riot directive to "shoot to kill arsonists" and "shoot to maim looters" discussed. In this respect, the committee did not deal critically with subjects that might prove embarrassing to the city administration.

The report was not unanimous. One of the 11 members of the committee, Charles Siragusa, executive director of the Illinois Crime Investigating Commission, objected to what he considered the committee's too lenient statement on the law and order issue and to its capitulation to blacks who threatened future disorders if corrective measures were not adopted.[111] The Chicago Committee's work was also challenged by groups which did not share the pro-city administration viewpoint of the committee. Black militants in Chicago formed a separate study group to interpret the 1968 civil disorder in terms of its meaning for the black community.[112]

The 1968 Akron Disorder

During the latter part of July 1968, a major civil disorder occurred in Akron, Ohio. Racial violence continued for six days and ended only after a citywide curfew was imposed and the National Guard called to riot duty. To the analyst of racial violence in America, Mayor John S. Ballard's response to the violent events was predictable:

> After peace was restored, the curfew lifted, and law enforcement units returned to their normal duties, one of the first actions of the Mayor was to appoint a commission of ten citizens to study the direct and indirect causes of the disorder and to make recommendations aimed at preventing similar occurrences in the future and, more generally, toward improving human relations in the city.

Mayor Ballard appointed the Akron Commission in July 1968 and the commission issued its final report some eight months later.

The Akron Commission faced problems from the beginning. Immediately after its appointment, the commission received considerable opposition from the black community because of Mayor Ballard's choice of commission members, delaying the commission's formal work for nearly two months. The commission began formal work by holding closed hearings, which again drew disruptive opposition from blacks. A written opinion from the city's legal counsel provided justification for

73

holding closed hearings, which were then conducted over a three-month time span. With hearings underway, additional problems arose because the commission, lacking investigative staff or subpoena power, had to depend on voluntary testimony. The militant black boycott of the hearings hampered the commission:

> It was most disappointing to the Commission to find the only persons who refused to appear were a small number of blacks who were not willing to share their information and ideas with the community through this report. Some of the refusers were persons who have been loudest in their insistence in having a voice in the planning and decision-making processes.[113]

Sixty-two recommendations for change were included in the final report. The commission took conscious steps to assure visibility for its report and recommendations. Its chairman elaborated:

> The Commission members and I were especially concerned with a public release of the report. This was successfully achieved as the Mayor and I held a joint press conference for radio, TV, and the press the morning I officially turned it over to him. I also placed copies in the public and university libraries. The Institute of Civic Education at the university has since printed a number of copies which are available to the public at no cost.

Concern over visibility resulted, of course, from commission members' desire to see the report's recommendations implemented. Although little evidence is available on this matter, the chairman claimed, "I believe this has been effective as many groups have referred to the report in their requests and/or demands for various programs."[114]

Historical and Contemporary Responses to Racial Violence

Confronted by past race riots and contemporary civil disorders, public officials' immediate concern has been to suppress the violence. Whether the racial violence involved whites attacking blacks or blacks attacking white property, race riots and civil disorders severely threatened domestic tranquility and introduced the specter of civic uncertainty. Public officials have accordingly attempted to suppress the violence as quickly as possible to demonstrate the inviolability as well as the might of public authority. A conspicuous exception to this pattern was the behavior of law enforcement personnel during race riots of the World War I and World War II eras. Here, where public antiblack sentiment was relatively unambivalent, police officers often encouraged the violence through conspicuous inaction and periodically joined the white mobs in attacks against blacks. Generally speaking, however, the main interest of public officials has been to put an end to violence and restore prior relationships.

When race riots and civil disorders end, public officials confront a new set of pressures. There is first the necessity to explain what happened and why. Public officials, whether actually surprised or hoping to deflect the implicit indictment of their administrations, commonly have expressed initial incredulity that what "couldn't happen here" actually happened. These statements rarely satisfy an anxious citizenry whose city has been torn by racial warfare. After the initial expressions of surprise, public officials generally develop interpretations of racial violence responsive to mass needs for reassurance. These interpretations usually minimize the severity of the violence, vastly underestimate the number of persons involved, describe participants as irresponsible troublemakers lacking stable social and economic attachments, and summarily dismiss as nonexistent or illegitimate the grievances that allegedly gave rise to the violence. The consistency with which public officials articulate such popular interpretations makes it unlikely that such explanations arise coincidentally. Rather, these interpretations may be said to arise from public officials' need to give the impression that the racial violence is not an indictment of the municipality or its political representatives, and that it will not happen again.

Although public officials' interpretations may be consistent with beliefs held by the general population, they usually are not enough to ease public anxieties. Influential community groups have generally insisted that "something be done" to assure that violence would not be repeated. Groups oriented toward white interests have petitioned for an improved capacity to suppress future violence. Groups oriented toward black interests, on the other hand, have demanded changes designed to alter economic and political conditions in the black community. These demands for action have usually been directed at municipal executives. Yet mayors often lack the authority and resources to produce the visible, immediate and meaningful actions envisioned by petitioning groups. Further, in the volatile political atmosphere generated by racial violence, they have also lacked clear signals concerning how their interests would be affected by alternative courses of action. Possibly because with few other alternatives to which they were willing to commit themselves, public officials created *ad hoc* commissions to investigate the racial violence and develop reform proposals. Thus, in a period of high tension public officials give the appearance of taking corrective steps without making binding commitments.

Public officials, it appears, attempt to assure concerned groups that their petitions for corrective action will be fulfilled by appointing representatives to riot commissions from established interests in the community. The appointing executive usually issues a formal charge to the commission detailing the areas to be investigated and suggesting broad guidelines for conducting the investigation. By placing representatives of dominant interests on the commissions and charging them with comprehensive duties, public officials try to reassure concerned groups and anxious citizens that a thorough investigation will be conducted by prestigious and representative study groups whose views will form the basis of future policy.

As *ad hoc*, temporary organization, riot commissions are often underfunded, limited in the time they are allotted to complete their work, faced with problems associated with the adequacy of staffing and sometimes fail to achieve consensus.

Despite their formal charges, riot commissions often choose between the incompatible quest for objective explanations based upon comprehensive evidence and sound inference—which we may call "scientific" explanations—and those calculated to be politically acceptable. Most of the commissions we have reviewed in this chapter emphasized politically acceptable explanations. The 1943 Governor's Commission in Detroit is an extreme example of such a choice, for it ignored available evidence in favor of explanations consistent with the law-enforcement career interests of its four members.

The orientation of riot commissions toward politically acceptable explanations is most apparent in two areas. Most commissions tend to exonerate public officials of blame—particularly the appointing executive. Few of the commissions reviewed here presented critical appraisals of the conduct of mayors, city councilmen, municipal bureaucrats or police personnel, either before or during the disorders. Rather, most riot commissions reaffirm norms of law and order and applaud police comportment even when these norms appear to have been violated by the police.

Additionally, riot commissions tend to defend or sympathize with the economic and political interests represented by commission members. Unrepresented interests, usually those sympathetic to blacks, tend to be singled out and condemned for contributing to the outbreak of violence. Likewise, reform proposals recommended by riot commissions at times seem less related to easing racial hostilities than to advancing the interests of groups politically represented.

Riot commissions have historically been relatively ineffectual. By and large their recommendations have not been implemented. This may be explained in part by the relative powerlessness of commissions as organizations. Commissions lack a budgetary base, continuing membership and enduring constituency and support. Nor have their proposals been supported by the executives who convened them. In part this is because they have failed to monopolize the role of explaining the fundamental causes of the riots. "Competing commissions" have usually arisen with alternative interpretations. In this sense the "opposition" of competing commissions and the riot commission process represents (to paraphrase a familiar aphorism) the continuation of long-term social conflict by other means.

Riot commissions have had some impact on city politics. In material terms some minimal proposals for reform have been adopted, generally in the area of employment and in the formation of biracial committees; recommendations urging increased weaponry and personnel for law enforcement agencies have also received considerable support. But more significantly, riot commissions provide public officials with recourse to immediate and visible action that they otherwise lack. The appointment of a commission buys executives precious time to formulate programs aimed at the causes of racial violence or, more likely, to allow aroused citizen concern to dissipate. Riot commissions thus seem to have a basically conservative impact on local community relationships. They provide a forum for debating controversial racial issues without forcing any public official or city agency to do anything about those issues.

NOTES, CHAPTER 2

1. Myrdal distinguishes between lynchings and race riots as forms of racial violence by noting that lynchings involve violence by whites upon blacks with the latter offering no effective resistance, while he reserves "the term 'riot' to refer to mass violence in which Negroes fight

as unreservedly as whites." Gunnar Myrdal, *An American Dilemma* (New York: Harper and Row, 1962), p. 566.

2. Masotti distinguishes between the two forms of racial violence by calling the earlier form "white-dominated person-oriented" and the later form "Negro-dominated property-oriented." See Louis H. Masotti, "Violent Protest in Urban Society: A Conceptual Framework," (unpublished paper presented at the 1967 annual meeting of the American Association for the Advancement of Science, New York City), p. 4. Janowitz similarly refers to the two forms respectively as "communal" and "commodity" riots. See Morris Janowitz, *Social Control of Escalated Riots* (Chicago: University of Chicago Press, 1968). On the general subject of labeling various forms of rioting see Allen D. Grimshaw, "Three Views of Urban Violence: Civil Disturbance, Racial Revolt, Class Assault," *American Behavioral Scientist* 2, no. 4 (March-April 1968): 2-7.

3. Here, and at other places in this historical chapter, we use the term *riot commission* generically, to refer to various organizations that have undertaken investigations of riots. At other times, particularly in the analysis that follows, we use the term in a more restricted sense; namely, to refer to an ad-hoc body with diverse membership that has been charged with investigating racial violence and making recommendations to prevent its recurrence. In the latter usage, a riot commission is not formally a branch of any governmental unit, although it is appointed by (an) official(s) holding public office, usually a political executive.

4. A survey of this kind suffers from the limitations inherent in summary accounts and reliance on secondary sources. To our knowledge, no comparable survey has been attempted systematically before. The closest attempt is Platt's review, which extends back to 1917, but of the ten "significant" riot commissions surveyed from 1917 through 1970 only four were prior to 1965. Cf. *The Politics of Riot Commissions*, ed. Anthony M. Platt (New York: Collier Books, 1971), pp. 8, 9.

5. That contemporary civil disorders coincide with the Vietnam War can be seen in Table 1.2 in ch. 1. Lieberson and Silverman identify 72 different race riots during the 1913-1963 period in Stanley Lieberson and Arnold R. Silverman, "The Precipitants and Underlying Conditions of Race Riots," *American Sociological Review* 30, no. 6 (December 1965): 887. Lieberson additionally records there were 37 separate events. . .that I would call riots. Five riots occurred in 1943." See Stanley Lieberson, "The Meaning of Race Riots," *Race* 7, no. 4 (April 1966): 373. Interesting, but as yet unexplored, hypotheses regarding connections between external national violence and internal

civil disorder are suggested by the coincidence of race riots with foreign wars. Such linkages are unfortunately beyond the scope of the present study.

6. An earlier riot of severe proportions is described in James L. Crouthamel, "The Springfield Race Riot of 1908," *The Journal of Negro History* 65, no. 3 (July 1960): 164-81.

7. Elliott M. Rudwick, *Race Riot at East St. Louis: July 2, 1917* (New York: Meridian Books, 1966), p. 35.

8. For an extended discussion of the Military Board of Inquiry's investigation, see chapter seven in Rudwick, *Race Riot at East St. Louis*, pp. 79-94.

9. Ibid., pp. 74; 78; 79; and 81.

10. From the report of the special House subcommittee assigned to investigate the East St. Louis riot. See Ben Johnson, John E. Raker, M.D. Foster, and Henry Allen Cooper, "East St. Louis Riots: Report of the Special Committee Authorized by Congress to Investigate the East St. Louis Riots," in *Racial Violence in the United States*, ed. Allen D. Grimshaw (Chicago: Aldine, 1969), p. 61.

11. From the congressional committee's report as quoted in Chicago Commission on Race Relations, *The Negro In Chicago: A Study of Race Relations and a Race Riot* (Chicago: University of Chicago Press, 1922), p. 75.

12. Johnson, et al., in *Racial Violence in the United States*, ed. Grimshaw, p. 72.

13. The congressional committee's final report suggested the possibility that it might take follow-up steps to insure action on its findings:

> Your committee has not adjourned *sine die* for the reason that it is possible, at least, that a supplementary report may be made showing the beneficial results of the exposures brought about by the investigation and also by the vigorous prosecutions hereinbefore referred to.

See Johnson, et al., in Platt, *The Politics of Riot Commissions*, p. 82. To our knowledge, no such steps were taken. Rudwick assigns the congressional committee's failure to have a substantial impact on post-riot politics in East St. Louis to the committee's exclusive reliance upon testimony for evidence and the failure to check this material against alternative information sources:

> a substantial portion (of testimony) was hearsay evidence requiring further investigation. Unfortunately, several factual errors appeared in the final report because some leads were not adequately explored by the Congressmen.

See Rudwick, *Race Riot at East St. Louis*, p. 140. However, in light of the low rate of implementation of riot commission recommendations historically, it is plausible to suggest that the committee would not have seen its recommendations implemented even if it had adopted the measures urged by Rudwick.

14. For a fourth investigation, by the St. Clair County Grand Jury, see ibid., pp. 95-132.

15. Following the race riot, East St. Louis, like other cities of the period, experienced some impetus toward reform government. The commission form of government was adopted by referendum and the business elite succeeded in electing sympathetic commissioners to replace the prolabor regime of Mayor Mollman. Efforts to reform the tax structure and the police force failed, and in a few years politics characteristic of the previous period again prevailed. Also as in other cities, the police department succeeded in translating criticisms of police practices into claims for salary improvements and a larger force. See ibid., pp. 93-94, 153-56.

16. The count is given in W. E. B. Du Bois, *Dusk of Dawn* (New York: Harcourt, Brace, 1940), p. 264. The "red summer" label is reported in James Weldon Johnson, *Along This Way* (New York: Viking, 1935), p 341.

17. Waskow presents excellent accounts of various commissions' investigations into racial violence in Omaha, Nebraska; Knoxville, Tennessee; Washington, D.C.; and Longview, Texas after the 1919 race riots. See Arthur I. Waskow, *From Race Riot to Sit-In: 1919 and the 1960s* (New York: Doubleday, 1967), chs. 1-3, 6.

18. See St. Clair Drake and Horace R. Cayton, *Black Metropolis*, vol. 1 (New York: Harper and Row, 1962; originally published in 1945), p. 65.

19. Immediately after the Chicago race riot ended, prominent national and local representatives of black organizations entered the unsettled post-riot environment and formed a Joint Emergency Committee to secure the legal rights of blacks who had been arrested and indicted during the violence. The Joint Committee issued a report at the end of the year charting the status of persons charged with criminal behavior. Additionally, at least two juries went beyond their assigned role to make seemingly authoritative pronouncements on riot causes and solutions. Waskow gives this description of the juries:

> In addition to functioning as agents of punishment and redress, the coroner's jury and grand jury tried to analyze the causes of the riot and recommended ways of preventing or controlling similar outbreaks. Both groups suggested that "voluntary segregation" would probably greatly reduce tension between the races. Both recom-

80

mended strengthening the police force, and the coroner's jury particularly warned that the police had acted with favoritism toward whites during the riot and must act impartially to prevent future trouble. The grand jury emphasized the connections of the "athletic clubs," of "vice of all kinds" in the "Black Belt," and of criminal gangsterism with local political organizations, and urged that the connections be severed and the dangerous activities rooted out. The coroner's jury, on the other hand, doubted that "politics. . .or catering to the white or colored vote, had much of anything to do with the production of race rioting" or that the athletic clubs had been responsible for the riots.

See Waskow, *From Race Riot to Sit-In*, p. 51.

20. Ibid., p. 60.

21. This appeal came from "a group of eighty-one citizens, representing forty-eight social, civic, commercial, and professional organizations of Chicago." See Chicago Commission on Race Relations, *The Negro In Chicago*, p. 15.

22. Waskow, *From Race Riot to Sit-In*, p. 63.

23. Chicago Commission on Race Relations, *The Negro In Chicago*, p. 17.

24. For a discussion of the commission's financial problems and its consequences for the commission, see Waskow, *From Race Riot to Sit-In*, pp. 66-70. For a more general discussion of the financial problems encountered by commissions as ad-hoc, temporary agencies, see ch. 3, below.

25. Ibid., p. 73.

26. Ibid., p. 66.

27. Many of the innovations produced by the commission's staff can be attributed to the influence of Robert E. Park. As a sociologist at the University of Chicago, "he influenced the research process not only indirectly through what he had previously taught his students, but directly, through constant consultation during both the investigation and writing periods of the staff's work" (ibid., p. 81). The methodology employed by the staff included door-to-door interviews in white and black neighborhoods, informal observation of interracial behavior in work and leisure areas, and the distribution of formal questionnaires to leadership groups in education, labor, social service, commerce, and among other elite groups in Chicago. Community leaders were also interviewed by commission staff at small conferences and informal hearings. A leading student of racial violence contends that the Chicago Commission's report is still "without question the best single source on social racial violence in the United States and quite likely is the best sociological study of a single case of social violence which is available."

Allen D. Grimshaw, quoted in Rudwick, *Race Riot at East St. Louis*, pp. 231-32.

28. The Commission held more than 75 meetings, but "forty of these were devoted to the consideration of the text of the report." Chicago Commission on Race Relations, *The Negro In Chicago*, p. 18.

29. Waskow reports that, "In September [of 1920] the commission replaced many of its data-gathering staff with new personnel equipped to digest and write up the data." Waskow, *From Race Riot to Sit-In*, p. 87.

30. Quoted in ibid., p. 89.

31. Chicago Commission on Race Relations, *The Negro In Chicago*, p. 18.

32. Ibid., p. 14.

33. See Drake and Cayton, *Black Metropolis*, pp. 69-76.

34. Harold F. Gosnell, *Negro Politicians* (Chicago: University of Chicago Press, 1967; originally published in 1935), p. 370. Gosnell's evaluation of the report's impact is reinforced by Waskow's assessment that: "By the second standard for measuring the commission's work, the extent to which its recommendations were adopted, the commission would not fare well." See Waskow, *From Race Riot to Sit-In*, p. 103.

35. Waskow, *From Race Riot to Sit-In*, p. 66; 104.

36. Ibid., p. 132.

37. Ibid., p. 14.

38. Alfred McClung Lee and Norman Daymond Humphrey, *Race Riot* (New York: Dryden Press, 1943), pp. 120-21.

39. One account of the rioting reads as follows:

Docile Harlem went on a rampage last week, smashing stores and looting them and piling up destruction of thousands of dollars worth of goods. But the mass riot in Harlem was not a race riot. A few whites were jostled by colored people in the melee, but there was no manifest hostility between colored and white as such. All night until dawn on the Tuesday of the outbreak white persons, singly and in groups, walked the streets of Harlem without being molested. The action of the police was commendable in the highest degree. The looting was brazen and daring, but the police were restrained. In extreme cases, when they fired, it was into the air. Their restraint saved Harlem from becoming a shambles. The outbreak was spontaneous. It was directed against the stores exclusively.

See Claude McKay, "Harlem Runs Wild," *The Nation* 140, no. 3639 (3 April 1935): 382.

40. See the description of commission members in Platt, *The Politics of Riot Commissions*, p. 161.

41. The Mayor's Commission on Conditions in Harlem, "Report of Subcommittee Which Investigated the Disturbance of March 19th," (New York City Public Library, unpublished, 29 May 1935), p. 1. The first report concluded:

We are now in a position to report, first, that the outburst was spontaneous and unpremeditated; second, that it was not a race riot in the sense of its being a physical conflict between persons of the white and colored groups; third, that it was not instigated by the Communists, though they sought to profit by it and circulated a false and misleading leaflet after the riots were well under way; fourth, that the work of the police was by no means beyond criticism. . . .

42. Ibid., pp. 3-4.
43. Ibid., p. 4.
44. Ibid., pp. 9-10.
45. Ibid., p. 6.
46. For sections of the second report see The Mayor's Commission on Conditions in Harlem, "The Negro in Harlem: A Report on Social and Economic Conditions Responsible for the Outbreak of March 19, 1935," in Platt, *The Politics of Riot Commissions*, pp. 165-82; also reproduced in Grimshaw, *Racial Violence in the United States*, pp. 119-28.
47. See Alain Locke, "Harlem: Dark Weather-Vane," in Platt, *The Politics of Riot Commissions*, p. 185.
48. See the *New York Amsterdam News*, 18 July 1936. Anthony M. Platt and Renetia Martin are presently working on a book-length treatment of the Mayor's Commission that promises to provide answers to several unanswered questions about LaGuardia's reception of the second report. See Platt, *The Politics of Riot Commissions*, p. 163 n. 1.
49. Walter White, "Behind the Harlem Riot," *The New Republic* 109, no. 7 (16 August 1943): 222.
50. Carey McWilliams, *Brothers Under The Skin* (Boston: Little, Brown, 1964), p. 3.
51. "Riots in Harlem," *The New Republic* 109, no. 6 (9 August 1943): 39. See also Allen D. Grimshaw, "The Harlem Disturbances of 1935 and 1943: Deviant Cases?", in Grimshaw, *Racial Violence in the United States*, pp. 117-19.
52. Thomas Sancton, "The Race Riots," *The New Republic* 109, no. 1 (5 July 1943): 10, 11.
53. For reference to these commissions see McWilliams, *Brothers Under The Skin*, p. 4.

54. Robert Shogan and Tom Craig, *The Detroit Race Riot: A Study In Violence* (Philadelphia: Chilton Co., 1964), p. 89.

55. One version of charges about police laxity toward and complicity with white mobs stated:

> Every one of the sixteen victims shot down by Detroit's predominantly Southern police force the first day of the rioting were Negroes. The news photographs of the flaming, exploding automobiles show the destruction of Negro property, not white. There are pictures of Negroes lying dead and wounded on the streets; begging for mercy; running like animals before white mobs armed with pipes and beer bottles. Almost without exception, the pictures of those arrested show only Negroes, men and women, lined up like cattle, hands above their heads. There is one revealing picture of a bewildered Negro man held by two policemen, and being struck by a white rioter; something speaks out from that picture beyond any force of argument; the white man knew the police were with him. There is a picture of a Negro cowering against a wall as two policemen came in fast with clubs. Twenty-five of the thirty-one dead are Negroes.

See Sancton, "The Race Riots," p. 9.

56. Shogan and Craig, *The Detroit Race Riot*, p. 100.

57. See Alfred McClung Lee and Norman D. Humphrey, "Race Riot," in Platt, *The Politics of Riot Commissions*, pp. 240-42.

58. Quoted from Rudwick, *Race Riot at East St. Louis*, p. 231.

59. H. J. Rushton, W. E. Dowling, Oscar Olander, and J. H. Witherspoon, "Factual Report of the Committee to Investigate the Riot Occurring in Detroit on June 21, 1943," in Grimshaw, *Racial Violence in the United States*, p. 139.

60. Ibid., p. 138.

61. Ibid., p. 139.

62. Shogan and Craig, *The Detroit Race Riot*, p. 107.

63. Thurgood Marshall, "The Gestapo in Detroit," *Crisis* 50, no. 8 (1943): 232-33.

64. See Grimshaw, *Racial Violence in the United States*, pp. 140, 141.

65. Shogan and Craig, *The Detroit Race Riot*, pp. 103, 104.

66. Lee and Humphrey, "Race Riot," in Platt, *The Politics of Riot Commissions*, pp. 236, 247.

67. Shogan and Craig, *The Detroit Race Riot*, p. 105.

68. Lee and Humphrey, "Race Riot," in Platt, *The Politics of Riot Commissions*, pp. 245, 246. Walter White of the N.A.A.C.P. clarified Dowling's threat to investigate the N.A.A.C.P.: "Dowling. . .hastily

disavowed (the extreme charge) when he found we were going to take him into court on libel."

69. Shogan and Craig, *The Detroit Race Riot*, p. 106.

70. Dean Harper, "Aftermath of a Long, Hot Summer," *Transaction* (now *Society*) 2, no. 5 (July-August 1965): 14.

71. P. W. Homer, "Report to the Rochester City Council on the Riots of July 1964" (Rochester, N.Y.: Office of the City Manager, 27 April 1965), p. 2.

72. Ibid., pp. 1, 8.

73. Ibid., p. 5. Here the report asserts that somehow the *number* of agencies was related to securing racial justice.

74. Ibid., pp. 6, 7, 9. The report notes:

New riot techniques have been taught members of the Police Bureau. New equipment has been purchased. Plans are near completion for a police tactical unit that can be brought to bear quickly in any potential trouble situation. Arrangements also have been made to insure quicker response by off-duty policemen and by the Sheriff's Office and State forces, if needed. All Rochesterians hope it will not be necessary to put into use any of the precautionary measures. The community is entitled, nonetheless, to know that these steps have been taken.

75. Here the report reads:

The [city] agencies, since the riots, have moved to meet the people more than half-way. The City-County Human Relations Commission has established field offices. The City-County Board has expanded its detached-worker program in the field. The local office of the State Commission for Human Rights has brought in more personnel. ...The private sector, as well as the governmental agencies, has moved to meet its responsibilities on a practical basis. Probably the most important actions have been the formation of a local chapter of the National Urban League, underwritten by local businesses and individuals and, through the Community Chest, by all Greater Rochesterians, and the creation of Action for a Better Community, Inc., to administer the various provisions of the Federal Economic Act in the City's war on poverty.

(Ibid., p. 6).

76. Ibid., p. 7. In ch. 1 we expressed doubts that recent civil disorders resulted from city characteristics. We have taken note of this aspect of the Rochester riot commission report to emphasize (1) if civil disorders do not arise from city characteristics, it is unlikely that they arise from suburban characteristics; and, more importantly, (2) in

Rochester as elsewhere, it is noteworthy not only that the riot commission reports or their equivalent tend to enhance the interests of their sponsors and members, but also that blame is continually cast elsewhere. This is seen in more detail in ch. 7.

77. Ibid.

78. The severity of the Los Angeles civil disorder is described in Governor's Commission on the Los Angeles Riots, *Violence in the City—An End or a Beginning?* (Los Angeles, Calif.: 2 December 1965), pp. 23-25.

79. Jacobs quotes the governor's executive assistant, Winslow Christian, to this effect:

What we needed was to rub the noses of the establishment in some unpleasant facts in order to get their acquiescence in and understanding of the changes that were needed to deal realistically with the problems. And the notion was that McCone was personally a rather conservative sort of man, and we accepted that.

See Paul Jacobs, *Prelude to Riot: A View of Urban America from the Bottom* (New York: Random House, 1966), p. 241.

80. Jacobs notes that:

McCone soon disabused everyone of the notion that he would play a purely passive role: not only had he insisted on veto power over the other members of the commission and, in addition, outlined the dimensions of its mission, but he also exercised a decisive voice on the appointment of key staff members, ran the commission with the same kind of discipline he had used in his CIA operations, dominated the commission hearings, and eventually made his personal stereotypes into the basic theme of the commission's report.

(Ibid., p. 245).

81. Scoble argues that Brown was motivated to impose this short-time limitation "in order that the discussion would be dead and buried by the time of the June 1966, primary in which the Governor intended to seek renomination." See Harry M. Scoble, "The McCone Commission and Social Science," *Phylon* 29, no. 2 (Summer 1968): 179.

82. Jacobs writes:

(The) full-time staff did not include a single professional working in the field of social sciences. One explanation for this lack of social scientists on the full-time staff was that it was difficult to get such people away from their assignments at the universities where most of them worked. As a substitute, therefore, the decision was made to hire them as consultants.

(Jacobs, *Prelude to Riot*, p. 253).

83. Governor's Commission on the Los Angeles Riot, *Violence in the City*, p. 2.

84. Scoble attributes this to lack of time in that social science consultants "had neither time nor interest in educating the staff and the members to old social science and they especially had no time to do anything new in the way of research" (Scoble, "The McCone Commission and Social Science," p. 180).

85. Robert Conot, *Rivers of Blood, Years of Darkness* (New York: Bantam Books, 1967), p. 416.

86. Jacobs, *Prelude to Riot*, p. 252.

87. Jacobs notes:

(The) commission's final report does not contain very much of either what some staff members produced for it or of the lengthy reports submitted to it by the consultants referred to in the final document. In the overwhelming majority of cases, the consultants' work was either ignored or contradicted in the commission's final document.

(Ibid., p. 262).

88. Governor's Commission on the Los Angeles Riot, *Violence in the City*, pp. 87; 85; 87-88. One statement in the commission's final report reads:

The accusations of the leaders of the national movement have been picked up by many local voices and have been echoed throughout the Negro community here. . . .(The) angry exhortations and the resulting disobedience to law in many parts of our nation appear to have contributed importantly to the feeling of rage which made the Los Angeles riot possible.

The defense of black political protest by Reverend Jones reads:

I do not believe it is the function of the Commission to put a lid on protest registered by those sweltering in ghettos of the urban areas of our country. . . .Protest against forces which reduce individuals to second-class citizens, political, cultural, and psychological nonentities, are part of the celebrated American tradition. As long as an individual "stands outside looking in" he is not part of that society; that society cannot say that he does not have a right to protest, nor can it say that he must shoulder a responsibility which he has never been given an opportunity to assume.

89. Jacobs, *Prelude to Riot*, p. 281.

90. Blauner argues that, "The McCone Commission missed the meaning of the Watts revolt due to the limitations inherent in its perspective. The surface radicalism of its language. . .cannot belie its basic status-quo orientation." Robert Blauner, "Whitewash Over Watts: The Failure of the McCone Commission Report," *Transaction* (now *Society*) 3, no. 3 (March-April 1966): 54.

91. Fogelson similarly concludes that:

(The) McCone Commission offered inadequate recommendations based on erroneous analyses derived from untenable assumptions. And in so doing it demeaned the rioters, belittled their grievances, misunderstood their ghetto, misconstrued the riots, and thereby discouraged efforts to devise imperative and more radical reforms. . . .(The) commission reflected middle-class, white American ideas and values so well that its findings and recommendations, or facsimiles thereof, have also appeared in many official observations about other recent riots.

(See Fogelson, "White on Black," p. 367). For an evaluation supporting this view see Bayard Rustin, "The Watts 'Manifesto' and the McCone Report," *Commentary* 41, no. 3 (March 1966).

92. Quoted in Jacobs, *Prelude to Riot*, p. 249.

93. The Southern California Advisory Committee later commented:

Following informal consultations with members and staff of the Governor's Commission on the Los Angeles riots (the McCone Commission), we decided to postpone making any recommendations until the McCone Commission had been afforded an opportunity to conduct its investigations and make its findings and suggestions.

(Southern California Subcommittee, California Advisory Committee, United States Commission on Civil Rights, "An Analysis of the McCone Commission Report," Los Angeles, California, mimeograph, January 1966, p. 1.)

94. Ibid., pp. 2, 6.

95. The McCone Commission found fault with California's Lieutenant-Governor Glenn M. Anderson because he allegedly "hesitated when he should have acted" in calling out the National Guard. The Southern California Advisory Committee countered this criticism

by stating: "Nor did it hesitate to criticize an individual by name when it appeared a scapegoat was needed. The individual the McCone Commission chose to criticize was the Lieutenant-Governor of California, Glenn M. Anderson, which criticism we find wholly unwarranted" (ibid., p. 7).

96. Ibid., p. 17.

97. This dissenting opinion had much the same effect as challenges to the McCone Commission by parallel commission investigations. Besides Reverend Jones's dissent, studies by Blauner, Fogelson, and Scoble show the limitations of the McCone Commission's analysis and Rustin challenged the commission's understanding of protest politics within the black community. See Blauner, "Whitewash Over Watts"; Fogelson, "White on Black"; Scoble, "The McCone Commission and Social Science"; and Rustin, "The Watts' 'Manifesto' and the McCone Report."

98. Governor's Commission on the Los Angeles Riot, *Violence in the City*, p. 2.

99. See Governor's Commission on the Los Angeles Riots, *Staff Report of Actions Taken to Implement the Recommendations in the Commission's Report: Status Report I* (August 1966), and *Status Report II* (18 August 1967).

100. Jacobs, *Prelude to Riot*, p. 282.

101. Fogelson, "White on Black," p. 367.

102. Conot, *Rivers of Blood, Years of Darkness*, pp. 417-24.

103. Ibid., p. 416.

104. J. David Greenstone and Paul E. Peterson, "Reformers, Machines, and the War on Poverty," in *City Politics and Public Policy*, ed. James Q. Wilson (New York: John Wiley, 1968), pp. 287, 288.

105. Cohen, "Los Angeles Riot Study," pp. 10, 11.

106. Mayor's Special Task Force, "Progress Report" (mimeo., n.d.), pp. 3, 6, 11. The report recommends:

This City and this region must muster an effort—unprecedented in this City's history—to bring about immediate, visible, and tangible change which can be produced in a matter of months in three principal areas: the Hill District, Homewood Brushton, the Manchester District of the North Side.

That short-range programs were consciously advanced by the task force is acknowledged in the report's conclusion:

The task force set out with a limited mission—to determine what can be done promptly in Pittsburgh to respond to the great crises which plague the slums and near-slums of every urban center in this nation.

In the interest of time, this report sets aside many of the longer-term philosophical issues, but they were not neglected or forgotten in the task force's deliberations.

107. See "Statement by Mayor Joseph M. Barr to City Council," (mimeo., 3 July 1968). Here we see two archetypical responses. Of two primary reform measures, one calls for enhancing the police, and another calls for financial assistance from another jurisdiction.

108. Chicago Riot Study Committee, *Report*, p. 1.

109. The chairman of the steering committee of the Chicago Committee was Daniel Walker, who later gained national attention as senior author of *Rights in Conflict*, better known as the *Walker Report*, and was elected governor of Illinois in 1972. The Walker Report, a staff report for the National Commission on the Causes and Prevention of Violence, dealt with the disruptive behavior surrounding the Democratic National Convention held in Chicago in August 1968. It critically assessed Chicago police conduct during the convention and concluded that Chicago law enforcement personnel had engaged in a "police riot" against political protestors in that city. See Daniel Walker, *Rights in Conflict* (New York: Signet Books, 1968). As discussed in the text of this chapter, the Chicago Committee found no similar instance of misconduct by Chicago police during the 1968 black civil disorder.

110. Chicago Riot Study Committee, *Report*, p. 3.

111. On the law and order issue, Siragusa's minority report reads, "The Committee's Report too briefly indicates that lawless actions have no place in our community. Too much emphasis was given to causative factors for the April disruptions, without a corresponding concern for the burning and looting" (ibid., p. 211). In objection to what he considered a sympathetic reception of black demands by the committee, Siragusa argued that, "I could not but help detect in the Report a feeling of warning by a few black citizens, youths and adults, that unless the white citizen immediately meet the demands of the militants, another disorder will result" (ibid., p. 213).

112. Note remarks to this effect by Charles Hamilton at the 1968 Annual Meeting of the American Political Science Association, Washington, D.C., 5 September 1968.

113. Akron Commission on Civil Disorders, *Report* (Akron, Ohio; Office of the Mayor, mimeo., 16 April 1969), pp. 4, 39.

114. Letter to one of the authors from Edwin L. Lively, Chairman of the Akron Commission on Civil Disorders, dated 19 August 1969.

3

The Analysis
of Riot Commissions

Commissions in Presidential Affairs

The appointment of a presidential commission, particularly one charged with studying racial violence, is simultaneously a routine and a unique practice.

As we have seen in chapter 2, it is routine in American politics to appoint a commission in the aftermath of racial violence. Presidents also routinely appoint commissions to seek advice and accomplish other presidential goals: Between 1945 to 1968, American presidents appointed 66 advisory commissions.[1] By a somewhat broader classification, fully 132 boards and commissions were appointed to advise the president, Congress and various executive agencies in the three-and-one-half year period from 1965 through the summer of 1968.[2] President Lyndon B. Johnson, the "great commissioner," appointed presidential advisory commissions at the rate of four per year during his five years in office. Among the most important, in addition to the National Advisory Commission on Civil Disorders (Kerner Commission), were those addressed to problems of automation and technology, the Kennedy assassination, crime and law enforcement, crime in the District of Columbia, selective service procedures, rural poverty, tenants' rights, urban housing and the causes and prevention of violence.[3]

If the creation of a presidential commission may be regarded as an ordinary event, particularly after riots, aspects of the creation of the Kerner Commission on July 29, 1967, were unprecedented.[4] A national, authoritative inquiry in response to American racial violence had never been undertaken before, for several reasons.

At least until the end of World War II, problems of segregation, discrimination and race-oriented brutality were considered a local, not a national affair. After the compromises of 1876 signaling the end of Reconstruction, national responsibility for black problems was minimized by political institutions and social conventions promoting local autonomy in racial matters.[5] These practices left blacks disfranchised and politically impotent, and meant additionally that black unrest was of little concern to politicians at the national level. Under such circumstances, only white discomfort with race relations could be expected to result in a national inquiry of concern.

Furthermore, the scope of race-related violence in which blacks took an aggressive or active role had never before been so extensive. The riots of 1919 engulfed not more than two dozen cities, but in 1967 hundreds were involved. Probably more important is the change in the character of the riots. Riots of previous periods had been white-initiated, interracial and interpersonal, while in recent times they have been initiated by blacks and directed against property and the police. For the first time race-related violence posed a threat to the white majority.

It is difficult to recapture the sense of threat that existed during the summer of 1967. The riots seemed likely to continue, myths of snipers and conspirators abounded, reports of soaring gun sales to white suburbanites proliferated and speculation as to when the rioters would "come downtown" (to white areas) was a subject of serious concern. This sense of foreboding and alarm is captured to some degree by a remark made by Robert Lilley, president of New Jersey Bell Telephone Company, and chairman of the N.J. Governor's Select Commission on Civil Disorders. As a member of an advisory committee to a Defense Department program, Lilley reports attending a meeting in Washington where army spokesmen admitted being worried that the riots could not be contained because of insufficient manpower. Lilley recalls shuddering in recognition that if the army was worried, "we should all be worried, for there was no force to back up the Army."[6]

A third major reason that an authoritative national study had not been previously undertaken concerns technological developments affecting perceptions of the scope of the problem and the potential of response by the federal government. Television creates an impression of the national scope of a problem which would otherwise be absent. Like radio, television is not only ubiquitous, but provides an unparalleled visibility for events as well. Although many national politicians tended to approach the riots as if they were local problems with local causes and solutions, television coverage substantially belied this orientation and created generalized pressures on national institutions for leadership and relief. Commissions are created in part to reassure anxious publics and reestablish more predictable political patterns, and they do so in proportion to their ability to communicate findings directly. Television permits public agencies and politicians to appear before broad publics with some frequency and intensity. Along with the tendency to project local violence as a national problem, television increases the capacity of commissions to reduce public apprehension.

Technological developments since World War II have also affected the ways in which commissions can operate—particularly those created in response to a crisis. Once a commission is appointed, the airplane and the telephone permit it to investigate many geographically dispersed riot sites without compromising the need to complete its work quickly. Commissioners can be recruited from throughout the country without being forced to suspend other commitments, and academics and public officials can be consulted wherever they reside, or flown to Washington for briefings. Without the telephone and the airplane, the speed, degree of authority, and breadth of participation which characterized the Kerner Commission and other recent commissions would have been substantially diminished. National commissions might have been considered during the eras of Presidents Wilson or Roosevelt, but they are more viable today, when the technological bases of nationhood are much advanced.

Commissions and Policy

In one sense the primary purpose of presidents in establishing commissions is to obtain innovative policy analysis, evaluations and recommendations.[7] Among the policy roles that commissions are asked to perform are: (1) fact-finding research, (2) developing policy, (3) evaluating policy or procedural alternatives, (4) recommending policy, (5) advising on continuing basis, (6) promoting—stimulating concern about problems, (7) educating the public.[8] Commissions have several advantages in fulfilling these roles. As temporary organizations they can fully identify with an attempt to resolve a specific problem and are not burdened by prior organizational biases and limitations. They are comprised of men and women with experience and skill. They can attract expert staff otherwise unavailable for government service.

But there are other ways in government to accomplish policy study. Cabinet departments and other governmental agencies have highly developed fact-finding, quasi-research capacities. (Indeed, for a time some federal agencies thought the Kerner Commission a competitor.) Policy development, evaluation and recommendation are normally the province of executive agencies and congressional committees. The president and his office certainly command extraordinary capacities to educate the public and draw attention to issues. Moreover, the executive can never be sure that the established instrument will not be a "runaway commission," stepping beyond the bounds originally prescribed or intended.[9] Thus, we must look elsewhere to understand why commissions are appointed in periods of severe racial conflict.

Commissions and Nonpolicy Functions

At times, presidents establish commissions to gain legitimacy for proposals they already favor, or to develop proposals for problems they have identified.[10] Commissions are able to achieve these ends because of their high status, their apparent representative quality and their presumed objectivity.

In another sense, however, commissions contribute to presidential politics *independent* of policy considerations. The creation of commissions permits an executive to defer action while appearing to act and allows him to appear to be a leader and fulfill the needs of his constituents without taking substantive action. These functions, both intended and unintended, seem most prominent in commissions convened in response to "crisis," where the importance of these functions may vary with the extent of executive need in these areas. In the following paragraphs we explore these functions in somewhat greater detail because of their implications for groups which may have high stakes in the outcome of crisis.

The extraordinary scope and intensity of the 1967 summer violence generated a variety of demands on the president. Those elites who regularly interact in policy matters affecting the status and welfare of blacks entered a period of heightened lobbying and jockeying for position. As tension and mass apprehension spread, policymakers, legislators, and representatives of various interest groups attempted to use the violent events to advance positions they had previously advocated. Politicians opposed to social welfare programs took the lead in demanding that violence be suppressed and condemning the leniency of past policies which they held responsible for the disorders. Because President Johnson was identified with the War on Poverty, these critics perceived the riots as particularly damaging to his administration.[11]

Civil rights leaders and advocates of social welfare measures, on the other hand, criticized the inadequacies of public programs and insisted that additional "massive" federal expenditures were required to stop the rioting.[12] Established black leaders were particularly challenged, for the riots demonstrated that their influence with the black masses was limited. In a sense both President Johnson and established black leaders had a mutual stake in maintaining the credibility of social welfare policies.[13]

The conflicting demands on the president were impossible to accommodate. One could hardly argue that the rioters should be punished severely or agree that expectations had been aroused beyond the capacity of the political system to fulfill them and at the same time advocate additional expenditures for programs which themselves were charged with contributing to the disorders. Any action became extremely risky, for it might have a severe impact on supporters of the other side.

There were two additional constraints. Great uncertainty in fact existed as to the actual causes of the riots. A nation unused to the idea that violence was inherent in its politics found it plausible to blame the violence on a small band of conspirators or on the discontent of a tiny and unrepresentative minority, rather than on underlying conditions of deprivation. Thus "objective" uncertainty prevailed in addition to the uncertainty about the costs of alternative actions.

The president himself imposed constraints. He was about to enter a preelection year in which he intended to pursue the war in Vietnam while developing impressions of prosperity at home. During this period the policy began of financing the war and continuing domestic programs while not raising taxes, initiating the inflationary spiral of the late 1960s and early 1970s.[14] The nature of this constraint may be judged by the report of a White House visitor who was scheduled to testify before a congressional committee the day before President Johnson announced the formation of the Kerner Commission. He reports that mayors were calling from many parts of the country, insisting that the riots were caused by a conspiracy. When he inquired what kind of congressional testimony might be useful to the White House he was treated to the following dialogue:

"No rewards for rioters."
"What else?"
"No rewards for rioters."
"Anything else?"
"No money."

The less involved and attentive to policy development is the general public, the more pressure groups can affect decisions. But with the general public actively attentive to riot events and making intense and often conflicting demands on decision makers about appropriate responses, the influence of formal pressure groups is muted. Since the New Deal, few aspects of domestic policy have engaged the American people as did the riots of 1967.[15] We must thus examine the relationship between political leaders and mass publics in these recent times of crisis to appreciate the role of riot commissions.

Social scientists have frequently remarked that in periods of great public insecurity people derive psychological comfort from explanations which appear to provide order, to "make sense" out of events. Under certain circumstances this proposition helps explain the acceptability of demagoguery, rumor and oversimplification in public affairs.

The assassination of President John F. Kennedy shows how anxiety is linked to the needs of mass publics, which in turn may be fulfilled by reassuring explanations. Assessing the finding that most Americans thought that Lee Harvey Oswald did not act alone, analysts recognized that "people need to have explanations of important events. . . .It is hard for most people to understand the psychic processes of a mentally ill person who seemingly acts at random; it is much easier to ascribe the event to an organized conspiracy with a conscious goal."[16] These analysts also note how such a belief may comfort people for whom the notion that the leader was cut down randomly or capriciously is threatening. In a study of immediate public reactions to the assassination in a New England community, similar explanations were offered for the rapidity with which people seized on the view that Oswald was guilty.[17]

From his intensive study of the structure of working-class ideology, Robert Lane provides another perspective on the human need to find

96

order in events. According to Lane, some of his subjects developed a theory of conspiracy in government affairs because they were

> unable to tolerate the idea of *no* social control, [were] too realistic to believe that society was in fact anarchic, [and were] moved by psychic needs and guided by projective interpretations that make one view more congenial than others—these men adopt a view of social control that we have termed *cabalism*, based on the term "cabal," "a secret association of a few designing persons."[18]

The relationship between mass uncertainty and the role of leadership has been convincingly explicated by Murray Edelman. He points out that people read their own meanings into unclear or emotionally provocative situations and will oversimplify and distort ambiguous or complex situations which are difficult to tolerate or assimilate into their world view. He also draws attention to the role of leadership in reducing mass anxiety.

> Because it is apparently intolerable for men to admit the key role of accident, of ignorance, and of unplanned processes in their affairs, the leader serves a vital function by personifying and reifying the processes. As an individual, he can be praised or blamed and given "responsibility" in a way that processes cannot.[19]

From another perspective, the search for leadership by an anxious public may be viewed as a *demand* on leadership for activity which (whatever its manifest content) will serve symbolically to satisfy groups that the threatening situation is being taken care of. One form this takes is the demand for *action of any kind*. On this point the pollster George Gallup has concluded that presidents may maintain their popularity in a crisis if they take some kind of action.[20]

The demands of a mass public troubled by the chaos and apparent meaninglessness of events may be expressed in a variety of ways. Prominent politicians will be made more or less aware that their constituencies are searching for answers and assurances that events are under control. Explicit demands for decisive action will be transmitted through newspaper editorials, letters and verbal communications. Other politicians will seize the opportunity to display their own capacities as leaders by trying to appear decisive. Spokesmen for various interests will advance views of the social order and governmental responsiveness which they have unsuccessfully championed in the past. This profusion of statements creates additional pressures for response, since to say nothing is already to contribute less than other politicians.

Our analysis suggests that riot commissions, created in times of severe crisis and conflict, initially function to provide evidence of action while postponing decisions.[21] They deflect attention for a time from the executive while organized groups focus their concern on the commission process. Political leaders sometimes *must* give an appearance of action; rhetoric may be insufficient to reassure anxious publics. Riot commissions are an ideal answer to the political leader's needs.

'The Commission Problem'

Riot commissions are established in significant degree to provide appearances of activity without necessarily committing leadership to a course of action. This imperative for creating commissions leads directly to the operational paradox that commissions simultaneously may expect, and may not expect, executive support. The difficulties of working within this dilemma substantially influence and somewhat undermine the commission's efforts.

On the one hand, riot commissions are manifestly designed to analyze and explain events and to make recommendations. The policy-related roles of commissions are emphasized at times of appointment when the president expresses utter confidence in the group and indicates his intention to rely heavily on its advice. These assurances are offered because the president believes that the commission will serve him well and because it would hardly be credible to say anything less. More importantly, his strategy of deferring action, deflecting the competing demands of organized groups, and offering reassurances to mass publics depends entirely on conveying the belief that the president will heed the commission's advice. For these and other reasons Wolanin is indeed correct when he observes: "Appointing a commission in general implies a commitment to presidential action."[22]

On the other hand, presidents are free to regard commissions as mere instruments in the policy process, sources of advice which may be freely taken or disregarded. Formally, commissions are merely a part of the presidential advisory system. *Advisors* have no right to expect that they will be influential; however, they may resign if they find their advice is regularly disregarded. Commissions, on the other hand, only receive reactions to their efforts after they have disbanded. There is no necessary relationship between the trust leaders express in commissions at the time of appointment and the implementation of commission recommendations. Thus riot commissions are instructed to act as if they were highly regarded advisors to the nation and the president, but are created precisely because the president wishes not to take any immediate course of action, or cannot find an acceptable resolution at the time. These conditions may continue to prevail, particularly if feelings remain high and the nation is divided on policy.

This is only one of many dilemmas that confront "crisis" commissions (and other commissions to some degree) in their organizational life. Others are discussed in the following pages.

Political Legitimacy

To be useful to presidents, commissions often must play some of the nonpolicy functions suggested above. But if they are to build a consensus, mobilize support, deflect attention or postpone action, executives must legitimate their commissions. They do this by expressing concern, approval and expectations that commission recommendations will be heeded. But executive support of commissions may gradually erode as commissions begin their work and public concern is eased. Executives may ignore the commission (as President Johnson did the Kerner Commission), actively oppose its findings (as President Nixon did with the findings of the Pornography Commission), or postpone action by asking another group to study the commission's study (as President Johnson did with the Selective Service Commission).

Initially, riot commissions are charged with generating objective analysis and impartial recommendations. If commissioners want their labors to have an impact, they must compete with other groups and individuals who are also trying to structure public understanding. But their ability to compete decreases as time goes by and executive attention focuses elsewhere. Thus, even while commissions pursue research and investigation, they must engage in an effort at public relations, although they may have little to say, and establish the legitimacy of their work.

A further dilemma of riot commissions is that maximizing the political legitimacy of their reports may at times conflict with their "scientific" orientation. The search for, and presentation of, information in objective, cautious and rigorous ways may not be compatible with the need to be convincing and persuasive. Furthermore, commis-

sions are not completely free to maximize the political acceptability of their efforts at the expense of a scientific orientation. To be credible a commission's work must be politically acceptable and have at least the appearance of scientific legitimacy.

Commission Integration

All complex organizations must find ways to get members to function together in pursuit of common objectives.[23] But the problem of developing such mechanisms is more severe for riot commissions than for other organizations. Commissioners are selected because they appear to represent diverse interests. The organization is also temporary. Commissioners and staff members anticipate that they will soon return to careers where norms and values perhaps antithetical to commission findings and recommendations will again prevail. Thus, the conventional development of group norms and orientations is inhibited.

Another peculiar dilemma of a riot commission is that its membership is recruited for diversity and for a limited task to be performed over a short and fixed period, while at the same time members are expected to agree on and support a meaningful report about a complex problem with clear ideological and value implications. This paradox sometimes leads the public to assume that the final report of any given commission will be little more than a collection of bland generalities, or an out-and-out "whitewash." Sometimes it is assumed it might be the former, because the commissioners, as representatives of diverse interests, were unable to agree on controversial matters. It sometimes might turn out to be the latter, because the commissioners were really chosen by the executive for their congruence of views. Either way, the commissioners must settle on a single report without substantial dissent, or risk jeopardizing their political legitimacy.

Historically, riot commissions have not conformed to a model of objectivity and neutrality. This should not really be surprising. In selecting riot commission members executives do not call upon all factions in the community. Furthermore, the functional political "community" in the past tended to exclude blacks and other minorities. And in any event, like most formal organizations, commissions gave expression only to represented interests in their reports. The history of past riot commissions and in a more subtle way of recent riot commissions is consistent with E. E. Schattschneider's well-known observation:

All forms of political organization have a bias in favor of the exploitation of some kinds of conflict and the suppression of others because organization is the mobilization of bias.[24]

Scarce Resources

Insufficient time and resources to accomplish tasks and goals are often primary determinants of bureaucratic behavior.[25] But advisory commissions, particularly riot commissions, are affected by these scarcities because of the narrow time limits under which they operate, the urgency of the issues they confront and the high visibility of their efforts. These problems are exacerbated if such commissions are uncertain of funding.

Riot commissions have to initiate a comprehensive search for answers to the questions with which they are charged and at about the same time begin to focus energies narrowly in order to concentrate on the production of a final report. They must simultaneously attempt to study widely, objectively and unhurriedly, while rushing to obtain answers. They must initiate a variety of research and data-collection activities yet appear judicious and deliberate. For a while the pressures and the excitement may be productive.[26] But this productivity diminishes as pressures grow, tempers become frayed, misunderstandings proliferate and directors increasingly scale their ambitions to the remaining time, available resources and personnel.

Riot commissions also encounter scarcities of trained personnel and confront the general inadequacies associated with a rudimentary state of knowledge in the areas of immediate concern. They expect to use the talents of the best available analysts, but these people are not always available for short-term employment on short notice. With few exceptions, commissions proceed by using such people (however inadequately) as advisors, while the actual work is done by people of presumed lesser competence and greater availability.

Commission directors may also discover that the sophisticated and comprehensive modes of analyses which they want to use are not reliable, cannot be completed within the limits of time and resources or simply do not exist. In the end they have to rely on considerably cruder analytic techniques, while the report is embellished with the trappings of the more sophisticated analytic technologies.

Implementation

Initially, crisis commissions are launched in an atmosphere where the major emphasis is on its "communal" obligations. They are supposed to act for the polity. Commissioners are asked to set aside parochial concerns and act as statesmen on its behalf. As time passes, however, commissions develop group or organizational identities, come to be associated with specific orientations or are seen as heading toward views that support particular ideological positions. The natural history of commissions is to become more and more identified with an organizational interest and to become merely another competitor in the governmental process. For this and other reasons suggested above, they tend to lose their relatively authoritative status and instead must compete for visibility, persuasiveness, legitimacy and, ultimately, effectiveness.

As commissions drift from under the executive mantle, they find themselves challenged by competing efforts which employ many of the same techniques and enjoy some of the same advantages. As commissions become merely other actors in an ongoing struggle, they find they cannot rely on executive support nor even anticipate whether it will be forthcoming. Theoretically recruited for their objectivity and impartiality, commissioners come to see their roles as requiring group (that is, commission) political action. But they are severely hampered in pursuing political action because they lack the resources and independent status to compete in a protracted conflict. Their strength is their weakness. Initially endowed with a legitimacy flowing from their "communal" obligations, their status and their temporary, *ad hoc* character, they have little capacity to affect implementation of their recommendations, particularly since they disband shortly after reporting.

These four subproblems intersect with each other. Scarcity of time and resources affects the scientific legitimacy of a study by placing pressures on data collection and analysis. The conduct of the study in turn affects commissioners' confidence in staff work, and hence, their willingness to agree with the products of the staff's efforts. The need to achieve commission integration further restricts the amount of time available to develop the materials necessary to secure the legitimacy of the report. The ability to secure implementation of recommendations is affected by the scarcity of organizational resources and the *ad hoc* nature of commissions. The desire to see their recommendations implemented at times leads commissions to choose political over scientific legitimacy. These four subproblems together generally suggest the contours of "The Commission Problem."

In the next three chapters we describe the activities of the Kerner Commission, analyze the actions undertaken in and by this organization and suggest the implications of these developments for interpreting riots in the United States.

NOTES, CHAPTER 3

1. Thomas R. Wolanin, "Presidential Advisory Commissions, 1945-1968" (Ph.D. diss., Department of Government, Harvard University, 1971). Wolanin traces the origins of the use of advisory commissions in their present form back to the presidency of Theodore Roosevelt, not to George Washington, as others have done (p. 7). This authoritative work is the only comprehensive contemporary study of presidential commissions. While the research and most of the writing for our study was completed before Wolanin's work became available, we have tried to take his work into account where appropriate.

Although we are not concerned with presidential commissions per se, our observations are generally confirmed by Wolanin's work. For those interested in commissions in the governmental process, our study may be viewed as a detailed analysis of one of the "crisis" commissions, a category suggested by Wolanin but not particularly developed by him. See, for example, Wolanin, pp. 38-41, 289, 381ff. Generally, see also Frank Popper, *The President's Commissions* (New York: Twentieth Century Fund, 1970).

2. Report of Gayle T. Harris, "Committees, Commissions, Boards, Councils and Task Forces Created To Advise The President, The Congress, or Executive Agencies Since 1965" (Washington, D.C.: The Library of Congress Legislative Reference Service, Government and General Research Division, 20 August 1968).

3. Other Johnson commissions and task forces ranged in subject matter from the Lewis and Clark Trail, the reconstruction of Alaska after an earthquake, interoceanic canals, political activity of governmental personnel, health manpower, food and fiber, architectural barriers in building for the handicapped, the American Revolution bicentennial, marine science, the Great Lakes basin, the observance of Human Rights Year 1968, and U.S.-Mexican border development. A commission on pornography was appointed by Johnson, although mandated by Congress (ibid.).

4. A possible exception to this generalization was the appointment of the President's Committee on Civil Rights, established by President

Harry S. Truman on 5 December 1946. Although several frightful lynch-ings preceded and may have motivated the appointment of the commis-sion, it appears that this body was established to head off potential postwar violence rather than respond to it. The example of the Com-mittee on Civil Rights appears to extend our analysis below by sug-gesting that executives may reassure anxious or aroused constituents by *anticipating* their concern or future mobilization. See Wolanin, "Presidential Advisory Commissions," pp. 50ff.

5. Note William Riker's conclusion that the fruits of American federalism are the enhancement of racism. William Riker, *Federalism* (Boston: Little, Brown, 1964).

6. Interview conducted with Robert Lilley, Newark, New Jersey, May 1968.

7. See Wolanin, "Presidential Advisory Commissions," pp. 23ff.

8. Ibid., ch. 2-3; see also Daniel Bell, "Government by Commis-sion," *The Public Interest*, no. 3 (Spring 1966), pp. 3-9; Elizabeth Drew, "On Giving Oneself a Hotfoot: Government by Commission," *Atlantic* 221, no. 5 (May 1968): 45-59; Popper, *The President's Commissions*, pp. 9-14.

9. The Johnson administration extensively used secret task forces precisely in order to avoid the problems associated with being forced to respond to public commissions. See Norman C. Thomas and Harold L. Wolman, "Policy Formulation in the Institutionalized Presidency: The Johnson Task Forces," in *The Presidential Advisory System*, ed. Thomas Cronin and Sanford Greenberg (New York: Harper and Row, 1969), pp. 124-43.

10. Wolanin, "Presidential Advisory Commissions," pp. 27ff.

11. See *Wall Street Journal*, 27 July 1967.

12. See, for example, New York *Times*, 22 July 1967; Washington *Post*, 29 July 1967.

13. A dramatic illustration of how the riots placed in jeopardy established black leaders' claims to speak for black masses may be seen in the following example of Congressman John Conyers's inability to persuade rioters along 12th Street in Detroit, which falls within his congressional district, to terminate the violence:

Shortly before noon Congressman Conyers climbed atop a car in the middle of 12th Street to address the people. As he began to speak he was confronted by a man in his fifties whom he had once, as a lawyer, represented in court. The man had been active in civil rights. He believed himself to have been persecuted as a result, and it was Conyers's opinion that he may have been wrongfully jailed. Extremely bitter, the man was inciting the crowd and challenging

Conyers: "Why are you defending the cops and the establishment? You're just as bad as they are!"

After being shouted down from atop the car, Conyers questioned whether he had established proper communication with many unfamiliar constituents. See National Advisory Commission on Civil Disorders, *Report*, p. 89. Confronted with such challenges after the rioting, black leaders appealed to the national administration for renewed support of existing and new social welfare programs. A graphic illustration of this appeal was the phrase, "You've Got To Give Us Some Victories," emblazoned across a cover photo of moderate black leader Whitney M. Young, Jr., on *Time* 90, no. 6, 11 August 1967.

The linkage of the interests of the president and established black leaders later found expression in the Kerner Commission's concern for reassuring blacks that the political system would be responsive to legitimate black needs. See ch. 6 below.

14. The essence of the Johnson policy was summarized by the New York *Times* headline appearing about that time: "Johnson Says U.S. Can Pay for War and Antiriot Aid," 1 August 1967.

15. The exception is perhaps the assassinations of the 1960s, but here, although public attention to political figures may have been high, the range of policy choices were minimal and not particularly conflictual in the short run.

16. Paul Sheatsley and Jacob J. Feldman, "A National Survey on Public Reactions and Behavior," in *The Kennedy Assassination and the American Public*, ed. Bradley S. Greenberg and Edwin B. Parker (Stanford, Calif.: Stanford University Press, 1965), p. 174.

17. Lewis Lipsitz and J. David Colfax, "The Fate of Due Process in a Time of Crisis," in *The Kennedy Assassination and the American Public*, ed. Greenberg and Parker, pp. 327-35.

18. Robert Lane, *Political Ideology* (New York: Free Press, 1962): 113-15.

19. Murray Edelman, *The Symbolic Uses of Politics* (Urbana, Ill.: University of Illinois Press, 1964), p. 78. See also pp. 30-31. Another response to mass anxiety may be avoidance of problem recognition. It is perhaps instructive that in mid-summer 1967 during the weekend when riots were tearing up Newark, the Gallup Poll reported that 78 percent of its respondents considered it unlikely that their communities would experience "serious racial trouble" in the next six months (New York *Times*, 25 July 1967).

20. *Opinion Polls: Interviews by Donald McDonald with Elmo Roper and George Gallup* (Santa Barbara, Calif.: n.p., 1962), pp. 34-35. Cited in Edelman, *The Symbolic Uses of Politics*, p. 78.

21. See also Wolanin, "Presidential Advisory Commissions," pp. 38ff.

22. Ibid., p. 43.

23. See Amitai Etzioni, "Organizational Control Structure," in *Handbook of Organizations*, ed. James March (Chicago: Rand McNally, 1965), pp. 650-77, and references cited there.

24. E. E. Schattschneider, *The Semisovereign People* (New York: Holt, Rinehart, and Winston, 1960), p. 71.

25. See, for example, Anthony Downs, *Inside Bureaucracy* (Boston: Little, Brown, 1967), pp. 1-4.

26. See James March and Herbert Simon, *Organizations* (New York: John Wiley, 1958), p. 116. For a brief discussion of "synthetic," ad-hoc organizations that resemble riot commissions in their rapid mobilization, unitary goal, and circumscribed organizational life pattern; see James D. Thompson, *Organizations in Action* (New York: McGraw-Hill, 1967), pp. 52-55.

4

Public Images
and Political Legitimacy

The riots in the summer of 1967 found President Johnson with no clear-cut alternatives. Burning, looting and reports of sniping from more than 100 cities demanded his attention. Aside from suppressing the disorders, there were no clear policy choices and it was difficult to make reliable judgments about the potential costs and benefits of various courses of action. Nor was the president completely free to set the national agenda. Political figures of all ideological shades were being called upon by their constituents to respond to the riots. They crowded the headlines with analyses and prescriptions.

The appointment of a commission has an impact on events quite independent of whatever information or analysis emerges from its deliberations. The symbolic aspects of commissions are not entirely the unintended or unanticipated consequences of actions taken for other purposes, but are to some degree deliberately produced and promoted by politicians interested in creating an image of leadership. Furthermore, once appointed, commissions take on the burden of reassuring the public that answers will be provided and policies prescribed and adopted to prevent the violence from recurring. They also have thrust upon them and accept responsibility for making the most of their influence upon policymakers and broader publics, although the executive appointing the commission formally retains this responsibility. A commission thus develops a concern for its public image which significantly structures its actions in ways that may have little to do with its official duties.

The Competition for Leadership

In the American political system, responsibility is often not fixed in specific branches or jurisdictional levels of government. Often conflicts over policy issues are translated into struggles over which branch or level of government will assume or accept responsibility. In the past two decades proper jurisdiction has been debated on issues ranging from integration of public accommodations, voting rights and welfare reform to pollution control and industrial regulation. In times of crisis, questions of jurisdiction may become increasingly prominent since the guiding voice of precedent is often mute.

The competition among various interests to secure interpretations of riots favorable to them[1] begins even before commissions are appointed. During what turned out to be the height of the 1967 riots, elected officials at all levels tried to present their own images of leadership.[2] In Congress, generally hostile public reactions to black-initiated riots were reflected as the "mood" of Congress turned against civil rights and social welfare legislation that might be perceived as "rewarding" violent dissent. For example, the House refused to debate President Johnson's $40 million antirat bill.[3] Instead, on July 19, 1967, it decisively passed an "antiriot" bill making it a crime to cross state lines with the intent to incite a riot.[4]

On the Senate side, the focus was also on conspiracy. The opening witnesses before the Senate Judiciary Committee hearings on an anticonspiracy bill—police officials of Cambridge, Md., Nashville, and Cincinnati—all testified that leaders of the Student Nonviolent Coordinating Committee incited riots in their cities. H. Rap Brown was identified by the police chief of Cambridge as the "sole reason" for the Cambridge riot during the previous week.[5] One month later the Senate Judiciary Committee finally agreed to hear witnesses opposed in spirit to the House measure.[6] Senate liberals eventually added various civil rights measures to the "antiriot" provisions and the legislation passed on March 11, 1968.[7] During this period the House approved the Omnibus Crime Control Act, which sharply revised presidential recommendations by emphasizing federal grants to help states pay for riot-control preparation.[8]

The poverty program had been the center of debate between liberal and conservative analysts of domestic policy since the founding of the Office of Economic Opportunity in 1964. The riots served to renew leadership competition over the fate of this agency. Director Sargent Shriver was severely criticized when he appeared before the relatively "friendly" House Education and Labor Committee. On the same day influential Appropriations Committee member Rep. George Mahon, Democrat of Texas and champion of the National Guard, addressed the House on the need for order and the ineffectiveness of much social programming: "Discipline, self-respect and law and order enforced at the local level is very important. . . .The more we have appropriated for these [social welfare] programs the more violence we have."[9] Members of the Senate Judiciary Committee engineered major headlines when Leonard Kowalewski, a Newark jailer and president of a policeman's fraternal order, testified that Newark's troubles could be blamed on the United Community Corporation (the Newark poverty program) as well as the Newark Legal Services Program, both funded by OEO.[10]

The Office of Economic Opportunity responded quickly to these charges. On August 9 the agency released a report indicating that, in 28 cities experiencing racial disorders up to that time, only seven persons out of 6,700 arrested worked for the poverty program, though over 12,000 people in these cities were employed—mostly in black ghettos—in community action programs funded by the OEO. Even so, Senator John McClellan announced that there was sufficient evidence that federal antipoverty workers were involved in rioting to warrant a full-scale investigation.[11]

The Newark disturbances which occurred July 12 to July 17 were the first to create general alarm. Pressures for congressional action increased as the riots continued and reached a peak with the disorders in Detroit. A frequent response to the pressure was to propose congressional investigations. Some senators suggested expanding hearings on the "antiriot" bill. The House Committee on Un-American Activities rose from the ashes to promise complete hearings on the riots.[12] The chairman of the Senate Rules Committee announced that his panel would consider proposals for a joint congressional investigation, or an independent Senate effort. Other congressmen reportedly considered turning a joint commission on crime into a vehicle to investigate the riots.[13] Senators Fred R. Harris (D-Okla.), and Walter F. Mondale (D-Minn.), proposed a commission investigation.[14]

The president came under fire. Republican congressmen, recognizing the political mileage to be made over presidential inaction, accused the chief executive of "unpardonable vacillation, indecision and even indifference" to the riots and said he feared "to offend any voter bloc."[15] A measure of the intensity with which congressional leaders felt they had to respond to the riots was the decision to charge McClellan's Permanent Investigations Subcommittee with conducting the primary congressional investigation of the riots. This decision came despite the appointment of the Kerner Commission some six days earlier with senatorial representation through Senators Brooke and Harris and despite the avowal of other congressional committees (Senate Judiciary, House Un-American Activities) to continue their investigations. Congress wanted to emphasize the law enforcement aspects of responses to riots, since the McClellan panel retained a permanent staff concentrating on law enforcement problems. When Senator John S. Cooper (R-Ky.) tried to direct the subcommittee to investigate "economic and social" factors involved in riots, this thrust was narrowed to order only that the committee focus on both short-run and long-run aspects of the riots.[16]

Like their conservative colleagues, liberals tried to turn the crisis to advantage. Senator Charles Goodell (R-N.Y.) and Rep. Albert Quie (R-Minn.) spoke out against recriminations over the causes of riots.[17] Hearings on extending the Elementary and Secondary Education Act provided a forum for Senator Robert F. Kennedy to relate ghetto discontent to problems of education. Hearings on Administration housing bills permitted Robert Weaver, secretary of Housing and Urban Development, to point out that only long-range, positive, substantial programs could overcome "decades of neglect and discrimination."[18]

Leaders and Followers in Response to Riots

The competition among politicians to command the symbols of leadership suggests that they are aware that they must respond to explicit as well as diffuse public needs for reassurance and must do so decisively or abdicate leadership roles. For example, the Kerner Commission was explicitly created to give the appearance of presidential action. As one White House assistant reported: "You can be damn sure that the President was not going to let the people think that he was not doing anything about the riots."[19]

Significantly, public officials tend to reinforce simplistic and stereotypic notions of the causes of complex events. It is not only that

110

mass publics are generally receptive to "cabalastic" views; elites who presumably know better or have access to better information and insights sometimes actively promote such explanations. The view that the riots were caused by a black militant conspiracy moving from city to city may have met the psychological needs of a mass public, but political elites and the media presented very few other perspectives to anxious citizens.

The very proliferation of investigations reinforced impressions that certain individuals and organizations might be blamed for causing the riots. Asking a riot commission to explain "to what extent, if any, there has been planning and organization in any of the riots"[20] also tends to confirm the view that a conspiracy requiring exposure exists, although the commission may later debunk such explanations.[21] Thus we must recognize the important role that elites often play in "cabalistic" thinking.[22]

Elite interpretations of disorders are often put to specific use as well. In justifying its views of the summer's violence, the Newark Police Department borrowed liberally from Governor Hughes's rhetoric, noting approvingly:

> The Governor said that the riots were not caused by a spontaneous uprising against unemployment, squalid housing and a general hopelessness—as Negro leaders insist—but were an outbreak by a "vicious criminal element."[23]

Thus the *ad hoc* opinions of prominent public officials help justify what otherwise might be tenuous positions.

Establishment of the Commission and the Functions of Recruitment

In periods of conflict, when opinion is polarized, most policy options are likely to offend one constituency or another. If an executive can postpone action, pressures may dissipate, particularly if the strengths of some groups are based on mass arousal and popular agitation, which are difficult to sustain. Postponement permits the chief executive to wait until the usual constraints of office again prevail.

This leadership strategy is clearly conservative. But it is by no means certain which groups benefit from postponement. For example, the antirat bill, defeated at one stage in Congress, was passed later when tempers were somewhat cooler and antiblack sentiments were less conspicuous. The emphasis in Congress on suppressing the riots and rooting out conspiracies also suggests that had the president taken immediate action it might well have been punitive.

Badgered by congressional critics to take action against the riots and by civil rights leaders to reassure blacks of the country's dedication to alleviating injustice, confronted by widely conflicting explanations of the causes of the riots, President Johnson addressed a national television audience at the height of the Detroit riots and announced the formation of a National Advisory Commission on Civil Disorders, proclaiming the following Sunday a national day of prayer. On the evening of July 27, 1967, he appointed an eleven-member commission, chaired by Illinois Governor Otto Kerner, with Mayor John Lindsay of New York City as vice-chairman. He basically asked the commission to do two things: "investigate the origins of the recent disorders in our cities," and "make recommendations—to me, to the Congress, to the State Governors, and to the Mayors—for measures to prevent or contain such disasters in the future."24

The president touched on the conspiracy question by reassuring his audience that the Commission would have access to materials collected by the Federal Bureau of Investigation and its director, J. Edgar Hoover (the ultimate in symbolic reassurance in this matter). He vowed that the FBI would "continue to search for evidence of conspiracy." He condemned the rioters as criminals who must be punished, in the process accepting and reinforcing the notion that snipers had been quite active during the riots:

> First—let there be no mistake about it—the looting, arson, plunder and pillage which have occurred are not part of a civil rights protest. There is no American right to loot stores, or to burn buildings, or to fire rifles from the rooftops. That is crime—and crime must be dealt with forcefully, and swiftly, and certainly—under law.25

He stressed riot control, insisting that public officials were responsible for halting the riots, not for analyzing them. He declared that the violence must be stopped.

The president recited the major accomplishments of his domestic policy, pausing to note that his critics did not want to fund some parts of his program. Then he stated his major themes: those who suffer most are people in riot areas; change must be sought, but peacefully; and there would be "no bonus or reward or salutes for those who have inflicted that suffering." He closed with a peroration on building faith among Americans and in America, so that the country might become "one Nation under God—with liberty and justice for all."[26] Throughout this speech the television cameras panned over the special audience the president had assembled to provide additional reassurances that the nation was united and prepared to defend itself. In addition to Secretary of Defense Robert McNamara (and other members of the Cabinet) he was applauded that evening by Cyrus Vance, former Deputy Secretary of Defense, his personal representative in the Detroit disturbances, and Lt. General John L. Throckmorton, commander of "Task Force Detroit," the military operations in that city.

In addition to Governor Kerner and Mayor Lindsay, the president announced the following appointments to the commission roster:

I. W. Abel, president, United Steelworkers of America.
Edward W. Brooke, U.S. senator from Massachusetts.
James D. Corman, U.S. representative from California.
Fred R. Harris, U.S. senator from Oklahoma.
Herbert Jenkins, chief of police, Atlanta, Georgia.
William M. McCulloch, U.S. representative from Ohio.
Katherine G. Peden, commissioner of commerce, State of Kentucky.
Charles B. Thornton, chairman of the board and chief executive
    officer, Litton Industries.
Roy Wilkins, executive director, National Association for the
    Advancement of Colored People.

Critical to the life and character of any organization are its recruitment patterns, which determine the kinds of people who will populate and direct it and the values and skills which they will bring to bear. Riot commissions are temporary organizations charged with a single set of goals and assigned a fixed time span in which to complete their work. Initial recruitment to such an organization is critical, because for the most part, there is little opportunity to change personnel (and direction) once appointments are made.

High-level recruitment to riot commissions is particularly interesting because of its *public* significance. Besides the obvious reasons—that they are judicious, informed or skilled at investigation and analysis— commissioners are chosen for what they are thought to stand for publicly.

The Kerner Commission was essentially moderate in composition, for which President Johnson "was severely criticized" by some at the time.[27] There were no representatives of highly conservative positions. In part this was to guard against excessively repressive commission orientations. As a White House official observed: "If you have Kerner, Lindsay, Brooke, Abel, and Jenkins on a commission, you know they are not going to say lynch blacks."[28] On the other hand, there were no spokesmen for radical solutions to black grievances.

In addition to its moderate character, the Kerner Commission appointments also displayed the following characteristics:

1. *The commission was comprised of high-status individuals.* Six were elected public officials, two held appointive positions in state and city governments and the others headed important organizations in the American economy. To judge from the implicit protocol rankings of the president's speech, Wilkins, Peden, and Jenkins (in descending order) had the lowest status among the commissioners. But Wilkins was the long-time director of the oldest, best-established and largest-membership Negro civil rights organization. Peden, the Kentucky Secretary of Commerce, was a state cabinet officer, owner of a radio station and past president of a prestigious businesswomen's organization. Chief Jenkins was widely known as a spokesman on police affairs and was former president of the International Association of Chiefs of Police. Although the commission needed a black, a woman and a police official, there was little in the Kerner Commission's assignment that accounts for the presence of these specific individuals on *this* commission. It would not have been surprising to discover these panelists on *any* commission of high status.

2. *The commission was comprised of men and a woman representative of potent institutions in American politics, or of large and visible constituencies.*

These individuals were representative in two senses. Wilkins, Jenkins, Abel and Thornton headed organizations with major stakes in the outcome of the Kerner Commission deliberations. Placing such individuals on the commission was intended to reassure specific publics that the interests of blacks, police, labor and business would be taken into account. These appointments would also deflect potential criticism that the commission had ignored certain viewpoints, and, if unanimous, would strengthen the impact of the report.

In addition to the congressmen, the governor, and the mayor, who were "representative" by virtue of holding elective office, there were people who had achieved recognition as and were identifiably, a black, a woman, a police official, a labor official and a business leader. These individuals were "descriptively" representative; that is, they reflected the characteristics of people whose interests were thought to be important to the commission.[29] The appointment of Peden, and to some extent Wilkins, suggests that commissions must include individuals who are like, in some respects, major portions of the American population. It would be considered "bad form" if no women were on the Kerner Commission, although obviously no individual can substantively "represent" half the population of the country. Similarly, while Roy Wilkins does not "substantively represent" one-tenth of the American population, his presence on this commission may be attributed to his organizational affiliation and status and his "token" descriptive representativeness.

Seven other major commissions appointed during the Johnson presidency also fit the pattern of including representatives of critical constituencies (see Table 4.1). Besides blacks, women and representatives of business and labor, big city mayors were also often appointed to these commissions, although the pattern here is more spotty.

Two other categories attract attention in the composition of these commissions. Texans were appointed to commissions rather regularly during the Johnson presidency. We are unable to account for this finding. College and university personnel also were frequently appointed (although not to the Kerner Commission), probably because of their high status, putative objectivity and neutrality, expertise on various subjects and the assumption that they have time to do the commissions' work.[30]

The Commission on Law Enforcement and the Administration of Justice (1965-67), analagous to the Kerner Commission in assignment and scope, illustrates these patterns. It was also comprised of a mayor of New York City (Robert Wagner), a leader of a moderate, high-status black organization (Whitney Young of the Urban League), a big-city police chief of national repute (Thomas Cahill of San Fransisco), and the leader of a national women's organization (Mrs. Robert Stuart of the League of Women Voters).

The impression that members are representative is critical to their public role. Commissions are supposed to work toward agreement on a document concerning a highly controversial topic, yet are chosen because they "represent" various institutions or social sectors. They must work together toward common ends, yet appear to be diverse in

Table 4.1: Constituency Representation on Selected Presidential Commissions

No. of Commissioners	Commission and date of appointment	Blacks	Labor	Big Business	Women	Big City Mayors	Texas	College Professors	College Presidents
11	National Advisory Commission on Civil Disorders 7/27/67	X	X	X	X	X	X	–	–
18	President's Commission on Law Enforcement and Administration of Justice 7/26/65	X	–	X	X	X	X	X	X
25	National Advisory Commission on Rural Poverty 10/21/66	X	X	X	X	–	X	X	X
20	National Advisory Commission on Selective Service 7/2/66	X	X	X	X	–	X	X	X
18	President's Committee on Urban Housing 6/2/67	X	X	X	–	X	–	X	–
12	President's Commission on Income Maintenance 1/2/68	X	X	X	X	X	X	X	–
13	National Commission on the Causes and Prevention of Violence 6/10/68	X	X	?	X	–	X	–	X

Legend: X indicates category represented on Commission.
? indicates marginal case.

their opinions. This helps explain their presumed legitimacy. A diverse commission which can reach agreement is thought, by example, to be able to unite a divided population. But this quality of representativeness, particularly when commissioners represent powerful interests and organizations, also helps explain why riot commissions are regularly criticized as being established to "whitewash" public officials. Commissions must provide a semblance of diversity to avoid accusations of a "whitewash," but share enough values to agree on a final product.

3. *The Kerner Commission was comprised of individuals for whom American society had produced substantial rewards.* Their backgrounds suggest little discontent with American society. The exception may be Wilkins, but in his case many of the measures for which the NAACP had so long struggled appeared to be on the horizon in 1967. Harris, with his "populist" orientation, might also be an exception to this generalization.

Conspicuously absent from the commission were individuals who might express fundamental discontent with American society. Black leaders more militant than Wilkins, young people who had not yet reached positions of eminence, members of other American minorities, spokesmen for interests resistant to further black advancement, "intellectuals" of various persuasions and social critics were all excluded.[31]

4. *The commissioners were relatively old, with a mean age of 53.* Yet an important segment of the population with a stake in the Commission's deliberations—the rioters themselves—were much younger. Fifty-three percent of all the rioters arrested were between 15 and 24 years old, and in Detroit, 61 percent fell in this category.[32] Indeed, the mean age of those involved in suppressing the riots—policemen—would fall substantially below 53. Only Harris at 37 and Peden at 41 were under 45 years of age.

5. *The commission, in a limited sense, was "balanced."* A Democratic senator balanced a Republican senator. A Democratic representative balanced a Republican representative. Labor balanced business. The police chief balanced the Executive Secretary of the NAACP. The commission was chaired by an elected Democratic governor, and the vice-chairman was an elected Republican mayor. Some appointments "killed two birds with one stone." Brooke, was both a Republican and black. John Lindsay was a Republican and a big-city mayor.

Some commissioners were representative by virtue of their occupation or position, yet none took an extreme position on racial issues within their occupation. Chief Jenkins's appointment somewhat mollified police antagonists because he was nationally known as a liberal among police chiefs. Roy Wilkins was considered a relatively conservative black leader in the sixties, however much respected for his past struggles. Senator Brooke was the country's only black senator, but was nationally known as a man who had submerged his racial identity in developing his party position in Massachusetts.

Of the other congressmen, Harris was a liberal from Oklahoma who had urged the president to appoint a commission. Representatives McCulloch and Corman were considered liberals; McCulloch was particularly remembered for his efforts on behalf of the Civil Rights Act of 1964.[33]

Commission members represent divergent interests yet are asked to suppress conflict and work for a common good. This is no real contradiction. Putative antagonists in American politics (Democrats and Republicans, business and labor) generally have a stake in prevailing political processes and patterns of resource distribution, even though they may compete over lesser issues. The commission-appointment process is the personification of the theory of "countervailing powers" enunciated by John Kenneth Galbraith with all of its contradictions and ambiguities intact.

The status of commissioners, superficial appearances of balance, inclusion of representatives of apparently concerned interests and exclusion of views that might be immoderate all reinforce appeals to nonpartisanship, patriotism and public interest, and objectivity and neutrality, in whose names commissions operate. These qualities also suggest assurances that the president (bound to display and respect these virtues) will respond favorably to the commission's recommendations.

Executive Staff Recruitment[34]

A critical initial appointment to the Kerner Commission was that of David Ginsburg as executive director. Ginsburg was a Washington attorney who had worked, like Abe Fortas and Clark Clifford, in the federal government in the 1930s. The influence of these "Washington lawyers" reached a peak with the presidency of Lyndon Johnson.[35] At the time of his appointment, Ginsburg was a senior partner in the firm of Ginsburg and Feldman, whose business with the government was as wide reaching as government itself. His firm had been retained, for example, by the Flying Tigers (an air-freight service with major military contracts) and over a dozen Washington embassies. The Virgin Islands, the Ford Foundation and various interests connected with the Kennedy family have also been clients of Ginsburg's firm. Ginsburg was socially prominent in Washington, appearing frequently on the guest list of conspicuous Capital affairs (including some at the White House) during both the Kennedy and Johnson eras. He was known as a person of skill and stature in official Washington circles and the president could expect his old friend and occasional aide to appreciate the problems of the White House.[36]

The second top staff position was filled by Victor H. Palmieri, a lawyer and president of the Janss Corporation, a successful building and development firm based in California. Palmieri was originally nominated for the job by Robert Wood, then Under Secretary for the Department of Housing and Urban Development. Palmieri had some ties to the liberal wing of the California Democratic party, had written articles on urban affairs and had experience with urban problems. He was appointed on August 16, 1967, after a number of other high-level staff members had been recruited.[37]

Ginsburg would have liked to hire a black for the position of deputy executive director, but reportedly could not find a highly qualified person willing to join the commission.[38] Originally, Theodore A. Jones, director of the Illinois Revenue Department and a member of Governor Kerner's cabinet, had been hired as the second-ranking staff member, with the title of staff director. However, he never assumed his duties in Washington and resigned under somewhat cloudy circumstances after a few weeks. Thus the only high-level black staff member was Merle McCurdy, who left his position as U.S. attorney in Cleveland to become the commission's general counsel.

Other problems in recruiting top staff resulted from extensive security precautions. Some potential staff members were denied commission employment because they had once been identified with left-wing causes. One highly regarded urban specialist, who at the time was withholding part of his income tax in protest against American military policy, was considered a security risk. It was impossible to hire well-known scholars and consultants, black or white, if they were discovered to have joined or supported various organizations considered suspicious by the American security apparatus. Moreover, time was scarce and even when checks were "cleared" valuable time was lost. And cynics' suspicions that the commission would produce a "whitewash" seemed confirmed when people discovered security checks were being made. To avoid security procedures, the commission began to hire solely on a contract-for-services basis, which did not require background checks.

The Public Commission

The manifest responsibilities of the Kerner Commission were to study the causes of the recent disorders, explain why they occurred and make recommendations to prevent their recurrence. But to political leaders the process is as important as the product. The Kerner Commission was to assure the public that the investigation of the riots was being conducted in a sufficiently reputable way that the resulting advice would provide meaningful guidance. Although on the surface there would be little if any contact, the commission throughout its existence in effect collaborated with the chief executive in reassuring the public.

Getting Started: The Appearance of Activity

The announcement of the commission and the appointment of members dominated the headlines for several days. Members were summoned to the White House where Vice-President Hubert Humphrey, Attorney General Ramsey Clark and Cyrus Vance, President Johnson's emissary to Detroit during the riots, were available for a meeting and a photography session. The president also called for a National Day of Prayer, established new training standards to better prepare National Guardsmen to cope with civil disturbnaces[39] and announced that the Small Business Administration had been ordered to offer attractive loans to home owners and businessmen whose property had been damaged in the Detroit riots.[40] These actions nicely illustrate the kind of appeals made by leaders during such times: the need for faith, particularly in America (surely one way to deal with a chaotic world); the need for improved techniques to suppress violence; and assurance that respectable victims of violence would not be abandoned by public authorities.

Before any substantial thought could be given to how to proceed, the commission held its first hearing (on August 1). Witnesses were called who could either speak to the problem of riot control, advise the commission on how to proceed, or who represented various departments in the federal government. Courtesy demanded calling the latter first; tapping their expertise and establishing liaison with their agencies

120

was an obvious requirement, and they would have to be called eventually, anyway. Perhaps most important, their prominence would call attention to the commission's efforts, and wrest the spotlight away from the violence itself as well as other post-riot analyses.

The most prominent witness during the first day of hearings was J. Edgar Hoover, director of the FBI. Hoover testified that he had no "intelligence" upon which to conclude that the riots were caused by a conspiracy. Other witnesses were Herbert J. Miller, Assistant Attorney General and Chairman of the District of Columbia Crime Commission; Fred Vinson, Jr., Assistant Attorney General, who consulted with the commission on Justice Department cooperation; and two high-ranking officers who discussed National Guard operations.[41]

Advising the commission on practical business were J. Lee Rankin, former General Counsel of the Warren Commission, and Warren Christopher, Deputy Attorney General and Vice-Chairman of the McCone Commission. Secretary of Health, Education and Welfare John Gardner also addressed the commission on the first day. The following day, August 2, Willard Wirtz, Secretary of Labor; Robert Weaver, Secretary of Housing and Urban Development (appearing with Assistant Secretary Ralph Taylor), and OEO Director Sargent Shriver, appeared.

Early testimony gave the impression that a diversity of opinion would be solicited. Hoover's testimony was the only information released about the first-day hearings. Then, as if to counteract the information that the chief criminal investigative official of the United States had no evidence of a conspiracy, Governor Kerner announced to reporters that Sargent Shriver and Robert Weaver both had evidence of unidentified strangers in neighborhoods shortly before riots broke out. At the same time, the press was told that the day before Hoover *had* indicated "outside agitators" had played a role in the riots.

Apparently members of the commission wanted to reassure the public that questions of law and order would receive high priority. Recognizing that reports of Hoover's early testimony appeared to preclude investigation of a theory widely held by some Americans, Governor Kerner "scrambled" the first messages in order to protect the commission from early criticism. He was able to do this because he fully controlled news media access to information about the hearings at that time.[42]

Continuing Pressures

Superficially, commissions seem to retreat into relatively isolated

121

deliberations and fact-finding once they are established. Actually, however, they spend a substantial amount of time assessing and anticipating political pressures. Like agencies with more stable structures and permanent governmental roles, commissions respond to outside influences even as they devote themselves to research and evaluation.

The Kerner Commission had to work in a political context in which: (1) a wide range of outside agencies conducted somewhat competitive investigations; (2) various political leaders and members of the commission's own staff attempted to shape interpretations of riot events and public policies that could affect the atmosphere in which the commission worked and how its report would be received; and (3) the president provided guidelines and constraints beyond those stated in his formal charge.

Competitive Investigations. Because the structure and staffing of the Kerner Commission was thought by some to predict the outcome of its deliberations, agencies which expected it to develop unfavorable or unflattering findings undertook competitive inquiries. They wanted to develop alternative statements on similar questions and see that questions they felt deserved emphasis would be researched and investigated. Commissions may be assigned "official" status and expected to provide authoritative answers, but they do not have a monopoly on research and high-status recommendations. Even before they report, competitive inquiries arise to insure that the commission does not report in an informational vacuum.

Virtually every federal government agency involved in domestic social-welfare policy recognized the crisis inherent in the 1967 riots and for diverse reasons committed resources to study the riots or policies possibly associated with ghetto unrest. The McClellan subcommittee, for example, continued its investigations, and, because of its methods of operation, continued to apply pressure on the Kerner Commission. Despite formal agreements to cooperate,[43] the aggressive and abrasive McClellan investigators sometimes made it difficult for Kerner field researchers to win the confidence of informants, who had difficulty distinguishing between the two investigative bodies.

The subcommittee continued to focus on the extent to which the riots were planned and the result of conspiracy. The McClellan subcommittee, not the Kerner Commission, provided a platform for the mayor of Plainfield, New Jersey, George F. Hetfield, to proclaim that the disorders "were organized, precipitated and exploited by a small, hard-core group," and that they "were planned, not spontanous."[44] Similarly, the Senate Judiciary Committee, temporarily chaired by McClellan (substituting for another conservative Southern Democrat, John O. Eastland of Mississippi), provided a forum for the Newark jailer's charge that poverty program employees encouraged and supported the riots.[45] Even after the Kerner Commission had released its final report, McClellan continued to try to influence public perceptions of the riots by announcing that he would hold hearings on the Detroit and Newark riots.[46] The McClellan subcommittee provided a constant reminder that an important potential constituency continued to view the riots in criminal or conspiratorial terms.[47]

Various federal agencies initiated investigations along lines similar to those pursued by the commission. The Department of Health, Education, and Welfare solicited papers from social scientists to help the department understand the events, which may also have been a "hedge" against the possibility of a report at odds with this agencies' interests.

For defensive reasons, many agencies undertook investigations of their performance in riot areas. Most prominent among these was the Office of Economic Opportunity's study of the riot participation of OEO employees, developed to counter congressional criticism.[48] The Public Health Service studied emergency health-care preparedness in selected cities.[49] The Community Relations Service of the Justice Department initiated a study of riot news coverage in Detroit, Newark and Buffalo.[50] Vice-President Hubert Humphrey was asked to chair a cabinet-level committee charged with framing proposals to deal with problems of the cities, despite the fact that the commission was scheduled to report on the same topic in two months.[51]

Competing Interpretations and Prescriptions. Another set of implicit pressures on the commission were the evolving interpretations of ghetto unrest. Few public officials involved in the problems of urban America could avoid commenting on the riots and suggesting solutions. Perhaps President Johnson acted typically when he delivered a speech strongly emphasizing law and order subsequent to appointing the commission.[52] Congressmen, big-city mayors and governors of urban states speculated about how to solve problems of black restlessness.[53] The commission witnesses contributed to these pressures to some degree when selected aspects of their testimony were released to the press.

During this period the causes of the disorders received considerable attention. Through scholarly and popular journals, interviews and reports, various commentators and social scientists self-consciously tried to influence the outcome of the deliberations. Their interpretations, they reasoned, would be more likely to be accepted by the commission if they received exposure. At worse it would be more difficult for the commission to adopt alternative explanations once they spoke up.

Among the most difficult pressures on the Kerner Commission executive staff were those prompted by staff defections and unintended publicity. At one point a social scientist-consultant made well-publicized efforts to warn that the commission would "whitewash" the problem of black insurgency and fail to propose long-term solutions.[54] At various times newspapers also ran stories based on "commission sources." The commission had to deal with "leaked" reports on its intention to blame city governments for ghetto unrest, its precarious financial situation despite presidential assurances, and its uncertainty about the costs of recommended programs.[55] Extensive security precautions had to be taken in commission offices at one point because of widespread pilfering of memos and other documents.[56]

Presidential Pressures. Commissions must appear to be free from executive interference if they are to develop widely acceptable, nonpartisan answers to important social questions. But however much chief executives respect this general injunction, *to some degree they will inevitably breach commission independence.* This occurs in part because the executive appoints commissioners in whom he has confidence, which guarantees that in general they will reflect a broad consensus supportive of contemporary social policy. It also occurs because commissions attempt to anticipate the needs or constraints of executives, to increase the likelihood that their recommendations will be adopted. Furthermore, commissions depend on the chief executive for their budget and for recommending that Congress fund any programs proposed.

Kerner Commission staff members frequently talked with members of the executive branch. David Ginsburg was regularly in contact with President Johnson's assistants, particularly Joseph Califano. Ginsburg also attended White House social events, but he reports that he only discussed the commission's work with the president "three or four times" during his tenure as executive director. However, he and members of the staff were frequently in touch with cabinet members and their immediate subordinates on information-sharing and budgetary problems.

Ginsburg may have been scrupulously nonpartisan, as he reports (an opinion generally shared by other commission participants), but the commission was still considerably influenced by the executive. The president's privately stated view that recommendations should not be costly significantly influenced early staff efforts. Eventually this restriction was disregarded, but not before it led to the abortive notion that an interim report should be filed, which meant that a great deal of staff energy was wasted on a false start.[57]

Originally, commission personnel were led to think that the president would seek a supplemental congressional appropriation to finance their work. But when the president began to enforce a policy of not seeking supplemental appropriations for any executive agencies, the commission eventually had to petition for funds from various departments and had to short-cut its ambitions for a longer-term study.[58]

Within limits commissions also try to ensure that their recommendations will be adopted by anticipating executive reactions. While this is more blatant among local commissions, it is also apparent in the work of the Kerner Commission. When the staff had to adopt housing goals, it exactly doubled the president's recommended rate of housing growth, permitting him to claim that his framework had been used to develop housing proposals. Similarly, staff members developed their employment proposals by seeking to expand the president's JOBS program. At one point Richard Nathan, who was responsible for developing ideas for short-term programs, was asked to comment on a letter sent him by sociologist Herbert Gans suggesting that short-term program innovations should not require new legislation or additional funding. Nathan indicated he supported this orientation, adding that it was consistent with the president's message to Congress, "The Quality of American Government."[59]

As the commission concluded its work, staff members alerted various federal departments and agencies to the content of the final document. Prerelease copies were sent to the White House and to those executive agencies which would be responsible for implementing many of the recommendations. Ginsburg himself discussed aspects of the *Report* with key members of the cabinet. In some cases the document was altered to accommodate their suggestions.

Even if there is relatively little overt executive interference, commission members and staff to some degree try to anticipate executive reaction. Because they had developed a subtle awareness of executive preferences and had tried to brief critical actors, Kerner

Commission members and staff were particularly dismayed when the *Report* was disregarded and implicitly rejected by the president. In concentrating on how to increase the likelihood of favorable executive action, commission participants lost perspective on the extent to which the report departed from Johnson's needs and expectations.

Politicians typically do not wait for commissions to report, although they may sometimes defend their reluctance to take a position by insisting that it would be premature to comment. (The same strategy is used by politicians who commit funds to study issues on which they do not wish to comment and those who claim that issues before courts of law should not receive public comment.) In the case of recent civil disorders, politicians and public and private agencies frequently attempted to structure the framework in which riots were perceived. These efforts compromised Kerner Commission activities in two respects. They influenced perceptions of the riots themselves, constricting the conceptual boundaries within which the commission documents would be received. And they limited the commission's monopoly in interpreting the disorders. Although riot commissions are formally charged with providing authoritative interpretations and recommendations, they must compete with others in manipulating the symbols of objectivity and high status on which commissions depend for influence. It is hardly surprising that other people attempted to influence public perceptions of the disorders. Yet it remains useful to specify the ways in which the commission was compromised along the way by pressures fundamentally challenging its hegemony in the area.

Keeping in the Public Eye

All government agencies thrive on favorable public images which they more or less deliberately cultivate. Commissions, however, encounter relatively unique public relations problems. As *ad hoc*, temporary bodies they enjoy few sources of support aside from the political legitimacy with which they are initially endowed or attempt to nurture. And a deliberate attempt to encourage publicity may put their objectivity in question. A commission seeks to influence public opinion through its investigation and to some extent it tries to reassure the public that the controversial issue which it is charged with examining will be dealt with clearly and forcefully. There is a tension between these goals. Reassurance requires visible activities and public reminders that the agency is at work, while in the long run acceptance is gained by objectivity and systematic study. Early announcement of results would satisfy the public need to know that issues are being taken in hand, but

126

would conflict with the image of commissions as deliberative bodies which report only after they have thoroughly weighed the evidence.

The Kerner Commission attempted to consolidate its command over the interpretation of the disorders in the following ways.

Creating Press Coverage. The commission sought to influence public perceptions of its activities by controlling publicity about the hearings it conducted. After reviewing testimony of witnesses called before the commission in secret session, staff members sought permission to release only portions of their prepared testimony to the press. At times, witnesses took this initiative themselves.

This policy represented a compromise between those who sought open hearings and those who favored closed sessions. The issue was raised at a September 13 meeting of the commission, occasioned by a newspaper column by Roscoe Drummond. Drummond had argued that the Warren Commission had failed to persuade the country of its findings because it operated behind closed doors, and then "in one quick burst. . .poured out to the nation such a volume of fact and finding that few could digest and fewer still could master what it had to say."[60] He advised the Kerner Commission that Americans would be most likely to accept its findings if it conducted open hearings and used them to educate the public.

Commissioners raised a number of objections to open hearings. Thornton argued that positions could be distorted and commissioners and witnesses could receive unfortunate publicity. Corman expressed the fear that open hearings might focus press coverage on personalities rather than on concepts and issues. Even those who wanted some open coverage were ambivalent. Jenkins favored admitting the press, but not the public. Harris urged that sensitive hearings involving political figures be closed, while those involving technical experts and specialists could be open.

Governor Kerner proved to be the most enthusiastic supporter of open hearings. Complementing Drummond's analysis, Kerner identified one of his primary goals as that of publicity: "My concern all the time about this commission has been that at the conclusion our greatest problem is going to be to educate the white, rather than the Negro."[61] Kerner was echoing a critical objective of the executive staff. In a memo written the previous day, Palmieri had proposed that a major commission objective should be: "To focus the attention of the American people—particularly the suburban white population—on the critical issues presented by the riots."[62]

Only Kerner and Harris favored limited open hearings when a show of hands was called. Brooke, Thornton, Jenkins, Corman, McCulloch and Peden were against the motion. The commission finally compromised along the lines suggested by Alvin Spivak, director of information. Hearings would be closed, but portions of testimony would be released when cleared, or when witnesses themselves chose to do so.

Public awareness of commission activity was also maintained by carefully arranging and publicizing most of the tours of ghetto areas and visits to cities undertaken by the commissioners. In addition to the other functions served by these tours, they provided "news" at an early stage of the commission's life, when staff had yet to be hired and a plan of attack had not yet been determined (see ch. 6). This publicity was useful even though at times members expressed concern that media coverage interfered with their ability to collect information and impressions. Most commissioners also commented on the riots in their public appearances, although deliberations often had not proceeded very far at the time. These activities served to keep the commission in the public eye and satisfy media demands for news, without compromising the commission by prematurely revealing a position on key issues.

Interim Recommendations. The commission decided at an early stage to make specific recommendations when appropriate. On August 10, 1967, it transmitted to the president recommendations pertaining to the National Guard, which was then encountering strong criticism. It urged that immediate steps be taken to increase black participation in the Guard, to provide improved riot-control training and to review Guard officer qualifications.[63] Coming so soon after the massive use of the National Guard to suppress riots in several cities in the summer of 1967, this recommendation received considerable criticism from Guard defenders in Congress.

In October the commission recommended to the president (with publicity) that the Department of Justice undertake training conferences for state and local personnel who might be used in riot control. Other interim recommendations included two statements in early February recommending that the Justice Department develop a program to encourage the use of radio equipment by patrolmen, and that the Federal Communications Commission take steps to alleviate the problem of insufficient frequencies available to police departments and other public safety agencies.[64] These recommendations were made after extensive consultations with the various agencies. The National

Advisory Panel on Insurance in Riot Affected Areas, a spin-off group of the commission, published its analysis in January 1968, two months prior to release of the main *Report*.

Contacts with Critical Sectors

The commission provided opportunities for staff members, and sometimes commissioners, to interact with potential allies and critics. Executive staff members toured prestigious universities seeking knowledgeable social scientists and soliciting their help and advice. Staff members served as liaisons with relevant executive agencies during the initial period when the staff thought it would be able to use data from agency sources. Agency personnel were also kept informed of progress, particularly toward the end when policy recommendations had been developed. On November 10-12, 1967, the commission sponsored a conference at Poughkeepsie, New York, to discuss problems of media coverage with representatives of the industry. The meeting was somewhat rancorous because industry representatives feared the commission would advocate policies that might abridge "free-speech" guarantees. Nonetheless, the conference helped to identify major problems. One recommendation to emerge from the meeting, included in the *Report* and widely adopted in the industry, concerned increasing media coverage of the black community during "normal" periods.[65]

During the fall and winter, at the suggestion of the commission, the Justice Department conducted sessions on riot-control techniques for police administrators. These sessions have been widely credited with minimizing the loss of life during the disorders which followed the assassination of the Rev. Martin Luther King, Jr., in April 1968.[66]

These contacts had mixed results. Meetings with academics generally convinced executive staff members of the inadequacy for their purposes of social science theory and research on riot causation and the general unwillingness of academics to undertake research projects on short notice. Agency representatives were cooperative to some extent, but relations deteriorated when they tried to deny the commission sensitive data, and when they became wary of providing it funds. Meetings with representatives of the media, initially somewhat hostile, later increased media treatment of black-related issues. In every case the commission received or imparted significant information. Less obviously, it showed deference to academic, agency and media representatives by seeking their advice and assistance, and seeking to incorporate their views.

Presenting the Report: Maximizing Political Impact

Commission and staff deliberations were conducted with one eye on the potential public reaction to commission activities and the other on its study and recommendations. Concern for its potential impact began as soon as the commission started to meet. Initial discussions quickly identified the two major, if broad, public targets of the final report: the white, middle-class, often suburban, population whose ignorance of black life poorly prepared it for understanding the revolts; and the country's black population, which needed reassurance that American political institutions had not abandoned them. There was early agreement, too, that the *Report* had to be written for popular consumption so as to capture public interest.

Tailoring the Report

The *Report* did not criticize major political and social institutions. Corporations, trade unions, school systems and police departments are rarely singled out for fundamental criticism. Problems associated with these institutions are always viewed as implicitly correctable. Their existing structures, practices and orientations remain unquestioned.

At least two reasons may be advanced to explain why the *Report* did not deal with fundamental practices of major American institutions. First, confrontations with such interests might have involved the commission in sparring matches which would ultimately have worked to the detriment of the *Report's* general acceptability. Second and more important, the organizational representativeness of the commission precluded represented interests and key institutions from major criticism. Anticipating hostile responses from the commissioner most closely associated with particular interests, staff would often be reluctant to submit critical materials. And in debates among commissioners, deference was usually accorded to the commissioner with career interests in an area under discussion.67

Closely related to the fact that various commissioners "defended" special interests is the importance of their concerns as public men and women. Virtually all of the commissioners would return to their careers after the panel concluded its work and were sensitive about being associated with controversial materials. According to staff members, commissioners gave the impression that they did not want to be associated with a report critical of institutions with which they would later have to deal.

130

These concerns may also explain the commission's conspicuous failure to discuss the war in Indochina. The *Report's* only reference to American Vietnam commitments appears in an oblique reference at the beginning of chapter 17, "Recommendations for National Action." On the question of finances the commission stated:

> The nation has substantial financial resources—not enough to do everything some might wish, but enough to make an important start on reducing our critical "social deficit," in spite of a war and in spite of current requirements.[68]

Yet the commission could hardly be ignorant of the impact of the war on domestic policymaking. The costs of the war, combined with the president's reluctance to raise taxes, had occasioned his original request to consider only inexpensive program proposals and had led him to rule out a supplemental appropriation for the commission. Witnesses at commission hearings frequently marked Vietnam as a reference point: Vivian Henderson, Rev. Leon Sullivan, Kenneth Clark, Ernie Chambers, Piri Thomas, Fr. James Groppi and David Hardy all mentioned the war in commenting on American priorities, the costs of domestic programs, or American moral commitments.[69]

The Government as Audience

To maximize the *Report's* impact within the executive branch, the commission pursued several strategies. As recommendations were developed, they were discussed with the appropriate departments. Conferences were held with Secretary John Gardner of HEW, with Secretary Robert Weaver of HUD and with Secretary Wirtz of Labor; and with the FBI and the CIA. Similarly Ginsburg maintained regular contact with the president's staff. A typescript version of the *Report* was sent to the White House as soon as it became available.

Attempts had been made to tailor the report to presidential needs. Commissioners who tried to bring up the relationship between the costs of the Vietnam war and the lack of money for urban areas had been outvoted. References to the costs of implementing commission recommendations had been deleted as diversionary. The plan for an interim report containing low-cost, short-term programs was in line with the president's desire not to seem to "reward" rioters, or to project hopes for additional spending.

Even more significantly the commission tried, as one staff member indicated, to "withdraw the focus from federal programs," to focus on "various levels of government, particularly on the local level," and to "concentrate attention of the country on problems of an underlying nature." As early as late October the commission planned to place major blame on unresponsive city governments: "primary emphasis," it was said, would be placed "on realigning and improving municipal government, rather than on massive federal spending programs for the urban areas."[70] Chapter 10 of the commission's *Report*, "The Community Response," reflects this theme. Thus the Kerner Commission, like most riot commissions, tailored its recommendations to fit the executive agenda and deflected criticism away from that branch of government which chartered it—in this case, the federal government.

Maximizing Publicity

Commission staff members paid considerable attention to public relations. A week before the *Report* was released, Ginsburg briefed representatives of the three television networks. Regular meetings with representatives of the black press were held during the commission deliberations and a special briefing was held for them just prior to release of the *Report*. The National Educational Television network's Public Broadcasting Laboratory was helped with a documentary based on the commission's work. Plans for the rapid publication and circulation of the *Report* were discussed with paperback publishers and, on the basis of its previous experience with the Warren Report, Bantam Books was chosen over two other houses.

On February 29, 1968, the commission distributed the *Report* to the media, with a release date of Sunday, March 3. However, as events demonstrated, the commission and its staff soon discovered that they were not in total control.

The (Lindsay) "Summary"

During the last two weeks of deliberations, John V. Lindsay, the most outspoken liberal on the panel, became increasingly concerned that the general fatigue of the commissioners and staff and the need under the pressure of deadlines to "lock up" sections of the document was working in favor of the more conservative commission members. At its last meeting Lindsay indicated that he felt the *Report* was losing focus. He suggested that a summary, serving as an introduction, might rectify this problem. Then he read a proposed version which Jay

Kriegel, his assistant, had drafted the previous night. At the conclusion of his presentation, the summary was accepted substantially as read. Some commissioners tried to propose changes, but lacking an alternative text they were unable to alter the summary substantially. Thus Lindsay succeeded in influencing public impressions of the tone of the *Report*.

The impression created by the *Report* when it is read with the summary is substantially different than it is without the summary. The summary stresses the commission's "basic conclusion" that: "Our nation is moving toward two societies, one black, one white—separate and unequal."[71] This statement does not otherwise appear in the introduction of the *Report*. It is a central theme of chapter 16, on "The Future of the Cities," where the commission spelled out the implications of three alternative strategies: continuing present policies; enriching the ghetto; and ghetto enrichment plus encouraging dispersion of blacks to the suburbs. But even here, it is a conclusion of "this" analysis[72] (i.e., the discussion of alternative strategies), not of the entire *Report*.

The Lindsay summary also accounts in part for the emphasis in the press on the commission's concern with "white racism." The expression appears once in the body of the *Report*, in chapter 4, "The Basic Causes:"

Despite these previously mentioned complexities, certain fundamental matters are clear. Of these, the most fundamental is the racial attitude and behavior of white Americans toward black Americans. Race prejudice has shaped our history decisively in the past; it now threatens to do so again. White racism is essentially responsible for the explosive mixture which has been accumulating in our cities since the end of World War II.[73]

The section then enumerates "three of the most bitter fruits of white racial attitudes": pervasive discrimination and segregation, black migration and white exodus, and black ghettos.

In this context the phrase "white racism" functions rhetorically as a synonym for the phrases "racial attitude and behavior of white Americans toward black Americans" and "race prejudice." Furthermore, "white racism" is here blamed only for the explosive mixture; the actual violence must be explained by racism in combination with other factors, among them "frustrated hopes," the "legitimation of violence," black "powerlessness," the "incitement and encouragement of violence. . .first heard from white racists" and echoed more recently "in the inflammatory rhetoric of black racists and militants," and "the police."[74]

Interviews with commission participants also suggest that the Kerner Commission did not intend to become so prominently identified with the "white racism" theme. Furthermore, in the discussion of the violence encouraged by "white racists," the commission was referring to Klansmen and their spiritual kin, not the more ubiquitous practitioners of "white racism" whom it has generally been credited with condemning. The result of the prominence given the subject in the summary, however, was that the press seized upon the "white racism" issue.[75]

To obtain maximum press coverage government agencies often release news with a Sunday release date. This makes coverage likely in widely circulated Sunday newspapers, facilitates programming for national TV news programs and minimizes competition with stories which break as a result of work-week activities. The Kerner Commission scheduled the release date of its report for March 3, a Sunday. To give the media time to study the *Report*, copies were distributed on the preceding Thursday. However, this careful orchestration of publicity was for naught. The *Washington Post* returned its copy and Ginsburg learned that the newspaper had received a copy from other sources and intended to publish the summary the next day, Friday. Ginsburg's efforts to persuade the editors to wait were unsuccessful. To avoid accusations of favoritism, and fearing the *Post* scoop might decrease other papers' interest in the *Report*, Ginsburg moved up the release date for the summary to Friday, March 1.

Thus the summary, never really planned by the commission and introduced by Lindsay after the rest of the document was completed, received exclusive coverage at the height of curiosity about the commission's work. The first two days of commentary about the *Report* were based exclusively on the summary and it structured public perceptions of the entire document.

For three full days the Kerner Commission received the commanding attention of the news media. On Friday, virtually every newspaper in the country reported on the contents of the summary. The following day reporters went into the background of the commission, interviewing commissioners and other public figures. On Sunday, March 3, the release date for the full text, newspapers devoted pages and pages to the commission. The *Boston Globe*, for example, devoted 14 pages to the subject, despite the fact that it had given it a full 20 pages two days earlier. The three television networks and the National Educational Television network devoted at least eight hours of programming to Kerner Commission affairs. NBC interviewed mayors of six riot-affected cities, CBS interviewed Lindsay on "Face the Nation," while ABC interviewed Kerner, Harris and Wilkins on "Issues and Answers."

Monday's press was devoted to reporting statements made on these programs. Through the week, press and television coverage concentrated on the reactions of President Johnson, Vice-President Hubert Humphrey, presidential hopeful Richard Nixon and local political figures. Columnists speculated on the implications of the *Report*; editorials were generally favorable.

The thoroughness of press and television coverage did not preclude distorting of the commission's message. This was particularly conspicuous in the case of newspaper headlines and articles. Many newspapers accurately reported the primary conclusion of the summary (that the nation was moving toward two societies, one black, one white—separate and unequal). But their headlines often stressed the white-racism theme. Table 4.2 charts (for selected newspapers) the paragraphs in which the apartheid theme and the white-racism theme are mentioned, along with the lead headline. In these five major newspapers the "two-nations" theme was considered more important than the white-racism theme, to judge by the lead paragraph. However, headline writers ascribed greater importance to white racism.[76]

On the day the report was released, Bantam Books published its "advance" copy of the *Report*. Its first edition of 30,000 was sold out in three days and, between March and June of 1968, Bantam sold 1,600,000 copies. Four years after the commission reported, the paperback edition had gone through 20 printings with a monthly reorder rate of approximately 2,500 copies. In April 1972, 1,900,000 copies were in print in paperback alone.[77]

While public attention focused on the *Report*, the response of the Administration was conspicuously guarded. The president withheld comment for a week, then (on March 6) praised only the scope of the *Report* and the energy and dedication of the commissioners. Vice-President Humphrey criticized the conclusion that the country was

Table 4-2.
Apartheid and White-Racism Themes in
Newspaper Coverage of Kerner Commission

Newspaper 3/1/68	Apartheid theme, paragraph	White-racism theme, paragraph	Main Headline
Washington *Post*	1	3	Racism, Poverty Blamed for Riots
Baltimore *Sun*	1,3*	4	Riot Panel Report Calls White Racism Key Cause of Violence in Ghettos
Richmond *Times Dispatch* (Associated Press Story)	1	(1),11+	Racism Could 'Split Nation,' Riots Commission Warns
Cleveland *Plain Dealer* (*L.A. Times*/Washington *Post* Service Story)	1	4	'White Racism' Blamed in Riots
Philadelphia *Inquirer* (Associated Press Story)	1	9	Racism Can Split Nation, U.S. Is Warned; Board Urges $24-Billion-a-Year Program

*Indicates theme stressed in first and third paragraphs
+Indicates allusion to theme in first paragraph, but main emphasis in eleventh paragraph

heading toward a divided society (on March 4). Secretary Weaver criticized the recommendations as unrealistic (on March 6). But the president, the one man who could have translated the Commission's *Report* into an agenda for the nation, remained silent and left the fate of the *Report* to the outcome of public debate.

Commission personnel were poorly prepared for the president's reaction. Instead of using the *Report* to advance agency programs, Administration officials condemned it for being unrealistic. Instead of reflecting on the extent to which the *Report* was consistent with previous Administration statements, officials balked at the narrower issue of the identification of white racism as the critical problem.

The commission had failed to anticipate executive needs in at least two ways. It had refused to accept White House hints that its efforts should focus on short-term programs which were not costly. And it had failed to praise the president for his progress in various areas. On the first point, the commission had decided that it could not realistically advocate only short-run, inexpensive programs and at the same time acknowledge the tremendous problems faced by black Americans. And it could not act effectively on the second point without raising partisan issues that might have jeopardized the entire commission process.[78]

Despite the president's virtual silence, the *Report* quickly became the touchstone for discussions of race relations. Church groups soberly committed resources to working on racial issues in its name. Black politicians applauded the identification of white racism as responsible for blacks' status in America. Politicians supported or criticized it depending upon their previous stand on racial questions. Entertainers evangelized for racial equality on late-night talk shows.[79] Conservative commentators found new evidence for the soft-mindedness of liberal thinking.

Throughout the country local efforts were initiated to build upon the work of the commission. Meetings of corporation executives were scheduled in various cities to discuss the *Report's* meaning for the business world. In Wisconsin, the legislature established a special citizen-legislative committee, known as the Little Kerner Commission, to do for the state what the *Report* had done for the nation.[80]

The Kerner *Report* remains the touchstone for race relations. The legitimacy of its origins and its wide circulation make the *Report* an invaluable compendium of American racial policy and a source of possible policy changes. More than four years after the *Report* was published, when Alderman Lois Morris was informed that other

Louisville, Kentucky aldermen would not vote to establish a civilian police review board because they did not know enough to vote for or against it, she reportedly "said she had answers to all their questions, and pulled out a report numbering more than 600 pages from the National Advisory Commission on Civil Disorders."[81] Mrs. Morris threatened to read the entire report to the board, but was ruled out of order.

Commission Participants as Advocates

Although their tasks were formally concluded with the release of the *Report*, to varying degrees commissioners and staff for a few months felt responsible for explaining and promoting it. Commissioners selected for their apparent diversity of interests came to identify with a single, relatively controversial document. This commitment was expressed in a variety of ways.

Some participants represented the *Report* before authoritative governmental bodies. Chairman Kerner, Vice-Chairman Lindsay and other commissioners testified before congressional committees. Staff member Stephen Kurzman worked with a committee of liberal Republican congressmen to develop proposals based upon the *Report*. Brooke and Harris took the lead in interpreting the *Report* to the Senate. Mayor Lindsay used the *Report* to identify critical priorities for New York City agencies. Chief Jenkins required all Atlanta policemen to read the document and write a report on their reactions.[82]

Mayor Lindsay and Senator Harris, the commission liberals, used the *Report* during the next few years to draw attention to domestic needs. Working through the Urban Coalition, they helped publicize the lack of progress revealed by a survey of domestic policy undertaken by the Coalition.[83] Lindsay had unsuccessfully advocated establishing a structure to monitor the rate of progress in implementing commission recommendations and he privately continued to draw attention to the gap between recommendations and policy through annual statements reviewing interracial progress.

Perhaps most significant, participants continued to "carry the flag" in their public appearances. In speeches, symposia, lectures and discussion groups, some staff members and commissioners continued to talk about the *Report* in the weeks, months and years to follow. The prestige of the occasions varied. In the three-week period following release of the *Report*, one staff member discussed the document in a speech or appearance on a Hershey, Pa., radio program; at Loyola

University in New Orleans; at an all-day meeting of the National Commission of Christians and Jews, National Capital Area Division; at a convention of the National Association of Chain Drug Stores in Bal Harbor, Florida; and at a meeting of the Executive Committee of the American Retail Federation.

That presidential advisory bodies become advocates when convictions are intense and needs apparent is not unique to riot commissions. The 1957 Gaither Committee, for example, presented President Eisenhower and the National Security Council with a comprehensive classified analysis of the nation's defense preparedness.[84] The high-status committee urged a reluctant president to undertake considerably greater defense spending in order to meet what it regarded as an underestimated Soviet threat. Initially failing to convince the president, the committee continued advocating its position in three ways: persistent efforts to reach the chief executive; enlisting the support of operating agencies; and attempting to arouse the public and elite groups to perceived dangers. Like the Kerner Commission, the Gaither Committee introduced a vigorous analysis of the problem for governmental (and through leaks) public consideration. Similarly, its efforts were finally thwarted. Military agencies were reluctant to accept the criticism implicit in the report and the president was unwilling to increase defense spending dramatically. Despite the efforts of committee members to launch public debate on the issue, the president opposed them, and he set the public agenda.[85]

The divorce of a riot commission from authoritative status, however, is qualitatively different from that of an advisory task force. Task forces, unlike commissions, are not given an implicit pledge that their advice will be used to establish policy priorities.

Policy Impacts: Through the Looking-Glass

During the hearings, Dr. Kenneth Clark made a deep impression when he questioned the usefulness of what the commission and staff were doing. He recalled that riot commissions in the past had issued reports and observed that the undertaking had an Alice-in-Wonderland quality, "with the same moving picture reshown over and over again, the same analysis, the same recommendations, and the same inaction."[86] Unhappily, the impact of the commission's work on public policy is substantially similar to Clark's bleak portrait.

139

It is generally hazardous to assess the policy impacts of a body with a scope of study as broad as the Kerner Commission. The number of influences on the policy process are so extensive that assigning weights is extremely risky. Moreover, it is difficult to assess what might have happened in the absence of a particular influence (in this case, to "think away" the influence of the Kerner Commission). Legislation, for example, might still have been enacted. Notwithstanding these difficulties, it is still possible to undertake an overall evaluation of the policy impact of the commission's work.

Virtually every assessment of the impact of the Kerner *Report* has come up with disheartening conclusions. The Urban Coalition's assessment of progress during the year after the release of the *Report* was grim: "a year later, we are a year closer to being two societies, black and white, increasingly separate and scarcely less unequal."[87]

Two years later the Urban Coalition convened another high-status group to report on the condition of urban areas. Chaired by Harris and Lindsay, the Commission on the Cities in the 70s declared:

> Despite the widely accepted Kerner finding that one major cause of the ghetto disorders of the 1960's was the shameful conditions of life in the cities, most of the changes in those conditions since 1968. . .have been for the worse. . . .The expressions of sympathy and concern that the Kerner Report elicited from a large number of those who, privately or publicly, wield the power that governs the United States, did not signify that they were willing to take the drastic action necessary to make American cities livable again.[88]

Wolanin, studying presidential commissions on a comparative basis, attributed only one piece of legislation to the Kerner Commission's work. Even this claim is questionable. The "Urban Property Protection and Reinsurance" section of the Housing and Urban Development Act of 1968 (Title XI) implemented the work of the commission's Advisory Panel on Insurance in Riot-Affected Areas. But this was a virtually autonomous subunit of the commission, whose report was not even included in the main *Report.*[89]

Initially, the *Report* may have helped persuade various political figures to favor ameliorative programs. For example, Senate sponsors of a bill for protection of civil rights workers and open-housing legislation were able to obtain cloture by a narrow margin on March 4 after previous failures. Yet the following day, Senate liberals were unable to defeat an amendment which made it a federal crime to cross state lines with intentions to incite a riot.[90]

An examination of federal-agency spending patterns reveals similarly mixed conclusions. James Button has found a positive relationship between riot severity and the tendency of the Office of Economic Opportunity to allocate money to cities. But he also found that the Department of Housing and Urban Development tended to *decrease* its funds the greater the riot severity, while the Law Enforcement Assistance Administration tended to focus support for riot suppression on cities with severe riot experiences.[91]

In the long run the *Report* has not fared well. While many observers believe progress has occurred in varying degrees in the four major policy areas identified by the commission—employment, education, welfare and housing—there have been no policy developments *consistent with the scope and urgency of the commission's recommendations.*

The basic recommendation for the unemployed and underemployed was the creation over three years of one million new jobs in the public sector and one million new jobs in the private sector. Public-sector programs have been infinitesimal; one and a half years after the *Report*, only about 17,000 unemployed and disadvantaged people had been placed in public-sector employment through New Careers and Operation Mainstream. In the private sector, the JOBS program of the National Alliance of Businessmen had enrolled 100,000 persons by June 30, 1969, but many lost their jobs after their federal subsidies (up to $3,500 per trainee) were claimed by their employers. Also, many of these jobs were merely filled with the disadvantaged rather than created for them, to qualify firms for the subsidy.[92]

Some progress had been made in reducing barriers to black employment such as discrimination and poor coordination of manpower training programs, but this progress is mostly attributable to general economic trends rather than deliberate employment policies. The generally robust economy of 1967 and 1968 induced employers to recruit the unemployed and underemployed, but the recession beginning in 1969 almost *doubled* the number of unemployed workers reported by the Kerner Commission. By the third quarter of 1971, black unemployment in large-city poverty neighborhoods had increased by 64 percent over the comparable figure in the fourth quarter of 1967. "Last hired and first fired," black workers who had been fortunate enough to get work under deliberate employment programs were likely to be on the streets again. Perhaps most significantly, the ratio of black and white unemployment rates was about what it had always been. Whatever progress toward integrating work opportunities may have been made by private employers, the aggregate results have been minimal.[93]

The desperate employment needs of blacks identified by the Kerner Commission have persisted. Black workers remain victims of the "present policies choice"[94] (as the Kerner Commission put it) toward unemployed black and other minority workers. As one observer noted, "the 'massive' investment in programs to meet the needs of the unemployed and underemployed suggested by the commission has not yet been made."[95]

In housing the commission advocated an overall goal of 600,000 low- and moderate-income housing units during 1968, as part of a five-year plan for the construction of six million new units. The Johnson administration had proposed the same goal, but over a ten-year period. The Kerner timetable for subsidized housing construction was rejected by the Johnson administration.[96] The Department of Housing and Urban Development argued, in rejecting the five-year orientation, that it would introduce economic instability. (This follows if one makes the critical assumption that other investment priorities will not be changed.) Though it failed to win recognition of a need for greater urgency, the commission may have provided additional support and legitimacy for the more modest Johnson administration projections.[97]

Implementation of low- and moderate-housing construction has been somewhat significant in the first years of the Nixon administration, but in other respects disappointing. Subsidized housing starts went from a yearly average of 60,000 in the 1960s to a high of 250,000 annually in 1972. Yet despite the fact that the ten-year projections call for more construction in the latter years (providing easier interim targets), approximately 25,000 fewer subsidized units were constructed in fiscal year 1969 than were required under the plan and an even bigger gap will occur in subsequent years. Despite its substantial accomplishments in encouraging subsidized housing starts, in its second term, the Nixon administration called a moratorium on subsidized housing.[98]

Moreover, a virtually exclusive emphasis on new-housing construction may not really mean improved housing for low-income blacks. During the 1960s, 6 million housing units—mostly low income—were removed from the housing supply, more than one-third of the 16.5 million constructed during this period.[99] Whole sections of America's largest cities, where blacks are concentrated, are being abandoned and some cities are losing as many units as they are building.[100]

The implementation of other commission housing recommendations has been extremely modest.[101] Open-housing legislation did pass but without granting HUD the resources to enforce it. Moreover, the Nixon administration displayed no interest in fostering open housing in the suburbs, although this is the heart of the Kerner Commission strategy to combat the cancerous development of "two nations."[102] The Model Cities program was expanded to cover more cities, but simultaneously its allocation was reduced in the early 1970s and was scheduled to be suspended indefinitely or substantially modified along with subsidized housing programs on July 1, 1973.[103]

Much has been made of the mobilization of private enterprise against ghetto problems in the housing field. For example, the life insurance industry pledged, on September 13, 1967, to lend $1 billion to ghetto homeowners and other black investors.[104] Yet subsequent study has shown that the program was implemented through relatively standard lending techniques and ground rules, substantially neglecting the "high-risk" black mortgagee whom the program was allegedly designed to assist.[105]

The thrust of the national response to housing needs remains mixed. The number of subsidized housing units under construction increased, but few subsidy dollars have actually reached the poor.[106] The Nixon administration encouraged subsidized housing (until 1973) with minimal attention to the problem of racial discrimination in housing availability.

Ghetto education is little changed. Aggregate indicators show that black students continue to lag behind their white counterparts in reading and drop-out rates. Northern schools are as segregated as they were before the riots. Resources devoted to ghetto education remain inadequate or have decreased since 1967.[107] More important, urban education remains inadequate even where deliberate policy changes have been made. This is only partly attributable to continued ignorance about effective ways to intervene. Compensatory funds for ghetto schools available through Title I of the Elementary and Secondary Education Act have been cut back substantially,[108] despite the fact that when the busing controversy reached its peak in 1972, [109] President Nixon rhetorically urged that emphasis be placed on ghetto educational enrichment rather than further integration.

President Nixon's welfare reform proposal, the Family Assistance

Plan, consistent at least in outline with the commission's views on the matter, languished in Congress for lack of support. Its demise was attributable in part to conservative intransigency on welfare and in part to liberal opposition to the punitively low levels of individual family funding proposed and apprehension about the plan's work requirements.[110]

In sum, there is no direct evidence that the commission had much impact on American public policy. Where ameliorative legislation emerged, it was contradicted by punitive measures developed by the same offices or bodies.

But it may be a mistake to focus too closely on specific program recommendations. The Kerner Commission was not likely to be more original or innovative than others who have thought about the problems; for the most part its specific recommendations only *illustrate* the ways problems might be solved. More important may be the goals established and the urgency with which they are pursued. In this respect our previous observation remains: at the national level the major reordering of priorities demanded by the commission did not emerge.

The commission may have had a more diffuse impact, however. The Kerner *Report* clearly served to punctuate dialogues in domestic political affairs. Political figures tended to use it to confirm or restate their previous positions or commitments, or to launch more vigorous efforts to pursue policies they sought anyway. Thus, the *Report* became a legitimating instrument for diverse public-policy proposals. It was also used symbolically. A black politician such as Representative Adam Clayton Powell, in addressing his supporters, could rhetorically document the view that whites are guilty of oppressing blacks by holding up a copy of the *Report* as he talked.[111] Similarly, a white politician such as presidential candidate Eugene McCarthy could endorse the *Report's* housing recommendations rather than develop his own program and rationale.[112] Church-related social action groups could, in the name of the *Report,* find new resolve to do what they had previously been pledged to do.[113]

Other diffuse impacts may be noted. The commission's major statement on race relations may have firmed the resolve of the individuals whose previous views were uncertain or ambiguous. It may have contributed to the general trend in the United States toward greater understanding and acceptance of blacks among whites. On the other hand, its focus on "racism" probably helped legitimate the use of this term and concept in public debate, particularly among blacks. In this respect the commission may have contributed to black mobilization and solidarity, as well as to a degree of racial polarization. Despite all this, there is little evidence that public policy toward American minorities would be much different today if the Kerner Commission had never been created.

Only in two areas is the picture more positive. First, the commission's assistance to police administrators and National Guard officials in planning procedures for handling civil disorders has been widely credited with minimizing loss of life during the riots of April 1968.[114] The commission's focus on media coverage and media employment of blacks has been similarly influential. There is a general consensus among analysts of the media that riot coverage has improved. Also, greater attention is currently paid to covering "everyday" news of the black community and there is greater emphasis on hiring blacks as reporters.[115] These developments might have occurred anyway, but there is some consensus that the Kerner Commission played a significant role in hastening them. The media have been somewhat dilatory, however, in responding to the commission's recommendations about the need for positive black images.[116] Similarly, the Equal Employment Opportunity Commission discovered widespread resistance to integration at many levels of media staffing.[117]

In a more speculative view there is another area for which the Kerner Commission may claim credit. In unambiguously rejecting the riffraff and conspiratorial theories of riot causation, the commission may have reduced the prevalence of these explanations among many people.

Riot Commissions in the Political Process

Why did the commission have such little success in obtaining its policy objectives? Two common explanations—that the United States is "racist" or that competing "pressure groups" thwarted blacks' efforts—are too general to be of much use. The former neglects the roles riot commissions may play in low levels of progress in race-related areas. It also neglects that even if one accepts that a majority of Americans oppose black progress, riot commissions (and other public and private organizations) contribute to black subordination independent of diffuse racist attitudes. The latter suggests that policy toward blacks is calculable solely in terms of the direction, intensity and duration of competing group pressures. We seek to examine structural aspects of the political system which help transform these pressures into greater or lesser influences.

Riot commissions are authoritative only in the sense that they are acknowledged to be the body to which the chief executive will look for answers. The appointment of a commission implies a pledge that it will set the policy agenda. But its recommendations are authoritative only insofar as the chief executive or others in authority accept and move to implement them. President Johnson, who in July 1967 appointed his commission with great fanfare, by the following March no longer was subject to pressures from anxious, angry or confused constituencies. The war in Vietnam was then absorbing his administration's energy and was restricting his policy options as he sought to avoid raising taxes or cutting domestic spending. And in an election year, the president was not in a position to welcome a *Report* which demanded higher spending levels and neglected to mention the achievements of his administration. The logic of the commission process led to a vigorous but vague report with global implications. The president had hoped for short-run and inexpensive suggestions.

Without executive support a commission's influence depends on the legitimacy that it can acquire and the political skills of individual commissioners. Here the probabilities of success are constrained by additional factors.

1. *The commission is not a permanent organization.* Once it delivers its report, it ceases to exist. There is no staff to answer inquiries, no way to follow up opportunities to participate in legislative or executive politics, no means of focusing attention on its recommendations.[118] Organizationally speaking it is entirely dependent in the postreport period on the continuing interest of individual commissioners.

2. *The kind of commissioner recruited usually mitigates against sustained personal involvement with the issues and recommendations in the report.* Since they are originally selected for balance and moderation, most commissioners have no career stake in promoting the *Report.* Only John Lindsay, and to a lesser extent Fred Harris and Roy Wilkins, manifested an interest in promoting the Kerner *Report* after the initial interest of the first few months had died down. Commissioners' busy schedules and conflicting career orientations do not make them reliable long-term advocates.

3. *The nature of press coverage and political rhetoric also influence the impact of the report.* We have already described how the summary achieved a prominent place in the Kerner *Report.* Press evaluations tend

146

to focus on narrow or limited disputes, to the neglect of larger questions. In the case of the Kerner *Report,* the press tended to focus on arguments about the costs of projected programs, the failure to condemn the rioters and the slogan of white racism.

4. *The resources of opponents are considerable.* Over time, those whom the report implicitly challenges have greater access to the media and to governmental agencies than the commission and its supporters. In writing a *Report* to appeal to conscience, the Kerner Commission aligned itself with relatively powerless interests. Shorn of the executive mantle, the commission faced the same pressures and constraints encountered by other advocates of black interests.

5. *Commissions to some degree attempt to tailor recommendations to harmonize with executive agendas.* They also try to avoid offending interests represented on the commission. Thus they pull their punches hoping to increase the likelihood that some of their recommendations will be implemented. Even if they fail, they may take comfort that their reports are educational. But this strategy may be compromised by the prior tailoring of the report to achieve concrete goals. Ironically, the Kerner Commission pulled some punches, but ultimately hurt its cause with the president by not being responsive enough to his needs.

6. *Without executive support, a commission must find other ways to translate its recommendations into a legislative agenda.* The Kerner Commission, however, found its early decision to develop a broad-ranging report incompatible with a more limited, specific agenda that might have attracted greater congressional support.[119] The multiple audiences perceived by the commission precluded development of a more focused and restrained document (see chapter 6).

In a way, Kenneth Clark's pessimism was justified a priori: whatever its educational impact, a commission helps deflect pressures for change. By enabling the president to claim that he awaited its recommendations, the commission helped him to postpone decisions until passions cooled. The commission provided a focus for various pressures which otherwise would concentrate on the president, even overtly undertaking to assure various publics that their interests were being considered.

By deflecting pressure in times of intensity, commissions contribute to a conservative, status quo bias—politics as usual. Those who are satisfied with the prevailing rate of black progress in America may applaud this role. Those who fear a white backlash against blacks and are alarmed at the possibility of repression may be relieved that commissions absorb pressures that otherwise might result in punitive policies. But those who believe that opportunity for decisive leadership and qualitatively different decisions about national priorities come only in crisis situations must regret the loss of an opportunity that may not soon arise again.

NOTES, CHAPTER 4

1. While we discuss here jurisdictional conflicts over interpreting riot events, another type of jurisdictional conflict occasioned by riots is observable in the jockeying over who will suppress them. Suppression of the Detroit disorder was complicated by the insistence of Attorney General Ramsey Clark that Michigan Governor George Romney declare the situation beyond his control. The governor was reluctant to make a statement which, he said, might jeopardize insurance policies in the city (and perhaps reflect on his leadership ability). For a summary of these events see *Report*, p. 95. Curiously, the last time federal troops had been used to suppress civil disorder was 1943, in Detroit.

2. For pressures from constituents on congressmen and their responses, see New York *Times*, 29 July 1967.

3. See Washington *Post*, 21 July 1967. Some months later, Congress, under severe criticism for insensitivity on this issue, rescinded its previous decision and passed the measure. See also *Congressional Quarterly Weekly Report*, "Special Report: Urban Problems and Civil Disorder," no. 36 (8 September 1967), p. 1,726.

4. Over liberal opposition, the House, by a vote of 347 to 70, sent the measure to the Senate as separate legislation. It had previously been detached from pending civil rights legislation under pressure from House Rules Committee chairman, William Colmer of Mississippi. Joining the appeal for this legislation was an old champion of civil rights bills, influential Republican William McCulloch of Ohio, who was asked to serve as a member of the Kerner Commission some 10 days later (Washington *Post*, 20 July 1967).

5. See the New York *Times*, 3 August 1967. That committees can manipulate what they are told by choice of witnesses is illustrated here, as it is throughout this study. When the Kerner Commission staff investigated the Cambridge disorders, they found the *police* to have been substantially responsible for creating the disorders.

6. Nathan Cohen, who had studied the Watts rebellion of 1965, and John McCone, chairman of the commission investigating this disorder, testified against the measure. So did Rufus Mayfield, young black

director of a Washington ghetto youth corps, and Dr. John Spiegel, director of Brandeis University's Lemberg Center for the Study of Violence. They argued that the bill would be practically valueless, that it reflected a severe misunderstanding of the causes of ghetto unrest and that it merely confirmed for black people that America was unwilling to reform itself. See Washington *Post*, 22-24, 30 August 1967.

7. As its critics had warned, the antiriot measure was never used to control riots. The first prosecutions under this provision of the Civil Rights Act of 1968 were used to harass leaders of the alleged antiwar "conspiracy" during the Democratic National Convention of 1968 in Chicago, as were most subsequent prosecutions.

8. Conservative Congressional reactions to the riots and punitive sections of the Omnibus Crime Control Act are described in detail in Michael E. Milakovich, "The Politics of Block-Grant Law Enforcement Assistance" (Ph.D. diss., Indiana University, 1972), especially pp. 14-20.

9. New York *Times*, 1 August 1967.

10. New York *Times*, 8 August 1967. Kowalewski was a minor figure in Newark, assigned to the "lockup" because he was considered extreme and unreliable. That the McClellan Committee selected this man to testify suggests it wanted to find a witness who would express a particular version of events.

11. New York *Times*, 10 August 1967. For a more complete account released during the first week in September, see "OEO and the Riots: A Summary" (Washington, D.C.: Government Printing Office, n.d. [GPO # 929.881]).

12. New York *Times*, 3 August 1967; Washington *Post*, 29 July 1967.

13. Washington *Post*, 28 July 1967.

14. Washington *Post*, 29 July 1967.

15. Ibid.

16. Washington *Post*, 31 July 1967; New York *Times*, 2 August 1967. The Senate charged the McClellan Committee "to make a full and complete study and investigation of riots. . .and measures necessary for their immediate and long-range prevention." U.S. Congress, Senate, Committee on Government Operations, *Riots, Civil and Criminal Disorders*, before the Permanent Subcommittee on Investigations, United States Senate, 90th Congress, 1st session, 1967, p. 1, part 1.

17. Washington *Post*, 29 July 1967.

18. New York *Times*, 25 July 1967 and 18 July 1967.

19. Thomas Wolanin, "Presidential Advisory Commissions," (Ph.D. diss., Department of Government, Harvard University, 1971), p. 39.

20. "Remarks of the President. . . ," *Report*, p. 536.

21. The Kerner Commission and the (N.J.) Governor's Commission, for example, both refuted the conspiracy theory. It is interesting to speculate on the implications for Detroit that the equivalent body to a riot commission dismissed the study of causes of disorders in order to concentrate on recommendations and proposals. We would hypothesize that the absence of an investigation into potential conspiracies may itself have allayed concern over the existence of a conspiracy. In comparison, the N.J. Commission may have contributed to anxieties over conspiracies by providing a forum in which this issue continued to be debated.

22. For an extended discussion of the theoretical bases for such inferences, see Murray Edelman, *Politics As Symbolic Action* (Chicago: Markham, 1971).

23. Newark Police Department, "Chronological Summary of Newark Riots, July 1967," document in files of the Governor's Select Commission on Civil Disorder, on deposit in the Governor's Office, Trenton, N.J.

24. President's Address to the Nation on Civil Disorders, Office of the White House Press Secretary, 27 July 1967, p. 1.

Documents cited in chapters 4-6 for which no published sources are given were obtained by the authors from commission sources and may be inspected for appropriate reasons on request. The papers of the Kerner Commission have been deposited in the Lyndon B. Johnson Presidential Archive in Austin, Texas, and many of these documents may be available there, although we have not verified that they were in fact deposited. For a very useful short treatment of the Kerner Commission see Andrew Kopkind, "White on Black: The Riot Commission and the Rhetoric of Reform," in *Cities under Siege*, ed. David Boesel and Peter H. Rossi (New York: Basic Books, 1971), pp. 226-58.

25. Ibid., pp. 1-2. On the (low) incidence of sniping in the disorders, see Terry Ann Knopf, "Sniping—A Pattern of Violence?" *Transaction* (now *Society*) 6 (July/August 1969): 22-29.

26. President's Address to the Nation on Civil Disorders, pp. 3-5.

27. According to New York *Times* writer Tom Wicker, in the Preface to the Bantam Books edition of the *Report*, p. 5.

28. Wolanin, "Presidential Advisory Commissions," p. 164.

29. The term is adapted from Hanna Pitkin, *The Concept of Representation* (Berkeley, Calif.: University of California Press, 1967), ch. 4.

30. These seven commissions all were charged with answering questions and making recommendations about pressing, sometimes controversial domestic issues and conflicts. The Warren Commission has

been omitted as a special case. There were only seven members. Chief Justice Warren chaired; the other members were senators, congressmen, the director of the CIA, and John McCloy, former chairman of the board of the Ford Foundation. The National Commission on Technology, Automation, and Economic Progress, appointed 14 November 1964, somewhat fits the pattern described below. It included in its membership one black; 3 labor leaders; 5 business leaders (one of whom was based in Texas); one woman; and 3 professors. Focusing on nine riot commissions since 1917, Platt notes that members of such commissions are typically white, male, relatively old (over 50), and lawyers (by profession); see Platt, *Politics of Riot Commissions*, p. 14. On recruitment to presidential advisory commissions generally, see Wolanin, "Presidential Advisory Commissions," pp. 163ff.

31. Significantly, the New York *Times* reported that the president did not want to appoint militant Negro leaders to the commission because (according to a "White House source") he "was interested in accomplishment and not in furthering 'a debating society' " (29 July 1967).

32. *Report*, p. 172.

33. Corman was relatively less well known; it is instructive that in providing the Kerner Commission with pertinent biographical materials he drew attention to the fact that he received an "[a]ward from the Jewish Federation-Council of Greater Los Angeles for 'outstanding service in fostering good will and understanding among religious and racial groups'. . ." *Report*, p. 543.

34. In the remainder of this chapter and in the two that follow we have relied heavily on interviews conducted with commission staff members primarily during November 1967 as the commission was in the midst of research activities and in March 1968, just after the release of the final *Report*. These interviews provide the basis for many of our observations, but have not been specifically cited because interviewees were promised anonymity.

35. On the influence of the Washington attorney, see Joseph Kraft, *Profiles in Power* (New York: World, 1966) pp. 69-76.

36. These assets in some respects were commission liabilities at first, since Ginsburg was often thought to be checking commission progress with the White House during the course of its deliberations. In recent years the roles of White House liaison have been specifically and overtly filled by presidential assistants. See Norman C. Thomas and Harold L. Wolman, "Policy Formulation in the Institutional Presidency: The Johnson Task Forces," in *The Presidential Advisory System*, ed. Thomas Cronin and Sanford Greenberg (New York: Harper and Row, 1969), pp. 137-38. However, public presidential commissions require

more oblique liaison work because of their putative freedom from interference. Hence the importance of someone "trustworthy" in the job of executive director.

37. See Washington *Star*, 16 August 1967.

38. One explanation for the absence of top-level black staff was the perceived risk to black professionals of working with a commission whose product might well compromise their future status in working with the black community.

39. New York *Times*, 28 July 1967.

40. See ibid., 29 July 1967.

41. See "Meetings and Witnesses," internal commission document, n.d.

42. See New York *Times*, 2-3 August 1967.

43. Memo, To: All Staff Members; From: John A. Koskinen, 12 October 1967.

44. U.P.I. story, 5 December 1967.

45. See New York *Times*, 8 August 1967.

46. *Wall Street Journal*, 8 March 1968.

47. The McClellan Subcommittee also may have helped the Kerner Commission gain access to relatively liberal, reluctant sources, since the commission appeared to be more favorable toward black interests when contrasted with the approach of the McClellan unit.

48. See New York *Times*, 1 August 1967; and "OEO and the Riots: A Summary."

49. Division of Health Mobilization, Bureau of Health Services, Public Health Service, "Metropolitan Area Readiness to Provide Emergency Health and Medical Services," December 1967, 9 pages.

50. New York *Times*, 6 September 1967.

51. *Wall Street Journal*, 6 October 1967.

52. Remarks of Lyndon B. Johnson on 14 September 1967, before the International Association of Chiefs of Police. *Public Papers of the Presidents of the United States, Lyndon Johnson, Containing the Public Messages, Speeches, and Statements of the Presidents*, 1967, Book II, 1 July to 31 December 1967 (Washington, D.C.: U.S. Government Printing Office, 1968).

53. Washington *Post*, 23 July 1967, 9 September 1967, 24 September 1967; New York *Times*, 9 August 1967. See also the statement of The Urban Coalition, New York *Times*, 2 August 1967.

54. Baltimore *Sun*, 31 December 1967.

55. Washington *Post*, 31 October 1967 and 19 November 1967.

56. Memo, To: All Staff Members; From: John A. Koskinen, 12 December 1967, p. 2.

57. This is discussed in detail in chapter 5. President Johnson had

requested similar austerity from his Task Force on Cities, chaired by Paul Ylvisaker.

58. President Johnson was reluctant to use funds available in the emergency fund for the president or the Special Projects fund, because of a general policy of not drawing from these sources so as to impress Congress with his frugality (Wolanin, "Presidential Advisory Commissions," p. 154).

59. Memo, To: Victor H. Palmieri; From: Richard P. Nathan, 13 October 1967; see also, *Congressional Record*, 20 March 1967.

60. Memorandum to David Ginsburg, on stationery of Deputy Executive Director [Palmieri], 12 September 1967, p. 4. Drummond's syndicated column appeared in the press around August 11.

61. Official Transcript of Proceedings before the National Advisory Commission on Civil Disorders (labeled "Executive-Confidential") 13 September 1967, p. 1,103. Hereafter, this reference will be cited as Transcript, and only the page reference noted.

62. Memorandum to David Ginsburg, on stationery of Deputy Executive Director [Palmieri], 12 September 1967, p. 1.

63. *Report*, Appendix I.

64. Ibid.

65. See *Report*, pp. 382-86. Controversy on the racial policies of the electronic media continues; see, for example, New York *Times*, 7 March 1972.

66. See, for example, New York *Times*, 14 April and 4 October 1968.

67. The "protective" roles played by various commissioners are revealed in interviews with key staff members and inferred from statements of commissioners during hearings. See, for example, Transcripts, pp. 2,998ff. (Abel); pp. 3,008ff. (Wilkins); pp. 1,599ff. (Brooke).

68. *Report*, p. 411.

69. Transcripts, pp. 1,181-82, 1,221, 1,266, 1,533, 1,538, 1,540, 1,547, 1,522, 1,554, 1,576, 1,594-95, 1,601, 1,611, 1,624, 1,657. Partially in reaction to the Kerner Commission's neglect of this subject, Jerome Skolnick and his staff, in preparing their report to the National Commission on the Causes and Prevention of Violence, *The Politics of Protest*, included a chapter on the relationship of riots to war in America; see Jerome Skolnick, *The Politics of Protest* (New York: Simon and Schuster, 1969).

70. Milwaukee *Journal*, 31 October 1967.

71. It is the fifth paragraph, *Report*, p. 1.

72. Ibid., p. 407.

73. Ibid., p. 203, 204-206.

74. Ibid., pp. 203-206.

75. In the summary the passage concerning white racism is essentially the same as the usage in chapter 4. See *Report*, p. 10.

76. Some newspapers did not stress the white-racism theme in headlines, for example, the New York *Times*, the Washington *Evening Star*, and the Chicago *Tribune*.

77. Personal communication from Jean Highland, the Bantam Books editor in charge of the project, 20 April 1972.

78. The commission's dilemma is illustrated by the relatively minor decision to introduce the *Report* with a quote from President Johnson's address to the nation of 27 July 1967. This statement was included in the printed version but not in the one signed by commission members. Put there independently by the staff either to praise the president indirectly or to appeal to him by stressing the congruence between the commission's work and his own previous statements, the quotation remained quite sensitive. When they discovered this insertion, Republicans associated with the commission questioned the propriety of using the commission's work to draw attention to the president's statements on domestic policy.

79. Actor Marlon Brando, appearing on the Joey Bishop television show on 25 April 1968, read aloud from p. 214 of the Bantam edition, instructing his audience on the history of segregation in America.

80. Madison *Capital Times*, 27 May 1968; and chapters 8-10 in this volume.

81. Louisville *Courier-Journal*, 28 June 1972, p. 1.

82. Herbert Jenkins, *Keeping the Peace* (New York: Harper and Row, 1970), p. 96.

83. Urban America, Inc., and the Urban Coalition, *One Year Later: An Assessment of the Nation's Response to the Crisis Described by the National Advisory Commission on Civil Disorders* (New York: Praeger, 1969). Lindsay and Harris continued this campaign at least through 1971. See Fred R. Harris and John V. Lindsay, *The State of the Cities* (New York: Praeger, 1972).

84. This discussion of the Gaither Committee is drawn from Morton H. Halperin, "The Gaither Committee and the Policy Process," *World Politics* 13, no. 3 (April 1961): 360-84.

85. The Gaither report was made public fifteen years after it was written (New York *Times*, 20 January 1973).

86. Transcript, pp. 1,288ff., and *Report*, p. 483. The same theme was expressed by Judge Leon Higginbotham, dissenting from the National Commission on the Causes and Prevention of Violence, *To Establish Justice, To Insure Domestic Tranquility* (New York: Award Books, 1969), pp. 119-20

87. Urban America, Inc., and the Urban Coalition, *One Year Later*, p. 118.

88. Harris and Lindsay, *State of the Cities*, p. 5.

89. See Wolanin, "Presidential Advisory Commissions," p. 374. Wolanin considers the Kerner Commission to have been relatively successful in achieving implementation of recommendations. But this is because he considers a commission successful if a single significant recommendation was implemented. However, from the perspective of commissioners, staff, or the public generally, this criterion is far too generous. The insurance panel was marginal to the commission's efforts and did not engage the attention of the commission. (The Kerner Commission summarized the insurance panel report in less than two pages, and endorsed its recommendations without comment; see *Report*, pp. 360-62.) In any event, this concern with insurance represents only a tiny fraction of the commission's efforts. Significantly, the presidential message supporting this legislation was submitted to Congress on February 22, *before the Kerner Report was released*; see Wolanin, p. 434.

90. New York *Times*, 5-6 March 1968. Compare this action with the *Report*, which found no evidence of the kind of behavior the legislation tried to prohibit. (The same ambivalence toward black needs is evident in actions taken by the House of Representatives later in the summer; see New York *Times*, 9 August and 17 August 1968.)

91. James W. Button, "The Effects of Black Violence: Federal Expenditure Responses to the Urban Race Riots of the 1960s" (paper presented at the annual meeting of the Midwest Political Science Association, Chicago, Ill., 3-5 May 1973).

92. Walter Franke, "The Kerner Commission Recommendations Revisited: Employment," *The Kerner Report Revisited*, ed. Philip Meranto (Urbana, Illinois: Institute of Governmental Affairs, University of Illinois, June 1970); these paragraphs on employment draw on this paper.

93. See Harris and Lindsay, *State of the Cities*, pp. 44-45.

94. *Report*, ch. 16.

95. Franke, "Kerner Commission Recommendations," p. 24.

96. The administration reiterated its support for a ten-year perspective, rejecting the five-year pace, in a report to the Subcommittee on Housing and Urban Affairs of the Senate Committee on Banking and Currency. See Message from the President of the United States, "First Annual Report on National Housing Goals" (Washington, D.C.: U.S.G.P.O., 1969), pp. 6-7.

97. The presidential report stated: the housing "needs estimate" of the Johnson administration "has been *endorsed* by the National

Advisory Commission on Civil Disorders, the National Commission on Urban Problems, and the President's Committee on Urban Housing" (ibid., p. 1; emphasis added).

98. Message from the President of the United States, "Second Annual Report on National Housing Goals" (Washington, D.C.: U.S.G.P.O., 1970), p. 12; Harris and Lindsay, *State of the Cities*, p. 70; New York *Times*, 9 January 1973, p. 1.

99. Harris and Lindsay, *State of the Cities*, p. 70.

100. Ibid. Note that the Kerner Commission stressed the problem of housing abandonment and deterioration in its analysis, but failed to stress rehabilitation and preservation in its recommendations. In this discussion of housing goals and performance we have profited from the comments of Arthur Solomon.

101. Michael Murray, "Responses to the Kerner Report Housing Recommendations," in Meranto, *The Kerner Report Revisited*, p. 56. This paragraph draws on Murray's full discussion, pp. 45-58.

102. Illustratively, see the dispute between H.U.D. Secretary George Romney and President Nixon over utilization of H.U.D. incentives and sanctions to force communities to cease discriminatory practices. This arose over Romney's efforts to force Black Jack, Mo., to practice open housing. See, for example, New York *Times*, 15 June 1971.

103. New York *Times*, 9 January 1973, p. 1.

104. For the industry's six-month proclamation of progress, see New York *Times*, 24 March 1968.

105. Karen Orren, *Corporate Power and Social Change* (Baltimore, Md.: Johns Hopkins University Press, 1974).

106. For a summary discussion, see Bernard J. Frieden, "Improving Federal Housing Subsidies: Summary Report," Papers Submitted to Subcommittee on Housing Panels, Committee on Banking and Currency, House of Representatives, 92nd Congress, 1st Session, June 1971, Part II, pp. 473-88.

107. Harris and Lindsay, *State of the Cities*, pp. 47-63; and J. Myron Atkin, "The Kerner Commission Report and Educational Change," in Meranto, *The Kerner Report Revisited*, pp. 25-30.

108. Ibid., pp. 53-55.

109. For example, New York *Times*, 17 March 1972.

110. Daniel P. Moynihan, *The Politics of a Guaranteed Income: The Nixon Administration and the Family Assistance Plan* (New York: Random House, 1973). See also Merlin Taber, "Welfare Recommendations on the National Advisory Commission on Civil Disorders and ADC in Illinois," in Meranto, *The Kerner Report Revisited*, pp. 25-30, 31-44.

111. New York *Times,* 24 March 1968.

112. New York *Times*, 29 May 1968.

113. On the National Council of Churches, New York *Times*, 30 March 1968; on the American Jewish Committee, New York *Times*, 3 April 1968; for a pastoral letter on the *Report* read in the New York Archdiocese, New York *Times*, 11 March 1967.

114. See Wolanin, "Presidential Advisory Commissions," p. 374. For a survey of organizational changes in various local public agencies during and after riots, see "Urban Civil Disturbances: Organizational Change and Group Emergence," an issue of the *American Behavioral Scientist* 16, no. 3 (Jan.-Feb. 1973).

115. See the Symposium, "Journalism and the Kerner Report," *Columbia Journalism Review* 7, no. 3 (Fall 1968): 42-65; William Small, *To Kill a Messenger: Television News and the Real World* (New York: Hastings House, 1970), esp. ch. 4; and Gene Graham, "The Kerner Report and the Mass Media," in Meranto, *The Kerner Report Revisited*, pp. 87-95.

116. See J. David Colfax and Susan Frankel Sternberg, "The Perception of Racial Stereotypes: Blacks in Mass Circulation Magazine Advertisements," *Public Opinion Quarterly* 36, no. 1 (Spring 1972): 8-18.

117. For the networks' equal-opportunity plan drawn up in response to the E.E.O.C. hearings, see New York *Times*, 26 February 1970.

118. On this point the Kerner Commission was actually well favored. Since the official life of the commission was to extend for one year, the commission did have authorization to maintain a shadow staff through the end of July 1968, even though the *Report* was released in March.

119. See Marvin Weinbaum, "Congress and the Commissioners: A New Species of Oversight," in Meranto, *The Kerner Report Revisited*, p. 10.

5

Research and the Commission: Dilemmas of Political and Scientific Legitimacy

President Johnson asked the Kerner Commission for two reports, one to be delivered no later than March 1, 1968, the other to be submitted after a full year of deliberations. This schedule was slightly revised during the first month of meetings when the commission agreed to advance the date of the interim report to December 15.[1] It took this action hoping to influence the president's State of the Union message and the congressional agenda in sufficient time to affect policy before the summer's expected "riot season." The commission also wished to avoid partisan quarrels in the upcoming presidential election campaign.

Less than three months later the investigations were convulsively reoriented and the form and content of the inquiry fundamentally changed. On Saturday, December 9, the commission abandoned plans to produce an interim report altogether, resolving instead to produce a single report on March 1. It altered the status and roles of key staff members, entirely reappraised staff efforts and discharged most staff members. The negative publicity generated by these events became an important concern.[2]

These actions resulted from failures to anticipate several dilemmas that arose in the research process. Essentially, the needs of the commission's social scientists for reflective and detached analysis was incompatible with the other needs of the commission. Similar conflicts occur in a wide range of agencies which conduct social research, but the severe time limits under which the commission operated and the public nature of commission activity focused these conflicts in extreme form.

Crisis commissions generally labor under three important constraints in conducting research:

1. *Temporal.* The limited time available for work shatters orderly procedures for collecting data, analyzing evidence and developing explanations. Commissions are expected to provide comprehensive analyses, but the schedule usually permits only cursory examinations. In this situation social scientists and others who conduct commission inquiries may be reduced to *ad hoc* advisory roles for which they have no special claim to expertise.

2. *Political.* To a large extent the impact of a commission's work depends upon its legitimacy. A commission's political legitimacy is determined by the extent to which its procedures, findings and reports, and role in the political process, are considered right and proper by a significant portion of active and aware publics.[3] We have already suggested some of the factors which bear upon a commission's political legitimacy. Social scientists also play a major part in determining the legitimacy of findings and reports. Commissions must search widely and objectively for evidence, analyze the results dispassionately and report their findings in accordance with the highest standards of objective social inquiry. The work undergirding such efforts is normally done by social scientists.

Sometimes, however, actions taken in pursuit of political legitimacy may conflict with the demands of scientific legitimacy, including standards of data collection, analysis, inference and presentation that social scientists, broadly speaking, impose on their work. Similarly, social scientists may develop findings which compromise the political legitimacy of the commission's efforts. Commission staffs also encounter conflicts between social scientists' methods and ways of presenting their findings and commissioners' need to feel confident in the final staff product and its acceptability. When efforts to secure the "best" social science research are thwarted by limited time and manpower, social scientists may understandably wish to hedge their findings with discomforting qualifications. Social scientists must somehow resolve these dilemmas, compromise professional judgment, or risk being repudiated by the commission. Ironically, the "ivory tower" social scientist may be more prepared to make do under commission pressures than other staff members who, to their later regret, come to expect a more impressive product than is reasonable under the circumstances.

3. *Conceptual and Methodological.* Social scientists may also find it difficult to fulfill their assigned roles because of limits on existing understanding of social causation; the questions they are expected to address sometimes do not have simple or precise answers. Despite this, commissions hope to gain access to previous social science research, to obtain the legitimacy that stems from consulting relevant experts, or simply to benefit from the experience and background of people who have studied certain phenomena extensively. Sometimes social scientists are asked to conduct research where no consensus exists on appropriate procedures and methodologies, findings and explanations. Under such circumstances it is particularly difficult to evaluate research and a premium may be placed upon superficial concerns of form, presentation and appearance.

The scope and approach of the commission's work clearly determines the nature of the demands on research. Thus we take up first how the Kerner Commission agenda was determined. Then we discuss the three major research tasks carved out by the commission: learning *what happened*; explaining *why it happened*; and investigating responsive *program alternatives*. The major tasks in these areas were to be undertaken "in-house," that is, within the commission as an organization, although significant contributions also were to be developed by outside consultants and contractors.

Establishing the Agenda

Presidential guidance concerning the Kerner Commission's tasks was provided in three stages. In his nationally televised speech President Johnson said only that the commission would investigate recent disorders and make recommendations.[4] The executive order establishing the commission called for the following investigation and recommendations:

1. The origins of the recent major civil disorders in our cities, including the basic causes and factors leading to such disorders and the influence, if any, of organizations or individuals dedicated to the incitement or encouragement of violence.

2. The development of methods and techniques for averting or controlling such disorders. . . .

3. The appropriate role of the local, state and Federal authorities in dealing with civil disorders; and

4. Such other matters as the President may place before the Commission.[5]

The president was most explicit in his statement to the commissioners at the White House on July 29. He asked them to consider three basic questions: "What happened? Why did it happen? What can be done to prevent it from happening again and again?" He then articulated 14 questions, the answers to which he believed would help maintain public order.

—Why riots occur in some cities and not in others?
—Why one man breaks the law, while another, living in the same circumstances, does not?
—To what extent, if any, there has been planning and organization in any of the riots?
—Why have some riots been contained before they got out of hand and others not?
—How well equipped and trained are the local and state police, and the state guard units, to handle riots?
—How do police-community relationships affect the likelihood of a riot—or the ability to keep one from spreading once it has started?
—Who took part in the riots? What about their age, their level of education, their job history, their origins and their roots in the community?
—Who suffered most at the hands of the rioters?
—What can be done to help innocent people and vital institutions escape serious injury?
—How can groups of lawful citizens be encouraged, groups that can help to cool the situation?
—What is the relative impact of the depressed conditions in the ghetto—joblessness, family instability, poor education, lack of motivation, poor health care—in stimulating people to riot?
—What Federal, State and local programs have been most helpful in relieving those depressed conditions?
—What is the proper public role in helping cities repair the damage that has been done?
—What effect do the mass media have on the riots?

The president asked for advice and recommendations in three

general areas: short-term measures to prevent riots, better measures to contain riots once they begin, and long-term measures to eliminate riots in the future. To accomplish this complex assignment, he specifically noted: "You will have all the support and cooperation from the Federal government. I can assure you of that."[6]

The executive order creating the commission provided that "[A]ll necessary expenses incurred in connection with the work of the Commission shall be paid from the 'Emergency Fund for the President' or such other appropriated funds as may be available for the purposes of the Commission."[7] Exective Director David Ginsburg was personally assured that sufficient resources would be available. Deputy Executive Director Victor Palmieri reports that the problem of financing was his greatest initial concern and that Ginsburg reassured him a number of times that the White House expected the commission to spend considerable sums. As we shall see, such assurances were not completely reliable.

These documents constituted the commission's assignment. The first tasks set by Ginsburg were to analyze the "charge" to determine specifically the areas in which the commission would have to report and to develop a working outline. Ginsburg consulted people who had served commissions before, such as McCone Commission staff director Warren Christopher, and began reading extensively about race riots and commissions in the past.

Some subjects, such as the responsibility of the media and the question of damage and insurance, did not fit neatly into the working outline. Ginsburg tentatively marked these for separate analysis. He considered the question of riots and conspiracy extremely delicate and immediately moved to establish liaison with the FBI and CIA.

On Friday and Saturday, August 4 and 5, 1967, he revised and sharpened his outline with the help of David Chambers, a young Washington attorney just appointed as his special assistant, and Richard Scammon, former director of the Census, whose engagement as chief research consultant was announced on August 2.[8] The outline provided the focus for a meeting held in Ginsburg's Georgetown home that Sunday with a panel of prominent urban experts, including Richard Boone, director of the Citizens Crusade Against Poverty and an architect of the poverty program; Christopher, then deputy attorney general; Jack Conway of the Congress of Industrial Organizations (CIO); Harold Fleming, president of the Potomac Institute; Oliver Lofton, director of the Newark Legal Services Project and recently appointed by Governor Hughes to the New Jersey Select Commission on Civil Disorder; Mitchell Sviridoff, soon to resign as New York City's Human Resources administrator to become vice president for national affairs of the Ford Foundation; James Q. Wilson, professor of government at Harvard University; Adam Yarmolinsky, professor of law at Harvard, also instrumental in creating the poverty program; and Paul Ylvisaker, former director of the public affairs program at the Ford Foundation, and at the time commissioner of the New Jersey Department of Community Affairs. Community organizer Saul Alinsky was invited but did not attend.

At this time Ginsburg received advice and general reassurance that the outline was useful. With relatively minor modifications, this outline guided the commission's work from then on. Later, when confronted with questions about the scope of the investigation, Ginsburg and other staff members would return to the "14 points" and the other documents for clarification. For example, as late as December, upon discovering that the commission had not prepared documents on the public role in rebuilding cities after riots—one of the 14 points—staff members were assigned to do so. Departures from the original outline were minimal. It anticipated more intensive investigations of the riot events than were eventually conducted. It also recommended studies of "nonriot" cities, statistical analyses of city characteristics associated with the occurrence of riots, and studies of white, nonracial riots such as panty raids and other college-student capers. But with these modest exceptions, the Ginsburg outline structured the commission investigations.

During this weekend Ginsburg also received advice on procedure. The importance of collecting information on the riots "first-hand" was brought home when he realized how widely Paul Ylvisaker's and Oliver Lofton's accounts of the Newark disorders departed from general newspaper and television coverage. Ylvisaker also stressed that the president could not be relied upon to support the commission's recommendations. As chairman of the president's confidential Task Force on Cities which had submitted its final report less than one month earlier, Ylvisaker had been assured that the White House wanted a report with "no punches pulled."[9] Yet in the end, the president received the report coldly and did not even formally accept it for many months.[10]

Other discussions during this critical organizing period focused on the basic posture the commission should assume. There was some debate on the appropriate tone for the interim report. Most of the participants advocated minimal discussion of police practices and controlling violence. A few disagreed, however, arguing that the white public needed to be reassured that widespread predictions about protracted sniping and violence were inaccurate. They argued further that the commission could take this direction because the average black person would not be paying as much attention to its work as the average white person. These key consultants thus explicitly recognized that a major role of a riot commission is to reassure various publics.

Other discussion at this meeting centered upon the proper focus for research. Some participants with social science backgrounds were skeptical that questions of riot causation could be definitively answered with statistical techniques. They urged attention to issues of riot control rather than explanation, since it might be easier to develop authoritative answers to questions in this area.

Staffing

In order to contribute to the president's legislative program and perhaps to influence congressional deliberations, the commission decided during these early weeks to produce a final report on March 1 and an interim report by January 15. This decision made the problem of finding and recruiting staff even more urgent. Palmieri later described recruiting staff as a "war strategy," in which many projects are initiated with the hope that enough will succeed to justify the effort. Richard Nathan, associate director for program research, compared the problems of commission staffing and staff work to those of a political campaign—overscaling the effort at first, then excising projects which do not develop successfully.

Regardless of which description is most appropriate, the Kerner Commission faced extraordinary staffing problems. Staff had to be hired quickly, without full assessment of qualifications and before the research agenda had been completed and major staff tasks identified. Even while they were recruiting, staff directors did not know precisely what the people they were hiring would have to do.

Finding qualified people who were available was perhaps the most severe problem. In late August, talented people in the academic world were already committed to teaching and various research projects. Or they were unwilling to speed up their normal research pace for the commission. However excellent the quality of research, a two-year project is not very useful to a one-year commission.

Another problem was the quality of staff members secured "on loan" from other agencies. According to one informant, federal agencies were often reluctant to "lend" black staff members and their best personnel to the commission and black bureaucrats were not anxious to accept temporary employment with the commission. Other potential recruits were skeptical about commission intentions and unwilling to accept temporary, dead-end employment, especially if it required moving to another city.

These factors in part may help explain the predominance of lawyers on the staff. Seven of the Kerner Commission members were attorneys, as were the two top-staff executives, their assistants, the deputy director for operations, the director of investigations, the general counsel and his staff, and others.[11] While the dominance of lawyers in commission affairs has been frequently lamented,[12] the tendency to hire them is hardly accidental. Indeed, in certain respects lawyers are the logical choice for commission operations, for at least the following five reasons:

1. Lawyers are generalists. They normally work in a client/ professional, problem-solving relationship requiring them to treat many matters in which they are not expert. The initially ill-defined nature of commission work makes the generalist desirable. Individuals who are already experienced in the Washington political milieu may be particularly attractive. In contrast, the social scientist/scholar makes a mark professionally by opening up new areas of inquiry. This may entail administering a small research staff but does not provide experience in accomodating the interests and perspectives of clients or colleagues.

2. Lawyers may be more available than others, since their client-centered firms often permit "leaves of absence" on relatively short notice. The great number of lawyers in Washington may increase the probability that they become involved in commission work. Others who seem to have been relatively available were free-lance writers and consultants, academics (but not for large-scale research) and graduate students.

3. When commissions begin to focus attention on producing a final document, the most important qualities are the ability to work all day and night, to absorb endless criticism without taking personal affront and to synthesize sentiments of commissioners or anticipate and then articulate their positions on various issues. Lawyers frequently have considerable experience working under pressure for clients regardless of

personal interests. Thus we have the contradiction that those often considered best able to gather and interpret socially relevant data (social scientists) may not easily accommodate the pressures that go into writing the final report.

4. Working for a commission requires a person to take some risk in exchange for possible high rewards. The eventual reputation of a commission is, of course, unknown, and employment is temporary with uncertain future prospects.

A number of inducements seemed to attract individuals to Kerner Commission employment despite the uncertainties. A young lawyer working for the commission might enhance his career through contacts and experience developed on the job. More established lawyers in politics already might have been unable to refuse a personal request from the president, particularly when accompanied by the possibility of favors in return. This might have been the motivation of Governor Kerner, appointed to the federal bench by President Johnson before he left office, and of Merle McCurdy, general counsel of the commission, who was appointed as the first counsel of the Office of Consumer Affairs in March 1968.[13] Others, such as criminologist and police expert Arnold Sagalyn, associate director for public safety, might have been attracted by the opportunity to employ their expertise in a new and important context. Still others were motivated by concern with racial problems in America and hoped to affect governmental action by influencing the final report. These motivations were, of course, not mutually exclusive. But one might expect considerable tension to develop among people induced to join for personal career enhancement and those recruited in hopes of affecting public policy.[14]

5. If the top staff of a commission is made up of lawyers, the dominance of the legal profession through the lower-staff ranks may be explained by the fact that lawyers are often more comfortable hiring other lawyers, with whom they share similar professional norms.

Using a White House office for the prestige it contributed to the search, Ginsburg (and later Palmieri) quickly developed a considerable staff. The first recruit, after Ginsburg and Jones, was Scammon. From the start Ginsburg felt a need to include someone experienced with quantitative analytic techniques. The engagement of the former director of the Census seemed to meet that need and Ginsburg was particularly impressed with Scammon's ability to popularize statistical materials.

Another important participant who had experience in providing "hard" data was economist Anthony Downs, who served as a consultant to the commission throughout its life. Ironically Downs had been a member of the confidential Task Force on Cities, chaired by Ylvisaker, whose report had been ignored and snubbed by the chief executive. Downs initially impressed Ginsburg by presenting the executive director with a detailed research agenda for the commission, partly derived from his previous Task Force experience.[15]*

The executive staff was quickly built up during the next month. The following men had relatively broad responsibilities in commission work:

- —Stephen Kurzman, deputy director of operations, a former assistant U.S. attorney from New York, with congressional experiences in the offices of Senator Jacob Javits and Congressman John Lindsay.[16]
- —Merle McCurdy, general counsel, on a leave of absence from his position as U.S. attorney for the Northern District in Ohio, the only black among the top staff members.[17] McCurdy's immediate assistant was a former subordinate from the U.S. attorney's office in Ohio, Nathaniel Jones, also a black.[18]
- —John Koskinen, special assistant to Palmieri, a young lawyer from Los Angeles.[19]
- —Richard Nathan, Ph.D. (Harvard, government), associate director for short-term programs.[20]
- —Arnold Sagalyn, on leave from HUD as a consultant on public safety, associate director for public safety.[21]
- —Milan Miskovsky, on leave as assistant general counsel of the treasury, and formerly connected with the Central Intelligence Agency, in charge of examining evidence of conspiracy. He held the uninformative title of director of investigations.
- —Robert Shellow, assistant deputy director for research, a social psychologist then chief of a special projects section of the National Institute of Mental Health, hired to direct the efforts of the staff social scientists.[22]
- —Myron J. Lefcowitz, a former OEO sociologist, initially charged with developing long-term proposals.[23]
- —Alvin Spivak, director of information, on leave from his job as a United Press International reporter.

* In the spring of 1968, members of the Ylvisaker task force held a reunion in Princeton, New Jersey. At the dinner the members of the task force toasted Downs for having taken virtually all its important recommendations, buried and denied recognition by the president, and inserting them in one of the most widely read American government documents ever produced.

Other critical staff roles were filled by Henry Taliaferro, a longtime associate of Senator Harris, in charge of congressional liaison, and Charles Nelson, who handled commission administrative matters.

Five commissioners obtained staff appointments for personal assistants. This, for example, was the primary role of Kieran McGrath, a former legislative assistant to Senator Paul Douglas, who served as Governor Kerner's representative. In other cases, commissioners made appointments to the working staff, as in the case of Taliaferro, or assigned their own staff members to work closely with the commission, as in the case of Mayor Lindsay's assistant Jay Kriegel.

Hundreds of applications and recommendations for employment poured into the commission's offices. This demonstration of interest was useful in limited ways (Nathan identified potential student assistants in this way), but the necessity of dealing with the correspondence proved a burden. Academic researchers and consulting firms began to volunteer to help the commission study riots. Overwhelmingly, no answers to riot problems were suggested in the proposals which flooded commission mail, just a willingness to study the problems for a fee. Staff directors would have liked to ignore these unsolicited applications and recommendations, but they could not give the impression they were unwelcome. The political sensitivities of commissioners and the need to demonstrate that they were making the widest possible search for expertise dictated that this mail be treated seriously. In response to such pressures[24] public information and congressional liaison staff were developed.

By December, at full strength, the Kerner Commission staff numbered 191. This included executive staff members, their assistants and associates, field team members, secretaries and research assistants, and individuals associated with the work of the insurance advisory panel.[25] By the end of December, over half of these people were informed of their impending dismissal, engendering resentment and concern over the direction of the commission's work.

The decision to rearrange commission schedules represented an abrupt departure from previous expectations and staff directions. The turnabout resulted in damaging newspaper and congressional speculation concerning the presumed conservatism the upheaval was thought to reflect. Dismissing the staff, changing directions and admitting the inefficiency of previous staff efforts indicated a major organizational crisis. To a significant degree the decision to change the dates the reports would be published resulted from challenges to the very credibility, integrity and unity of the commission. We now turn to the problems in staff research which were at the root of the difficulties.

Structuring Research

The Kerner Commission had no easy mandate. It was asked to do no less than thoroughly analyze the history of American race relations, the impact of domestic social policy and develop answers to a problem of social causation of extraordinary complexity. The intensity of passions required that commission staff work be particularly sound and invulnerable to attack. Anything less risked alienating commissioners who expected reliable evidence and an airtight case. Corman, for example, noted that the commission's task was not so much public education as it was "more seeking valid information and drawing reasonable conclusions from it." Similarly, Brooke expressed concern about whether sufficient evidence existed on which to base recommendations and Thornton warned that it would be a mistake to offer any statement unless the commissioners became authorities on the subject.[26] These expressions were shared by executive staff members, who reminded the commissioners that the president "expected all [the commission's] findings and conclusions to be fully supported in the record of the Commission's work."[27]

To provide an interim report by mid-December, the staff developed a research schedule in the first month which, with few exceptions, permanently structured the commission's efforts. Subsequent attempts to change the commission's orientation came up against the fact that the proposed subjects had not been researched. Analysts who have studied the exercise of power often concentrate on the influence that individuals may be *observed* to exercise. They would focus (as we do later in this book) on the issues raised, debated and resolved by commissioners. But this focus alone would distort Kerner Commission politics. Many vital decisions were implicitly made, with commissioners playing passive roles, essentially ratifying early staff work. Later commission debates were held in a framework previously set.[28]

The first fully elaborated outline of the interim report was developed by Downs.[29] His agenda called for scenarios and re-creations of the riots; studies of the immediate responses of control forces (police and national guard); advanced planning studies; analysis of police-community relations; and studies of short-range options. The scenario studies would include classification of 1966 and 1967 riots and incidents, field studies of 20-25 cities, a synthesis of these data and studies of the effectiveness of the police and National Guard. Advanced planning would include studies of intergovernmental relations, the courts and the administration of justice. For short-run program development studies Downs recommended concentrating on manpower, recreation, education and Defense Department planning.[30]

Ginsburg and Palmieri spent August and the beginning of September attempting to hire a staff, establishing liaison with government agencies, and identifying potential research personnel. A dinner meeting on August 21 concerning riot control was designed to permit staff members and Commissioner Jenkins to consult with knowledgeable people in the criminal justice area.[31] A similar meeting was held in late October to consult with sociologists about problems of survey research.[32]

On September 12, as the commission prepared for a hearing on Negro history and employment problems, its first on a substantive topic, the staff started to review and discuss its efforts with the commissioners. In a memo to Ginsburg, Palmieri listed the commission's basic objectives as follows: to answer the president's questions; to provide guidance for officials at all levels of government to help prevent future outbreaks; to make recommendations for social and economic "action" programs for all groups and levels of government;[33] and "to focus the attention of the American people—particularly the suburban white population—on the critical issues presented by the riots."[34] The intention to address the *Report* to the white, middle-class, suburban American infused staff thinking almost from the beginning (see ch. 6).

According to the memorandum, the commission would study selected cities, survey pertinent research by experts and conduct new research where necessary. Hearings would be held with "outstanding practitioners and experts, scholars, Negro leaders and militants and representatives of the ghetto community, such hearings to be held in part on a regional basis with the Commission sitting in panels." To meet the schedule for the interim report would require a "concert of views on the basic tone and approach of the document and a minimum of editorializing to meet individual problems."[35]

Nine sections were envisioned for the interim report. Palmieri proposed to begin with an outline of the presidential mandate and background on events leading up to the establishment of the commission, and a summary of the document. He then suggested the following general topics:

1. What Happened and How it Happened: What Did We Learn?
2. The Historical Perspective.
3. The Apparent Causes of Grievance, Tension and Disorder.
4. Recommendations Relating to the Community's Capability to Maintain Law and Order.
5. Social and Economic Action Programs.
6. Recommendations with Respect to Media Problems.
7. Recommendations with Regard to Insurance Problems.[36]

Some of the topics were straightforward and including them caused little controversy. Historian John Hope Franklin's essay on black protest in the past was eventually included as chapter 5, "Rejection and Protest: An Historical Sketch." Because some commissioners did not appreciate the difficulties of drawing an analogy between earlier European immigration to America and more recent black migration to northern cities, sociologist Herbert Gans was asked to develop an essay on this subject, which provided the basis for chapter 6, "The Formation of the Racial Ghettos." The essay was solicited in response to some commissioners' views that blacks should be able to rise in American society like other urban immigrants in the past.

Both of these contributions were summaries of existing knowledge and theory and required no new data or analysis. But considerable difficulties emerged when original data had to be collected, or where existing theory was relatively diffuse or contradictory. Palmieri was particularly concerned with the social science aspects of the staff's efforts. When he joined the commission the only social scientists at work were individuals from the Census Bureau, who were preparing to develop a factor analysis of the characteristics of riot cities. He doubted their ability to do research on ghetto issues because of the bureau's regular undercounting of black-ghetto populations.

Researching What Happened

Available reports on the riots were so contradictory that it was quickly clear to Ginsburg that the commission would have to conduct its own research.

Ginsburg hoped to have the story of the riots told dramatically. At an early date he approached writer John Hersey, a friend, whose

172

treatment of the devastation of Hiroshima Ginsburg thought might serve as a model. When Hersey declined, Robert Conot, whose book on the Watts uprising had recently appeared, was asked to develop riot city profiles using journalistic skills.[37] Ginsburg also felt the description of the riots had to be comprehensive, which meant covering enough riot cities to capture salient patterns and important details. Also, investigations had to be initiated quickly while memories were fresh. The general lack of success in efforts to contract out this research to university personnel reaffirmed inclinations to develop an "in-house" research capability.

The kinds of questions the commission sought to answer were suggested in Palmieri's memo to the staff on September 21. In addition to the composite profile, the report would compare characteristics of riot and nonriot communities; preriot climates (levels of grievances, sources of tension, outside agitators); types of disorders and severity; types of rioters (including roles of participants—"looters, snipers, etc." and degrees of organization); possible patterns by which riots spread among cities; types of riot-control responses; intergovernmental interaction; and the nature of damages.

Selecting a Sample

As assistant deputy director for research, and chief resident social scientist, Robert Shellow was asked to select a "sample" of cities for intensive analysis. Shellow began by combining an FBI list of 56 cities experiencing racial disorders between January 1 and August 1, 1967, with a relatively unsystematic and somewhat inaccurate supplementary list derived from news clippings provided by the Lemberg Center for the Study of Violence at Brandeis University. With the assistance of Downs, Shellow devised a classificatory scheme which distinguished among riot episodes along several dimensions: degree of violence or damage; duration; number of participants; and law enforcement response. A five-point scale was developed to distinguish levels of intensity of riots. This scaling procedure yielded a continuum of riot intensity on which three were classified as most serious (Class A), eight fell into the next category (Class B), and 18, 15 and 14 were listed in the other categories in descending order of severity.[38] This scheme was eventually used to structure staff work, despite Shellow's cautions concerning continua and the use of noncontinuous variables and the problems of arbitrary classification with unreliable data.

Charting the disturbances by time and geography revealed linkages between riot occurrences. Two riot "clusters" developing out of the

Detroit and Newark disturbances and four "circumscribed" chains seemed to emerge from this exercise.[39] The latter linked disorders in Cincinnati and Dayton, Ohio; Buffalo and Niagara Falls, New York; Riviera Beach and West Palm Beach, Florida; and Tucson and Phoenix, Arizona. The remaining cities were residually classified as "isolates."

In selecting a sample for the first phase of the study, the Class A cities (Cincinnati, Detroit, and Newark) were automatically included, as were the eight Class B cities (Atlanta; Buffalo; Cambridge, Md.; Grand Rapids, Mich.; Minneapolis; Plainfield, N.J.; and Tampa, Fla.). The final panel of 26 cities was selected on the basis of geographic representation, severity and origin of the riot. One cluster chain was included—the New Jersey cities of Elizabeth, Jersey City, Paterson, New Brunswick, Englewood and Bridgeton. Dayton, Ohio (in combination with Cincinnati), and Phoenix and Tucson, Arizona, were to provide an opportunity to study the hypothetical "circumscribed cluster" effect. Three cities—Nashville, Houston and Jackson, Miss.— were selected to study disturbances originating in university settings. Also included in the original sample of 26 were New Haven, Conn., which experienced relatively mild (Class D) disorders during three days in late August; Atlanta; San Francisco; and (as a nonriot-city comparison) Pittsburgh.[40]

The study of university-related riots was contracted out to investigators at Peabody College in Nashville and never incorporated into the commission's work as a special type. San Francisco, Buffalo and Pittsburgh were eventually dropped from the analysis, although as late as October 31, Ginsburg continued to tell the commissioners that plans called for conducting surveys in 12 more cities.[41] Thus the commission eventually studied 20 cities which experienced disturbances, although its original research design called for investigating 26.

The method of selection simply used common sense, choosing the most severe events or those which might reveal the significance of additional variables. But it was not a "sample" which could permit testing of theory, for the simple reason that it was unclear of what the 20, 23 or 26 cities were samples. One measure of the atheoretical nature of the sampling and later research may be seen in the failure to make any use of the major theoretical questions implicit in the "sampling" procedures. The commission had nothing to say about riot-city clusters, circumscribed clusters or university-oriented disturbances above and beyond what was known when the cities were initially picked.

In the back of its *Report* the Kerner Commission reproduced charts characterizing various riots on dimensions of violence, duration, number of participants and suppressive official response. These charts appear to represent considerable investigation and analysis. In fact, however, they are the most fragmentary representations. The data were not a result of research but were developed from news reports as an aid in determining which cities should be studied in the first place. This "symbolic" research seems intended not so much to convey information as to create the *impression* that valid data had been collected and sophisticated analysis conducted.

The Elusive Nonriot City

In 1966, the Lemberg Center for the Study of Violence initiated a study of three riot and three nonriot cities to try to account for the fact that disturbances had occurred in some cities and not in others. The study had been significantly compromised in 1967, when civil disorders broke out in two of the three control cities, and in 1968 when the remaining nonriot city experienced disorders. Despite the Lemberg Center's experience, the Kerner Commission remained committed to identifying the characteristics of nonriot cities, in part because the presidential mandate had included a charge to do so. Pittsburgh was included in the original sample of 26, and other cities, such as Atlanta, Rockford, Tucson and New Brunswick were included in order to examine factors affecting the level of severity. Palmieri's preliminary outline of the December report indicated that an attempt would be made to provide "[A] more detailed analysis of the riots in terms of. . .[t]ype of communities (demographic and other statistical characteristics) which experienced riots as compared with those which did not."[42] In Ginsburg's late October summary of research, he continued to stress the desirability of investigating cities "which have been free of disorders altogether."[43]

In statistical sampling, the number of cases selected for analysis is primarily related to the desired reliability of the analysis and the size of the universe to be sampled. If there is no possibility of statistical reliability, however, the importance of feasibility in sampling increases. If there is no theoretical justification for sampling, one might investigate as many cases as is efficient or convenient. Yet Shellow was required to sample according to the idealized image of social science investigation held by his staff superiors. Shellow recalled in an interview that he had to try to counteract unsystematic approaches to selecting which cities to study. Some staff members wanted to determine the sample size by such logic as "a respectable number—50 perhaps." Certain high-level staff members hoped to identify a "control" group in the manner of a quantitative study. He pointed out that Philadelphia represented no "control," statistical or otherwise; moreover, it was likely to experience disorders in the near future. The inclusion of Pittsburgh also represented obeisance to a model of "control" which is not applicable to nonexperimental social science research. (Pittsburgh, at the time regarded as one of the best examples of a nonriot city, experienced a major riot in April 1968).

The search for the nonriot city reflected inappropriate deference to inapplicable models, but it provides insight into prevailing concepts of civil disorders. It suggests that riots are seen to result from specific, localized conditions which vary to such an extent that cities may be dichotomously conceived as "riot" and "nonriot." While this approach is hypothetically plausible, it obscures the alternative hypothesis that riots express attitudes and behaviors with national dimensions and that blacks are treated sufficiently uniformly throughout the country that local considerations are relatively immaterial in explaining the outbreak of violence. According to this formulation, if riots have not occurred in a locality, it is due either to time lag or random and idiosyncratic factors. In a relatively short time period, with limited resources, it would of course be impossible to demonstrate conclusively the validity of either approach.[44] Thus the commission's basic approach and working assumptions became all the more significant.

The commission's interest in explaining factors potentially affecting the level of violence held more promise. Here the continuum on which riot severity was scaled did seem potentially fruitful, however shaky the evidence on which cases were assigned. The investigation of disturbances in New Brunswick, for example, particularly the responsiveness of Mayor Patricia Sheehan did seem to help explain why violence was minimized. But as Shellow explained: "the fact that a city did not experience a major disturbance may testify to the effectiveness of early control attempts; it may also indicate the absence of high levels of grievances in a city *or any number of other factors, including a large element of chance.*"[45]

Field Investigations and the Problem of Incremental Concreteness

To collect data on the chronology of various riots as well as on factors hypothetically related to their occurrence, the commission hired

30 investigators in mid-September to conduct interviews in teams of six in 23 riot cities. The teams were to review statistical summaries and "back up" files on the cities prepared with the help of various federal agencies. Then, divided into three subteams of two, each was to spend a week to ten days interviewing public officials, people in the area of disorders and representatives of the private sector. Using a loose open-ended questionnaire, team members were to return to their hotel rooms in the evenings to transcribe interviews and discuss strategy. Upon returning to Washington they were to finish transcribing their notes and participate in "de-briefing" sessions. These sessions, directed by Stephen Kurzman, were to be conducted with the help of staff social scientists, members of the short-term-program operation team and the law-enforcement study group. The sessions were designed to elicit additional information and identify data "gaps" which could be filled on subsequent visits. These "first cuts" into the field were intended to provide data for the interim report. Only six to seven weeks could be spent in the field if November was to be set aside for a draft of the interim report.[46]

The field investigations were conducted in a loose and hurried manner. Interviewers assigned to public officials discovered that they had to "touch base" with almost every city agency, although their time might have been more fruitfully spent pursuing leads or interviewing subordinate officials. Despite these concessions to protocol, the teams frequently bruised local officials' feelings and jeopardized the possibility of future cooperation with the commission.

Interviewers in the riot areas also encountered problems. Black residents often refused to talk to black staff members. On the other hand, when interviews were granted, interviewers were sometimes hustled from barroom to pool hall in an outburst of cooperation that made the interview schedule irrelevant, the list of respondents chaotic and notetaking impossible. This undoubtedly resulted in considerable insight, but at the expense of comprehensiveness. These problems only added to the difficulties encountered in interviewing unsystematically, in coding responses without a theoretical framework and in recreating 10 hours of breathless interviewing in a fatiguing late-night session.

In conducting long-term studies preliminary field investigations may be required to develop hypotheses for further investigation and formulate relevant policy recommendations.[47] The commission's strategy was to encourage broad-scale collection of data, receptivity to various viewpoints and flexibility. But the field investigations were ultimately marred by wholesale abandonment of the premises and limitations under which they were originally mounted. What started out as a "first cut" at the data became virtually the only "cut" on which the commission ultimately relied.

Although little if any additional data on the riot cities were ever collected, the commission staff, driven by a need to impress the commissioners with the reliability of their findings, fashioned parts of the report by a process which we may call "incremental concretization." This involves the gradual adaptation and molding of initial analyses based on admittedly shaky data into increasingly "harder" analyses by ignoring the qualifications and caveats upon which the original investigations and conclusions were based, even though no new evidence is introduced to make the findings more reliable.

As successive drafts were written, they became a little sharper, a little more definite, as qualifying words and phrases were eliminated by writers and editors striving for a "hard" tone. By a series of marginal changes successive versions became more definitive, but no additional data or sources were employed to justify such a resolution.

The process of incremental concretization is probably familiar to anyone who has attempted to write descriptive or analytic narratives of complex events. Any single change is relatively slight and unlikely to be subjected to criticism. Indeed, writers and editors may not even realize that their efforts to develop a more definitive tone have resulted in a distinctive bias toward the general but uncertain direction of the original effort. It also results in providing the arguable impression that riots have a linear simplicity which may be captured in a narrative description. Contradictory facts are rarely considered. And when available such evidence is used to challenge the interpretation, not to offer alternative formulations. At the very least, incremental concretization results in the appearance of certitude when uncertainty better characterizes the state of knowledge.[48]

When the commission decided to concentrate on a single report scheduled for March 1, there was no time to go back into the field. Even if there had been time, financial constraints would have precluded doing so. Although the general counsel's staff did reinterview people to obtain sworn testimony where controversial findings seemed to require documentation, the staff had no opportunity to reexamine or further develop materials. This experience suggests the importance of encouraging the inclusion of qualifying statements in research with the built-in limitations described above.[49]

Researching Why it Happened

To ask why riots occurred in some cities and not in others is to pose a complex question. The Kerner Commission developed three ways to deal with it: (1) civil disorders could be explained dramatically; (2) they could be explained by identifying contributing causal factors and assessing the importance of these factors without reference to the whole; (3) they could be explained through development of a multi-factor theory.

Dramaturgy

Ginsburg originally hoped to produce a composite description of a riot by recreating the main causes on the basis of evidence gathered in many cities. This was to be the contribution of Robert Conot. In Palmieri's September 21 memo to the staff he described the objective as follows: "The Composite Profile: A narrative account of the prototype, full-blown riot, indicating each major stage."[50] Ginsburg never fully abandoned his quest for the prototype riot profile, even when the data suggested that no central tendency among disorders existed.[51]

Limited Hypotheses

The contribution of the media to riot causation had been widely speculated on and represented one of the few "simple" explanations of why riots occurred when they did. The president had asked the commission to report on the effect of mass media on the violence and, inferentially, for recommendations about changes that might be made in the organizational behavior and influence of the media.

The question seemed to be answerable through content analysis, which required highly specialized skills that the staff did not have. A contract for this research was awarded to a private consulting firm, Simulmatics, Inc., headed by Ithiel de Sola Pool of the Massachusetts Institute of Technology. As Ginsburg originally told the commissioners, the $221,000 contract provided for a study of 19 cities:

> many of them overlapping with the cities studied by the commission's field research teams. All racial and riot news reported on television and in newspapers, and a selected sample of radio programs, will be studied in each city for the period from March 1 to September 20, 1967. Simulmatics will also analyze the content of a selected sample of national periodicals and a cross-section of the Negro press in the subject cities. The study will address itself to

179

several major questions, including the manner in which the media presented information regarding the 1967 riots, the degree to which the media contributed to polarization of attitudes and behavior, and the manner in which the media differentiated between the different levels of attitude and behavior within the ghetto.[52]

In addition, the commission sponsored a conference on the media and civil disorders at Poughkeepsie, New York, on the weekend of November 10 to 12, inviting representatives from newspapers, news magazines, radio and television.

The compression of the commission's schedule and its financial difficulties meant that the scope and comprehensiveness of the content analysis had to be considerably scaled down. Simulmatics limited its coverage to 15 cities and its sampling of media content to the disorder period and a few days immediately preceding and following the events. More significantly, Simulmatics agreed to deliver descriptive statistical analysis on such questions as the space or time media devoted to riot activity, the kind of display accorded, the types of stories presented and the subject focus of riot-oriented stories.[53]

On the basis of Simulmatics' content analysis the commission was able to reject the hypothesis that the media bore much blame. It found that for the most part media coverage tended to be factual and relatively calm and that newspapers did not give disproportional coverage to militant black leaders who supported the disorders. The analysis did, however, reveal a relatively excessive coverage of law enforcement activity compared to stories describing grievances or tensions in the black community.[54] The content analysis permitted the commission to attack a common view of the disorders, puncturing neatly the "devil theory" of the media's role.

However, a noteworthy aspect of the chapter on the media is that the recommendations concerning media coverage of the riots had little relationship to the research. Because of changes in the schedule the Simulmatics research was watered down analytically, and submitted late in the commission's deliberations. There was little time to formulate recommendations on the basis of the research whatever the findings.

As it was, the commission developed a thoughtful chapter on the media based primarily on commissioner and staff perceptions supplemented by the Poughkeepsie conference. A number of recommendations were made, including better police-media relations to secure greater reporting accuracy; more and better coverage of day-to-day ghetto activities to provide (mostly white audiences) with better perspectives on black affairs; and desegregation of the journalism profession.

An ironic contrast to the background of the media chapter is the commission's profile of the rioters and research on people arrested during the riots. Robert Fogelson's extremely critical article on the McCone Commission was required reading by the Kerner staff.[55] Fogelson, a young historian, was invited to Washington to discuss a variety of matters. Although skeptical about working with the commission, Fogelson offered to help analyze the records of riot arrestees, in order to further test and refine his theory that the riot participant was much like the average ghetto resident.

In contracting to have Fogelson and his collaborator Robert Hill analyze the riot arrestees, the commission was "buying" a controversial thesis which had not yet been documented for the 1967 disorders. Because it took considerable time to collect and analyze the data, and the commission moved up its final report date, evidence which might confirm or disconfirm the "riffraff" theory was not available until very late in the deliberations. When staff members consulted Fogelson about his progress he reported only that the analysis was proceeding and that he was working with his original set of propositions. The commission, by its commitment to Fogelson, became in effect committed to Fogelson's ideas, developing its riot analyses and policy recommendations in accordance with his theory, but without supporting evidence. In the end, Fogelson's report did confirm his original position,[56] but the commission was forced to take a supporting position before his evidence was in.

Under ideal circumstances of rational inquiry, recommendations follow analysis, which in turn follows data collection. While publicly subscribing to this model, the Kerner Commission was forced to cut corners to complete its assignment in the time allotted. As these cases illustrate, research, analysis and development of recommendations may take place simultaneously and out of sequence, despite verbal deference to a "scientific" model of investigation.

The Politics of Theory Construction

The third approach, and the one in which the commission initially placed most confidence, was to use social science techniques to construct a theoretical statement on why the riots occurred. Because the commission's dependence on completion of this task was too great to run the risks involved in outside contracting, it decided to develop an "in-house" social science team for this and other assignments. To direct the social science group the commission hired Shellow as assistant deputy director for research.[57]

Two of the social scientists' tasks were to assist in contracting for outside research, and to provide a "social science input" for staff work. At times the input would consist of advice on research procedures. The early selection of a "sample" of riot cities for investigation was one such assignment.

At other times Shellow and the social scientists were expected to participate in general staff activities, introducing social science insights into the proceedings and distilling social science theory when it was called for. In this "paprika role" they assumed responsibility for spicing investigative activities with social science findings and wisdom. Like the chef who sprinkles paprika on a dish, the social scientists on the team contributed color but little substance. Although the social scientists participated in debriefing sessions and other staff conferences, there is little evidence that they had much influence on them.

Shellow's main tasks, however, were to examine the data that came into the commission, to draw from whatever body of theory proved useful and to prepare an analysis of why riots occurred. He understood that this would play a major part in the commission's work. The technique employed by the social scientists was to identify central themes that emerged from data on individual cities and organize analytical profiles of individual disorders around those themes. The profiles required an analytic chronology as well as an analysis of background factors (such as economic conditions, history of the city's race relations and the educational system).[58] An imaginative and discursive focus seemed appropriate, since Conot and his staff were providing narrower, descriptive profiles.

These city-by-city analyses provided the basis for some of the most fruitful encounters between staff and commissioners. At one point Shellow helped salvage a crisis of confidence in commissioner-staff relations. At a mid-October meeting, the staff had conducted a debriefing session for the commissioners to demonstrate data-collection techniques. It had been disastrous. Many of the commissioners expressed concern that the impressionistic nature of the evidence would result in a *Report* that would not be solidly grounded. The following week Shellow presented two of the city profiles which had been developed by his staff—on Plainfield and Cambridge, Md. The Cambridge report identified the cause of the disturbances as a "state of siege mentality" governing Cambridge police reactions. H. Rap Brown's inflammatory speech was reported to have been rejected by black residents, but the police, not realizing this, precipitated the riot by overreacting to his rhetoric. Although the analysis was controversial, the commissioners reportedly appreciated Shellow's insistence on staying close to the facts and not letting speculation prevail. This session revived commissioners' respect for the staff.

Following the creation of the 20-city riot profiles, the social scientists were to turn to a comprehensive theoretical analysis of riots. The presumed importance of the social scientists' contribution is illustrated by Ginsburg's description of the work only two weeks before a draft was scheduled for completion. Ginsburg indicated that of the three kinds of analytical studies being prepared, the one

> by Dr. Robert Shellow's group, is being concentrated on collective, or crowd behavior, the leadership structures, and the bargaining processes operating in the disorders. This analysis seeks to describe and explain the disorders in social-psychological terms and to identify operative factors during the period of disorder itself.[59]

Working under tremendous pressure—Shellow reports working 18 hours a day for 41 straight days at one point—using thousands of pages of unsystematically collected and processed raw notes, the social scientists produced their analysis of riot causation on schedule. This document, titled "The Harvest of American Racism," generated extraordinary controversy. Shortly after it was presented to staff executives, the commission rejected the document, downgraded or dismissed the social scientists, dismissed almost 100 people and changed its schedule.

For some staff members, these events confirmed their suspicions that the commission had little respect for their skills and wanted a conservative report at odds with their analysis. Leaks to the press followed. At least one commission consultant held a press conference to bring public attention to the anxieties of the staff.[60] The commission was attacked by Congress and top staff members frequently had to defend the integrity of the commission during this period.

"The Harvest of American Racism" was central to this controversy.

To our knowledge it has never been published;[61] yet the document lies at the heart of a number of subsequent commission developments.

The first section of "The Harvest" was a classification of recent civil disorders. The first category, called "massive upheavals," including those in Detroit, Newark and Watts, was regarded by the social scientists as too complex for any single line of analysis.

Category 2 was described as containing "political confrontation in which goals and processes were more explicit, form and structure more explicit, form and structure more evident." The disturbances in Cincinnati, New Brunswick, Englewood and Plainfield were so described. Indeed, the Plainfield uprising was called a "focused political rebellion."

Category 3 included riots caused by official anticipation of disturbances, such as in Milwaukee when 4,800 national guardsmen joined the police for a show of force after a group of 150 black youths broke some windows after a dance.[62] The events in Cambridge, Maryland, provided the clearest case of riots caused by official anticipation.

Category 4, not necessarily incompatible with the others, was the expressive rampage, analogous to the seasonal disorders of white college students who bring notoriety to Fort Lauderdale, Fla. These disturbances, not instrumentally motivated, were characterized as lacking in political effort or consciousness.

The fifth category, the race riot, characterized by interpersonal, interracial conflict, was mentioned as significantly absent from the riots of 1967.[63]

Throughout, the document expressed interest in whether or not the riots displayed political content and form. It urged recognition of the fact that behavior may range from a "spree" at one pole to a politically oriented crowd at the other. The document provided a table analyzing the political content of riots. Disorders in six of the 20 cities were thought to have displayed considerable political content: Detroit, Newark, Plainfield, Englewood, New Brunswick and Cincinnati. Riots in four cities displayed "some," the others "little or no" political content. At least one hypothesis stemmed from this classification: political riots are more likely to take place in cities with an established black middle class, in areas that are relatively stable and in areas moderately well-off. Further, it was hypothesized (correctly) that participants in riots would tend to be residents raised in the north.[64]

Another subject of major concern to the social scientists was the impact of riots. This interest stemmed in part from the presidential charge to investigate both the "causes and effects" of riots. But it also was fostered by the insistence of many black leaders that the riots were rebellions and were likely to have positive consequences.

The social scientists concluded that the riots were neither profitless nor a warning of permanent warfare that white society dismissed at its peril. The picture was more mixed. To illustrate, they compiled a table classifying cities along two dimensions: polarization of racial attitudes; and interracial communication and elite efforts to affect change. On these characteristics alone the riot cities tended to be distributed fairly evenly.[65]

A third major theme of the document was "America on the Brink: White Racism and Black Rebellion;" in this section the document went beyond analysis to prescribe a solution to racial polarization and conflict. It argued that the present course of American domestic progress was dangerously inadequate and equally rejected the development of a garrison state, concluding with a plea for accelerated racial change and enthusiastically supporting higher levels of expenditures for programs such as the War on Poverty.

It concluded by observing that black youth retained considerable goodwill toward American society:

> There is still time for our nation to make a concerted attack on the racism that persists in its midst. If not, then Negro youths will continue to attack white racism on their own. The Harvest of Racism in America will be the end of the American dream.

"The Harvest" also dealt with the social characteristics of rioters, white rioters and alternative theories of riots and general black discontent. But its political themes fundamentally countered the expectations of executive staff members. The document supported the view that the police helped to instigate disorders and that sometimes riots had positive results. It also seemed to provide support for controversial and partisan legislation then under attack in Congress and the press. For the commission to accept such views under the best of circumstances would require careful argumentation and extensive documentation. Here the expectations of Ginsburg, Palmieri and other top staff members, and the working assumptions of the social scientists, proved to be incompatible.

The Harvest report was completed in first draft on November 22, 1967, and a meeting to discuss the paper was scheduled for the following Tuesday. Palmieri and Ginsburg reacted with shock and dismay. Their objections were more formal than substantive. The document, they said, was unsuitable. It was too long; it was diffuse and poorly organized; contradictorily, it was more authoritative and confident in tone than the data warranted. Most of all, it was "too speculative and not sufficiently documented." To ask commissioners to put their signatures to such a document would be folly. To present the document for their consideration would seriously impair confidence in the staff.

Shellow pointed out that the document was being presented to other staff members as soon as possible to maximize discussion (the reverse paprika role?). He insisted that the 172-page paper could be much more extensively documented. It was, in short, a first draft. These arguments proved fruitless. Palmieri could not see how another draft version would be acceptable to the commissioners and command the desired authoritative tone.

Much of "The Harvest" did find its way into the final *Report*; the emphasis on racism, on the attitudes of ghetto youth and even the notion of the garrison state (inserted by Mayor Lindsay in the summary), were eventually included. But as a whole "The Harvest" spurred the first in a series of reappraisals of staff capabilities and commission requirements that led directly to changes in staff and plans and negative commission publicity.

Great controversy was generated by the "rejection" of the "The Harvest" as a working document.[66] The rejection may be attributed to faulty and costly miscalculations about what social scientists are capable of doing. The social scientists had been working on an analytic essay, aiming for a theoretically coherent ordering of diverse materials in order to "make sense" of otherwise confusing events and suggest categories for future analysis. Recognizing the complex nature of riot causation, they were content to draw attention to aspects of the events where something sensible might be said or where it would be useful to concentrate future attention. They assumed that a more pedestrian, descriptive analysis would be provided by Conot.

To a certain extent the document was also a personal one. Individual members of the social science team had pursued topics in which they were particularly interested. This was both predictable and under-standable, given the lack of specific direction from above, the problems of staffing, the character of the recruitment process and the apparent approval of the social science effort by executive staff directors up to that point. It was also probably desirable to the extent that people are often most productive when they are interested in a subject. Prior censorship might have meant greater difficulties in recruitment, negative publicity, or severe inter-staff conflict.

The executive staff's original expectations are not so clear. Shellow's early outline was certainly well received, but the potential for conflict might have been anticipated by Shellow's earlier stated intention to discuss "concrete gains—economic, political access, symbolic victories, *vis á vis* power structure," under the topic "Aftermath: Post-Riot Consequences."[67]

An elementary classificatory scheme should generate insights and provide economy in managing data. Testing whether a scheme succeeds in these tasks depends upon further analysis using similar but different data. The executive staff seems to have wanted both classification and demonstration of the validity of the classification at the same time, employing the same data. One cannot do both.

Under the limits of time, data collection problems and previous theory inadequacy, "The Harvest" was pretty much what the executive staff should have expected: a loose, imaginative document which attempted to order disparate events into useful and manageable categories. Though they had originally requested a theoretical statement, Ginsburg and Palmieri began to anticipate commissioner needs and look for the kind of reliability provided by a lawyer's brief. As Shellow has pointed out:

> The final product [ch. 2, "Patterns of Disorder," *Report*] was dryly atheoretical; a pseudo-statistical tallying of events and characteristics of cities. At best it was a layman's conception of what a respectable social science analysis should look like. . . .[68]

The commission again opted to secure its political legitimacy at the expense of its scientific legitimacy.

If staff directors had known what social science was capable of doing, they might have overlooked "The Harvest's" conclusion and extracted what was useful from the document without "rejecting" it and creating a crisis of confidence in the staff. They might even have excised controversial sections.* In the end, the harvest of "The

---

*As indeed was done: Many aspects of "The Harvest" found their way into the *Report*, but treatment of police riot provocation and beneficial results of riots are conspicuously absent.

Harvest" was dismay with staff work, convulsions in commission and staff schedules and procedures and outside criticism when these developments became public knowledge.

Research Program Recommendations

While the commission could and did make recommendations about suppressing disorders once they broke out and preventing incidents from exploding into full-scale conflicts, preventing disorders was presumed to require attention to the design of government programs and their effectiveness.[69]

The expected short-term recommendations, which were to appear in the interim report, were to have immediate implications. Palmieri's September outline of the December research report shows two topics to be discussed under the heading "Social and Economic Action Programs." "What Are We Doing Now?" would include descriptions and analysis of major program areas, in terms of service delivery, effectiveness and relationship to civil disorders. "What We Can Do Immediately" was to develop principles of the report, existing program reforms, new program directions, and funding considerations. The latter would include redirecting existing federal commitments, increasing efficiency of federal and local programs, private-sector participation and additional joint federal-state-local funding.[70] Nathan, a research associate at the Brookings Institution in Washington, was engaged to direct this staff effort.[71]

Nathan declined to hire experts to do research on short-run program recommendations because it was difficult to recruit such people on short notice. He also felt that experts might be too involved in their own field, committed to their own perspectives and fail to provide a comprehensive and objective view of it. Drawing on his experiences as director of domestic program research for Nelson Rockefeller in his 1964 Republican presidential nomination campaign, Nathan fixed on a strategy of hiring bright, young, nonspecialists. These staff members were to provide an inventory of current programs and "action options" by reading widely and interviewing knowledgeable people. The inventories would later be refined by experts with the research assistants serving the experts as staff. Meanwhile, the short-term-program team would be developing a unit capable of responding fairly quickly to a wide variety of commission policy needs and demands. Seven women, all recent college graduates selected from among the many applicants for commission employment, were hired.

The research assistants were to prepare "central research documents" on the following nine topics: the role of private enterprise in the inner city; the role of minority communities in action programs; education; welfare; civil rights enforcement; manpower; urban renewal and rehabilitation; recreation; and sanitation. Papers on consumer protection and programs for women were scheduled to be written by staff members not connected with Nathan's unit. In addition to individual research, assistants were instructed to use testimony provided in commission hearings, data gathered in field investigations of riot cities, materials collected from government agencies,[72] and, as informants on programs in individual cities, newspaper reporters.[73]

At first Nathan's staff was constrained by the requirement that recommendations should be limited by existing budgetary allocations. This directive fit the president's policy of pursuing an undeclared war without raising taxes. This limitation was acceptable to Nathan, who viewed tight money situations as opportunitites for fundamental governmental reform. Nathan, for example, urged the commission to

> say that in areas the problem today is not so much a need for new policy and legislation as a need to do the job better under the many policies and Acts of Congress which now exist. The groundswell of legislation on civil rights up to 1964 and on domestic programs in 1965 has given the government powers and responsibilities in many areas. The questions today are increasingly, not what needs to be done, but how to do better the jobs we are already doing. . . .[74]

At the beginning of November, however, just as final drafts of the program chapters were being completed, Ginsburg changed signals: recommendations for increased expenditures were now in order, although they should not require new legislation. Commissioners were increasingly aware that the problems before them required some government spending.[75]

After his staff had submitted "action option" papers in the various fields, Nathan reduced the recommendations to a 61-page paper, "Proposed Short Term Domestic Program Options."[76] The report proposed a "$4.55 billion opportunity program:" $1.5 billion for employment, $1.1 billion for schools and $1.7 billion for welfare and associated services. Other program recommendations would require expenditures of $250 million. The report also proposed adopting an emergency tax program to finance the recommendations.[77]

The Nathan group, with commission consent, had been unable to hold itself to President Johnson's request for low-cost programs. The commission eventually chose to obscure the costs of its recommendations, developing the *Report* with extensive financial implications but refusing to attach cost estimates. In the controversy surrounding the eventual release of the commission's *Report*, some critics focused on the failure to provide cost estimates.[78]

The Nathan document was never submitted to the commissioners for discussion; Ginsburg and Palmieri were disappointed with it. The program inventories were dismissed as amateurish, no better than high school or college freshman theses; they lacked the crispness and profundity that the commission required. The summary prepared by Nathan was similarly rejected.[79] Like the Shellow group, the Nathan team was victimized by changes in expectations. Created only to provide the commission with the resources for further study and analysis of programs, the Nathan effort was dismissed as sophomoric in its lack of specificity. Created to prepare recommendations for cheap, incremental changes in existing program structures, the Nathan effort produced recommendations which were "short-term" in name only.

The Nathan effort did, however, contribute to the final *Report*. On the matter of jobs, for example, Nathan's $1.5 billion job-stimulation program to provide work for an estimated 400,000 people in the first year compares favorably with the president's recommendation to Congress for one million jobs in three years and is relatively conservative compared to the commission's final recommendation for two million jobs in three years. Although the press speculated that the commission had rejected the report because it recommended a specific funding level for certain programs,[80] the long-run result of the Nathan episode was to provide still another reason for reassessing the direction and timing of commission staff efforts.

The "failure" of the short-term-program effort contributed to the commission decision to abandon the interim report and take more time to produce a single report in a few months. The decision to change the schedule and condense the two reports to one and the recognition of the difficulties of distinguishing between long- and short-term changes made the Nathan staff expendable.

The Commission Changes Direction

In the early rush to develop the interim report, planning for the final report was neglected, although it was still scheduled for late spring, no later than the end of July. Three factors combined to force the commission to reconsider this schedule and by implication critical aspects of its planning: disappointment with the staff, uncertainty about the feasibility of the schedule and the condition of the commission's finances.

Executive Staff Disappointment

Under pressure to respond to the president's questions about riot characteristics, causes and prevention, Ginsburg and Palmieri had initiated a number of staff efforts in a short period of time, gambling that one or more would bear fruit. At times they even seemed to be protecting themselves by initiating parallel staff efforts. Henry Taliaferro, for example, assigned to congressional-liaison functions, began to develop independent program proposals until Nathan objected to this duplication of effort and threatened to resign. Major portions of such research efforts proved disappointing, as we have described above. In some respects staff weaknesses or failures must be blamed for these disappointments, but unrealistic executive staff expectations and their changing conceptions of the purposes of documents presented to the commission also played a part. "Quick and dirty" preliminary surveys of riot cities proved inadequate as comprehensive statements, and their shortcomings had to be obscured to get them into acceptable form. The social scientists' analysis of riot causation was rejected in first-draft form because the classification, loose and somewhat unstructured as befit the problem, proved "unacceptable." Similarly, Nathan's short-term-program inventories were criticized as superficial and amateurish, although they were supposed to be rehashes of current practices and proposals.

Uncertainty about Current Schedules

Ginsburg's proposed schedule change came at a time when commissioners were increasingly hesitant about issuing a report which described the riots and their causes at length and then provided only short-run proposals for change. Skeptical about issuing a final report during "the riot season," they reasoned that if the commission issued its report in the summer their efforts might be lost in the heat of emotions. Concerned liberal commissioners recognized that focusing the interim report on inexpensive short-term measures and riot control meant that proposals for progressive legislation would have to appear in the final report. However, it appeared that the commission would receive most attention from the initial statement rather than the projected final document, regardless of the importance attached to it by the commission. A summer report would also embroil the commission in the politics of the presidential-nominating conventions. And an early interim report of some policy urgency might no longer fit the needs of a president under severe budgetary pressures and distracted by a war.

Preparation of an interim report was proving exhausting and time-consuming for commissioners as well as staff. It was difficult to imagine recreating the same sense of urgency when the final *Report* had to be prepared. These reasons, combined with disappointment with the staff, created a situation where those most involved in shaping the commission's work wanted more time to work on drafts of the *Report* and were reluctant to "go down to the wire" a second time.

The Problem of Finances

When he took the job of executive director, Ginsburg was assured of full funding for the commission. The president had indicated this privately and had told the commissioners: "You will have all the support and cooperation you need from the Federal government. I can assure you of that."[81] Palmieri too had been assured that the commission would have unlimited resources at its disposal. But promises made in the heat of summer evaporated when it came to financing guns and butter without a tax increase.

The commission was initially funded with a $100,000 allocation from the Emergency Fund for the President. At least a month went by before the commission could estimate its research (and thus financial) needs and so it never sought a special congressional appropriation during the period when attention and concern were focused on the riots. By the time the commission was able to identify its needs, the political winds had shifted. The president could not support a supplementary appropriation request and deny that privilege to established federal agencies. But if policy guidance were the president's primary interest, adequate commission financing would be pre-eminently important. This supports the view that the crisis-reduction aspects of some commissions may be more important than the policy guidance they may provide.

Other than the emergency-fund allocation, full federal cooperation meant that funds for commission support would come from current agency budgets. Kurzman, Palmieri and Ginsburg were forced to go "hat in hand" to various agencies for contributions at the same time that agencies were under pressure to cut their own budgets by as much as 10 percent. Understandably, agencies forced to fire employees of long standing might be reluctant to contribute from their already shrunken budgets to a temporary commission hiring almost 200 employees for less than a year. Departments also balked at financing what many considered research efforts which duplicated theirs. Nonetheless, a total of approximately $900,000 eventually was secured from other agencies. It was, however, almost impossible to return to these agencies for additional funds, and obtaining presidential assistance for additional financing was out of the question.

The change in schedule conveniently solved the commission's hidden financial problems. If the commission did not have to return to the cities to collect additional data, the field teams were superfluous. If "The Harvest" was judged inadequate, the social science team could be disbanded. If the final report was to be consolidated with the interim and published around March 1, then all but a skeleton crew could be released five months early. The problem of incorporating contracted studies in an accelerated research schedule remained, but this could be resolved by asking the researchers to abbreviate their work or complete it on schedule as "supplemental studies." The financing of these studies, a remaining financial burden, could be assumed by outside sources.[82]

The decision to change schedules was made on Saturday, December 9. The following Tuesday, 36 members of the professional staff were given notice of termination during the next month. Most had expected employment through July, although no formal promises had been given. Those released included two social scientists from Shellow's staff, Nathan's research assistants and 12 members of the field-investigation teams.

Confronted with extraordinary time pressures, the commission had still managed to launch investigations in three critical research areas, which produced a considerable body of data, evidence and interpretation. The problems resulting from this research process stemmed from the conflicting expectations of the executive staff. The model of social science research to which they deferred was incompatible with the demands of rapid staffing and the need to complete research efforts almost as soon as they were begun.

Conflicting role demands had been placed upon staff members and executive-staff personnel. Staff members were constantly confronted

193

by tensions between professional standards and recognition of the political, subprofessional needs of the commission. Some, who had hoped to affect the outcome of the commission's deliberations, found it difficult to decide whether to act as professionals providing skills to the commission or as advocates, performing so as to increase the likelihood that the final report would conform to their own conclusions about civil disorders.

The executive staff was also torn by role conflicts of a particular sort. At the beginning, executive staff members were most concerned with establishing an agenda and hiring and fielding a staff. Later, however, as commissioners began to lend direction to staff efforts and began to establish the parameters of the report, executive staff began to serve as liaison between commissioners and staff. They then tended to caution staff about commission expectations or to anticipate them for the staff. At the same time they had to alert commissioners to staff directions and findings.[83]

Period of Consolidation

When the Shellow and Nathan teams were disbanded and the interim report scrapped, Ginsburg directed attention to producing a document as expeditiously as possible. But the hope and expectation that outside scholars and experts could develop positions for the commission died hard.

To write the chapter explaining riot occurrences—the role previously allocated to the Shellow group—the commission recruited Hans Mattick of the University of Chicago Law School. For a six-week period beginning January 22, 1968, Mattick was engaged to provide an analysis of the riot process, incorporating the materials collected by the commission staff and developed by the social scientists, but not repeating the "error" of their ways. This was to be chapter 2 of the *Report.*[84]

Mattick worked under the same incessant time pressures as other staff members.[85] In a month's time he reviewed general works on rebellion and riots, the FBI reports, the field notes collected by the staff and the materials generated by the social science team. Mattick, discovering that he thought the social scientists were on the right track, developed a series of riot ideal-types, labeling disorders "rational," "expressive," "reified" and "irrational." He submitted his first draft on February 15, *scarcely two weeks before the Report was to be published.* Aware of Ginsburg's and Palmieri's criticism of "The Harvest," Mattick sent along 45 pages of footnotes.

Mattick's efforts in many ways got the same reception as "The Harvest." Staff directors were still concerned about the acceptability of the *Report* to the commissioners. Ginsburg and Palmieri told Mattick that his efforts represented "a very good synthesis—even brilliant" but that it was doubtful whether the material could be published in the *Report* in that form. He was told that the commissioners would reject the position that riots could be viewed as "rational," that the draft contained too much jargon and that the assertions seemed plausible but were not proved.

Mattick tried to respond to the criticism, changing the term "grievance bank" to "grievance network," substituting "overly antici-pated riot" for "reified riot," and changing other terms which were thought to be too technical. Ultimately he decided to retain the conception of "rational" riots. Informed that the commission would reject the idea that the authorities or the media created riots, Mattick agreed to refer generally to riot "themes" rather than to a riot typology.[86]

In the end, the executive staff rejected the entire manuscript. Mattick had made the same "mistake" as the social scientists: he had seen that public officials were sometimes primarily responsible for the outbreak of violence and that riots at times may be related to the existence of genuine grievances. He developed a typology reflecting these insights but the discussion was considered too delicate for commission consideration.

Mattick was ultimately pleased with the development of chapter 2. His emphasis on the publication of as much data as possible and his focus on interactions in riot processes helped to focus the commission's work. But compared to the Mattick manuscript, the ultimate product, redrafted by Stephen Kurzman and others, was indeed "dryly atheo-retical."[87]

Similar difficulties arose in attempts to salvage the staff efforts concerning program recommendations. The papers written by the Nathan team had been rejected as sophomoric. The long-run plan to assign the Nathan staff as research assistants to prominent experts now seemed less inviting. Among other things, these women were being fired as part of the general staff cutback. To develop program recommen-dations after the Nathan debacle, Palmieri created a task force consisting of Mitchell Sviridoff of the Ford Foundation, James Tobin, a Yale economist with the Office of Economic Opportunity; Lewis Winnick of the Ford Foundation; and Kermit Gordon, president of The

Brookings Institution. Downs, a prime consultant to Palmieri from the beginning, was to serve as the working member of the five-man committee.

The Downs's document which emerged from this effort aggressively advocated a strategy of ghetto dispersal. Written from a systems approach, the document showed the interrelationship of various policies in contributing to or detracting from the goal of an integrated society. It boldly advocated specific federal policies to promote ghetto dispersal—for example, rewarding suburban schools which encouraged integration while allocating low-income housing subsidies to those communities which promised integrated schooling.

This dispersal approach tied everything to a basic strategy, challenging the commissioners to consider the merits and demerits of policy alternatives in terms of one set of goals. Ginsburg presented the document to the commission and urged the members to debate the issues it presented even if some conflict developed. The commissioners debated the document, and discovered that they were not prepared to advocate a single, primary solution.

The final *Report* presents the Downs's document shorn of its policy recommendations (chapter 16, "The Future of the Cities").[88] Where Downs had linked policy recommendations to a set of goals oriented toward ghetto dispersal, this chapter outlines general alternatives open to American society (The Present Policies Choice, the [Ghetto] Enrichment Choice, the Integration Choice, including interim enrichment efforts) without vigorously indicating which the commission favored. Most importantly, where Downs developed policy proposals as a strategy in pursuing a general goal, the commission's policy proposals are presented in a subsequent chapter (chapter 17, "Recommendations for National Action") without reference to the three alternatives the commission said were confronting the nation. Indeed, choosing policy recommendations without referring to the alternatives facing the nation calls into question the one general conclusion on which the commission seemed to agree. While at one point it rejected the present policies choice as "most ominous,"[89] the commission's later recommendations concerning employment, education, welfare and housing may be considered advocacy of "more of the same" (albeit much more) since there is no explicit acceptance of a primary goal.[90]

Conclusion

Social scientists have played critical roles on many recent presidential commissions.[91] They have been asked to produce theory and data for commissions charged with providing answers to questions of complex social causation. Just as commissioners are selected by the president in part to represent diverse constituencies, so the presence of social scientists on the staff provides the impression that relevant professionals have been consulted.

However, the deliberate pace of social research is incompatible with the urgency and haste under which recent commissions have operated. Under pressures of time, acceptability of findings and limitations of theory and methodology, the contributions of social scientists are reduced to three types: synthesizing existing research and theory and preparing it for presentation; conducting original research or developing new theory according to conventional, professional timetables and methods of work; or conducting original research or developing new theory with compromises of work procedures consistent with the requirements of commission schedules.

Most commissions using social research implicitly admit that existing knowledge is either sufficient or will have to suffice and organize work around educating commissioners and affirming existing data and theory. When commissions adopt the second mode, they usually hire consultants or contract for research which will not be available in time for examination by commissioners but may contribute to public understanding through subsequent publication. Such researchers may be asked to anticipate their findings or provide preliminary reports, although these may represent no more advanced understanding than was available when the research was originally contracted.

The most significant research conducted for the Kerner Commission was produced in this way. The supplemental studies published under the commission's signature, including the Fogelson-Hill refutation of the riffraff theory, represent important contributions to understanding aspects of the preconditions of civil disorders. But they were largely irrelevant to the commission's deliberations.

Research on riot participants and the responsibility of the media suggests that social scientists can probably make their most significant contribution to commissions as social scientists when the question is relatively narrow. When the question is "How broad was participation of blacks in riots?" or "To what extent did television present biased coverage?" social scientists can provide responses that are professionally and politically acceptable. As the "Harvest of Racism" episode suggests,

197

however, social scientists may not be able to produce politically acceptable or authoritative answers to broad questions.

In the third mode, in which social scientists accept the necessity of compromise, they are placed in essentially advisory roles. Here, research becomes a marginal contribution to otherwise independent staff efforts. On the Kerner Commission, social scientists operating in this way contributed insights concerning police responsibility for riots under some circumstances, and general cautions concerning the variations in riot types. It is uncertain whether their contributions derived from their status as social scientists, or their different underlying attitudes toward riots—which may have accounted for their interest in joining the staff in the first place. However, social scientists' more substantial efforts to contribute to the commission's work were less successful. The theoretical statement on why riots occur was rejected as flimsy when staff directors imposed new standards of proof and documentation. Their attempts to provide structure to data-collecting efforts were similarly unsuccessful, when rigor was subordinated to the need to complete work under severe time pressures.

Whatever insights were provided by social scientists on the Kerner Commission staff, they clearly played an important role in legitimating staff efforts. Internally, they provided assurances that critical theory and insights would not be neglected. To a public attentive to commission activities, they represented the profession whose expertise was presumed to deal with the issues under investigation.

NOTES, CHAPTER 5

1. Memo, Palmieri to Ginsburg, 12 September 1967.

2. For a brief treatment of some of the issues discussed here, see Michael Lipsky, "Social Scientists and the Riot Commission," *The Annals* 394 (March 1971): 72-83.

3. For similar usage of the term *legitimacy*, see Robert Dahl, *Preface to Democratic Theory* (Chicago: University of Chicago Press, 1956), pp. 46, 138.

4. Lyndon B. Johnson, "President's Address to the Nation on Civil Disorders" [27 July 1967], *Report*, Appendix C.

5. Executive Order 11365, 29 July 1967, *Report*, Appendix A.

6. Transcription of Lyndon B. Johnson, "Statement by the President" [29 July 1967]. A modified version of these remarks appears in *Report* in Appendix B.

7. Executive Order 11365, *Report*, p. 537.

8. Scammon, like several other early consultants, soon faded from prominence in commission affairs.

9. Like the Kerner Commission, the Ylvisaker task force during its life received veiled instructions from the White House concerning the amount of money that might be available for programs and which subjects should be covered.

10. The Ylvisaker task force submitted its report on 7 July 1967. It was released by the White House almost a year later when President Johnson was preparing to leave office.

11. Others disproportionately recruited to commission staff work included residents of Washington, D.C., and returned Peace Corps volunteers who had not yet found steady work.

12. For example, remarks of Amitai Etzioni in *Wall Street Journal*, 9 July 1968.

13. Officially, McCurdy was appointed as a special assistant to the attorney general in the Justice Department (New York *Times*, 21 March 1968).

14. On the relationship between goal diversity and intra-organizational conflict, see Anthony Downs, *Inside Bureaucracy* (Boston: Little, Brown, 1967), pp. 223-36. For a general discussion of inducements to participate in organizations, see James March and Herbert Simon, *Organizations* (New York: John Wiley, 1958), p. 78.

15. Much of this agenda was incorporated into the commission's work. For example, the commission's chapter 16, "The Future of the Cities," was indicated in the original Downs outline. Downs later expanded on this chapter, which he wrote for the commission, in "Alternative Futures for the American Ghetto," *Daedalus* 97, no. 4 (Fall 1968): 1,331-78.

16. In 1966 Kurzman resigned his position as minority counsel to the Senate Committee on Labor and Public Welfare, to which he had been appointed by Senator Javits, to open his own law firm in Washington with Ronald Goldfarb. The author of several books on the administration of justice (for instance, Ronald Goldfarb, *Ransom: A Critique of the American Bail System* [New York: Harper and Row, 1965]), Goldfarb was also appointed to the commission as a consultant on that subject. For a period in 1967 Kurzman had been a consultant to the Subcommittee on Employment, Manpower and Poverty, chaired by Senator Joseph Clark, which conducted inquiries into the poverty program. On the commission Kurzman supervised the collection of data from riot cities and later assisted in writing and compiling a number of chapters on a crisis basis.

17. McCurdy's greatest contribution to the commission's work was

his skillful orchestration of the hearings, trapping labor leaders, bank presidents, and others with subtle interrogation.

18. Jones was appointed general counsel of the National Association for the Advancement of Colored People in October 1969 (New York *Times*, 2 October 1969).

19. Koskinen had clerked for liberal Judge David Bazelon, yet more recently had worked for a conservative California law firm. As it was with Ginsburg's assistant David Chambers, Koskinen was close to the action because of his association with Palmieri. Following his stint with the commission, Koskinen was hired by John Lindsay to staff New York City's Washington office.

20. Formerly employed in staff capacities by liberal Republicans, Governor Nelson Rockefeller (N.Y.) and Sen. Kenneth Keating (N.Y.), Nathan at the time was a research associate of the Brookings Institution in Washington and retained his affiliation with Brookings through this period. He withdrew from involvement in commission affairs after his staff work was completed in December. In January 1969, Nathan was appointed by President Nixon as a top staff official in the Bureau of the Budget. Nathan's commission title was later changed to associate director for program research.

21. A personal friend of Ginsburg, Sagalyn's background in police administration and crime control extended back to 1939. Sagalyn was in charge of the riot-control aspects of the commission staff work.

22. Following his work with the commission, Shellow was appointed director of the Pilot District project in Washington, D.C., an experiment in decentralizing police work. See Robert Shellow, "Social Scientists and Social Action from within the Establishment," *Journal of Social Issues* 26, no. 1 (Winter 1970): 207-220. For Shellow's account of his experience as consultant to the Upper Marlboro, Md., police force when confronted with an incipient invasion of motorcycle enthusiasts, see Robert Shellow and Derek Roemer, "No Heaven for 'Hell's Angels,' " *Transaction* (now *Society*) 3, no. 5 (July/August 1966): 12-19.

23. On the staff of the Institute for Research on Poverty at the University of Wisconsin, Lefcowitz's involvement declined after a few months in part because of the difficulties of working effectively as a commuter on a fast-moving staff.

24. An illustration of the problems of processing the plethora of unsolicited offers of assistance is provided by the case of a prominent research-oriented psychiatrist who submitted his name through his senator, commission member Edward Brooke of Massachusetts, for a top research position on the commission. He did not receive a reply until some months after the commission was thoroughly staffed. Then

he received a formula response, thanking him for his inquiry concerning a "job" at the commission, but explaining that positions were no longer available. The man was insulted, and subsequently did not fully cooperate with the commission when later asked to share data he had collected. The peremptory posture assumed by top staff members of the Kerner Commission of necessity, given the strain under which they operated, was resented in many quarters—both in academic circles and in staffs of subnational riot commissions. Especially irksome to the Kerner Commission was the fact that from the outset there was general recognition of the haste with which the commission would have to work; this "marked" the commission for exploitation by individuals convinced they could help (or convinced that the commission could help them).

25. "Telephone Directory," National Advisory Commission on Civil Disorders, Federal Building 7 (for December).

26. Transcripts, pp. 1,100, 1,112ff.

27. "Memorandum to the Commission," from the executive director [Ginsburg], 31 October 1967, pp. 1-2.

28. For a recent discussion of problems of studying the exercise of power, see Raymond Wolfinger, "Nondecisions and the Study of Local Politics," and Frederick Frey, "Comment," *American Political Science Review* 65, no. 4 (December 1971): 1,063-1,101. A parallel illustration may be found in the development of legislation founding the Office of Economic Opportunity. Those who have tried to determine the origin of the legislation's most controversial component—the provision calling for "maximum feasible participation" of the poor—have discovered that it was never debated by Congress, but inserted without particular discussion by the framers of the legislation. See, for example, Daniel P. Moynihan, *Maximum Feasible Misunderstanding: Community Action in the War on Poverty* (New York: Free Press, 1969), and various essays in James Sundquist, *On Fighting Poverty: Perspectives from Experience* (New York: Basic Books, 1969).

29. Formally, Downs worked through his consulting firm, Systemetrics, Inc. This agenda was a refinement of an earlier staff memo, "Re: Direct Controls; Police-Community Relations," 21 August 1967.

30. Outline, "Research Studies Oriented Toward the First Major Report in December," [from] "Systemetrics—9/7/67."

31. Guests at this meeting included Fred Vinson, chief of the criminal division, Department of Justice; Patrick Murphy, then with the Department of Justice; Cartha DeLoach and William Mooney of the FBI; and Joseph Lohman, dean of the School of Criminology, University of California at Berkeley.

32. Invited to the October meeting were, among others, John Morsell of the National Association for the Advancement of Colored People; Peter Rossi and James Coleman of the Johns Hopkins University; and Herbert Gans, then associated with Teachers College of Columbia University.

33. An *action* program, as the term was used in the commission, was one that could be implemented relatively quickly, with a minimum of legislative initiative, and for very little money, certainly without major federal appropriations.

34. Memorandum from Victor Palmieri to David Ginsburg, 21 September 1967.

35. Ibid. (In the end, no regional hearings were conducted.)

36. "Memorandum for the Staff from: Victor H. Palmieri," 21 September 1967. That Palmieri proposed a summary does not negate the assertions in ch. 4 regarding Lindsay's proposals for a summary with specific contents.

37. John Hersey later accepted the challenge, without commission affiliation, through his work in *The Algiers Motel Incident* (New York: Knopf, 1968), a chronicle of the events surrounding the assassination of some black men and white women during the Detroit disturbances. Conot's book is *Rivers of Blood, Years of Darkness* (New York: Bantam, 1967).

38. The staff ultimately utilized these and three other sources to rank a total of 164 disorders for the first nine months of the year; see *Report*, p. 113.

39. Cf. the rejection of the relationship between the Newark and Plainfield, N.J., disturbances by commission witness David Hardy, in *Transcripts*, pp. 1,706ff.

40. This account draws upon "Selection of Cities for Intensive Study, Staff Paper No. 1," Office of Assistant Deputy Director for Research [Shellow].

41. "Memorandum to the commission," 31 October 1967, on stationery of the executive director [Ginsburg].

42. "Memorandum for the Staff," 21 September 1967, p. 2.

43. "Memorandum to the Commissioners," 31 October 1967, p. 3.

44. See generally, chapter 1 above. For a quantitative analysis that rejects the hypotheses on which the commission analysis rested and tends to confirm the significance of widespread, nationally distributed black feelings of frustration and resentment, see Seymour Spilerman, "The Causes of Racial Disturbances: A Comparison of Alternative Explanations," *American Sociological Review* 35, no. 4 (August 1970): 627-49.

45. "Selection of Cities for Intensive Study," p. 6, emphasis added.

For another account of some of these matters, see Shellow, "Social Scientists and Social Action from within the Establishment."

46. Appendix B, "Summary of Field Research Program," "Memorandum to the Commission," 31 October 1967; and the work schedule for the interim report included in "Memorandum for the Staff," 21 September 1967.

47. In fact, a number of excellent profiles of individual riot cities was developed (notably of Plainfield and Cambridge), considerable data were gathered, and direct staff exposure to ghetto life was useful for further staff efforts.

48. This certitude may be associated with complicated findings. The commission asserted: "We have been unable to identify constant patterns in all aspects of civil disorders. We have found that they are unusual, (sic) irregular, complex and, in the present state of knowledge, unpredictable social processes" (Report, pp. 109-110).

49. Although the tone of the Report does not otherwise reflect uncertainty, the commission's disclaimer concerning the adequacy of its data is quite apt: "We have examined the 1967 disorders within a few months after their occurrence and under pressing time limitations. While we have collected information of considerable immediacy, analysis will undoubtedly improve with the passage and perspective of time and with the further accumulation and refinement of data" (ibid., p. 110).

50. "Memorandum for the Staff," p. 2.

51. He finally settled for the narratives that comprise chapter 1, "Profiles of Disorders." These profiles were drawn from many sources, primarily the field notes of the investigating teams and the chronological summaries prepared under private contract.

52. "Memorandum to the Commission," 31 October 1967, pp. 16-17.

53. Report, p. 368.

54. Ibid., pp. 369-71.

55. Robert Fogelson, "White on Black: A Critique of the McCone Commission Report on the Los Angeles Riots," Political Science Quarterly 82, no. 3 (September 1967): 333-67.

56. Robert Fogelson and Robert Hill, "Who Riots? A Study of Participation in the 1967 Riots," Supplemental Studies for the National Advisory Commission on Civil Disorders (Washington, D.C.: Government Printing Office, 1968), pp. 217-48.

57. Others in the group included Ph.D. candidates David Boesel of Cornell and Louis Goldberg of Johns Hopkins. Gary Marx, assistant professor of social relations at Harvard, worked three days a week for two months, spending more time when the final drafts of the report

were in preparation. Elliot Liebow assisted one day a week from his position at National Institute of Mental Health. The team was further aided by consultants: sociologists Neil Smelser, Ralph Turner and Kurt Lang. Like the entire top commission staff with the exception of the general counsel, all were white.

58. For examples of such profiles as later revised, see David Boesel, Louis C. Goldberg and Gary T. Marx, "Rebellion in Plainfield," and David Boesel and Louis C. Goldberg, with a chronology by Jesse Epstein, "Crisis in Cambridge," in *Cities under Seige: An Anatomy of the Ghetto Riots, 1964-1968*, ed. David Boesel and Peter H. Rossi (New York: Basic Books, 1971), pp. 67-83, 110-36.

59. See "Memorandum to the Commission," 31 October 1967, pp. 5-6. The other two were the analysis of arrest records by Fogelson and Hill, and the contribution of Conot using "the reporter's method of identifying and classifying the key actors and the critical points in the action and asking hard, common-sense questions about why things happened as they did."

60. See New York *Times*, 30 December 1967; also, T. M. Tomlinson, "The Development of a Riot Ideology among Urban Negroes," *American Behavioral Scientist* 2, no. 4 (March/April 1968): 27-31. See also Gary Marx's letter, New York *Times*, 7 February 1968, and Knight Newspaper correspondent Philip Meyer's article, for example, Tallahassee *Democrat*, 15 January 1967.

61. However, it is available in the National Archives, Record Group 282, filed under "Commission Research Studies," housed in the Lyndon Baines Johnson Presidential Library, University of Texas, Austin, Texas. See also Louis C. Goldberg, "Ghetto Riots and Others: The Faces of Civil Disorder in 1967," in *Cities under Siege*, pp. 137-57. This article provides a sense of the original analysis.

62. See Harold R. Wilde, "Milwaukee's National Media Riot," in *Urban Government*, rev. ed., ed. Edward C. Banfield (New York: Free Press, 1969), pp. 682-88.

63. As indicated in ch. 2 above, such riots were typical of previous eras.

64. See *Report*, ch. 2, part 3, for later confirming data.

65. Polarization and increased communication were observed in Detroit, Newark, Plainfield, Chicago, and Milwaukee. Polarization without increased communication was observed in Cambridge and Jersey City. No polarization and increased communication (the most desirable combination) was noted in Atlanta, New Haven, Grand Rapids, Tampa, and New Brunswick. Neither polarization nor increased communication were seen as resulting from the riots in Rockford, Tucson, and Phoenix.

66. The document was never truly rejected as such by the commission because it was never formally submitted to it, as commission spokesmen literalistically pointed out.

67. "Summary Analysis of Twenty-Six Disturbances (Working Outline for Interim), Office of Assistant Deputy Director for Research [Shellow]."

68. Shellow, "Social Scientists and Social Action," p. 212.

69. See "Appendix B: Remarks of the President," *Report*, p. 537.

70. Paraphrased from "An Outline of the December Report," accompanying Palmieri's "Memorandum for the Staff," 21 September 1967, p. 8.

71. His work was to dovetail with the work of sociologist Myron J. Lefkowitz, who was to direct research efforts for long-term program recommendations, but Lefkowitz gradually withdrew from commission involvement.

72. "Program Research Staff, The National Advisory Commission on Civil Disorder."

73. Memo, "To: Al Spivack; From: R. P. Nathan; Subject: Program to Set up a Network to obtain information from Newspaper Reporters in Selected Cities."

74. Memorandum, "To: Victor H. Palmieri; From: Richard P. Nathan; Subject: Herb Gans's Letter of October 7, on Short-Term Action Programs, 13 October 1967."

75. The Nathan staff paper on education illustrates the proposed scope of the short-term, program-unit goals. Most of the paper concentrated on reviewing federal programs assisting education, with an introductory section summarizing the findings of the Coleman Report and the U.S. Civil Rights Commission Report on racial integration in education. The short-run programs advocated in this document included: encouraging year-round educational programming; rewarding school systems that attempt to eliminate de facto segregation; encouraging community participation in education; developing ways to individualize ghetto teaching techniques; improving ghetto teaching techniques; and improving ghetto teaching through an expanded Teacher Corps, greater use of volunteers and paraprofessionals, and recruitment of Vietnam veterans. Each program recommendation was accompanied by a brief statement and documentation. Carol B. Liebman, "Short-Term Action Options in the Education Field," preliminary draft, "For Official Use Only," 1 December 1967.

76. Dated 11 December 1967.

77. Because of the importance of two nonprogrammatic themes related to the proposals, the document also treated in separate sections problems of increasing citizen participation in the programs and

increasing the priority of allocating resources to the inner city. In the area of employment, the Nathan group concentrated on increasing efforts to end racial discrimination in employment; creating the Private Job Development Corporation to engage private enterprise in hiring the hard-core unemployed; and developing the Public Service Job Program to expand opportunities in the public sector. The welfare recommendations focused upon adopting national standards; extending the program of Aid to Families of Dependent Children—Unemployed Parents (A.F.D.C.-U.P.) to all states; eliminating punitive policing practices; training welfare workers to render services to clients; and removing residency requirements. In education, the report reflected the recommendations of the "Action Options" paper described above, except for an increased emphasis on a program to increase the verbal skills of ghetto residents and elimination of the recommendation concerning Vietnam veterans.

78. See, for example, the views of Rep. George Mahon, in the Washington *Star*, 3 March 1968.

79. One confirmation of this view of the Nathan document subsequently offered by other staff members was the staff's ability to improve the evidential and argumentative basis for the commission's recommendations.

80. See, for example, Philip Meyer's Knight Newspapers column, in the Charlotte *Observer*, 3 March 1968.

81. "Statement by the President," The White House [29 July 1967]; for the modified statement, see *Report*, p. 537.

82. The Ford Foundation continued its support for the Campbell and Schuman study, and the Rossi, et al., study. The National Institute for Mental Health assumed the financial burden for the Fogelson-Hill study; see *Supplemental Studies.*

83. Still later, executive staff members on the Kerner Commission again shifted roles and effectively substituted themselves for subordinates who were dismissed or discredited.

84. The following paragraphs are largely based on memoranda dictated by Mattick at the time of his involvement with the commission. We are indebted to Professor Mattick for making them available to us.

85. Although the hotel in which he stayed was across the street from commission offices, Mattick and other staff members slept on cots in their offices during the most hectic times.

86. For Mattick's conception of the riots see his article drawing on his experiences with the commission and materials made available during his tenure in commission employment: Hans W. Mattick, "Form and Content of Recent Riots," *Midway* 9, no. 1 (Summer 1968): 3-32.

87. Shellow, "Social Scientists and Social Action," p. 212. Kurzman was not the only executive staff member to work on drafts. Both Ginsburg and Palmieri tried their hands at various times and Jack Rosenthal, a former newspaper reporter with extensive experience in Washington as a press officer, was specifically hired to assist with the writing process.

88. Cf. Downs, "Alternative Futures for the American Ghetto."

89. *Report*, p. 397.

90. Much of chapter 17 of the *Report* may be read by a sympathetic observer as consistent with an integration/enrichment strategy. But in the absence of specific language drawing attention to the primary goal, the discussion of recommendations for national action otherwise appears to be a peroration for refinement and expansion of present policies. The choice of a strategy might have provided the *Report* with an element otherwise glaringly absent—a sense of what kinds of programs should be given priority. It may be argued that any one of the three strategies was too simplistic to encompass the necessary policy proposals. But then one may wonder why the commission included the Downs chapter at all.

91. Other commissions on which social scientists have played important roles include the National Advisory Committee on Selective Service; President's Commission on Law Enforcement and Administration of Justice; Commission on Obscenity and Pornography [see James Q. Wilson, "Violence, Pornography and Social Science," *The Public Interest* (Winter 1971) pp. 53-57]; National Commission on the Causes and Prevention of Violence [see Jerome H. Skolnick, "Violence Commission Violence," *Transaction* (now *Society*) 7, no. 12 (October 1970): 32-38]; and Commission on Campus Unrest [see Martha Derthick, "On Commissionship—Presidential Variety," *Public Policy* 19, no. 4 (Fall 1971): 623-38].

6

The Education of Commissioners and the Management of Learning and Consent

All complex organizations require mechanisms of integration to resist tendencies toward fragmentation and inertia. Members of such organizations must develop attitudes toward their work that contribute to the success of the organization, even if this means curbing other orientations or inclinations.[1] While all organizations and members of organizations experience such imperatives to some degree, riot commissions confront them in extraordinary fashion.

Commissioners are specifically recruited for the diversity of interests they represent. A commission must have balance and diversity of membership if it is to carry political weight, reassure various publics and generate popular support for proposals.

Riot commissions must also work within a short time span. Created in response to crisis, they have to report relatively quickly. Thus they may not depend upon the gradual development of norms, role expectations or personal relationships which lend cohesion to stable, long-lasting organizations.[2]

Like all presidential commissions and task forces, riot commissions are temporary. Organizations with potentially high levels of intra-organizational conflict ordinarily develop integrative mechanisms—inducements and sanctions which affect members' career goals, personal loyalties and organizational norms.[3] But these are limited when the organization has a fixed, short life. The inducements to riot commission harmony are ambiguous at best. For example, while the status of people in public life is often enhanced by appointment to such a commission,[4] they may not necessarily be cooperative or otherwise supportive of the organization. Moreover, commissioners and staff are unlikely to abandon personal values and perspectives; indeed, if they are to remain "representative" of important, relevant interests they are in theory precluded from doing so. Thus any rewards stemming from participation in commission activities (as opposed to appointment) from this perspective are not likely to be relevant to commission cohesion.

The temporary nature of riot commissions has other implications. Inherited organizational norms are obviously nonexistent. Sanctions against deviant members are, for the most part, unavailable. Personal affinities conducive to organizational harmony surely develop within commissions, but compatability is not essential to performance or advancement in the organization. In any case, such friendships must almost always be developed from scratch. In some temporary organizations, such as those which arise to deal directly with crisis (flood-relief units,[5] emergency fund-raising) a sense of mission and unity of purpose contribute to organizational cohesion. But riot commissions are temporary organizations without such clarity of direction, whose sense of mission is at least partially precluded initially by the apparent diversity of commissioners.

The theory implicit in appointing riot commissions reveals sensitivity to the possibility of fragmentation. It is reasoned, for example, that if high-status individuals ostensibly representative of diverse interests can agree on a commission's explanations and proposals, then it may be possible to mobilize popular support for them. Conversely, if a commission is unable to agree, it will be extremely difficult to gain a politically effective consensus.

As suggested in chapter three, the fact that its membership is diverse yet agreement is expected often leads to predictions that the report will be bland or an outright "whitewash." Bland reports are sometimes predicted because commissioners are assumed to be protecting diverse interests. "Whitewashes" are sometimes predicted when critics think commissioners have been chosen because their views are congruent with those of the chief executive. Sometimes, "whitewashes" are predicted because if commissioners are moderates, they are assumed to support political institutions which come under attack. These predictions are sometimes borne out.

Yet, despite the inherent "logic" of the commission process and the dire predictions of critics, the Kerner Commission's efforts were not neatly predictable.[6] The *Report* was a remarkable document. Rejecting punitive responses, 11 prominent citizens put their names to a report extremely critical of the performance of American society as a whole. Given their moderation, the diversity of interests they represented, the demands for order which developed after the riots (which many commissioners shared) and the president's concern for inexpensive programs, how can the tone, scope and message of the Kerner *Report* be explained?

In answering this question we must return to our discussion of organizational integration. Approaches to commission work which reflect members' experiences and loyalties prior to their appointment we shall call *career orientations*. Attitudes, experiences and loyalties which developed through exposure to and simultaneously with commission activities we shall call *commission orientations*. Simply put, the factors affecting the shift in the balance from career to commission orientations is the key to the answer.

Three interrelated processes characteristic of official investigative bodies contributed to the Kerner Commission's cohesion. First, commissioners were helped or induced to learn about the problems they were charged with addressing. Second, commissioners were helped to gain confidence in what they were asked to affirm. Finally, remaining conflict was resolved in ways consistent with commission solidarity.

Initial Assumptions

When the commission was initially appointed, several commissioners seemed to take a hard line on riot control. Thornton and McCulloch, for example, told the commission that they felt the group's major role was to "stop the riots." "Law and order," Jenkins told the commission, "is the first order of business." Similar views were expressed by Peden shortly after her appointment.[7] Despite these members' views, the commission assumed responsibility for developing a report that would, among other things, review the setting in which civil disorders emerged. A number of factors contributed to the decision to take a comprehensive view.

One obvious influence was President Johnson, who asked the group to investigate long-term as well as short-term factors causing riots. In so doing, the president helped structure the commission's work in ways which later brought it into conflict with him. Although he later tried to

signal them to make only inexpensive, short-run policy recommendations, he had established a framework in which it became impossible to
accept those limitations. As various commission participants came to
realize later, one could hardly describe fully the plight of black Americans and then recommend only short-term reforms and better programs to suppress violence.

The president's original call for a comprehensive study also strengthened the hand of those commissioners who sought a broader view and
structured staff efforts before commission sentiment had hardened. For
some commissioners, the group's major role was to bridge the gap in the
understanding of the problems of blacks in America.[8] Governor Kerner
insisted: "My concern all the time about this commission has been that
at the conclusion our greatest problem is going to be to educate the
white, rather than the Negro."[9] Senator Harris similarly argued that the
"worst problem in America is nobody is talking to each other about
this problem." Corman agreed: "Nothing is going to happen, seriously
without a change of attitudes on the part of most of the people in this
nation." Even Thornton described the problem as one of understanding
and education, although he used this position to reject a governmental
role in creating better race relations. In questioning Omaha civil-rights
leader Ernie Chambers, Thornton observed:

> I understand what you say, the government attitude has to change.
> You mean the white community, their attitude has to change, as we
> have heard before, the attitudinal problem is perhaps the biggest
> problem. *And the government can't force that to change. The atti-
> tude of whites.*[10]

Another factor affecting the decision to serve an educational role
was the desire to keep faith with black moderates. Some members perceived black politicians as competing for the loyalties of the black
masses. Keeping down the influence of "militants" was seen to depend
on maintaining the black population's faith that working within the
system offered the best prospects for change. Focusing on educating
white publics was in part a response to the needs of moderate black
leaders such as Commissioner Wilkins.

Focusing on the education of white America did not necessarily imply a radical or vigorous orientation. This was clearly illustrated when,
on September 13, 1967, the commission reconsidered a proposal by
Mayor Lindsay to hold hearings on the Neighborhood Youth Corps

(NYC) with a view toward possibly addressing a statement to the White House about the program. The NYC part of the poverty program administered by the Department of Labor was then in jeopardy in Congress, heavily criticized because the jobs available seemed to offer little future. Although the commission had already made an "action" recommendation concerning the National Guard, there was considerable opposition to the Lindsay proposal. Thornton, McCulloch and Jenkins argued that suppressing the riots was the commission's first task and making recommendations concerning social programs would undermine their priorities and create an unfortunate impression. Thornton put the matter succinctly:

> Now, the thing that I think we ought to do to keep credibility of this Commission, that it is really getting in profound areas, that we should not come out with any interim report unless the next one has a strong flavor in it of some sort of law enforcement, or something that stops the riots.
>
> Now, we can have in there some of the social programs, or some attack on the underlying causes. But unless we establish ourselves, that we are facing realistically with the number one charge given by the President, which is stop the riots, we are going to discredit ourselves, because the next thing we come out with is spend more money.
>
> Many people believe that is the only conclusion we are going to arrive at—that we are not going to face up realistically to the problem.[11]

McCulloch and Corman further argued that Lindsay's proposal would have little impact on Congress. Thornton also insisted that the commission should first establish expertise in an area on which it commented.

Senator Harris, the only commissioner to endorse the Lindsay proposal,[12] argued that because riots cannot be stopped "by police action or law enforcement alone," the commission should balance its public statement on the National Guard with one supportive of social programs. He agreed with Thornton, however, that the commission should not take a stand unless it held hearings on the subject and developed a record of investigation. Brooke and Jenkins gave the proposal lukewarm support and it was rejected by the chairman without a vote.[13]

In addition to the preceding initial assumptions about the commission's role, members also had aspirations for the organization which to some degree reflected their own career orientations. At least four dimensions of such orientations were apparent in their approaches to their work.

1. *The commissioners remained responsive to their original constituencies.* This is reflected in some commissioners' attempts to identify the source of their convictions: when McCulloch indicated that he thought the first task of the commission was to stop riots, he explained "that is what the people in my section of Ohio are looking for us to do." And Jenkins defended his relatively ameliorative position by explaining that more jobs and better communications are the highest priorities of "the people that I am in contact with—those of us, the chiefs of police and the mayors who are in the middle of these things. . . ."14

Allusions to constituents of course may be regarded in part as ploys. McCulloch and Jenkins, for example, gained legitimacy for their views by claiming to speak for others.

2. *Members' commission roles were consistent with their expertise.* McCulloch and Corman regularly took the lead in advising the commission on how to gain influence with Congress and expressed interest in the design and desirability of additional legislation. Corman showed particular interest in witnesses' views on open-housing legislation scheduled to come before Congress in the coming months and Jenkins took an interest in police matters.

Wilkins demonstrated his interest in and experience with civil rights matters by particularly incisive questioning of representatives of the National Association of Real Estate Boards. Abel was extremely gracious and friendly to labor representatives. Wilkins also was receptive to labor representatives, perhaps preferring not to jeopardize carefully developed relations with critical questioning. Thornton, who chaired the commission's Advisory Panel on Private Enterprise, questioned witnesses closely on employment in the private sector and the fiscal implications of recommendations for higher levels of public spending. Kerner called upon his experiences as governor in vetoing "stop-and-frisk" legislation when the commission took up this subject.

Generally, commissioners took the lead in discussions of issues on which they were expert. Perhaps even more important, members reviewed staff work carefully in their various areas of specialization, the staff tended to develop materials in anticipation of their potential criticism and commissioners regularly deferred to other commissioners in their areas of competence. Thus representativeness, far from being divisive, contributed to organizational integration. Moreover, the informal division of commission work according to career specialties allowed for short-circuiting the usually tentative and time-consuming processes by which small groups establish the roles of individual members.

3. *Because the commission has a brief life, commissioners can never wholly neglect the views their constituents are likely to have in the future.* This consideration, if operative, represents a continuing source of strain because it undermines the development of commission orientations.

Illustratively, a severe conflict arose over fears that one commission member was acting to enhance his career prospects. In one of the few intercommission memos drafted by a commissioner, Corman expressed the view that the commission should deal with a limited range of problems and not try to respond to all the problems of American cities. This memo was regarded as a rebuke to Lindsay, who at the time was vigorously championing a more reform-oriented version of the *Report*. In response, the mayor—also without mentioning any names—insisted in a memo that the problems of cities were equivalent to American racial problems and criticized narrow restriction of commission perspectives.

4. *For commissioners no less than for other people, previous experiences and observations color the ways they perceive events.* When Thornton referred to experiences in his enterprises or when Harris illustrated a point by making reference to a particular Oklahoma county familiar to him, they were exhibiting the personalized, experiential ways people come to hold convictions. The unreliability of this mode of cognition can be embarrassing. In Wilkins's absence, Thornton at one point delivered a dissertation on the role of business in hiring minorities. He asserted from experience and personal knowledge that blacks were at the time favored in employment over whites of similar and even greater ability, even suggesting that the integrationist NAACP hired white workers only because it could not find qualified blacks for some of its key positions.[15]

Sometimes personal experiences which had no relation to careers provided the basis for opinion. Brooke, for example, praised the New Deal Civilian Conservation Corps camps, mentioning the assistance his brother received from this program. Thornton, skeptical of the value of government employment programs, referred to the willingness of his generation to work during the Depression.

It is hardly surprising that men and women hold opinions based upon experiences and we have certainly not established in any precise way how prevalent this kind of thinking was in commission deliberations. But to some degree at least, commissioners signal their preferences and orientations to staff members through such informal, untestable and unsystematic thinking. It is not that they should censure themselves and refuse to express their personal convictions and prejudices. But it does suggest that it is desirable to appoint individuals with varied backgrounds to commissions so that for every commissioner who insists that he "knows" from personal experience that blacks are not discriminated against in employment, there will be one who argues with equal conviction that it is often difficult or impossible for blacks to get jobs equivalent to their skills and training.

Although there was some initial agreement that the *Report* should educate whites on the condition of blacks in America, a number of commissioners strongly disagreed with this orientation. While these commissioners viewed themselves to some degree as representative of different constituencies, they also shared a stake in American society and institutions. There was disagreement, too, about the role of the commission and which programs it might appropriately prescribe. Despite these disagreements, the commission managed to gain and sustain consensus and resolve continuing differences in a number of ways.

The Management of Learning and Commission Integration

Although riot commissions substantially lack characteristics that ordinarily contribute to organizational integration, the urgency of the problem with which riot commissions are charged and the short period of time they have to complete their work can contribute to feelings of solidarity and dedication among staff and commissioners. Commission integration is also promoted by the desire for a unified report. To the extent that commissioners come to identify with their report, either because they believe in it or want to be associated publicly with a highly visible undertaking, they will have a stake in minimizing organizational dissent. A commission split by a substantive minority report is less influential, revealing by implication that the issues remain divisive, even for those charged with developing a common view of the conflict. To avoid a minority dissent, commissions may compromise or soften interpretations and recommendations.

Within limits, the threat of a minority report is one with which some commissioners can persuade others to modify their views. Mayor Lindsay was prepared to rely on this tactic if the Kerner Commission had refused to accept his "summary." If commissioners intensely disagree on fundamental points, the commission will try to isolate these views as dissenting commentary. At the same time, they will try to persuade the dissidents to sign the majority document, subject to the reservations they may express in an appendix or footnote.[16] On a day-to-day level, the threat of a minority report keeps staff within boundaries established by strongly held beliefs and convictions of commissioners. Kerner Commission staff members deliberately attempted to nurture a sense of unity and purpose. Work was structured to provide commissioners with direct exposure to ghetto conditions and simultaneously to develop a sense of shared experiences. Toward this end the Kerner Commission placed great emphasis on visits to riot areas.

The importance of direct exposure had been established when Dr. Leonard Duhl, then working for the Department of Housing and Urban Development, arranged a trip to New Haven with commission Deputy Executive Director Palmieri. At the end of a day spent interviewing local officials, Palmieri was surprised to discover that the two were advised by these same officials not to speak to ghetto leaders. Despite this advice, Palmieri met with black leaders and was reportedly impressed by the frank, free-wheeling and honest exchange that ensued. He reportedly left New Haven sobered by the problems of gaining reliable information. Other staff members were troubled by different interpretations of specific riot situations provided by press accounts on the one hand and public officials on the other. First-hand visits became one way of gaining direct information and multiple exposure to sources.

On August 16, scarcely two weeks after the commission was appointed, Lindsay and Ginsburg visited Newark without prior announcement. To the amusement of curious residents who quickly recognized New York City's mayor, they toured poverty-program offices and the riot area walking up and down Springfield Avenue, the scene of the previous month's most severe rioting. The two also met with city officials, including Mayor Hugh Addonizio, on the one-day excursion.[17]

On the same day, Kerner, Peden and Thornton made an unannounced visit to Detroit, while Wilkins and Abel toured East Harlem and Bedford-Stuyvesant in New York City. Newspaper reporters were intrigued with the cloak-and-dagger techniques used by the Detroit contingent to meet in seclusion with various informants. Later that month, on August 20, McCulloch visited Detroit; Abel and Peden traveled to

Cambridge, Md.; and, on August 30, Lindsay and Harris investigated conditions in Cincinnati. Later, various commissioners toured Milwaukee and Los Angeles; others revisited some cities. In all, commissioners personally surveyed eight riot cities, talking with ghetto leaders and public officials with varying levels of responsibility.

Comprehensive learning about conditions in American ghettos can hardly be accomplished with half-day guided tours of major American cities. Yet these tours exposed commissioners to living conditions and enabled them to confront black leaders directly, contributing to the process of commissioner orientation and learning. Two incidents illustrate the importance of this exposure. In Cincinnati, Lindsay's staff arranged for the mayor and Senator Harris to meet clandestinely with 15 of the city's black militant leaders. They encountered civility but not courtesy. The black spokesmen stressed that the commissioners were wasting their time, that the American system had long ago proved itself corrupt and that they were dedicated to destroying that system. What was particularly meaningful to these liberal commissioners was that these black leaders were professional men and college graduates and had all tried to work within the system.[18]

Another incident reflects the kind of "learning" that may take place in the streets. In the decaying, "bombed-out" neighborhood of Brownsville in New York City's Brooklyn, one participant on a ghetto tour stopped to question a woman sitting in the doorway of a run-down building, surrounded by four young children, all, like her, in tattered clothing. The staff executive began to question her (as recollected by our informant):

Do you live here?
Yes.
Do you live alone?
Yes.
How many children do you have?
Five.
How long have you lived here?
Five years.
Where do you come from?
Mississippi.
Why did you come?
To find a better life.
Did you find it?
Yes.

In a few words the woman had confounded her questioner's under-standing of the black urban experience. He had expected his respondent to despair of her current situation, regret her move to the North and wish to return. If this way of life was an improvement over what she had experienced before, what must life for blacks in rural Mississippi be like?

These trips also gave commissioners something to do while staff members developed hearing schedules and otherwise initiated research. Commissioners were able to learn about ghetto conditions before policy papers had been prepared and before it became necessary to "take sides." In addition, these trips permitted the commission to project an image of a concerned, busy commission while there was still much public anxiety over riots, but before the commission was prepared to make statements.

Staff members hoped that commissioners would get to know each other during these trips and would feel that they shared a common basis of understanding aspects of American cities. That this goal was realized to some degree is suggested by the frequency with which commissioners alluded to the city tours in questioning witnesses.[19]

A second way in which commissioners "learned" was through exposure to witnesses at closed hearings. The commission first heard from cabinet officers, Justice Department and FBI officials and National Guard spokesmen.[20] Paul Ylvisaker, secretary of the New Jersey Department of Community Affairs; Governor George Romney of Michigan; Mayors Jerome Cavanaugh (Detroit) and Hugh Addonizio (Newark); and city and state officials accompanying these men provided the commission with what Palmieri termed "a total expurgation of the city [officials] point of view."[21]

Following the testimony on cities, the commission met on an average of twice a week through November 9 to hear witnesses discuss: black history; employment and ghetto conditions; police-community tensions and community relations; action programs and citizen participation; manpower and job training; the employment service and ghetto employment; the role of business and labor; rural-urban migration; education, youth, welfare and consumer protection problems and programs; the ghetto family; and the administration of justice during civil disorders.

Witnesses with dramatic testimony were particularly instrumental in creating a sense of commission urgency. The commission took note of this when it called attention to the impact of Kenneth Clark's testimony, in which he expressed skepticism that the commission's efforts would result in substantive change.[22] What the commission did not convey was that witness after witness, black scholars, intellectuals and representatives of minority opinion expressed the same kind of doubt and despair. Ernie Chambers, the Omaha barber and civic leader; economist Vivian Henderson, president of Clark College in Atlanta; Father James Groppi, the advisor to the Milwaukee NAACP Youth Council; Piri Thomas, the Puerto Rican author—all expressed the same resignation and cynicism that Clark communicated so eloquently.[23] In their own ways these men reinforced the doubts expressed by Ylvisaker and Downs when they first told Ginsburg about their disappointing experience with President Johnson's urban task force.

Sometimes direct confrontation with witnesses enabled staff members to make dramatic points. Commission counsel Merle McCurdy was able to pillory AFL-CIO president George Meany by citing specific instances in which white building-trades workers walked off when blacks were brought in to work on a job. McCurdy's close questioning of Alexander Summer, former president of the National Association of Real Estate Boards, concerning NAREB's opposition to open-housing legislation, was similarly effective.[24] McCurdy explicitly extracted from witnesses David Hardy, a New York *Daily News* reporter, and Roger Wilkins, head of the Justice Department's Community Relations Service, testimony that neither in Plainfield, N.J., about which Hardy testified, nor nationally, according to Wilkins, was there evidence that riots were caused by planned conspiracies or outsiders.

In their field trips and hearings the commissioners were confronted with experiences which for most were relatively new and certainly different. The anger, passion and need to which the commissioners were exposed could only be transmitted through experiences such as these. But to express sympathy for the black position in America, the commissioners still had to develop a report which they could defend.

The Management of Confidence

Commission unity is threatened at all stages. Initially, the organizational problem is getting members to think of themselves as commissioners, not as individuals motivated by career orientations. In later stages, the problem becomes one of structuring staff work so that politically sensitive commissioners will be willing to put their names to what the commission as a whole chooses to say. To a significant degree, commissioners are willing to make assertions only when they are confident staff work has been responsible. Thus nourishing commissioner confidence becomes a primary staff concern, subservient (although not necessarily in opposition) to its pursuit of information and analysis.

We have already discussed how social scientists' controversial statements and inadequate documentation led to rejection of the "Harvest of American Racism." Although it was regarded as a working document by the social scientists, staff directors feared the commissioners would take it as definitive staff work. This husbanding of staff reputation was reflected in many decisions and procedures of the executive directors. The management of confidence has two components: *the initiation and establishment of the commission process and the process of learning and commitment itself.*

Initiation and Establishment

An important potential point of tension is the commissioners' need to feel that staff members are unbiased. The fear that some staff members will be biased ideologically is reinforced by the nature of lower-level staff recruitment. In lower-status commission jobs, individuals may be interested in employment for ideological reasons and this factor may not have been screened out in hiring.

Furthermore, staff members may rebel against commissions if they feel unfairly treated or if their views are ignored. On the Kerner Commission, staff members with commitments to certain interpretations of the disorders drew public attention to what they felt at the time were conservative aspects of the commission's research methods and procedures.

The uncertainty over staff loyalty was apparent even earlier on security matters. Staff members anxious to preserve a memo for posterity or hoping to exert outside influence through a judicious "leak" to a receptive newspaper reporter created problems for the commission quite early in its life. At one point the pilfering of documents got so far out of hand that field reports and other sensitive materials were stored in safes and department heads were instructed to enjoin personnel from photocopying documents or taking them out of the building. A high-level staff committee was also established to make recommendations for increasing building security.[25]

It is difficult to assess the costs of fears about staff bias. In theory it is important for commissioners to communicate their values and preferences to the staff, just as it is necessary for staff members to

221

anticipate correctly the commissioners' convictions. Staff departures from commissioners' preferences, if carried too far, will result in embarrassing and costly demands for substantially different kinds of staff work. This was the experience of the President's Commission on Campus Unrest (Scranton Commission), whose staff consistently produced materials more conservative than a majority of commissioners considered appropriate.[26]

On balance, staff members' anticipation of commissioners' preferences tended to encourage moderation; staff directors and presentations which were at all speculative or beyond the bounds already established by the commissioners were excluded.

A second misgiving of commissioners toward the staff focuses on staff partisanship. The Kerner Commission was vulnerable to this problem because of speculation associating the commission with the interests of the president. The selection of Ginsburg as the commission's executive director led to concern that the chief staff officer would be fronting for the president. Ginsburg was a partner in one of Washington's most prestigious law firms, had extensive government connections and was a participant in White House social circles.

Republicans' concern about a "whitewash" were alleviated in part by the appointment of a Republican to the unique position of vice chairman of the commission and by the high-level staff appointments of Nathan and Kurzman, both of whom had worked for Republican congressmen. Although both insist that they did not function in a partisan manner (indeed Nathan says he specifically refused to do so when asked to serve by a Republican commissioner), these appointments reassured Republicans that their interests would be accommodated or defended. The deep involvement in commission affairs of Lindsay's assistant, Jay Kriegel, also helped to alleviate these anxieties.

Learning and Commitment

The second stage in the management of commission confidence is accomplished in small steps throughout the life of a commission. By exposing commissioners to new kinds of learning experiences, by developing their regard for staff procedures and by allaying anxiety over the final product, the Kerner commissioners were persuaded to sign a report in March that few would have endorsed nine months before. The incremental nature of commission work in describing what happened (which we have labeled *incremental concretization*) and developing interpretations and conclusions (which we may call *incremental consensualization*) constitute the political aspects of social research by commission.

To increase commissioners' confidence in staff work several mechanisms were employed. Commissioners were continually asked for suggestions about witnesses, hearings and personnel. For example, H. C. (Chad) McClellan, president of the Management Council for Merit Employment, Training and Research, was invited to testify when one commissioner suggested that it would be useful to hear from employers who had attempted job-training programs.

Ginsburg's role in inducing commissioners' confidence in staff work was considerable. According to all accounts, Ginsburg conducted himself without regard for partisan concerns. Ginsburg fully embraced the commission as his client, creating an atmosphere of openness which was simultaneously tough-minded. He would invite suggestions, while demanding that commissioners be specific in their criticisms. He would show patience in debate, but was willing to cut it off with exclamations that the staff had discussed the subject at great length. He relieved Republican anxieties by avoiding positions which could be interpreted as particularly favorable to the president. And, because he was thought to be well-connected with the White House, relatively conservative commissioners may have thought he was in a position to protect their interests, even though more liberal commissioners seemed to dominate proceedings.

Perhaps most important, Ginsburg's emphasis on "making a record" encouraged confidence that the commission would not take positions it could not support. Hearings were designed not only to inform commissioners, but also to demonstrate that the commission had studied deeply. This concern carried over in the writing of the *Report*. Frequent and somewhat gratuitous references in the *Report* to witness' statements were intended to call attention to the information-collecting in which the commission engaged. Allegiance to "the record" also helped Ginsburg slide over what was perhaps the most potentially controversial commission concern—the scope of the *Report*. By referring to the president's statements in creating the commission, Ginsburg was able to develop the foundation for a wide-ranging document.

Indicative of Ginsburg's role as mediator and choreographer of commission consent was the way he approached the final writing. As final drafts were prepared in February, Ginsburg read them, aloud, word for word, to the entire commission. Only in this way, he felt, could he obtain the signatures of all the commissioners. Where obvious conflicts arose, the staff could try to resolve them. But when commissioners expressed only vague feelings of uneasiness they had to be specific if their complaints were to be accommodated. On questions of "tone," Ginsburg shifted the burden of proof onto recalcitrant commissioners, whose resources to put together a counter-argument in such circumstances were obviously limited.

Towards the end of the commission's work serious disagreement and conflict arose. The staff effort prior to this stage—partly by design—had emphasized procedure and minimized the extent to which commissioners had to commit themselves to specific positions. But during the last few weeks, considerable conflict developed over what the commission could say with confidence. Commission liberals, for example, sought to endorse proposals for a negative income tax; more conservative members insisted that they were not expert on income maintenance, had not studied the problem in depth and should not make statements outside their limited range of expertise. In the final *Report*, the commission commended recent experimentation in this area and drew attention to a recently created commission to study income maintenance.[27]

The issue of community control of schools also divided the commission. Led by Mayor Lindsay, a liberal minority favored decentralization in education, but a more conservative majority again prevailed. Some objected that such a recommendation was too complicated for full commission endorsement. Corman, joined by McCulloch and Thornton, led the opposition, pointing out that the commission was not qualified to endorse structurally radical proposals in education. Still others generally objected that it would be destructive to condemn institutions as basic as the public schools. The commission finally recommended "maintaining centralized control over educational standards and the raising of revenue, while decentralizing controls over other aspects of educational policy. The precise mix must be determined locally."[28]

Thus the commission endorsed vague and general recommendations to accommodate commissioners uncomfortable with specific endorsements. Ginsburg also introduced a universal disclaimer to accommodate this concern:

We do not claim competence to chart the details of programs within such complex and interrelated fields as employment, welfare, education and housing. We do believe it is essential to set forth goals and to recommend strategies to reach these goals.

That is the aim of the pages that follow. They contain our sense of the critical priorities. We discuss and recommend programs not to commit each of us to specific parts of such programs but to illustrate the type and dimension of action needed.[29]

Prior to the final weeks, commissioners were not required to take positions on matters of policy. Because of the time required in the writing process and the executive staff's desire to withhold consideration of drafts until the end, only Ginsburg, Palmieri and perhaps a few other top-staff members had any reasonably solid impression of what the final *Report* might look like. Commissioners' views of the emerging *Report* were at best fragmentary. While Ginsburg continually informed the commission of research progress and the projected design of the *Report*, he kept to himself his uncertainties concerning the adequacy of the work and anxieties over whether the commission would accept staff efforts.

The executive staff approached the final weeks—when the pieces would have to come together—with some trepidation. Both commission liberals and conservatives grew apprehensive as fragments of the *Report* were consolidated. When commissioners were confronted with specific findings or proposals, career orientations again became salient.

Lindsay, frequently defeated in his efforts to get the commission to accept strong, specific policy recommendations, salvaged his position by forcing the commission to adopt the summary. While some commissioners expressed anxiety that the *Report* did not sufficiently condemn the rioters, there were few specific changes they could recommend. The commission had long before consented to the basic dimensions of the *Report*, to address itself to the white community and to take a relatively broad look at the causes of black discontent. In its preface it had summarily condemned violence and paid homage to respect for law and order.[30] The staff had failed to uncover evidence of conspiracy and outside agitators. Efforts to moderate the *Report's* ameliorative tone fell against the logic of Ginsburg's arguments that the final document had to address a broad range of questions if the commission were to fulfill its assigned tasks. Unable to mount specific criticisms, commissioners with doubts remaining signed the *Report*.

The Kerner Report: A Solution to the Commission's 'Problems'

The Kerner Report was hard-hitting. It was widely applauded by a broad spectrum of elite opinion and received extensive publicity. It went considerably beyond what most observers thought it would say. Whatever its strengths and weaknesses, it is primarily a product of the organizational and political processes we have outlined.

The liberal tone of the *Report* is attributable to the relatively broad mandate provided by the president, the liberal bent of at least some of the commissioners and the processes of learning and gaining a consensus in which staff and commissioners engaged. Some might hold that in a society riven by a legacy of injustice and brutality, political men and women could only conclude that: "Race prejudice has shaped our history decisively in the past; it now threatens to do so again."[31] Nor could any reasonable investigator dispute, in 1967 and 1968, on even the most superficial examination the "basic conclusion" of the commission: "Our nation is moving toward two societies, one black, one white—separate and unequal." The contribution of the staff directors was to structure that examination in ways which would permit commissioners to insist on or acquiesce to a vigorous statement of concern.

In some ways, however, the failures of the commission are more instructive. The commission substantially failed in its hopes to establish a policy agenda for the nation. Only as an educational document did the commission have any substantial success. Although the *Report* created confusion in many places, and focused attention on itself rather than on the conditions it attempted to describe, it did obtain significant distribution (although the long-range impact of this circulation is difficult to assess).[32]

The weaknesses of the *Report* may be largely explained by examining the ways in which it solved the commission's organizational tensions. Allan Silver has aptly observed that riot commissions in the United States historically have located the causes of civil disorders in the social conditions of the disrupters. The focus on underlying conditions as in the Kerner *Report* permits commissioners and middle- and upper-class readers of commission reports "to maintain broad political sympathy for the urban Negro 'underclass' and simultaneously come to terms with popular unruliness, riot and violence even though these things are especially disturbing to them."[33] This observation specifically applies to the Kerner Commission, which deliberately sought to inform whites about the grievous conditions under which

226

black people live and to establish credentials with a black public by affirming the identity of the oppressor.

This same perspective also permits elites to ignore or avoid acknowledging the political content of civil disorders. By attributing disorders to social causes the commission inferentially denies that they result from purposive political action or from a loosening of the political and social bonds which otherwise restrain people from seeking to solve problems by violent means. This perspective is the opposite of, but the functional equivalent to, the riffraff theory which also deflects attention from the political content of violent protest by attributing riots to criminals, the uneducated or the socially dislocated. It is one thing to say a problem is rooted in social backgrounds and historical developments; it is quite another to acknowledge that disruptions express profound dissatisfaction with the arrangement of power and the distribution of values.

We are not suggesting that the black riots were as articulate as a petition of the League of Women Voters. But if oppressed groups act in such a way that they may be calling attention to profound injustice, it is debilitating to have their appeal officially translated into questions of the injustice of previous generations or nonpurposive behavior. The commission, for example, failed to discuss the meaning of the riots for blacks, although it had data on this subject and used attitudinal data for other purposes.[34]

In its demands for change and reform without identifying specific culprits, the Kerner *Report* solved the commission's needs. The commission viewed the political system as failing to practice what it calls for in theory. Although many programs are advocated or endorsed, on the subject of reform the fundamental, exhortative commission posture is summarized in these words: "Our basic conclusion. . .[is that] the need is not so much for the government to design new programs as it is for the nation to generate new will."[35]

Just as Silver argues that past commissions have tended to "objectify the causes of violence, to show their roots in environment and social structure, to depersonalize the connection between particular violent groups and the specific content of violent acts,"[36] we would argue that the Kerner Commission *ignored how purposive actions create preconditions for violence.* There is little or no discussion in the *Report* of how institutions and bureaucracies sustain the racism that is condemned. While institutions and agency performances are sometimes found wanting, no one is responsible, no one is blamed or urged to act as individuals any differently.

The commission was concerned with maximizing the political legitimacy and acceptability of the *Report* and avoided criticizing those people and institutions on which it would have to depend for implementation. It thereby sought to avoid the divisiveness which might follow from such specificity. On the whole the commissioners were intrinsically supportive of basic American institutions in which they continued to have a major stake and within which they had built substantial careers. Whatever the mix of reasons, the "shining" Kerner *Report* is but an introduction to American racial problems. The chapters in which the agencies of stagnation are named and the strategies to end oppression are outlined remain to be written.

NOTES, CHAPTER 6

1. For an excellent review of literature bearing on the problem of organizational integration, see John F. Manley, *The Politics of Finance: The House Committee on Ways and Means* (Boston: Little, Brown, 1970), chs. 1, 3. Another study that focuses on problems of integration in potentially conflictual organizations, although from a somewhat different perspective, is Richard Fenno, Jr., "The House Appropriations Committee as a Political System: The Problem of Integration," *American Political Science Review* 56 (June 1962): 310-24.

2. As suggested above (ch. 3), the pressures of time and the perceived urgency of the task may partially substitute for the opportunities available to less pressured organizations to develop integration mechanisms.

3. See discussion in Manley, *Politics of Finance*, chs. 1, 3.

4. Status may be enhanced by the publicity surrounding a commission and the recognition implicit in such an appointment. Or it may be manifest more concretely in the rewards that are expected to accrue after service on the commission has ceased.

5. See James Thompson, *Organizations in Action* (New York: McGraw-Hill, 1967), pp. 52-55.

6. This presumably accounts for the surprise of Tom Wicker (who wrote the preface to the Bantam Books edition of the *Report*), that the Kerner Commission, comprised of "moderate" individuals, could produce the document it did. See the *Report*, pp. 5-11. See also Martha Derthick's proposition "that the origins of a commission. . .and its

composition. . .foreordain" a more liberal account of events than would be forthcoming from a local agency of opinion, in "On Commissionship—Presidential Variety," *Public Policy* 14, no. 4 (Fall 1971): 633.

7. Washington *Post*, 29 July 1967.

8. As early as September 12 the theme of white education had been incorporated into commission planning. See "Memorandum, Palmieri to Ginsburg, 12 September 1967," p. 1; and above.

9. Transcript, p. 1,103. For full reference see n. 61, ch. 4, in this volume. Our discussion of commissioners' initial and preliminary orientations is drawn from examination of the transcripts and interviews with informed observers of the commission's work. We were unable to conduct interviews with commissioners before and after the commission's work, which would have provided more valid and comprehensive data on attitudinal change. Thus we regard the evidence presented in this chapter as illustrative of a developmental process.

10. Ibid., pp. 1,100, 1,263, 1,621. See also p. 1,276; emphasis added.

11. Ibid., p. 1,107.

12. Lindsay, who had made the proposal at a dinner meeting the previous evening and was under the impression that a positive decision had been made, was not in attendance.

13. See Transcripts, pp. 1,106-1,115.

14. Ibid., pp. 1,110-1,111.

15. Transcript, pp. 1,143ff.

16. In this way the National Commission on the Causes and Prevention of Violence obtained the signatures of black commissioners Leon Higganbotham and Patricia Harris, who strongly disagreed with some of the emphases of the main document. See National Commission on the Causes and Prevention of Violence, *To Establish Justice, To Insure Domestic Tranquility* (New York: Award Books, 1969), pp. 119-20. For a discussion of some centripetal tendencies observed in President Nixon's Commission on Campus Unrest, see Martha Derthick, "On Commissionship," pp. 628-29.

17. From contemporary press reports. Kerner followed much the same itinerary during a four-hour tour of Newark on September 28.

18. Through a leak of a staff memo recounting this experience, this incident was reported widely in mid-November by columnists Rowland Evans and Robert Novak.

19. See, for example, Brooke's allusion to talks with "Mau Maus" (a militant group) during a trip to Harlem (Transcript, p. 1,590); McCulloch's statement that he felt in Detroit that the absence of consumer banking institutions contributed to the development of the

riots (Transcript, p. 2,927); Thornton's "reminder" to Wilkins of an aspect of public housing that they had discussed on their trip to Newark (Transcript, p. 2,019).

20. 1, 2, 9 August and again on 20 September 1967.

21. 9, 15, 22 August and 12 September. Testimony was taken on 5 October from Mayors Henry Maier (Milwaukee), Alfonso Cervantes (St. Louis), Thomas Whelan (Jersey City), and Theodore McKeldin (Baltimore). On 12 October the commission heard from representatives of Cincinnati, on 23 October from Los Angeles Mayor Samuel Yorty.

22. See the *Report*, pp. 29, 483.

23. See Transcripts, pp. 1,622ff., 1,121, 1,518-1,519, 1,583ff.

24. Transcripts, pp. 3,020, 2,932ff.

25. See "Memorandum, To: All Staff Members; From: John Koskinen; Subject: Meeting of Department Heads, Tuesday, October 10, 1967"; 12 October 1967, p. 2.

26. The experience of this commission thus suggests the hazards of thinking that staffs invariably tend to be more liberal than commissioners. See Derthick, "On Commissionship," p. 625.

27. Rather than endorse specific income-maintenance schemes, the commission limited its recommendation to the encouragement of a system of income supplementation with the general goals of supplementing workers' incomes and providing for those who could not work. See the *Report*, pp. 461, 466.

28. *Report*, p. 451. Robert Fogelson, a consultant to the commission, is most critical of its failure to deal more forcefully with issues of community control. See Robert Fogelson, *Violence as Protest* (New York: Doubleday, 1971), ch. 7.

29. *Report*, p. 412.

30. Ibid., p. 31.

31. Ibid., p. 203.

32. For example, one popular view is that large circulation is suggestive of widespread positive impact on white attitudes; alternatively, another popular interpretation is that extensive circulation represents an opportunity for mass catharsis and thus diminishes or at least does not improve the probabilities of material change.

33. Allan Silver, "Official Interpretations of Racial Riots," in *Urban Riots: Violence and Social Change*, Proceedings of the Academy of Political Science, ed. Robert H. Connery, vol. 24, no. 1 (New York, 1968), p. 151.

34. See *Report*, ch. 2.

35. Ibid., p. 412.

36. Allan Silver, "Official Interpretations of Racial Riots," p. 150.

III
RIOT COMMISSION POLITICS IN THREE AMERICAN CITIES

7 Official Investigations in Newark, Detroit, and Milwaukee

By the end of the 1960s, racial violence in American cities had reached unprecedented levels. During the "long, hot summer" of 1967, rioting affected more American cities with greater intensity than in any other year of our history: the Kerner Commission recorded a total of 164 civil disorders in 128 American cities. The number of deaths, injuries, arrests, amount of property damaged or destroyed and number of law enforcement personnel deployed to suppress the violence indicate that the three most severe civil disorders, in descending order of intensity, took place in Detroit, Newark and Milwaukee.[1] This ranking is confirmed if duration of rioting is used as an additional indicator of severity.[2]

Even though these disorders were national in scope and received a good deal of attention from the Kerner Commission, it would be a mistake to ignore the local-level response to them. At least four considerations compel us to examine political developments in the three cities which experienced the most severe riots. First, a major emphasis in most post-riot analyses was the extent to which local governments had been severely tested and found deficient in maintaining order. Second, the violence called into question the extent to which local governments set the stage for racial tensions through their educational policies, police practices and housing policies (formal

231

and informal). Moreover, the president and the Kerner Commission attempted to focus attention to some degree on local government responsiveness to black needs. Finally, if riot commissions as we have argued help to reassure the public and return political influence to the status quo, this must also happen on the local level.

The Newark civil disorder began on the evening of July 12 after the arrest and beating of John Smith, a black cab driver, and continued through July 17 until the combined forces of national guardsmen and city, county and state police succeeded in quelling the violence. The Newark civil disorder claimed the lives of 24 black civilians, one white fireman and one white policeman (see Table 7.1). Black citizens constituted 95 percent of the 1,500 persons arrested. Additionally, over $10 million worth of property damage occurred and estimates placed the number of injured persons at over 1,000.[3]

Five days later the most severe civil disorder of the decade began in Detroit after a police raid on an illegal social club in the black ghetto. For two days and nights violence raged, despite efforts of local, county and state police and national guardsmen. On July 24, President Johnson federalized the Michigan National Guard and dispatched 2,700 Army paratroopers to Detroit, the first time federal troops had been used to quell a domestic disturbance since President Roosevelt sent federal troops to suppress the 1943 Detroit race riot. The 1967 disorder continued for nearly two weeks, claimed the lives of 33 blacks and 10 whites, injured over 300 persons, accumulated property damage of $40-$45 million and resulted in the arrest of nearly 7,000 people (see Table 7.1). On July 27, while violence continued in Detroit, President Johnson called for a national day of prayer and announced the creation of the Kerner Commission.

Only three days after the president had made his announcement, the third most severe civil disorder of 1967 began in Milwaukee. It extended over eight days, although most of the looting, burning and personal injuries occurred during the first four days. Official control forces, including county and city police and national guardsmen, received assistance in suppressing the violence when Mayor Henry W. Maier imposed a strict curfew on the entire city.[4] The disorder resulted in four deaths, over 1,500 arrests and undetermined injuries and property damage.

The intensity and duration of racial violence in these cities, particularly in Detroit and Newark, and the helplessness of local and state law enforcement agencies before it, shocked an uneasy public and

TABLE 7.1

Data on the Three Most Severe Civil Disorders in 1967

Riot City	Dates of Duration	Number of Deaths	Number of Injuries	Number of Arrests	Property Damage
Detroit	July 22-August 2	33 Blacks 10 Whites 43 Total	300+	7,000	$40-45 million
Newark	July 12-July 17	24 Blacks 2 Whites 26 Total	1,000+	1,500	$10 million
Milwaukee	July 30-August 6	4	Undetermined	1,500	Undetermined

Sources: National Advisory Commission on Civil Disorders and Governor's Select Commission on Civil Disorder

focused the nation's attention on the issue of black rebellion. When the violence finally ended, the nation began the tasks of interpreting and acting upon the civil disorders. Within the riot cities themselves, doubts, antagonisms and uncertainties generated by the rioting created demands on public officials to develop acceptable interpretations and responses.

Pre-Commission Politics: Imperatives to Investigate

Because of the common belief that "it couldn't happen here," citizens as well as elites were incredulous when riots broke out in their city. The relative absence of race warfare since the end of World War II contributed to the shock at black violence against white institutions and representatives of white authority. Awareness that the police and the Army had been ineffectual engendered the spread of rumors, heightened concern for ending the violence and generated demands that something be done.

Numerous uncertainties arose during the last days of the disorders and immediately after order was restored. Elites and citizens alike wanted to know why the disorders occurred when and where they did, who took part in the violence, why local police proved unable to control the rioting and what measures might prevent a recurrence of the violence. The unsettled environment in the aftermath of racial violence contributed to mass uncertainties, as did the simplistic, contradictory and at times inflammatory interpretations of the events made by elites.

In this chapter we attempt to account for the seemingly uniform imperative to convene investigations of civil disorders by focusing on the interplay between mass needs and elite behavior in the aftermath of racial violence. In the three cities with the most severe disorders, several patterns of elite response were observable. But the creation of municipal riot investigations seems to have been the most appealing recourse available to public officials and the most effective way to reduce mass anxieties and conflicting claims.

Mass Demands On Leaders

An initial implication drawn from the outbreak of racial violence was that city administrations and especially municipal executives were responsible because they had failed to adopt programs addressing needs in black neighborhoods or were unable to control and suppress racial violence. At times the indictment of municipal administrations came from national sources. While violence continued in Newark, an emergency resolution by the NAACP, meeting in national convention in

234

Boston, charged Newark's city administration with failure "to take corrective action to meet many of the grave social ills of the Negro community."[5] Local residents attributed similar inadequacies to city officials in Detroit, castigating the administration not only for its failure to develop social programs for blacks, but also for placing too many constraints on local police.

Sixty-four leading Newark religious, civil rights and education leaders formed the "Committee of Concern" and charged that black people were "shot, beaten and brutalized...without regard to wrongdoing" by city police and national guardsmen. Mayor Hugh J. Addonizio granted a hearing to the committee, which then proposed that a massive reform program be adopted. The mayor responded, "Now that the violence has ended, perhaps city hall can get back to normal." But a committee member pleaded, "No not that! Normalcy is what got us in this trouble."[6] In Detroit, despite the presidential call for a national day of prayer and a national riot commission, various citizen groups demanded tougher police responses to violence while other groups insisted that Mayor Jerome P. Cavanagh adopt corrective programs.

On a national level, Mayor Henry W. Maier was acclaimed for his role in suppressing the Milwaukee disorder. In 1966 the mayor had formulated a "Manual of Procedure in Civil Emergency" which provided for a citywide curfew, immediate call-up of the national guard and a "hot line" between the mayor's office and the governor's office. The immediate deployment of the emergency riot plan elicited widespread praise:

Like no other mayor of a northern city, Mr. Maier responded quickly with a tough, detailed plan for a curfew written last year. It had the city transformed within hours.
—*New York Times*

Mayor Henry W. Maier views himself as a "municipal scientist" but behind his articulation of clinical solutions to the city's ills lies the muscle of a German general.[7]
—*Chicago Sun Times*

But local citizens and groups did not receive the mayor's actions with such uniform applause. The Greater Milwaukee Conference on Religion and Race, for example, expressed the fear "that what Milwaukee and the rest of the country will learn is that Milwaukee can achieve the championship for controlling a riot [and] that it will be the only lesson learned."8 A spokesman for the conference urged reforms in employment, housing, education and police policies affecting blacks.

Groups in Milwaukee's black community claimed that the mayor was more concerned with suppressing violence than addressing its causes. Even as violence continued, black organizations interpreted the disorder as positive proof that the city administration had failed to pay attention to problems affecting Milwaukee's black community. At the height of the violence, 23 representatives of some 15 black-oriented groups formed an organization called "Common View" to express their version of what the disorder meant and to prescribe appropriate responses. They blamed the disorder on the city administration, with particular reference to the mayor:

> The mayor and city administration have circumvented the constant needs for equality of opportunity. (Education, housing, employment, police community relations, etc.)

> Local government has ignored studies citing the causes of riots, the sub-standard conditions that have long existed, yet has continued to exploit the community through lack of enforcing housing ordinances, providing equal employment opportunities, creating equal educational opportunities, etc.

> The city administration and the white system called the shots and set the guidelines for communications in the traditional paternalistic manner which was acceptable to them, with no intention to follow up with affirmative action.

> The mayor heads a structure which is the most segregated and discriminating institution in the community.

The group called for massive reforms in education, housing, employment and police-community relations. The Common View statement concluded with the threat: "If the black voices in the community remain unheeded and affirmative action programs are not implemented, the Milwaukee community will continue to suffer. Black people want control of their community."9

Mayor Maier responded to the statement by challenging the group's representativeness: "We don't have what I consider to be any single, valid, effective Negro leader. There is a divergence of leadership." Common View members interpreted the remark not as a description of Milwaukee's black leadership structure, but as criticism for the absence of a single, valid, effective black leader. Wesley L. Scott, executive director of the Milwaukee Urban League and a member of Common View, stressed the positive aspects of the group's actions: "What Henry refuses to acknowledge is that we are not here to fight with him but to offer our co-operation."[10] The mayor's office did schedule a meeting with representatives from Common View, but Maier failed to attend. In response, the representatives walked out on the mayor's aides, with one black leader protesting, "We've been trying for months to get in touch with the mayor, but it ain't done us no good. This riot ain't gonna stop until he comes to us."[11]

The civil disorder aroused the concern of other groups about appropriate responses. The Urban League of Milwaukee called an emergency meeting of 45 representatives of ten voluntary groups from the black community to discuss the shooting of an 18-year-old black and brutality by police and National Guardsmen during the civil disorder. The Urban League's research director, Corneff R. Taylor, summarized the meeting by criticizing the mayor: "A lot of people are concerned as well as angry. Everybody recognizes the need for something to be done which is not being done. The thing seems to point to the second floor of city hall."[12] Father James E. Groppi, adviser to the Milwaukee NAACP Youth Council, charged that the shooting of the 18-year-old constituted "murder" and that the violence was not a riot but a rebellion in which "these young people were fighting for what they believe to be a noble cause."[13] Representatives from Milwaukee's community action program voted to lodge written protests against police behavior during the disorder and against Maier's stringent measures in putting down the violence. Finally, the executive board of the Milwaukee Labor Council called for education, housing and employment reforms in respect to conditions it blamed for the disorders.

Public officials viewed the disorder in different ways, creating conflicting interpretations of appropriate postriot responses. Wisconsin Governor Warren P. Knowles committed himself to "an all-out campaign" to deal with problems of Milwaukee blacks. He emphasized improved communication and increased job opportunities as priority items. His appointed chairman of the State Industrial Commission, Joseph C. Fagan, urged Maier to open a dialogue with inner-city blacks.

Former Milwaukee Socialist Mayor Frank P. Zeidler accused Maier of ignoring black problems of which he had been warned earlier. Alderman Robert O. Ertl used the disorder as an occasion to revive the city's Model Cities application which the Common (city) Council had previously refused to approve. Other public officials opposed "rewarding" rioters for their violent behavior. County Executive Robert Doyne, for example, interpreted the disorder as "a conspiracy against law and order aimed at the police department," which should not be followed by special programs for blacks.[14] Some city aldermen called for programs to rebuild predominantly white-owned business establishments destroyed during the riot.

Mayor Maier's interpretation of the disorder differed from those of aroused black groups and led to quite different recommendations for appropriate responses to the violence. After lamenting the absence of a single, valid, effective black leader, he placed blame for the disorder on "so-called civil rights leaders who have been encouraging defiance of the law."[15] Pending further study, he withheld concluding that the riot was an organized disruption, but did say that 99.8 percent of Milwaukee's 90,000 Negroes did not participate in the disorder.[16]

Both national and local sources thus implicitly or explicitly criticized the city administrations for their alleged shortcomings. Some censured city administrations for failing to upgrade the status of blacks; others indicted municipal executives for not providing sufficient police power. In response to both types of criticism, the mayors tried to appear "cool" under conditions of crisis and escalating mass demands. Maier responded to the news of violence in Milwaukee, for example, by announcing: "I was not astonished we had a riot. I am astonished it did not come sooner. I had it down [pinpointed] to about within one week."[17] During the early stages of Newark's rioting Mayor Addonizio similarly tried to seem fully in control of events. The following account describes his handling of initial demands that "something be done":

The Mayor called in civil rights leaders, including both moderate ministers and some of his more militant opponents. Concessions were made. Addonizio decided to ask for City Council funds to allow additional police captaincies so that a qualified Negro officer, Eddie Williams, could become the first Negro captain. He requested that Human Rights Director James Threatt and Police Director Dominick Spina separately investigate Wednesday's conflict. He reassigned the two patrolmen who beat Smith to "administrative positions." He referred the Smith case to the county prosecutor and FBI. He announced formation of a Blue Ribbon Commission, like the McCone Commission that investigated Watts, to examine this "isolated incident." The Mayor was doing what militant politicians were demanding. But when someone told him point blank that the people had lost confidence in his administration, Addonizio replied: "That's politics. Sit down. You've said enough."[18]

The mayor's attempt to project an image of being in control failed; the "isolated incident" escalated into the second most severe civil disorder of 1967.

Public officials attempted to treat the disorders as commonplace, to deemphasize the violence and in a limited fashion to satisfy their aroused constituencies. But the severity of the violence, the intensity of attitudes and the enduring the heightened conflict rendered such actions unacceptable to citizens who demanded comprehensible explanations and visible, acceptable actions. The genesis of riot investigations may be traced to unresolved mass uncertainties and elite needs to provide an image of responsive action.

Elite Response To Mass Demands: "False Starts"

In Newark, Detroit and Milwaukee, demands for investigations into the violence were directed primarily at local public officials. Eventually, for reasons suggested earlier, "official" investigations were launched, followed by the development of what we have termed "competing" investigations. Significant insight into the development of riot investigations and the functions they serve may be gained by reviewing the "false starts" toward "official" investigations initiated by public officials groping their way toward the management of public conflict. Each of the "false starts" constituted a "competing" investigation to the extent that it threatened to capture the field of investigation at the expense of the official riot commissions.

The usefulness of convening a commission to investigate Newark's disorder was recognized by Mayor Addonizio, who promised to create a "Blue Ribbon Commission" the day after what he labeled an "isolated incident" began. The promised commission aborted, however, when racial violence escalated into more severe dimensions during the next five days. A second false start was initiated in an effort to submit to investigation sensitive charges concerning improper state police behavior. In response to allegations of unlawful activity by the state police, particularly brutality against black citizens and indiscriminate firing into black-owned stores, Governor Richard J. Hughes promised a thorough inquiry into the charges. He ordered a senior officer of the state police to investigate charges of official misconduct by Newark police, state police and National Guardsmen. On July 16, the day before the disorder ended, Hughes promised that "all reports of excessive behavior would be handled by the troopers' own investigative unit. If charges were proven true. . .'justice will be done.' "[19] The promised investigation remained unpublicized, however, until the main riot commission in Newark condemned the state police for engaging in official violence. At that time the state police defended itself by alluding to an investigation conducted by and on itself.

As violence continued to escalate in Detroit, demands on public officials also increased. The Michigan Civil Rights Commission urged an official inquiry into the rioting. It circulated a two-page proposal on how the inquiry should be conducted and suggested a group like itself to sponsor the study.[20] Detroit's only black city councilman, Nicholas Hood, charged the police with brutality and called for a complete investigation for which "he offered to produce affidavit upon affidavit in support of the charges." Law enforcement officers responded to the allegations with counter charges that "professional agitators, both from Detroit and outside, instigated Detroit's devastating riot," and said they welcomed a neutral and thorough investigation of the disorder.[21] The Detroit city council asked Mayor Cavanagh to appear before it to explain how he planned to respond to the violence.

While charges and questions mounted, no less than four state legislative committees threatened to preempt the field of study. State Senator Robert J. Hubor, a Republican, suggested that his Municipalities Committee could most appropriately study the disorder because it was composed primarily of former mayors and township supervisors. James Del Rio, a black legislator from Detroit, had already been authorized to head an inquiry into Detroit's poverty program and other lawmakers expected him to expand his study to include at least some aspects of the Detroit riot. On August 2 the State Senate broadened the scope of Senator James G. Fleming's Crime Investigation Committee to include civil disorders, added two members and boosted its appropriation from $3,000 to $10,000. Finally, a "supercommittee" or "coordinating committee" composed of five members from each chamber of the state legislature began attempts to supervise the various legislative inquiries into Detroit's disorder. The chairman of this committee explained the proliferation of investigations: "The minute something like this (disorder) happens, you know how politicians want to go out and make headlines."[22] Headlines were indeed made; nevertheless the preceding studies were never completed.

The initial suggestion for an investigation of the Milwaukee civil disorder came from Governor Knowles. After the first day of violence he released a statement commending law enforcement officers and urging formation of a study group to investigate the causes of and remedies for racial violence. Concurrently, Milwaukee state Senator Martin Schreiber proposed an investigation by the State Board of Government Operations. This proposal drew opposition from Republican board members who feared that partisan politics would dominate the inquiry. Republican state Senator Walter Hollander, chairman of the board suggested instead that Governor Knowles appoint a "blue ribbon" citizens' commission. Knowles said the suggestion had merit, but wanted to discuss it with Mayor Maier before taking action. Maier then requested the governor not to appoint an investigative commission until his office had gathered and processed information on the education, economic and residency characteristics of those arrested during the disorder. Neither the proposed gubernatorial commission nor Maier's promised study were ever completed.

In an address carried on local television and radio two days after Milwaukee's disorder ended, Maier again urged that the city council fund a study to be conducted by a local team of experts. Maier proposed the study in language consistent with depicting the rioters as riffraff:

> We must find out who the lawless are. We must find out where they came from, and how long they have been here. We must find out why they took up the gun and the torch and acted outside the law. To accomplish this, we will need a factual, detailed profile of the lawless. We will need to know as much about them as possible. Such a profile might dictate meaningful programs to help remedy some of the basic causes of the disturbances and thus prevent civil disorder in the future. There are hundreds of records that will have to be gathered and sifted. Policemen can furnish some of this data. A team of experts—possibly volunteers from our universities—should be established to prepare the kind of questions that will be needed to get an accurate profile of the lawless. I will ask the Common Council tomorrow to underwrite the gathering of this necessary information.[23]

Maier followed up the speech by submitting a resolution to Milwaukee's common council requesting $3,000 to fund the study. The common council created a special committee to study riot-related matters, including the mayor's request. This committee rejected the mayor's request because a similar study had been announced earlier by the Milwaukee Urban League. Mayor Maier's proposed study of rioters' characteristics thus died for lack of funding.

The numerous false starts toward investigations in each of the riot cities emphasize public officials' attraction to bodies of inquiry into severe disruption of established routines in the life of municipalities. The crises created by civil disorders could not adequately be addressed by rhetoric or initial interpretations. The public propensity to demand immediate, visible and formal action (although usually inchoate as to actual content) was matched by their leaders' predilection for attempting to convene *ad hoc* bodies of investigation. This pattern of demands for action and attempts at response varied little from city to city or from group to group within the cities.

The Official Riot Commissions

While many of the attempts to set up commissions of investigation ended up as false starts, some did not. The investigative imperative appears to be inexorable as a post-riot-response pattern, even on the local level. The appointment, deliberations and recommendations of local riot commissions that did not end up as false starts were easily the most significant political developments initiated by local officials following the racial violence in Detroit, Milwaukee and Newark. The process of commissioning and the commissions' end products received greater attention than any other official postriot development in the cities. These locally focused riot commissions shared several common characteristics. All were "official" commissions by virtue of the status assigned to them by the appointing political executives. Reflective of the themes suggested earlier, each commission experienced important constraints on its internal proceedings and external relations because of its temporary, *ad hoc* nature. Additionally, the commissions' recommendations tended to favor some political interests and disadvantage others in a pattern consistent with the interests represented on the commissions. All three riot commissions engaged in activities within several of the seven performance areas outlined earlier, but they did so at different times and to varying degrees. While one riot commission primarily recommended policy, another mainly evaluated and developed policy alternatives. The third took fact-finding and research as its primary role. The local commissions exhibited important differences in organization, the thoroughness of their investigations, the extent to which they claimed to be representative and the degree of outside intervention in their deliberations.

Newark: The Governor's Commission

Newark did not have a municipal riot commission. Mayor Addonizio's "Blue Ribbon Commission," proposed after what Addonizio said was an "isolated incident," proved to be a false start. Governor Hughes's promise to have the state police investigate allegations of police misconduct failed to mollify public concern. As rioting continued in Newark, Hughes decided to appoint his own commission of leading citizens to study the violence.

After announcing his intention to appoint a commission, the governor immediately began to recruit members for the study panel. He contacted two former New Jersey governors about their willingness to serve on the panel, and after receiving positive responses from them, he selected as chairman the president of the New Jersey Bell Telephone Company. Just two days after he withdrew National Guard forces from Newark, Hughes announced the appointment of his 11-member blue ribbon panel, which consisted of seven white and four black members:

1. Chairman Robert D. Lilley of Short Hills, N.J.; president of New Jersey Bell Telephone Company and director of Fidelity Union Trust Company.
2. Vice-chairman Raymond A. Brown of Jersey City, N.J.; member of the New Jersey Bar Association and past president of the Jersey City NAACP.
3. Alfred E. Driscoll of Mendham, N.J.; Republican governor of New Jersey from 1947 to 1953 and president of Warner-Lambert Pharmaceutical Company.
4. The Rev. John J. Dougherty of South Orange, N.J.; president of Seton Hall University and Auxiliary Bishop of the Roman Catholic Diocese of Newark.
5. Dean Clyde Ferguson of Washington, D.C.; dean of the Howard University Law School.
6. John J. Gibbons of Short Hills, N.J.; president of the New Jersey Bar Association.
7. Ben Z. Leuchter of Vineland, N.J.; editor of the Vineland *Times-Journal.*

8. Oliver Lofton of Newark, N.J.; director of the Newark Legal Services Project.
9. Robert B. Meyner of Princeton, N.J.; Democratic governor of New Jersey from 1953 to 1961 and a lawyer practicing in Newark.
10. The Rev. Prince A. Taylor of Princeton, N.J.; Bishop of the New Jersey Area of the Methodist Church.
11. William A. Wachenfeld of Orange, N.J.; former Essex County Prosecutor and Justice of the New Jersey Supreme Court from 1946 to 1959.[24]

Hughes was unsuccessful in recruiting at least one other panel member, the noted psychologist Kenneth B. Clark. In choosing the panel's chairman, Hughes avoided possible partisan connotations by passing over both former governors in favor of the established businessman Robert Lilley.

Although announced to the public on July 19, the panel did not receive its formal charge from Hughes until three weeks later. In the interim, Hughes continued to refer to the group as a "blue ribbon" panel until giving it (on August 8) the formal title of the Governor's Select Commission on Civil Disorder. The study group's tasks as well as its title remained in doubt during the interim period.[25]

The formal charge to the commission specified three primary areas of inquiry: "Examining the causes, the incidents, and the remedies for the civil disorders which have afflicted New Jersey."[26] Six months later the Governor's Commission produced a unanimous 200-page report, divided into three sections, on "the sources of tension," "the disorders" and "recommendations," which parallel the three areas of the governor's charge. In producing its *Report for Action*, the commission held 65 meetings, heard 106 witnesses, developed a transcript of 5000 pages, collected 121 exhibits, conducted 700 staff interviews and made several field trips into riot neighborhoods. This was accomplished despite many of the usual organizational obstacles encountered by riot commissions. Indicative of difficulties encountered in attracting qualified staff, the commission was unable to appoint an executive director until after it had conducted several meetings and one formal hearing. On August 16, Hughes appointed Sanford M. Jaffe as the commission's executive director.[27] Jaffe and chairman Lilley in turn recruited Robert B. Goldman as deputy director. Lilley, Jaffe and Goldman assembled the remaining 28 staff members over a three-week period. Thus, the commission's staff did not begin research work until mid-September, nearly two months after Hughes had announced formation of the panel.

The kinds of staff the commission wanted to hire led to further delays. It desired qualified persons with proven expertise, but could offer such people at a maximum only three months of employment and, like the Kerner Commission, the recruitment effort took place in August when university-affiliated persons were already committed for the academic year. The commission thus revised its criteria and accepted availability as the most important qualification for employment. Those who tended to meet this primary criterion were law students, graduate students, staff from other government agencies and unemployed community residents with prior involvement in specialized areas of interest to the commission. The Governor's Commission recruited heavily from the Woodrow Wilson School of Princeton University and made liberal use of specialists from the New Jersey Department of Community Affairs. Only about one-third of the staff were full-time.

Conscious efforts were made to promote harmony between staff and commissioners. Selected staff members attended commission meetings and Jaffe invited some staff members to attend commission dinners. These and other informal techniques promoting cordial relations between staff and commissioners may partially account for the absence of publicized staff resignations or public criticism of the commission's work, in contrast to the McCone and Kerner Commission experiences.

Research papers on specialized areas, varying in length from 25 to 50 pages were developed by the staff. Each staff person responsible for a specialized area presented his or her paper before commissioners and defended it. The staff's performance received almost uniform praise from commissioners with the single exception of staff research on public welfare. A typical assessment of staff input into the final report by one commissioner contends that:

> The staff's factual material was, in large part, accepted by the commission and incorporated into the report. However, the transcript of the report and especially the recommendations were the making of the commissioners themselves. We rejected staff suggestions for recommendations more often than not.[28]

Although the commission resolved early problems involving staff recruitment, it lacked a clear statement of tasks beyond the governor's charge. Jaffe developed an outline charting areas of investigation that closely paralleled the governor's suggestions calling for inquiry into sociological conditions in the black community, a description of riot events and recommendations for action. The outline was approved by commissioners and became the agenda for commission deliberations. Like Ginsburg's original outline for the Kerner Commission, Jaffe's outline defined boundaries beyond which the commission would not venture and focused staff work on immediate problems requiring research. One comissioner observed: "If you look at the tentative outline and compare it with the *Report for Action* in its final form, you will see how closely the two match."

The Governor's Commission was constrained by the disparity between Hughes's expectations of the commission and the time and resources he allocated to fulfill those expectations. When Hughes appointed the commission, he anticipated a December 1, 1967 deadline for a final report. The commission wanted to meet the projected date so that its recommendations could be considered in the governor's budget message to the legislature. It also wanted its report to be a matter of public record before the Kerner Commission released its findings. Rumors that the Kerner Commission's interim report would take a "hard line" on the disorders made this all the more urgent. Moreover, the Governor's Commission anticipated (probably correctly) that its work would receive greater visibility if it reported before the Kerner Commission.

Unexpected delays in receiving its charge and recruiting staff effectively prohibited the commission from releasing a final report by December 1. The commission moved the target date up to January 1, then January 15 as staff hearings continued as late as January 4. February 1 then became the commission's target date. On February 10, six and one half months after appointment, the commission released its final report.

Time limitations affected the commission process in important ways, forcing the commission to define its tasks during the initial meetings and to accept compromises in staffing arrangements. Time limitations also precluded investigation by staff and commissioners into questions peripheral to the outline but of possible relevance. In searching for information the commission deferred to other groups on some questions[29] and contracted for research on other questions.[30] In other areas of study, the commission could not overcome its time limitations.

In considering public welfare issues, for example, the staff produced what most commissioners viewed as a clearly inferior document, but it had to suffice.[31]

While insufficient time may have impaired performance of some tasks, it fostered harmony among commissioners during deliberations and contributed to unanimity on the final report. With a deadline confronting it virtually from its appointment, commission members tailored their divergent interests to permit agreement on a final report. As deadlines passed, the drive for unanimity increased. The chairman described the impact of time limitations: "We did more in six months than we could have in two years as an ongoing commission. The time deadline made us work. Also this produced closer feelings of in-group belonging than would otherwise have been the case." The staff director concurred:

> We aimed for January 15, 1968. We missed that. At this point everyone had reached the point of just getting done with the thing—the commissioners, all of them prominent men, had taken hours and hours from their business practices. The staff was reaching its end of the rope. So, we just wanted to finish the report and get it out. This aided in the resolution of the differences we had and led to the issuance of the report.

Riot commissions, as suggested earlier, tend to receive fewer operating resources than they require and than they are initially promised. The Governor's Commission confronted such problems. Initially Hughes estimated that $15,000 would cover expenses. Commission members and high-level staff argued during the appointment process that between $150,000 and $200,000 would be necessary to fulfill the governor's expectations and some made increased finances a condition of appointment. On August 18, one month after creating the commission, Hughes made $100,000 immediately available from his emergency fund and indicated additional finances could be obtained if needed. At mid-point in the commission's life, chairman Lilley petitioned the governor for an additional $50,000, but the request was not immediately acted upon. Lacking operating funds, Lilley tapped the resources of New Jersey Bell Telephone Company for secretarial personnel and meeting facilities. Hughes eventually provided the requested $50,000, bringing the commission's total public funds to $150,000, but only after repeated delays which precluded research in certain areas and deflected attention away from pressing work in order to secure necessary funding.

The Governor's Commission also encountered difficulties concerning issues of immunity. Safeguards against possible lawsuits directed at commissioners became an issue in late November. Evidence gathered concerning misconduct by city and state police and national guardsmen forecast unequivocal condemnation of law enforcement officers' conduct in the final report; but this opened up the possibility of legal costs and damage suits.

The commission requested and the Hughes administration drafted a bill granting legislative immunity to commissioners and staff. Essex County (which includes Newark) Democrats sponsored the bill in the New Jersey Assembly, where it passed; but on December 11 it was defeated in the State Senate by six votes with all four Essex County Democrats among those abstaining. Their rationale was conveyed by the leader of the Essex County Senate delegation who "told reporters that police spokesmen were opposed to giving the commission a blank check to make any kind of charges against the police as a result of their role in the Newark and Plainfield riots last July."[32] The State Senate reconsidered and passed the bill in late December after Hughes expended considerable effort on its behalf.[33] The commission's difficulty in obtaining immunity illustrates problems of scope of power persistently encountered by riot commissions.

The *Report For Action* is essentially a unanimous document, yet the commissioners represented diverse and often conflicting interests. Hughes appointed commissioners ostensibly because of their social position, group membership and leadership. The commission included prominent lawyers, businessmen, church officials, academicians, public officials and civil rights figures. Ideologically they ranged from conservative former New Jersey Supreme Court Justice Wachenfeld to black militant, poverty program director Lofton.

The requirement for representation of diverse interests, as we have previously suggested, builds in tendencies toward fragmentation. The Governor's Commission countered this tendency in several ways. A first order of business was to read Robert Fogelson's critical study of the McCone Commission, which introduced staff and commissioners to the nature of their tasks and to the possibility of a minority or dissenting opinion.[34] Early in the commission's life, tours through Newark's ghettos introduced commissioners to conditions in the black community; some members credited the tours with creating a sense of urgency among more conservative members. Dramatic testimony by black businessmen whose stores were shot up by state police and National Guardsmen also disturbed those initially inclined to defend police action. The chairman commented:

> It is fair to say that it was the attitudes and opinions of the whites that changed on this commission. As they were exposed to what goes on in the black man's life each day, they changed. As an example, one man came to the commission being entirely in support of the State Police, and when he left the commission six months later, he was their severest critic.

Public testimony at hearings also was influential, as the recital of wrongdoings by the police gained an impact.[35]

The commission's schedule helped commit members to the group enterprise. The commission averaged between three and four meetings each week during actual operations,[36] which usually lasted all day and sometimes late into the night. Individual commissioners claimed that this work schedule produced a report authored by commissioners with the assistance of staff, rather than vice versa, and they attribute willingness to compromise on strongly felt positions to the amount of time spent in deliberations.

Concern that the report have maximum impact contributed to agreement on disputed points and to support for the final document. One commissioner explained that "this unity in the report is important, especially in terms of our ability to put pressure on the legislature. Any legislature will attempt to exploit a split in commission recommendations. Even if it's not an apparent split, but a difference over philosophy—they will get to it." All ten commissioners signed the *Report for Action* with no dissenting comments.

Sharp differences of opinion among commissioners did surface during the writing stage. The most divisive issue was a proposal for metropolitan consolidation in Essex County. It recommended that "the administration and financing of certain basic services, such as the police, should be consolidated throughout Essex County." One faction of the commission argued, however, for additional consolidation of governmental units as the only hope for relieving Newark's intractable problems and their arguments were expressed in the commission's final report.[37] Other commissioners argued against consolidation on the ground that Newark's black population would lose its recently achieved majority status; their arguments were also included in the final document.[38]

Commissioner Gibbons's description of the consolidation controversy offers insight into internal commission divisions and bargaining:

> The commission was split evenly, with five members favoring political consolidation and five members opposed to it. I led the faction favoring political consolidation while Governor Meyner led the faction opposed to it. My argument was that the center city had lost its capacity for solving its financial problems, and all social problems that depend on that financing, because of the movement of new industry and persons with a larger taxable base to the suburbs. I felt very strongly on this issue and fought rather hard for it. At one point in the commission's deliberations I had a majority and thought that we would carry the day. At that point Governor Meyner threatened a minority report. He felt as strongly about the issue as I did. He is one of the leading candidates for the governorship now and he saw political dynamite in this issue. He argued that consolidation would prevent Negroes from getting elected to major offices, such as mayor, when they were numerically reaching that possibility. I guess that proved to be a fairly effective argument because I lost my majority and then notified Governor Meyner that we would file a dissenting statement if they reached a majority. We finally compromised on this, the most heated issue that arose before us, by offering our recommendations on political consolidation in the rather fuzzy language that we did.

Differences on political consolidation remained, but at the same time they did not publicly rend the commission through dissenting opinions, minority reports or resignations.

The bargaining among commissioners over the issue of metropolitan consolidation, with each side calculating the consequences of its position and eventually compromising, illustrates the attention the commission devoted to establishing the political legitimacy of its findings and recommendations. It did not devote a comparable degree of attention to establishing its scientific legitimacy. In fact, early in its deliberations, the commission consciously disavowed the view that it need explain in any profound way the underlying causes of the disorders. Instead it relied on descriptive characterizations of controversial issues and events that preceded the rioting and chose to give a relatively innocuous narrative of the riot events themselves. These sections of the report provide only the most rudimentary understanding of why the disorders occurred, how many people participated and what their characteristics were. Again, this strategy was deliberate, in part because of insufficient time to conduct highly technical research, but also because it had learned that the Kerner Commission would address these subjects. Choosing to either ignore controversial subjects in this area or report on them in a somewhat bland manner also enhanced the likelihood that commission recommendations would be accepted.

Although it avoided potentially controversial items, the Governor's Commission tried to give its investigation the appearance of being based upon scientifically defensible foundations. Assuredly, minimum requirements for scientific validity were portrayed. The commission contracted for survey data on attitudes in Newark, retained consultants in specialized areas and gave the impression of thoroughly searching for relevant information throughout the hearings. But the report presents only isolated findings obtained through the $27,000 survey of Newark residents,[39] relies only inferentially on consultants' papers[40] and derives most of its information from testimony compiled during public hearings; usually a less systematic data base than survey evidence or consultants' papers. This also demonstrates the minimal threshold of scientific investigation acceptable to the commission. These particular commissioners, seven of whom were lawyers, relied in the end upon familiar, conventional and "political" learning processes.

The title of the final document, *Report For Action*, testifies to the commission's concern for the political acceptability of its recommendations. So too does the language used throughout the document: "We have not engaged in studies for studies' sake," and "in the spirit of practicality that motivated us, we focused our attention on what the people of our State and our communities can do." The commission introduced its report in language conforming to traditionally accepted beliefs. It condemned those who engage in violence and emphasized the goals of "equality" and "integration" in prescribing the American creed as its framework of beliefs.[41]

Despite its concern about political legitimacy, the commission did not shy away from politically controversial subjects. The relationship between the city administration in Newark and the black community there received close scrutiny. The commission devoted several sections of its report to shortcomings of the Addonizio administration. It critically reviewed inadequacies in city agencies' performances, condemned the city administration for displaying insensitivity to the black

251

community and concluded that "distrust, resentment and bitterness" characterized police-community relations in Newark. A second politically controversial area was the behavior of law enforcement officers and agencies during the disorders. Police forces, the commission noted, had expended ammunition in amounts "out of all proportion to the mission assigned to them"; and it strongly condemned the conduct of state police and National Guardsmen for firing into black-owned stores with "no possible justification."[42]

The seeming contradiction between the concern for political legitimacy and the involvement with politically controversial subjects may be resolved in part by recalling the jurisdictional level at which the commission operated. The Governor's Commission was created at the state level and received funding and other assistance from Hughes. It is not coincidental that the Addonizio administration in Newark received the main brunt of criticism. An analysis of the governmental levels targeted for reform in the 99 recommendations contained in the *Report For Action* shows that the largest number of recommendations were targeted to the city level; no fewer than 33 reform proposals were aimed at Newark (and if Englewood and Plainfield are included the total number of municipal recommendations is 38) (see Table 7.2). In addition, reforms proposed for the city level were much more comprehensive than those aimed at the state jurisdiction (see chapter 9). The number and kind of recommendations directed toward different governmental jurisdictions shows that the quest for political legitimacy need not be immune from the representation of certain interests at the expense of others.

The character and number of recommendations addressed to the city and state level respectively embroiled the commission in considerable controversy and in part undermined its claim to political legitimacy. Critics discerned in the *Report For Action* the visible imprint of Governor Hughes. Besides appointing the commission's members (none of whom directly or indirectly represented the Addonizio administration) and charging it with a formal set of tasks, Hughes helped the commission recruit a staff director and other staff assistants, assisted it in securing legislative immunity and granted it necessary money from his contingency fund.

This close relationship generated claims that Hughes had edited the final version of the report to his liking. Addonizio's administrative assistant Donald Malafronte charged:

There is absolutely no question in my mind but what Governor

TABLE 7.2

**Governor's Commission's Recommendations
by Jurisdiction Targeted for Reform**

Governmental Jurisdiction	Number of Recommendations
Newark	33
Essex County	6
State of New Jersey	29
Federal Government	4
Combined or no jurisdiction specified	22
Englewood	2
Plainfield	3
Total	99

Hughes edited the riot commission report to his own liking. How else could they single the mayor out and whip him as badly as they did while at the same time not touching the governor at all? You see, these commissions are really rigged. That is, the guy who appoints them puts his people on them, tells them what to look at, instructs them how to do it, gets them financing and all the rest. Of course, these types of commissions will only deal favorably with the men who create them. This is natural.

Commission members and staff personnel categorically denied the charge. As one commissioner put it:

Governor Hughes issued some communications to the commission during our deliberations, but he in no way interfered or tried to influence our work. The report was submitted to him, but he made absolutely no revisions of the draft. The draft that was printed as *Report For Action* is exactly the same document as the draft that was submitted to the governor. In fact, on Friday, February 9th, the press was given the draft at 10:00 a.m., the governor got his copy of the draft at 4:00 p.m. and the next day—Saturday, February 10th—the report was issued to the public at our press conference. Now, how could the governor influence the report under these circumstances?

Although Malafronte and other commission opponents were probably mistaken in alleging that Hughes edited the final report, their charge nevertheless contains more than a grain of truth. The commission severely criticized Newark public officials, but did not mention Hughes's behavior or public statements during the disorder, although black residents perceived them to be highly inflammatory.[43] The commission gained information about these inflammatory remarks by collecting transcripts of five separate public statements by Hughes during the disorder and six speeches by and interviews with him after the disorder.[44] It also received unsolicited reports from city agencies which had adopted the governor's remarks to legitimize their own inappropriate behavior during the disorder.[45]

The commission's obvious reluctance to criticize the governor's inflammatory rhetoric may be explained by the fact that he had appointed each commissioner. Commissioners also realized that implementation of proposed reforms depended, to an extent, upon the governor's favorable reception of the report. To criticize his behavior during the disorder could by this logic violate the political legitimacy the commission sought at the state level and jeopardize future support.

Concern about the implementation of its recommendations led to an additional exchange between the commission and Hughes. As deliberations came to an end, several commissioners seized upon the idea, not unique to this commission, of extending the commission's life to assure that its efforts would be heeded. A letter from chairman Lilley to Hughes conveyed the commissioners' sentiments:

> In accordance with this Commission's closing deliberations, I was asked to convey to you informally their feeling that a body be appointed to concern itself with the implementation of all or part of the report's statements, and recommendations. There is a strong feeling on the part of the Commissioners that the great amount of time and effort that they have expended would have no results unless some interested body was concerned about implementation. It is not suggested that the present Commission be continued as such, and it is not intended that a paid staff be involved. It is hoped, however, that a smaller group, including in its make-up some individuals on the Commission, will be considered. I will be happy to discuss this matter at further length if you so desire.[46]

Hughes did not discuss the matter with Lilley, nor did he appoint the proposed review body.

Three days after Lilley's request, the commission released its report at a press conference. The commission chose a Saturday for its release date because of the relative absence of news then and the wider distribution of Sunday newspaper editions. Commission representatives placed calls to the editors of major newspapers announcing the press conference, arranged press conference ground rules and distributed advance copies of the report.

Use of the press conference and other transactions with the press resulted in some unanticipated and unintended consequences. Time and space limitations common to all news media precluded full coverage of the report and the press overplayed controversial aspects of the report that were marginal to the commission's concept of the document. The Governor's Commission devoted only one and one-half pages of its report to "a widespread belief that Newark's government is corrupt," and one of 99 recommendations called for "a special grand jury to investigate allegations of corruption in Newark."[47] Yet the press, especially Newark newspapers, gave more attention to allegations of official corruption and the call for a grand jury than to any other item in the report.[48]

The peril posed by news media coverage is that issues central to commission concerns may be lost in sensational reporting of peripheral issues. One commissioner spoke about this issue some four months after release of the report:

> In terms of what has happened to the report, we made a mistake in calling for a grand jury investigation of corruption in city hall. Not that that doesn't need to be done, but our discussion of that issue was picked up by the news media and given all the publicity. That single point in the commission's report has been given more publicity than all the other issues combined.

Critics charged the commission with naivete for not anticipating press reaction to the corruption charge. Mayor Addonizio's chief assistant argued:

> Even though the corruption charge was fairly minor in the report, it became the dominant one in the way the local press handled it. Here was the issue the press longed for. Especially the *News*. It just goes to show you how naive people like that are. They didn't know inclusion of a small statement on corruption would set the fire. Well

it did, and now it's too late to correct that. In fact, I think that some people like Jaffe wanted to play corruption down or leave it out all together. But that damn Meyner had to have it in there and the *Newark News* is his newspaper, so not only did it go in the report, but it got all the headlines after the release of the report.

When the commission inquired into politically controversial subjects, it often proved impossible for commissioners to endow their report with the legitimacy required for universal acceptance. Commission findings and recommendations necessarily dealt with controversial matters that could not be dealt with in a manner acceptable to all interests in the state. On employment, for example, the commission relied exclusively on the testimony of Joel R. Jacobson, president of the New Jersey Industrial Union Council, who alleged "denials of opportunities to Negroes in the building trades because of the prejudices of certain individuals."[49] No other testimony on union practices and no discussion of black employment opportunities in industrial unions was provided in the report. This prompted the president of the New Jersey Building and Construction Trades to condemn the commission for taking "the adverse, caustic and unfounded testimony, unilaterally, of a man whom the building trades refused to support in his quest for the presidency of the State AFL-CIO." The statement further accused the commission of accepting hostile testimony "for the furtherance of the gubernatorial aspirations of a member [Meyner] of your commission, for otherwise there is no explanation."[50]

Similar controversy surrounded political consolidation. To advocate consolidation would assure blacks in Newark an adequate tax base to solve local problems; all three black commissioners (by this time Ferguson had resigned) took this position. Other commissioners argued that advocating consolidation risked disturbing white suburbanites upon whom the commission felt dependent for implementing recommendations directed at state government. They also anticipated hostility toward consolidation by some blacks in Newark who perceived (correctly) imminent black control of city hall. The commission split (five to five) on this issue and expressed both positions in its recommendations.

Internal divisions within the Governor's Commission are less impressive in the end than the fact that it was able to produce unanimity on what happened during the rioting, what the disorders meant and what programs would be appropriate to prevent future violence. This unanimity projected an image of authoritativeness. Attempts to challenge the commission's interpretations of riot events and recommendations for corrective measures are assessed in chapter 8 of this volume.

Detroit: The Mayor's Development Team

The 1967 Detroit civil disorder ranks as the single most severe instance of racial violence in the 1960s and for that matter among the most severe of the twentieth century. It continued unchecked for nearly two weeks, finally ending after the combined forces of city, county and state law enforcement agencies, the National Guard and the Army quelled the looting, burning and other acts of violence. If civil disorders over the prior months and years created mass uneasiness and elite concern, the staggering toll of deaths, injuries, arrests and property damage in Detroit shocked citizens and public officials alike. The severity of rioting in Detroit also cast the problem of racial violence in national terms, eliciting a presidential response beyond simple assistance in suppressing the riot.

Some continued to try to explain the "isolated" outbreak of violence by discerning malfunctioning city processes and characteristics. However, in many respects Detroit was quite progressive. It possessed one of the most reformed municipal structures in the country, immunizing the city from some of the disabilities of machine politics; it received sizably more than its fair share of federal monies for programs aimed at inner-city problems; and its private sector boasted an enlightened automobile industry pursuing integrated employment practices and its counterpart, the United Automobile Workers Union, incorporated blacks to a degree unmatched among trade unions in the country.[51]

Detroit residents, recalling the quick termination of a minor racial flare-up in 1966, were surprised that what "couldn't happen here" had in fact happened on an unprecedented scale. Local residents' astonishment was compounded by the widely held belief that Detroit had, in Jerome P. Cavanagh, one of the most forceful and enlightened mayors in the nation. Elected and re-elected as a reform mayor with the overwhelming support of blacks, Cavanagh's policies had met with the approval of Detroit's black community to such an extent that racial violence was thought to be precluded.[52] Bewilderment about massive violence in Detroit's streets soon engendered demands for immediate action and meaningful explanations from city officials. Consistent with his past behavior, Cavanagh responded by explicitly rejecting law enforcement interpretations of the Detroit violence and by reassuring the black community that "each of these claims [of police misconduct] will be thoroughly investigated."[53]

Mayor Cavanagh actually participated in the appointment of two study groups in response to the Detroit riot. The first study group, the New Detroit Committee, came into existence on July 27 through a joint declaration by Cavanagh and Michigan Governor George Romney. It included 37 prestigious members, mainly from the private sector, and was intended to marshal private resources to rebuild Detroit. Creation of the New Detroit Committee did not, however, quiet demands for an official public investigation into the civil disorder. In a statewide speech discussing the Detroit violence, Romney announced on July 30 that "the mayor and I plan to appoint a joint group of top experts to searchingly investigate the causes of the riot, the actions taken to end it, and the programs needed to eliminate state and local conditions that helped trigger it." Three days later Cavanagh called for a "distinguished but small panel of experts to conduct a comprehensive inquiry into last week's six-day riot."[54] Without waiting for the governor, Cavanagh created the second study group, the Mayor's Development Team, on August 3. As we shall see in chapter 8, the New Detroit Committee eventually competed with the work of the Mayor's Development Team.

The Mayor's Development Team soon became the official riot commission in Detroit: the New Detroit Committee was to mobilize *private* resources in the community's reconstruction effort and the Mayor's Development Team was to mobilize *public* resources in the rebuilding of Detroit. The Development Team's official nature is shown in its threefold charge from Cavanagh:

To coordinate city departmental activities to assure that the appropriate measures are taken to restore public and community services and alleviate hardship.

To coordinate long-range planning by city departments in creating a blueprint for the social and physical redevelopment of the city.

To act in a liaison capacity with the "New Detroit Committee" and to coordinate all city agencies in their relationships with other governmental and private entities as they affect the carrying out of the Mayor's Development Team assignments.[55]

Each of the three charges single out city agencies as controlling the resources to be used in responding to the civil disorder.

Noticeably absent from the charge to the Development Team was a directive to investigate certain areas usually assigned to riot commissions. The charge does not, for example, ask the Development Team to inquire into the causes of disorder or the nature and number of participants. Cavanagh, in this sense, directed the team away from traditional investigative questions that have preoccupied most national, state and local political executives.[56] Instead of primarily being a fact-finding or investigative body, the Detroit study group was concerned with developing reform measures to prevent the recurrence of civil violence.[57]

The rationale behind its unique role has been explained by Richard Strichartz, the chairman:

> We gave consideration to creating a formal study commission. In fact, the mayor consulted with Pat Moynihan about the advisability of an investigative commission. We even went so far in our thinking on this as to discuss who would name the commission, what form it would take, and so forth. Well, after President Johnson appointed the National [Kerner] Riot Commission, we decided against an investigative riot commission and in favor of a development commission. We said, let's get on with development in the future and forget the mistakes of the past. This needed to be done. But, we saw it as more important to get on with the work of the day in development. We wanted to set new goals.

Time considerations also influenced the kind of study group appointed:

> We felt that to be a good, investigative riot commission—like say the one in Chicago after the 1919 riot—would take two years of deliberation and a considerable amount of manpower. The question that faced us was, what about the community during this two-year period? We wanted an action oriented development team that would have an impact and produce results. So we moved to the Mayor's Development Team concept.

The existence of other investigative riot commissions and the desire to show a rapid response help account for the Development Team's unique character. Its orientation also stemmed from Cavanagh's desire to use the civil disorder to launch major programs intended to heal racial divisions in Detroit.[58]

Having set the tasks, Cavanagh turned to two former high-level staff aides to head the Development Team. Richard Strichartz, general counsel of Wayne State University in Detroit, became coordinator (or chairman) of the Development Team; he had previously served three years on the mayor's personal staff and two years as his City Controller. Fred J. Romanoff, a vice-president of Michigan Bank, the Development Team's deputy coordinator, had been the mayor's executive secretary and before that his law partner. Appointing former staff assistants coincided with Cavanagh's objective of making city agency structures and services the Development Team's immediate concern.

The close association of the Development Team with the mayor's office extended beyond the choice of study group heads. Five of the remaining seven members of the Development Team came from the Cavanagh administration; and brought with them a high degree of knowledge about and experience with city agency operations. These included:

1. James D. Wiley, acting director of the Community Renewal Program, later to become its director.
2. Arthur Yim, from the Auditor's General Office, later appointed by the mayor to the position of Corporation Council.
3. Peter C. McGillivray, director of the city Civil Defense Department.
4. John Kanters, from the staff of the Detroit Budget Bureau.
5. James T. Trainor, press secretary to the mayor and the only member of the mayor's staff to serve throughout both Cavanagh administrations.

Paul Borman came to the Development Team from private law practice, but later became a special legal counsel to the mayor. The only Development Team member not serving the city administration at any time was Harold Johnson, who came from a voluntary group, the Neighborhood Services Organization.

The Mayor's Development Team recruited all 12 of its professional staff from city agencies.[59] The staff director explained how staff personnel were recruited:

We relied heavily for working staff on city agency people. The mayor gave us blanket approval to get them to work for us. It was the only way we could do the job. And he provided that we could get any we wanted. So we turned to the ones we thought were the best people. The agencies would say when asked for X person, "He is our best man, can't you take somebody else?" Our reply always was, "The reason we want him is because we know he is your best man!"

The Development Team also recruited specialists within and outside city agencies. Development Team member Wiley, for example, used more than half of the employees of his Community Renewal Program to help formulate recommendations aimed at consolidating existing housing, urban renewal, building code enforcement and Model Cities programs. Additionally, outside specialists were selected from lists of prospective appointees to high-level city agency positions. The staff director explained:

We knew all the professional assistants who came on board from outside city government. Most of them were about to be appointed to some position in city hall. This experience on the Development Team helped them to become familiar with city operations and obviously it gave us top talent that we needed.

Two such assistants were later appointed to the Model Cities Program as director and deputy director.

Other forms of assistance for the Development Team's work came directly from the mayor's office. Following a minor racial clash in the Kercheval section of Detroit in August 1966, Cavanagh formed an *ad hoc* Summer Task Force to act as a trouble-shooting group in tense racial confrontations. After the 1967 disorder, the Summer Task Force information and personnel were transferred to the Development Team. The mayor also provided six of his top assistants to aid the work of the Development Team. The staff director commented on the importance of this:

The people on the mayor's staff came in and out of the Development Team as they were needed or interested in what was being done. These people are the eyes and ears of the mayor for the various city departments. They oversee agency performance in separate areas. They knew what was going on in the departments and how to get them to respond. When they talked to the agencies, they [the agencies] responded.

Finally, the Development Team retained six outside consultants and received technical assistance from a private systems research firm largely through the efforts of the mayor's office. None of the consultants were paid for their services and all had some previous contact with Mayor Cavanagh.

The narrowly conceived objectives and shared interests of members allowed the Mayor's Development Team to avoid internal problems. Threats of fragmentation did not materialize, no minority reports were filed or threatened by Development Team members, no staff member resigned during the commission's life and only minimal criticism of the Development Team by members and staff followed release of its report. Relations between members and staff remained cordial throughout the Development Team's existence. One member elaborated on the importance of shared orientations among personnel:

> We all knew each other fairly well so there was a good deal of harmony on the Development Team. We were all action-oriented rather than being deliberative. There were no minority reports from the group and none were threatened. In fact, it was a consensual type of commission. We were a group of professionals who had been recruited by the mayor to address a major problem. Each of us had considerable experience in a specific issue area and we knew the ropes of city hall. No one on this team really wanted or dared to raise philosophical issues. We wanted results.

Because of its limited tasks and the shared interests of its members, the procedures of the Mayor's Development Team similarly departed from those employed by other riot commissions. No formal hearings were held, witnesses from riot-affected areas of Detroit were not sought out and the search for information did not extend beyond questioning agency performances. Coordinator Strichartz explained the relevant information which the Development Team sought:

> Once having decided to look just at city agencies we then chose to zero in on three questions of each agency. They were: 1) what is the nature, level, and quality of city services from the agency; 2) is the structure of the city agency proper to meet the new needs it faces; and, 3) what are the attitudes of city agencies in forming programs?

To secure and process information on these three questions the Mayor's Development Team divided into research teams. Four research teams were created to deal with city agencies under the general categories of social services, business services, physical planning and

262

emergency planning. Members and staff personnel assigned to each research team knew a great deal about each city agency's past performance because of their past involvement in programs from the mayor's office or within city departments (see Table 7.3). The interlocking relationship between the Development Team and the mayor's office is also demonstrated in Table 7.3, to the extent that each research team reported directly to Romanoff and Strichartz, two of Cavanagh's closest associates and most trusted advisors.

Mayor Cavanagh committed himself to providing the resources and authority necessary to implement its charge. He assured the Development Team of unlimited access to key agency personnel, ordered city agencies to pay the salaries of Development Team staff and to provide equipment, office space and incidental expenses. Probably the most important resource was information. Under Mayor Cavanagh's executive order creating the Development Team, all city agencies were required to provide written statements about their short-range and long-range plans for responding to the civil disorder.[60] The Development Team made additional requests when initial submissions were unsatisfactory and used its former city agency staff to corroborate the submitted information.

The city agency information gave the Development Team a basis on which to initiate its analysis. The amount and kind of information the Development Team received from city agencies is illustrated in Table 7.4, which lists the reports submitted by one city agency, the City Plan Commission. The table shows that the City Plan Commission complied with the request in Cavanagh's executive order and provided additional information at somewhat regular intervals. In all, the City Plan Commission's submissions totaled well over 500 pages.

This provision of the mayor's executive order, coupled with executive support of the order in spirit as well as letter, provided the Development Team with the functional equivalent of subpoena power within government, a resource for obtaining information most riot commissions lack.

Like most other riot commissions, the Mayor's Development Team encountered severe time pressure in pursuing its work. It released its final report on October 27, 1967, just 85 days after its appointment. In doing so, it acknowledged: "Confines of time and the magnitude of the task were limiting factors in the preparation of the report by the Development Team."[61] One member emphasized the importance of time limitations:

TABLE 7.3

Mayor's Development Team Organization

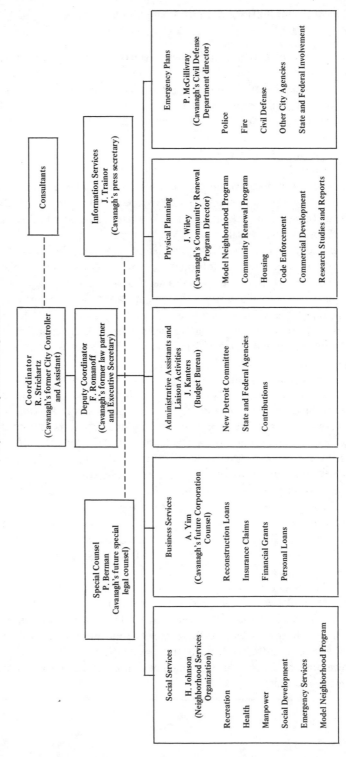

TABLE 7.4

Summary of Reports Submitted to Mayor's Development Team
by City Plan Commission

Date	Description of Report	Length
3 August 1967 - - - -	Complete set of reports for each building damaged or destroyed during the July 1967 civil disturbance.	300 pages
3 August 1967 - - - -	"Estimated Quantities for Damaged and Destroyed Structures Resulting from Riot in July 1967"	1 page
8 August 1967 - - -	"Report to the Mayor's Development Team, 80 pages City Plan Commission"	80 pages
9 August 1967 - - -	"Preliminary Estimate of Riot Damage, July 1967 Riot; Totals Summary"	3 pages
10 August 1967 - - -	"Civil Disturbance, July 1967 Map" (this is the map which the Mayor took to Washington for a committee hearing)	1 page
10 August 1967 - - -	"Some Suggestions as to How the City May Better Relate to Community Organizations"	2 pages
16 August 1967 - - -	"July 1967 Riot Damage: Revision of Assessors Estimates"	1 page
21 August 1967 - - -	Ritzcraft Homes as Permanent Housing on Interim Sites	5 pages
23 August 1967 - - -	"Riot Affected Establishments—Address—Order, August 23, 1967"	13 IBM pages
23 August 1967 - - -	"Riot Affected Establishments—Name of Firm—Order, August 23, 1967"	30 IBM pages
23 August 1967 - -	"Riot Affected Buildings, August 23, 1967"	32 IBM pages
8 September 1967 -	"Riot Damage Report—Establishment Listing"	17 pages
8 September 1967 -	"Riot Damage Report—Real Property Parcel—Listing"	

TABLE 7.4 (Cont.)

Summary of Reports Submitted to Mayor's Development Team by City Plan Commission

Date	Description of Report	Length
1 October 1967	"Redevelopment Possibilities for Ten Riot Sites"	36 pages
3 October 1967	"Memo to Mr. Richard Strichartz, Mayor's Development Team regarding New Detroit Committee Request of September 11, 1967"	11 pages
6 October 1967	"A Report on the Status and Progress that has been made on the Short- and Long-Range Planning Activities in the Areas Affected by the Civil Disorder of July 23, 1967"	11 pages
August through November 1967	Analysis of many maps, aerial photographs and field surveys were given verbally on many occasions during this period.	

Source: Letter from Detroit City Plan Commission to Mayor Jerome P. Cavanagh, dated 22 November 1967, pp. 42, 43.

> We operated under one hell-of-a time constraint! We put out a 700-page document in less than 90 days. The last days were frantic. We were scheduled to submit the document on a Thursday morning. We still had people writing the report the night before. Then it had to go on mats and be printed and bound. We did make it on time, but the writing style suffered for it.

Time constraints also precluded consideration of several studies which were completed after release of the report.[62]

Such problems were compounded for the Development Team because its members and staff served full time, unlike members of the Kerner Commission and the Governor's Commission in New Jersey. While staff personnel may have felt that full-time service on this important panel was a welcome relief from the routine of agency business, it created additional pressure to finish the assignment quickly so they could return to the departments they headed. To expedite its tasks, the Development Team divided into research teams and concentrated on formulating recommendations with only passing attention to more general questions about race relations, addressing the three tasks outlined in the mayor's charge sequentially. These procedures may have saved time by "short-circuiting" the commission process, but lack of time was still emphasized in interviews by members and staff personnel.

Mayor Cavanagh intensified problems of time scarcity by assigning three additional tasks to the Development Team. He asked it to formulate legislative presentations requesting assistance in reconstructing Detroit from the state and national government, to prepare the City of Detroit's statement (delivered by Cavanagh) before the Kerner Commission and to write Cavanagh's postriot "Report to the People" speech.

In effect, the Mayor's Development Team functioned as an extension of the mayor's office. Its presentations before special and general sessions of the Michigan legislature all related directly to the mayor's plans for rebuilding Detroit. The Development Team made its presentations for federal assistance before the Michigan congressional delegation and several federal agencies, requesting release of pending funds from federal agencies and additional funds.

The Development Team's work on the second task consumed its first two weeks of existence. In Detroit's statement before the Kerner Commission, the Development Team carried its analysis into areas that had previously been exempted from its charge, attempting to answer questions about what happened in Detroit, why it happened and what needed to be done to prevent racial violence from recurring. The Development Team listed a chronology of disorder events gleaned from city agency reports and personal observations and, in a 70-page section, gave an exhaustive account of fires, arrests, injuries and deaths during the disorder. As to why Detroit experienced a riot in 1967, the Development Team maintained that, "There has been no discernible relationship between the location or degree of violence in these disorders to social or economic or governmental factors," but that, "The explosion in Detroit was one flame in a nationwide fire."[63]

The Development Team rejected reports of a conspiracy, asserted that police repression would impair race relations and called for massive social programs to reduce racial tensions. In recommending preventive measures the commission described activities of the Development Team and the New Detroit Committee and advanced 17 proposals, ranging from specific recommendations for housing, employment, education and police assistance for Detroit to more general proposals such as "the need to consider and accept a new principle on which to base federal programs—the principle of reparation for long-standing injustice dating back to the generations preceding ours."[64] The federal government was asked to match local efforts.

The Development Team acted most explicitly as an arm of the executive in preparing Cavanagh's "Report to the People."[65] In the speech, Cavanagh revealed a "Detroit Plan" for responding to the civil disorder, much of which was later included in the Development Team's final report. Cavanagh also singled out city agencies, as the Development Team would do later, for criticism:

> City government needs some shaping up. I know that some local government agencies dealing with general city problems can be more efficiently and effectively conducted and organized than they have been. There have been unjustified delays in essential programs because of confusion over responsibilities, jurisdictional and even ideological disputes between agencies. In ordinary times, some of this may be justified by the benefits of interagency competition. These are not ordinary times. I am studying moves to remedy these weaknesses through appropriate reorganization or otherwise, as the situation demands.[66]

The threat to reorganize the municipal bureaucracy to improve the delivery of city services immediately drew opposition from agency directors. The Development Team's recommendations to this effect met with a similar response two months later (see chapters 9 and 10 of this book).

The Development Team's final report consists of an agency-by-agency review of Detroit's executive departments. It critically assesses the quality of services delivered, the departmental structures for service delivery and the performance of personnel in each agency. The report describes the Development Team's role in providing emergency assistance to riot-affected neighborhoods[67] and, in line with its desire to reform city agencies, literally hundreds of recommendations for changing city agencies are included. The proposals were intended to redirect municipal resources to achieve greater impact on previously intractable problems in the inner-city with particular emphasis on agency services to blacks.

The myriad of recommendations are overshadowed by three more fundamental proposals to reorganize and consolidate city departments. The first recommends consolidation of all social service agencies in Detroit under a "super agency," termed the "Social Development Agency," which would be indirectly responsible to the mayor's office. Second, the report recommends consolidation of all city agencies dealing with physical development in Detroit into a "City Development Agency," which likewise would be indirectly responsible to the mayor's office. Finally, the report calls for creation of a "Community Renewal Program" in the mayor's office that would assume responsibility for research and evaluation of ongoing agency programs, a function previously performed independently by city departments. Consistent with the interests represented on the Mayor's Development Team, all three proposed consolidation measures promised a great increase in control over city agencies by the mayor.

Although these recommendations promised to decrease city agency autonomy, the Development Team tried to reassure city departments and their clientele by acknowledging departmental "enlightenment and aggressiveness in this area" and asserting that its recommendations promised to introduce greater efficiency.[68] Similarly, it attempted to justify creation of a "City Development Agency" by criticizing the existing "division of authority and responsibility [which] results in delays and lack of coordination and responsibility."[69] Concentrating all research and evaluation of city departments in the mayor's office would prevent duplication, allow interchange of information among agencies and provide a means for agency heads to monitor progress by other city departments.[70] Moreover the Development Team attempted to dispel city agency fears that the report advocated a wholesale reorganization of existing departments.[71]

The cordial and direct relationship between Cavanagh and the Development Team was highlighted during a press conference at which the commission's report was released. In accepting the report, Cavanagh called it "the most significant city document ever produced in Detroit," and said it would be "a blueprint for the future." The extent to which the mayor's forecast proved accurate is assessed in chapter 9 of this volume.

Milwaukee: The 39-Point Program

Although in the 1960s it ranked as the tenth largest city in the nation, in several important respects Milwaukee is a unique metropolitan center. The significant impact of the progressive movement in Wisconsin left municipal structures in Milwaukee among the most reformed in the country. A relatively autonomous municipal bureaucracy is governed by strong civil service regulations, the electoral system is nonpartisan and a weak mayor-strong city council arrangement literally eliminates any possibility of patronage from the municipal executive. Milwaukee also enjoys, and prides itself in, a tradition of efficiency, good government with little municipal corruption and an heritage of socialist domination of local politics in the twentieth century up to, and including, the 1950s. The strength of socialist candidates for public office rested (along with the city's reputation for "gemütlichkeit," old world traditions and good beer) on the heavy concentration of recent immigrants from central and eastern Europe. This heritage convinced local residents that the racial turmoil affecting other cities would not take place in Milwaukee. The fact that only slightly over 10 percent of Milwaukee's population was black made this conviction all the more persuasive to local residents.

Characteristics peculiar to Milwaukee did not protect the city from racial violence, however. On July 30 rioting broke out and continued sporadically for one week, resulting in four deaths and the arrest of more than 1,500 citizens. The violence shocked local residents, but disbelief soon yielded to a demand for explanations:

A major disturbance occurred in Milwaukee when other cities with far more serious problems managed to avert trouble. Many Milwaukeeans wonder why a city which takes pride in its clean streets, beautiful parks, low rate of fire losses and its staid, "old world atmosphere" would experience a major disorder. Others wonder why Milwaukee, having been amply warned of its problems by local leaders as well as by studies sponsored by governmental and civic agencies, did not take steps toward solving them. Answers ranged from belief that outsiders came into Milwaukee to instigate the violence to belief that existing frustrations, lacking legitimate avenues to create change, inevitably resulted in violence.[72]

Bewilderment about why their city experienced violence was immediately answered: Mayor Maier raised the possibility of outside organization to the rioting, concluding that civil rights leaders were also to blame for the violence for "encouraging defiance of the law." He claimed that only two-tenths of a percent of Milwaukee's blacks took part in the disorder.

Such official comments, as we have suggested in chapters 1 and 3, provide confused, anxious and apprehensive citizens with simple, convincing and readily accessible understandings of civil disorders. But they also can guide and even manipulate political responses to violence to serve the objectives and goals of the political leadership.

The behavior of Milwaukee's chief executive before, during and after that city's civil disorder dramatically demonstrates the extent to which political leaders may structure responses to violence for their own ends. H. R. Wilde depicts the mayor as calculating how he could be sure to retain control over emergency procedures long before the expected crisis occurred:

> He began preparing for it fifteen months before it occurred by working out elaborate contingency plans. Among other things, he installed a "hot line" to the Governor's office, worked out the legal and other preliminaries to imposing a curfew, and established a procedure for calling out the National Guard on very short notice. These contingency plans were a source of great pride to him and his associates, and during the second day of the riot he released them to the press to show how well the city government had prepared for what happened.[73]

Wilde pictures Maier as inaccessible to the local press and black leaders and content to let the preriot plans self-deploy. After the rioting, the mayor continued to abide by strategies he had conceived several months in advance:

271

While he waited for the riot to occur he drafted a long statement for use after it was over. The statement said, among other things, that the American metropolis could have no future until the walls separating the central city from the suburbs were torn down and it called on Congress to help tear them down.[74]

Wilde concludes that Maier was less concerned with averting a riot than capitalizing upon it to further his municipal programs.[75]

Maier continued to manipulate his own and others' responses after the rioting. He repeatedly rejected demands for a local riot commission made by representatives of militant black organizations. After refusing to meet with members of the Common View organization during the violence, Maier countered by proposing "a new biracial organization in Milwaukee for many purposes" which would be "absolutely representative of the economic and social groups in the Negro community."[76] Five members of the Greater Milwaukee Conference on Religion and Race met with him to spearhead the biracial organization. Conference members reported after the meeting that the new organization would use "moral force" to change police, employment, housing and education policies affecting blacks. Consistent with Maier's definition of influential black leaders, the organization would "be composed of Negroes and white clergymen, tavern owners, barbers, lawyers, union stewards and probably others."[77] Conference members also announced that Maier had scheduled two meetings to set up the new biracial organization. This time Maier attended the meetings.

Instead of creating the promised organization, however, the two meetings led to formulation of an official response to the civil disorder. The first meeting was a conference between Maier and "grass roots Negro influentials," the second, a marathon session between the mayor and the Interdenominational Ministerial Alliance. They produced a set of 39 official recommendations for responding to the violence. Maier thereafter repeatedly referred to the proposals, known as the "39 points" or less commonly as "Milwaukee's Little Marshall Plan," as his city's assault on problems that caused the rioting within Milwaukee's black community. Testifying before the Kerner Commission, he commented: "During that emergency period, working with grass roots representatives from the Negro community, we worked out what we might call 'Milwaukee's Little Marshall Plan'—a 39-point program for action to build that greater city of trust and confidence and hope for all."[78]

The 39-point program represents Milwaukee's equivalent of riot commission recommendations, for there was no official riot commission as such, only the meetings between the mayor and two black groups he consulted during the immediate postriot period. In effect, the mayor bypassed formal appointment and delays inherent in the commissioning process by imposing a set of previously advocated programs on the two groups. He thus obtained a set of official recommendations with the trappings of legitimacy conveyed by the groups' endorsements. Maier later explained why he acted as he did: "After going so slowly for years, I finally had the chance to unroll this plan. . . .The opportunity was there: The suburbs were frightened by the riot, so they would have gone along. And Washington was worried, of course."[79] How Maier unrolled "this plan," obtained endorsement for it from the two groups and presented it as an official set of recommendations offers insight into the ways elites structure political responses to disorders.

On August 4 Maier held the first of two meetings with "grass roots Negro influentials" suggested by the Greater Milwaukee Conference on Religion and Race. The meeting took place in city hall and drew 47 residents of the Inner Core, Milwaukee's black section, who had been selected and invited by the mayor's office. Members of the group included barbers, bartenders, union stewards and ministers, but they were mostly small businessmen. At the meeting, Maier presented his proposal for a new biracial organization and discussed his plans for responding to the violence. The new organization, he indicated, would seek ways to implement programs aimed at the causes of the violence. The plans he presented to the meeting included many programs he had previously sponsored without success.

After this first meeting, Maier reported to the press that a show of hands revealed 44 members of the group approved his program while only three disapproved. One day later he summarized the August 4 discussions:

I said one thing to this group yesterday—47 wonderful people there—I got some hell, but it was a different kind of hell. It wasn't something made up by somebody else and then transposed and shipped into Milwaukee, to raise hell with the devil at city hall. They didn't figure I was the devil. They figured I was the mayor and they were citizens and they were going to raise hell with the mayor—there is a difference. I hate somebody for pretending that I'm responsible

273

for Detroit, or Atlanta, or New York's troubles or Watts, because I'm not. . . .Now the only difference we had yesterday at that meeting was a question of my appointments, that one joker from the poverty board, he was the only dissenter, and they got him on television of course and quoted him in the newspapers. Forty-seven people, one guy came to cause trouble and dissent, one woman had an honest disagreement and it was modified. She went through it after the vote and got her answer. The other person was part of the organized group. So 47 people, 44 of 'em voted for a new biracial council to be formed by the Conference on Race and Religion. Tavern keepers mostly and barbers—they want in on the act, they want to keep out of trouble, they want a good community, they want to make money and they know that you are not going to have bread by burning down the bakery. . . .We had a good meeting, we had a great meeting. The thing was we took a vote, lasted three and one half hours.[80]

The mayor and the black group did not release any formal program or statement of objectives at this time. That awaited the second meeting from which the 39 points were generated.

The second meeting drew 58 black clergymen from the Inner Core who belonged to the Interdenominational Ministerial Alliance. The meeting between the mayor and the Ministerial Alliance lasted over seven hours and produced a set of official recommendations, but without the elaborate procedures of investigation, hearings, evaluations, analyses and compromise over reform proposals engaged in by formal riot commissions. Maier brought to the meeting a package of measures he had previously advocated, offered it to members of the Ministerial Alliance for adoption and then publicly presented the 39 points as the recommendations decided upon by himself, the Ministerial Alliance and grass roots Negro representatives. Thus, even more than in Detroit, the chief executive was able to control and coordinate the character of the response to the riots, while maintaining the fiction of obtaining consensus on controversial policy.

Reverend Louis Beauchamp, moderator of the Ministerial Alliance, opened the meeting by stating his group's modest objectives:

I don't think we have any business meeting here today, except that we were one of the first ones I think to try to get to you [Mayor Maier] on Monday and we had no right to your time on Monday either, when you were in the middle of just trying to organize all these things. But we had put in a bid and there were around eighty to a hundred of us that first day who felt that something should be, the climate should be helped, and who of us knows what should be done? We should have a program and we have resolutions here which anybody can draw up and they don't really mean a great deal except to focus attention on the fact that there has to be a listening post from the higher echelons.[81]

Maier interjected to reassure the assembled clergymen:

I want to tell you gentlemen something. I'm happy to meet with you because you are the only friendly group that I have liaison with. So nobody has gone to the mayor of Milwaukee and superseded this group with me because to me this is the only place that I have found a gentle voice. And this whole problem with the last several years. So, it's no imposition to me, I'm very happy to meet with this group.[82]

This interjection shows how comfortable Maier felt with this group of moderate black church leaders, deliberating about policies yet to be decided upon in response to the violence. It also reflected his need to surround any forthcoming recommendations with some semblance of legitimacy, which was not likely to be forthcoming from other black organizations or leaders in Milwaukee.[83] The mayor went on to explain his reasons for rejecting demands of more militant groups and confided that "we did more good yesterday on television and last night with tavern keepers and barbers walking out of that meeting," than had occurred in all his meetings with militant civil rights groups from the Inner Core.

Maier introduced his package of proposed reforms by commenting:

What do we have to work for? This is the program I'm going to ask you to consider. I'd like to have it said that we worked it out together. Not a statement of what, but a statement of how. . . . I got a hell-of-a-program here if you stop and consider it. We have been going at this thing and I've been having this thing in the hopper and I'm going to announce this myself, but I'd just as soon announce it with you. If you don't take it, I'll announce it myself as exclusively mine. Otherwise, we can work it out together here today and approve it together, and let her go.[84]

The program consisted of proposals that had been introduced more than one year earlier, under his highly publicized "Campaign for Resources."

The clergymen reacted with only one mild objection and that dealt with the mayor's reluctance to visit the black Inner Core which he had not done for over a year. The following exchange between the alliance's moderator and Maier illustrates the point of objection:

> *Moderator:* Some people take that [ghetto tours] as a matter of concern, Mr. Mayor, that is the point. You and I and some others understand some of the more important fine lines [of the program]; but the common man involved—it's a matter of showing concern, so far as he is concerned. Now that is an elementary point, that has very little to do with some of the basic problems, but it is important to the man who only knows what he can see. He has to have a picture.
>
> *Mayor Maier:* Reverend, when you go out of here this morning and the television cameras focus on you, the meeting yesterday focused on 'em; that is two nights in a row and I have a meeting next week and everybody walks out with television cameras focused—they gonna know I'm concerned without me going up there looking at the damage done.
>
> *Moderator:* Of course the clergy is facing this, too. What do you tell the people just now in language that they can understand and how do you win their confidence to know that their mayor is not only concerned on a long-range basis but immediately, that he is demonstrating some kind of immediate concern that they can understand.
>
> *Mayor Maier:* I've got to depend on you for that.[85]

Maier thus sought not only the endorsement of the alliance of clergymen, but also wanted them to explain his program to residents of the Inner Core. They promised both, and the 39 points were released to the public. Maier gave representatives of the press the following account of how the program was formulated:

> I have had the pleasure of working with this group of clergymen here today who had been working earlier in the week. . . .They had been working on a number of specific points that they believed would vastly improve the racial relations of our city and make general improvements for our city. We entered into an extremely long termination dialogue today. We met here from eleven o'clock until

now. A great many things were discussed, many things were agreed to, a program was outlined. I am happy to endorse the program. I think the meeting was most constructive, some of the points came out of the meeting which I held yesterday with a representative group of nonwhite citizens of our community; businessmen, union stewards, among them, barbers, tavern keepers, others who are influential with grassroots people in the nonwhite community. Some of their ideas were incorporated into this statement. I think it is a good summation and I think it speaks well for the future.[86]

A day after the meeting, the Milwaukee *Journal* headlined "Maier, Clergy Map Action" and noted that, "Mayor Maier met Saturday with a group of inner core ministers and announced a 39 point assault on Milwaukee's racial problems.[87]

The 39-point program dramatically reflected the political interests of its primary author. Maier seized upon the crisis in Milwaukee to advance his previously unsuccessful "Campaign for Resources" to a more visible place on the civic, state and national agenda. After successfully obtaining the desired attention for the program, Maier acknowledged: "These measures are being proposed because they are measures long needed to build a better city. Many of them, most of them, have been proposed time and time again."[88] Not only had the 39 points previously been advanced by the mayor's office, but they were also aimed mainly at governmental jurisdictions other than the city of Milwaukee. Table 7.5 shows that the burden for producing the changes called for in the 39 points fell on the federal government in 13 of the points, the state government in 14, combined federal and state governments in two, the county in three and the city of Milwaukee in only seven. Moreover, of the recommendations aimed at the city of Milwaukee only two called upon the mayor's office for reform and these were relatively innocuous proposals. Maier termed the recommendations his assault on Milwaukee's black problems and took direct responsibility for implementing them.

Announcement of the 39 points did not satisfy everyone. The lack of a formal investigation into two riot deaths stimulated immediate concern. Black groups charged that Clifford McKissick, an 18-year-old black college student, had been unjustifiably shot to death by police. Others questioned the circumstances surrounding the shooting death of a 77-year-old black woman. Police Chief Harold A. Breier refused to talk about the two incidents to reporters or representatives of concerned groups or to make public the information his department

TABLE 7.5

Milwaukee's 39-Point Program
by Jurisdiction Targeted for Reform

Governmental Jurisdiction	Number of Recommendations
Federal	13
State	14
Federal and State	2
County	3
City	7
TOTAL	39

had obtained. Spokesmen for black groups demanded that Maier take action and condemned the absence of any mention of the cases in his 39 points. The mayor's strategy of meeting with self-selected groups with which he felt comfortable did not convince other aroused groups that a thorough investigation would be conducted.

Maier was strongly criticized by some black leaders who insisted that he should select black community representatives to formulate postriot plans. The mayor earlier had been the object of Common View's attack for his handling of the disorder and for not addressing conditions in the Inner Core. Two requested meetings between Maier and Common View failed to materialize in the immediate postriot period.

Common View responded to the announced 39 points by counter-proposing a 24-point program to alleviate conditions it said caused the riot and by asking for a meeting with Maier to discuss the two sets of proposals. As opposed to the 39 points, Common View's proposals dealt almost exclusively with the city of Milwaukee and many were aimed at the mayor's office.[89] Maier agreed to meet with Common View, but requested that representatives of nine other governmental jurisdictions also be invited.[90] Common View immediately rejected

278

Maier's request, insisting on a meeting with him alone. The executive secretary of Milwaukee's Commission on Community Relations and the Conference on Religion and Race prevailed upon the mayor to agree to a meeting.[91]

Maier reluctantly met with Common View one week after releasing the 39-point program. Nearly every civil rights group and voluntary service agency from the Inner Core had representatives at the meeting. Over the one-and-one-half-hour meeting Maier answered questions posed by the 100 persons in attendance. The questions focused on the 24-point program developed by Common View. The following exchange is typical of the questioning:

> *Questioner:* If you, with your leadership and aggressiveness and vigorous attitude about things, could pursue open housing for Milwaukee, I think we would be quite pleased, quite pleased.
> *Mayor Maier:* If I must give you my convictions on this, after next April you will be talking to another mayor.
> *Questioner:* I can appreciate this.
> *Mayor Maier:* This is not a political proposition. As mayor of this city I feel I cannot support a city-only open housing law. . . .
> *Moderator:* The question was asked of you a moment ago as to your position in terms of a city open housing law. You stated very clearly that you would not go along with a law for the city only. These are citizens of Milwaukee and this is all they are concerned about in terms of leaders of the city of Milwaukee—where you stand as far as city open housing laws are concerned. You have given us your answer, I think at this point, and in order to try to justify that answer, there is no justification at this point, because I think if we move into this area here, of trying to justify your position as to why you are for a county open housing law, the people of the audience are not concerned. . . .
> *Mayor Maier:* They are Milwaukee citizens aren't they?
> *Moderator:* Yes, but they are interested only in the city.
> *Mayor Maier:* Then they ought to be interested in this answer because it's a Milwaukee answer and it relates sharply to the problems of this city in their greatest extent. . . .
> *Moderator:* What is the opinion of the group, does it want the mayor's explanation at this point?
> *Audience:* NEXT QUESTION, NEXT QUESTION![92]

Common View members concentrated on the city's responsibilities regarding Inner Core problems. Each time Maier attempted to draw attention to his 39 points or other programs at the federal and state level, questioners brought the issue back to the city's responsibilities. At times the questioning had a harshly bitter tone.[93] Unanswered questions regarding the death of Clifford McKissick prompted expressions of concern from some members about the absence of a formal investigation. Common View members also repeated their displeasure at Maier's statements about black leaders, as the following excerpt from an exchange illustrates:

Questioner: You have suggested or alluded to the fact that there is no adequate or responsible Negro leadership in this community, with the understanding that we have that there is no single white leader that can speak for all the white community...we would like, though, since there is inferred an Anglo-Saxon air of superiority, a slandering, a derogatory type presentation...what is your concept of leadership within the black community?

Mayor Maier: That reference was made once, once! It was made in a press conference, it was not in the context in which the *Milwaukee Sentinel* put it. We protested on the record the paper's use of it. This was a question of analysis on Negro leadership in the press conference—the reporters assumed there was one. I said there is no single, valid leader. I said there is a diversity of leadership. I said there is a polylithic structure just as there is in the white community. This was my exact language....There is no white power structure as such. There is [sic] several white power structures. It is many, many structures. The word is polylithic. It's a big word.

Questioner: But they are all white!

Mayor Maier: Huh?

Questioner: But they are all white![94]

On the issue of black leadership, the overarching concern was why the mayor listened to and consulted with less representative groups, such as the alliance of clergymen, instead of Common View. The mayor's meeting with barbers, tavern keepers, union stewards and businessmen during and immediately after the rioting effectively screened Common View members out of the decisions taken at the time. The following exchange is quoted in full because it reveals the particular concern expressed about Maier's use of the Interdenominational Ministerial Alliance:

Questioner: It appears that, from the perspective of the community

280

—the Negro community—that the mayor is afraid of the Negro community, or is not really willing to rely upon the influence and the help that the black leadership in this community can give. You know it is not all negative, it is not all anti-Mayor Maier, and the analysis which leads to a divide-and-conquer tactic in the Negro community has created considerable resentment. One of the things we are concerned with is the way in which you might use this potent force in the community for good, not only to support the programs that you want to push, but also to accomplish the general good of the community. . . .

Mayor Maier: . . .Now what do you mean by trying to divide the community? What do you mean by that? Do you mean I'm trying to divide the community?

Questioner: Statements in the paper concerning Negro leadership, not recognizing the existing leadership, but using your efforts to secure the kind of leadership which presumably. . . .

Mayor Maier: What are you referring to specifically, Lou? I don't know what you are talking about. What are you talking about specifically?

Questioner: What we are speaking of, and I must move into this tactfully because it is extremely important to all of us that we maintain our unity. The selection of the clergy as were chosen I'm sure with your best, good offices at heart. . . .

Mayor Maier: I did not choose them.

Questioner: They came forth?

Mayor Maier: Yes. They invited me to a meeting. And I came to the meeting. Then they invited me to another meeting.

Questioner: I appreciate that, sir. Now let me hold up to say this much. Does this ordinarily happen? And what may be against those we say, Mr. Charlie and his black and white friends then move to print things, and what was printed was that the clergy as they appeared were the leaders of the Negro community, and those of us who are not ardent church goers did not accept that these were religious leaders for those people who were in their flock, but there is many of us who undoubtedly did not have a religious leader of our own, so we thought that there was another element in the Negro community that had been ignored. And many of us thought that we were that group. So now we have this group which encompasses everyone, and I think this is what we are saying, that we felt that this had been a hand-picked, docile, intelligent, educated real nice group of people who were going to sit down and then you would have the vocal man who would always start talking and say just what you wanted him to say—and that is what annoyed us.[95]

Common View members uniformly reacted against Maier's reliance on black groups he defined as representative and they similarly refused to recognize as legitimate the proposals for reform sanctioned by those groups.

The meeting ended less than satisfactorily to all parties present. The Common View moderator summed up the meeting:

> We want to let the mayor know at this point that there is a lot of feeling in the community about a lot of things that ought to be done now. He has answered some questions, many of the questions I think from my reaction to the group have not been answered as specifically, mayor, as they want. I think the Common View group would have to use another media to get at some of these problems in a more concrete way. The Common View group wants you to also know, mayor, that if they can be of any help to you in pushing some of these problems in other areas that we want some immediate action on, that we want you to let us know, because I think you all understand that this group of citizens from the community are determined to get some of these problems solved.[96]

Common View released a similar statement to the press summarizing the meeting: "The mayor came to meet with the black community and the Common View group. The mayor agreed that our points were good. The mayor was asked specific questions and responded with general answers. We of the Common View group expect the mayor to work with us in the future in resolving the city problems that the community sees."[97] Immediately the mayor's chief administrative assistant took issue with the press release by saying: "He [Maier] answered specific questions with specific answers."[98] Significantly, one month later Maier appointed Common View's chairman to the Milwaukee Community Relations Commission, but the nominee declined the appointment because of differences between his group and the mayor's office. The extent to which continuing controversy surrounding the 39-point program impaired its implementation is assessed in chapters 9 and 10 of this volume.

The immediate response to Milwaukee's civil disorder followed patterns similar to those described for Newark and Detroit, and also parallels response patterns we discussed in chapter 2. Black groups demanded reforms aimed at basic causes of the disorder while some whites warned that violence should not be rewarded through adoption of such reforms. One version of the demands by aroused black and white groups called for an official investigation of the disorder, its causes and its remedies. Unlike the response in Newark and Detroit, however, no formal riot commission was appointed to investigate the racial violence. Instead Mayor Maier assembled a list of 39 programmatic recommendations, most of which had been unsuccessfully proposed earlier, and advanced them as the "official" set of reforms. A group of moderate black clergymen was assembled by Maier and it endorsed the 39 points, but black organizations not involved in formulating the official set of recommendations immediately challenged the representativeness of the clergymen and the appropriateness of the reform package. Thus divergent political interests, even in the absence of an official investigation, competed for control of authoritative explanations, interpretations and recommendations in the aftermath of racial violence.

Official Municipal Response To Severe Racial Violence

In the summer of 1967, public officials in Newark, Detroit and Milwaukee were confronted with civil disturbances that fundamentally challenged their capacity to lead. The riots mobilized public sentiments in unparalleled ways and polarized attitudes about race relations and policy usually expressed in much more muted tones. Black leadership in the cities seized the occasion to demand attention to long-standing grievances; white leaders rallied to the defense of police organizations charged with confronting the rioting directly; and citizens generally searched for explanations about why the rioting occurred and what could be done to prevent its recurrence. Whether sympathetic with black aspirations or not, white leaders and white populations in general condemned lawlessness and reflexively criticized supporters of persons who might engage in property destruction and mayhem.

In such cases as these, when the claims of competing "sides" are particularly intense and cannot be resolved in satisfactory fashion, an "independent" investigation and an "independent" interpretation of the events in question becomes highly appealing to public officials. Equally apparent is the simultaneous, but sometimes incompatible, desire to control the legitimate, postriot civic agenda. Thus, in each city, executive activity was directed toward formulating the authoritative interpretation of disorders and developing programs to prevent future disorders.

Study groups, committees of investigation and riot commissions proliferated because political executives needed means to answer the demands of aroused groups. These *ad hoc* organizations reassure concerned citizens generally, and aroused interest groups specifically, that something is being done and deflect demands for action away to the investigative organizations and subsequently to an agenda established by a group endowed with the legitimacy of high status, objectivity and public spirit. For a variety of reasons these groups perform the functions of reassurance for which they were originally created, attempt to consolidate their claim to authoritative status with which they were originally endowed and in varying degrees advance the agenda of the appointing executive.

While we recognize the hazards of generalizing from a limited number of cases, the following observations appear to characterize official riot investigations. After severe civil disorders, public officials attempt to organize authoritative governmental activities which maximize the extent to which interpretations of disorders compatible with their interests and recommendations consistent with their own political agenda are forthcoming. However, the more balanced the influence of the "sides" in the conflict, the less public officials are able to "direct" the verdicts, and the more public officials will need to cloak the investigations in the aura of independence with which full-blown riot commissions are often endowed.

Despite the existence of a national commission called upon to study the disorders, public officials in New Jersey, Detroit and Milwaukee sought to command local interpretations of the disorders and subsequent recommendations. This proved to be a much easier task in Milwaukee, where blacks constituted a small proportion of the population, relatively recently arrived and significantly neglected by the politics of that city. In contrast, in Newark, where blacks comprised in excess of a majority, the investigation had greater independence.

These observations also suggest the consistency between riot commissions in previous eras and the investigations of more recent times. In earlier epochs, when the status of blacks in America was lower, their numbers fewer and their tenure in cities of shorter duration, investigations (with a few notable exceptions) tended to be antagonistic to black interests. In the current period, when blacks' civic influence is more commanding, public officials tend to develop more neutral investigations. These observations parallel those of Arthur Waskow regarding the greater (although many would argue still flawed) neutrality of police conduct in civil disturbances when comparing the protests of the early 1960s with race riots of the World War I period.[99]

Although dispassionate inquiry free of particularistic interests may be claimed, although recommendations developed in the "public interests" may be asserted, riot investigations consistently are characterized by indentifiable biases.

These biases reflect the group interests of commission members who in turn have been selected by political executives with a stake in the outcome of commission deliberations. The degree of overt bias varied, of course, among the three cities. The Governor's Commission in Newark reflected the interests of the state executive by ignoring Governor Hughes's inflammatory rhetoric. The Mayor's Development Team in Detroit acted as an arm of the municipal executive by undertaking several tasks for Mayor Cavanagh in addition to those initially assigned. In Milwaukee the 39-point program was virtually an extension of the mayor's office and a moderate group of black leaders was coopted to advance it virtually unrevised.

The mobilization of bias, perhaps observable in all organizations, is clearly evident in the structuring of official inquiries into racial violence. Even in apparently "neutral" inquiries, representatives of interested groups were omitted and representatives likely to "protect" selected interests were appointed to the panels. However, the pluralism of elites in these cities finds expression in the creation of "unofficial" investigative panels that challenge the hegemony of official investigations and the interests articulated in official interpretations.

NOTES, CHAPTER 7

1. See ch. 1 n. 69.

2. See National Advisory Commission on Civil Disorders, *Report*, pp. 611-59, for type and duration of civil disorders.

3. Governor's Select Commission on Civil Disorder, *Report for Action* (Trenton, N.J.: State of New Jersey, February 1968), pp. 124-41.

4. The far-reaching curfew is described by the Kerner Commission: "Milwaukee imposed a citywide curfew restricting all persons to their homes, closing all streets to vehicular and pedestrian traffic, and permitting no one in or out of the city," National Advisory Commission on Civil Disorders, *Report*, p. 525.

5. Detroit *News*, 16 July 1967.

6. Quoted in Milwaukee *Journal*, 23 July 1967.

7. Both news accounts are quoted in Milwaukee *Journal*, 6 August 1967.

8. Milwaukee *Sentinel*, 3 August 1967.

9. Quoted from the Common View's text in Milwaukee *Sentinel*, 2 August 1967.

10. Milwaukee *Sentinel*, 3 August 1967.

11. Milwaukee *Journal*, 3 August 1967.

12. Milwaukee *Sentinel*, 4 August 1967. The mayor's office is on the second floor of city hall.

13. Quoted in the Milwaukee *Journal*, 10 August 1967.

14. Milwaukee *Sentinel*, 1 August 1967.

15. His description of civil-rights leaders' activities leading to the civil disorder reads: "The evolution has gone from marching and demonstrating to breaking windows and looting to killing"; both statements quoted in the Milwaukee *Journal*, 6 August 1967.

16. By this logic, no more than 180 blacks participated in the civil disorder. This figure is difficult to reconcile with the more than 1,500 citizens arrested during the violence.

17. Milwaukee *Journal*, 6 August 1967.

18. Tom Hayden, *Rebellion in Newark: Official Violence and Ghetto Response* (New York: Vintage Books, 1967), pp. 23, 24.

19. The governor also added, "I felt a thrill of pride in the way our state police and National Guardsmen have conducted themselves"; quoted in Tom Hayden, ibid., p. 50.

20. The document proposed that:

The study should seek to learn what caused the riots; who participated in them and in what manner; vital statistics of the rioters, including income and education; and to what extent existing government programs are relieving the causes of riot. Also why there was so little hostility between whites and Negroes in comparison with previous outbreaks; what are riot warning signals; is there a better way to quell riots, and how can the full metropolitan area get involved in reorganizing the cities. The study should employ public hearings, group workers, social psychologists and even psychotherapists.

(Quoted in the Detroit *News*, 31 July 1967.)

21. Detroit *News*, 3 August 1967. Colonel Frederick E. Davids, director of the Michigan State Police, quoted in the Detroit *News*, 24 July 1967.

22. Quoted in Detroit *News*, 8 August 1967.

23. From a press release, "Mayor Maier's Report to the People on

Recent Civil Disorders, All TV Stations," (mimeo.; Milwaukee, Wisconsin; 8 August 1967), p. 5.

24. These biographical sketches of commission members are taken from the Newark *News*, 11 February 1968, and the New York *Times*, 11 February 1968.

25. Thus the governor, on July 23, projected roles for the commission other than those it actually performed: "I have appointed a blue ribbon committee of people whom the people in New Jersey trust, Negro community and White both—Governor Meyner, Governor Driscoll, Bishop Doherty [*sic*], a lot of other people, including many prominent and outstanding Negroes, Oliver Lofton, Jr.—to work very closely with me and very cooperatively with me in establishing communication to the Negro community during these riots, especially the young militants." See Richard J. Hughes, "Transcript of Interview over CBS' Face the Nation," 23 July 1967, p. 12; files of Governor's Select Commission on Civil Disorder, Governor's Office, Trenton, N.J.

26. Governor's Select Commission, *Report For Action*, p. 199.

27. The governor was instrumental in gaining Jaffe's release as special assistant in the U.S. Attorney General's office in Washington. Jaffe had previously served as an assistant prosecutor for Essex County for two years and for four years as chief of the U.S. Attorney's Criminal Division in New Jersey.

28. Throughout this and subsequent chapters direct quotation of principal participants in riot commission activities is made. These are derived from focused interviews with over 175 persons in the three cities. Copies of the interviews remain in the files of the authors and can be made available upon request. Hereafter in this study, materials drawn from the focused interviews will be noted by the absence of citations.

29. The Governor's Commission received information that the Kerner Commission intended to develop a thorough investigation into background causes. Accordingly, it chose to concentrate on background features distinctive to New Jersey cities. Similarly, on the conspiracy question, it discounted any organized plan to the disorders and deferred to "other authorities, armed with stronger powers and conducting investigations into the matter, [who] may have more to say on the subject"; Governor's Select Commission, *Report For Action*, p. 142.

30. The commission retained two consultants to conduct research on housing conditions in Newark and the politics of Newark. Six additional consultants advised the commission on education, police, housing, and health issues. Seven of the eight consultants came from university-affiliated positions. The commission also contracted with the

Opinion Research Corporation for a $27,000 attitudinal survey of Newark residents.

31. The section on welfare in the commission's report is shorter than other sections and is prefaced with the reservation that, "Guided by its general policy, and in accordance with Governor Hughes's charge not to make 'studies for studies' sake, the Commission sharply circumscribed its investigation of welfare problems"; Governor's Select Commission, *Report For Action*, p. 83.

32. New York *Times*, 13 December 1967.

33. Commission chairman Lilley later expressed written appreciation to Governor Hughes for "your interest and your successful effort to obtain legislation covering our activities on a safe, harmless basis." He wrote that "they [commissioners and staff] greatly appreciate the confidence displayed by your willingness to obtain the legislation under difficult circumstances." See Robert D. Lilley to Governor Richard J. Hughes, dated 7 February 1968, files of the Governor's Select Commission on Civil Disorder, Governor's Office, Trenton, N.J.

34. Commission chairman Lilley and staff director Jaffe also met with their counterparts on the McCone Commission. From these sessions they report being forewarned of procedures to avoid.

35. One account of the impact witnesses before the commission had describes the changed opinion of one member: "The Select Commission also gave voice and respectability (two former governors signed its report) to decades of black resentment of police methods. 'You should have seen Governor Alfred Driscoll's face,' says another commission member, Raymond Brown, a top criminal lawyer rated as Jersey's most astute black leader, 'when we brought in those white-haired Negro shopkeepers who told how their small stores were shot up by men in blue trousers and white helmets! As governor, Driscoll professionalized the state police and has remained proud of them. And then one of these old men said—'Governor, do you think a policeman should call a man 64 years old a boy?' " The account describes a similar impact on another former governor who also served as a commissioner: "Another former and doubtless future governor, Robert Meyner, was at first incredulous of the black community's view of the disaster that struck Newark's Central Ward two summers ago. A long procession of eyewitnesses, rounded up by Brown and by commission member Oliver Lofton, lawyer and former aide to Robert Kennedy in the Justice Department, persuaded Meyner to sign the commission report. . . .Son of a frugal German mother who walked miles along Jersey City streets to save on grocery bills, Meyner was visibly shaken by witnesses' reports of the prices and credit charges exacted by white shopkeepers in the

ghetto. . . .Meyner [now] finds his role in the commission report his only real card with New Jersey's big Negro voter bloc." See Louise Campbell, "Profile: The Workings of Urban Politics, Problems and Alleged Payoffs Within Paul Ylvisaker's New Jersey," *City* 3, no. 3 (June 1969): 16. Interviews with commission members confirm these statements. For similar dynamics affecting the Kerner Commission, see ch. 6 of this volume.

36. Indicative of how the work schedule departed from Governor Hughes's expectations of the commission was Dean Ferguson's resignation as a commissioner. Hughes had anticipated sufficiently infrequent meetings to allow Ferguson to commute from Washington. Early in the commission's life, as its work schedule lengthened to all-day meetings, three and four days a week, Ferguson resigned.

37. Governor's Select Commission, *Report For Action*, p. 162. The report reads, "Some Commissioners, while they approve this recommendation, believe that it falls short of what is required in the present circumstances. . . .In their view consolidation of municipalities and school districts, and regionalized zoning and planning are the essential first steps toward any permanent relief of these parallel sources of urban tension."

38. The report reads: "Some Commissioners feel that many municipalities which are now seeking to build new sources of strength and vitality will be deprived of their ability to do so through political consolidation." (ibid.).

39. Survey data provided supporting evidence for arguments made in the report. Where the opinion survey is mentioned, often the actual data obtained are not included. When included, systematic presentation and analysis are notable for their absence. See Governor's Select Commission, *Report For Action*, pp. 2, 3, 16, 35, 55, 67, 68, 78, 79.

40. Studies by consultants provided the commission with marginally helpful materials. Leonard Chazen, a consultant on housing, noted that his report "appears, condensed and disemboweled, in the Commission's public statement." Letter from Leonard Chazen, School of Law, Newark to one of the authors, 6 February 1968. Nathan Wright received a contract for a study of "A Black Point of View of Newark's Political Dimension." Files of the Governor's Commission include a letter to Wright dated 5 January 1968, requesting the overdue study. It did reach the commission before the report was released, but too late to be considered. The study provided the basis for a later book. See Nathan Wright, *Ready to Riot* (New York: Holt, Rinehart and Winston, 1968).

41. Governor's Select Commission, *Report For Action*, pp. 5, 12. For example, the report's Preface argues that, "The illusion is that force

alone will solve the problem. No group of people can better themselves by rioting and breaking laws that are enacted for the benefit and protection of everyone. Riots must be condemned. The cardinal principle of any civilized society is law and order."

42. Ibid., pp. 143, 144.

43. During the disorder Hughes characterized the events as "open rebellion. . .criminal insurrection. . .an atrocity. . .plain and simple crime and not a civil rights protest." See Allen D. Grimshaw, "Three Views of Urban Violence: Civil Disturbance, Racial Revolt, Class Assault," *American Behavioral Scientist* 2, no. 4 (March-April 1968): 4. He also said: "The line between the jungle and the law might as well be drawn here as any place in America," and noted a "carnival-like" atmosphere that "is like laughing at a funeral." To charges of police brutality the governor commented: "I'm not surprised. It is great fashion and almost standard operating procedure"; quoted in the Newark *News*, 17 February 1968.

44. See documents under "Governor's Statements at Newark" and "Governor's Statements after Newark" in files of the Governor's Select Commission on Civil Disorder, Governor's Office, Trenton.

45. See ch. 4 in this volume.

46. Robert D. Lilley to Governor Richard J. Hughes, 7 February 1968; files of the Governor's Select Commission on Civil Disorder, Governor's Office, Trenton.

47. Governor's Select Commission, *Report For Action*, pp. 20, 21, 162.

48. This overplay of the corruption issue particularly characterized the Newark *News'* coverage of the commission, its report and developments subsequent to release of the report. Even before the disorder, the Newark *News* had conducted a campaign against official corruption, gambling, and vice.

49. Governor's Select Commission, *Report For Action*, p. 72.

50. Quoted in the Newark *News*, 18 February 1968.

51. Banfield goes so far as to characterize Detroit as follows: "Detroit was a city of relative prosperity and opportunity for the Negro; it had no real 'ghetto' and its police had for several years been under very enlightened and determined leadership"; Edward C. Banfield, *The Unheavenly City* (Boston: Little, Brown, 1970), p. 197.

52. One of the best descriptions of Cavanagh's relationship with blacks in Detroit is: J. David Greenstone and Paul E. Peterson, *Race and Authority in Urban Politics* (Beverly Hills, Calif.: Sage, 1973).

53. Quoted in the Detroit *News*, 5 August 1967. Contrary to most political executives, Cavanagh said outside agitators and conspirators did not play a part in the disorder, blamed instead long-standing and

unmet grievances among blacks for causing the violence and summoned the community "to jointly resolve to build this city up from the ashes of the present conflict into the kind of urban environment in which every man can say with dignity and self-respect that he is a Detroiter and proud of it"; quoted in the Detroit *News*, 27 July 1967.

54. Detroit *News*, 31 July 1967 and 2 August 1967.

55. The charge is contained in Executive Order Number 17, 3 August 1967, files of the Mayor's Office, Detroit.

56. The mayor's decision to exclude traditional investigative concerns and to focus instead on reform of city agencies was made after consulting with three urban specialists; Daniel Patrick Moynihan, director of the M.I.T.–Harvard Joint Center for Urban Studies; Adam Yarmolinsky of the Harvard Law School; and Julius Edelstein, director of urban studies at the City University of New York.

57. For a discussion of alternative policy roles riot commissions play, see ch. 3 in this volume.

58. The Development Team's final report allows that, "When the Mayor formed the Development Team, his desire was to reassure the citizens of Detroit that what appeared to be the lowest ebb in the city's history could become its finest hour. His intention was that change born of the conflict would bring the government closer to all the members of the community." See Mayor's Development Team, "Report To Mayor Jerome P. Cavanagh" (Detroit, Michigan: City of Detroit, October 1967), pp. 9, 10.

59. Mayor Cavanagh made this possible by including in the executive order creating the Development Team the provision that, "All departments will cooperate to their fullest extent in providing information, personnel, and other needs requested by the Mayor's Development Team"; see Executive Order Number 17.

60. The mayor's executive order included the following provision:

All departments will submit to the Mayor's Development Team, 1108 City-County Building, the following information by August 8, 1967: 1. A description of all departmental activities to date concerning the recent civil disorder. This information should contain available data and the evaluation of same. 2. Short-range plans for departmental participation in the restoration and redevelopment due to the recent civil disorder.

(Ibid.)

61. Although this statement appears in the original version of the report released to the press on the date mentioned, it was subsequently deleted from the published version.

62. This particularly affected consultants, some of whose submis-

sions did not reach the Development Team until after its report had been released.

63. "Appearance of the City of Detroit before the President's National Advisory Commission on Civil Disorders" (mimeo.; Detroit, Michigan; Office of the Mayor; 15 August 1967), pp. 5, 6.

64. Ibid., recommendation no. 2.

65. Cavanagh explicitly acknowledged that the address was prepared by the Development Team; see Detroit *News*, 6 September 1967.

66. From the text of Mayor Cavanagh's "Report to the People," reprinted in full in ibid.

67. A document reviewing "Emergency Response Plans" formulated by the Development Team is not included in the final report and has not been released because, in the report's words, "Obviously, it would be best not to make public the details of this specific proposal"; Mayor's Development Team, "Report," p. 4.

68. Mayor's Development Team, "Report," p. 218. The Development Team argued that its proposals "would represent a major step toward the creation of a more effective system of services and should result in the more efficient utilization of personnel and reduced administrative costs" (ibid., pp. 218, 219).

69. Ibid., p. 57.

70. A single research center promised, from the Development Team's perspective, to be more efficient: "The Mayor's Development Team recommends that the efficiency and effectiveness of the City's program could be increased if the responsibility for program evaluation, and social and physical research were vested in a single agency" (ibid., p. 12).

71. The report states, for example, "Many of the new government functions recommended may be absorbed by existing departments or agencies. Some are merely expansions of efforts already begun or under study within the present structure. It was never the intention of the Development Team to create additional governmental units" (ibid., p. 12).

72. Karl H. Flaming, *Who "Riots" and Why? Black and White Perspectives in Milwaukee* (Milwaukee, Wisc.: Milwaukee Urban League, 18 October 1968), p. 1.

73. H. R. Wilde, "Milwaukee's National Media Riot," in *Urban Government*, 2nd. ed., ed. Edward C. Banfield (New York: Free Press, 1969), p. 685.

74. Ibid.

75. Wilde suggests Maier consciously pursued this strategy:

From the mayor's standpoint it may have been less important to avert a riot than to handle one well if it occurred. The national audience that he most wanted to reach would be impressed by a city administration that had done a first-rate job of planning to cope with a riot; in the nature of the case this audience would not even be aware of a city administration that succeeded in preventing a riot from occurring. It was a fact, too, of course, that a riot would dramatize the need for new revenue sources and programs to deal with fundamental problems. . . .Whatever his motivations, the mayor hastened to use the riot to propagandize for measures that he, along with most national opinion leaders, had long favored.

(Ibid., p. 686.)

76. Milwaukee *Sentinel*, 3 August 1967.

77. See Milwaukee *Sentinel*, 4 August 1967. One day later, Maier made a plea for greater attention to black influentials, by whom he meant, "the barbers, tavernkeepers, clergymen, and businessmen who daily come in contact with a greater number of Negroes" (Milwaukee *Journal*, 6 August 1967).

78. Mayor Henry W. Maier, "Statement to President's Commission on Civil Disorders" (mimeo.; Milwaukee, Wisconsin: Office of the Mayor; 5 October 1967), p. 5.

79. Quoted in Ralph Whitehead, Jr., "Milwaukee's Mercurial Henry Maier," in *City* 6, no. 2 (March-April 1972): 16.

80. Tape recording of meeting between Mayor Maier and the Interdenominational Ministerial Alliance, 5 August 1967. This tape recording, and others cited below, were made available to the authors by Richard Budelman, press secretary to the Mayor of Milwaukee, and can be supplied to others upon request. These tapes record, verbatim, important aspects of Mayor Maier's handling of the municipal crisis following the civil disorder.

One black businessman who attended this first meeting offered the following dissent about the nature of the discussions: "(A) pitiful waste of time. That fellow is the Mayor of a city that is about to burn down around his ears, but all he talks about to Negro businessmen is the tax structure" (see Milwaukee *Journal*, 5 August 1967).

81. Tape recording, 5 August 1967.

82. Ibid.

83. The sorry state of Maier's relations with blacks in Milwaukee is described by Wilde: "Negro leaders also found him inaccessible. During the riot he was too busy to talk to them. But he had not paid much attention to them in the months before either. For well over a year he had not made a visit of any length to the black 'core.' Nor had he established close ties with any of the recognized Negro leaders in the city" (Wilde, "Milwaukee's National Media Riot," p. 868).

84. Tape recording, 5 August 1967.

85. Ibid.
86. Ibid.
87. Milwaukee *Journal*, 6 August 1967.
88. Milwaukee *Sentinel*, 9 August 1967.
89. Wilde describes the mayor's reaction to Common View's program as follows:

> The Mayor's list [39 points] contrasted sharply with another list that had been put forward by a coalition of militant and other leaders. This list said nothing of county, state, and federal programs; it called for actions that the city government itself could take: put a Negro on the fire and police commissions, suspend without pay policemen involved in fatal shootings, appoint a Negro to command the police of the Fifth District, pass an open occupancy ordinance, and so on. The mayor brushed these demands aside preemptorily; he had no time for people who wanted to play the old-fashioned game of locally oriented politics, bargaining about specifics.

(Wilde, "Milwaukee's National Media Riot," p. 687.)
90. The Mayor justified this request by singling out one of the 24 points, dealing with the appointment of black judges, and saying, "Obviously, this request is more properly placed before the governor, who actually makes the appointments" (Milwaukee *Journal*, 9 August 1967).
91. The conference urged, "We call upon the mayor of Milwaukee to meet with representatives of 'common view' at the earliest possible date to listen sympathetically to their understanding of the problems of the central city and to consider carefully their proposals for dealing with these problems" (Milwaukee *Sentinel*, 8 August 1967).
92. Tape recording, 12 August 1967.
93. One questioner declared: "Mr. Mayor, you said that the City of Milwaukee was an equal opportunity employer, and I'm here to call you a liar, because it is not, because the only thing that is equal is in hiring laborers and the question is, are you going to upgrade these Negroes that are qualified and if so, how and when?" Maier did not respond (ibid.).
94. Ibid.
95. Ibid.
96. Ibid.
97. Milwaukee *Journal*, 13 August 1967.
98. Ibid.
99. See Arthur I. Waskow, *From Race Riot to Sit-In: 1919 and the 1960's* (Garden City, N.Y.: Doubleday, 1967).

8

Competition Over Authority and Legitimacy in Riot Investigations

Official investigations of the riots in Newark, Detroit and Milwaukee claimed to provide authoritative answers to questions prevailing in the wake of racial violence, including what kinds of recommendations might prevent a recurrence of violence. Interpretations of riot events and reform proposals have to appear authoritative partially because the public demands certainty, but also because an image of authoritativeness enhances the political appeal of reform proposals. But on what basis and to what extent were the answers and recommendations authoritative?

Conventionally, a policy or group may be considered authoritative "when the people to whom it is intended to apply or who are affected by it consider that they must or ought to obey it."[1] In this usage, authority implies that a group or policy will command obedience from those to whom it applies either because they feel it *must* be accepted (the coercive basis of authority) or because they feel it *ought* to be accepted (the legitimacy basis). There is no necessary relationship between official status and authoritative status, but in practice the distinction is often ignored. Platt, for example, attributes authority to riot commissions by definition:

Riot commissions are authoritative tribunals, financed and/or supported by a governmental body, established temporarily to investigate and explain specific outbursts of illegal collective violence by private citizens, notably urban blacks.[2]

Platt's elaboration shows clearly that what he really means by "authoritative" is "official":

> Riot commissions are *authoritative* in the sense that they are created at the request of or with the approval of governmental representatives and are composed of professional experts, "leading citizens," and high-level members of political, economic, and religious interest groups.[3]

Appointment by governmental officials does assign "official" status to riot commissions, and elite members may contribute to the "legitimacy" of commission efforts. But neither of these factors vests riot commissions with authoritative status. Platt concludes that "the sources" of riot commission authority are public funding and sponsorship by city, state and federal governments and by the president,[4] but these "sources" actually only establish the "official" nature of such inquiries.

Our concern about the analytic consequences of equating authoritative status with official status may be illustrated by two hypothetical cases. Suppose a mayor sponsors a riot commission, appoints its members and finances it through executive contingency funds, and the city council also creates a riot commission, selects its members and appropriates funds for its work. The two commissions come to diametrically opposed findings and recommendations. Which commission would then have authoritative status? According to Platt's criteria both investigations would be authoritative. Or say a mayor sponsors and funds a riot commission, and a governor, reacting to the same riot events in the same city, does the same—but the two commissions come to opposite conclusions and urge different reforms. Again, for Platt both commissions would have authoritative status. His interpretation renders the concept of authority virtually meaningless.

We have called the riot investigations discussed in chapter 7 "official" investigations because they were appointed by public officeholders and used public finds and facilities. Each investigative group indeed *claimed* authoritative status for its findings and recommendations on the basis of its official position. In reality, these riot inquiries had no monopoly on the authoritative interpretation of the violence or the proposal of reforms. Instead, their claims to authoritative status prevailed to a greater or lesser extent.

Two significant factors circumscribed the official investigations' claim to authoritative status. First, like all riot commissions, these bodies were purely *recommendatory* or *advisory* study groups, as specified in the charge from the appointing executive. Assuredly they could and did attempt to surround their work with symbols of authority, partly on the basis of their official standing, but such attempts should not be equated with authority itself. Advisory and recommendatory riot study groups have no legal, political or other assurance that their work will be binding upon or accepted by the public, nor that public officials will feel bound by or inclined to accept their findings and recommendations. Rather (although this contradicts popular assumptions that riot commissions will significantly structure the post-riot civic agenda), riot investigations possess only the authority they can develop or others are willing to acknowledge.

Second, the claim to authoritative status by official riot investigations is circumscribed by the controversy and competition that surround their studies, findings and recommendations. Since riot commissions cannot compel compliance, they must gain acceptance for their findings and recommendations by establishing their legitimacy. That is, they must show that their findings and recommendations are entitled to acceptance because they are right and proper.[5] In Newark, Detroit and Milwaukee "competing" riot commissions arose, seeking to undermine the validity of findings and the appropriateness of reforms proposed by the official study groups. In addition, they attacked the work methods used by the official investigations, which provided one basis for the latter's claim to authoritative status. In this chapter we shall examine the origins, procedures and reports of the competing riot commissions to illuminate the continuing controversy and competition over authority and legitimacy in riot investigations.

Contradictions are built into riot commissions. Their attractiveness to political executives simultaneously provides the basis for invalidating their claim to authoritative status. When faced with crisis conditions and conflicting demands for immediate action, political executives are attracted to the temporary, *ad hoc* riot commission device. Executives can assign them official status without at the same time assigning authoritative status. The commission mechanism, moreover, is also available to political executives in other jurisdictions, public officials within the same jurisdiction and private groups. Thus the potential exists for multiple and competing riot commissions.

In each of the three cities, the appointing executive named prestigious citizens and representatives of established interests to the official riot panels. Few commissioners had previously engaged in activities critical of the appointing official or antagonistic to his administration. These recruitment criteria tend to ensure that the administrations of appointing executives will be exonerated of any wrongdoing and recommendations will be advanced favorable to represented interests. But they also create the potential for disaffection among unrepresented interests.

The *ad hoc* riot commission was apparently as attractive to political interests excluded from membership on official study groups as it was to political executives who originally created the official investigations, and in each of the three cities competing commissions were formed. To interests not represented on official study groups, the logic of creating a competing commission appears to be as follows: if it could be shown that opposite conclusions might emerge from the same kind of riot investigation, then it could be argued that the findings and recommendations of the official study group resulted from the biases of the commissioners.

In Newark, Detroit and Milwaukee, the political interest responsible for creating a competing riot commission turned out to be the major interest that was without representation on the official bodies. In Newark, where police officers felt they were not represented, the New Jersey State Patrolmen's Benevolent Association formed a competing commission. The New Detroit Committee was actually formed several days prior to the official Mayor's Development Team, and at first the two groups were ostensibly cooperative. But as the business-dominated New Detroit Committee saw the direction being taken by the Mayor's Development Team, their relationship evolved into competition over appropriate post-riot courses of action. Republicans in Wisconsin's state government created a "Little Kerner Commission" to represent partisan interests antagonistic to those in Milwaukee's Democratic-controlled city administration, particularly as given expression in the 39-point program.

These competing riot commissions employed many of the strategies used by official study groups to manipulate symbols of legitimacy and establish their authority to interpret the disorders and recommend corrective reforms. They followed closely the procedures of official

298

investigations by: assembling a staff, holding formal hearings, conducting inquiries, hearing witnesses, collecting documents and offering recommendations. The representative nature of their membership and the thoroughness of their investigations were asserted. Their findings and reform proposals vary considerably, however, from those of the official investigations. An examination of the competing riot commissions illuminates the full range of local efforts to manipulate public opinion and the background of policy determination in the post-riot period and highlights the competition for legitimacy among antagonistic study groups which sought authoritative status for their work.

Newark: The PBA Commission

As the official riot study group in New Jersey, the Governor's Commission attempted to establish authority for its interpretations and reform proposals by using the legitimating symbols of objectivity, neutrality and scholarship. In assembling an investigative staff, contracting with respected consultants, holding formal hearings, conducting survey interviews, hearing witnesses, collecting documents and offering comprehensive recommendations, the Governor's Commission sought to fulfill its assigned tasks with particular attention to the acceptability of its work. Parallel study groups, convinced that the Governor's Commission would be antagonistic to their interests, contested its monopoly on the study of racial violence.

An early parallel study group was appointed by the state police, when it was asked by Governor Hughes to investigate widespread allegations of official misconduct by Newark police, state police and National Guardsmen. On July 16 Hughes promised swift punishment of any law enforcement officer who had engaged in illegal behavior. Internal investigations conducted by the state police were not publicized until after the Governor's Commission released its highly critical findings, which concluded that "State Police elements were mainly responsible" for shooting into stores marked with "Soul" signs, and recommended that "State authorities should immediately conduct an exhaustive investigation into the violence committed against persons, and against Newark stores that displayed 'Soul' signs."[6]

Three days later the state police countered with an interim report contending it "had not been able to identify any troopers accused of firing indiscriminately at stores owned by Negroes."[7] New Jersey Attorney General Arthur J. Sills characterized the state police study as an "exhaustive investigation" and commented "we can't just line up all

the policemen and pick out every fifth one and say 'you're guilty.' "8
The Governor's Commission's recommendation for an "exhaustive
investigation" thus was squelched by the assertion that a thorough
investigation had already failed to reveal any misconduct.

The primary competing riot commission came into existence two
months after Governor Hughes appointed his "blue ribbon" panel.
Delegates to the annual convention of the 1,600-member New Jersey
State Patrolmen's Benevolent Association (PBA) unanimously adopted
a resolution on September 24, 1967 authorizing formation of a PBA
Riot Study Commission. "(I)ts primary task" was to conduct a "study
and investigation of the riots of Summer, 1967, as they related to law
enforcement and the responsibility of police under such circumstances."9 According to the PBA, the reasons for creating this study
group were as follows:

> Whereas, law enforcement officers have been charged by various
> groups in the news media and otherwise as being the cause of riots,
> insurrections and civil disturbances, and Whereas, in the course of
> said riots, insurrections and civil disturbances, charges were made
> against law enforcement officers as to their actions in attempting to
> quell and suppress the riots, insurrections and civil disturbances, it
> was felt to be consonant with the continuing duty and purpose of
> the NJSPBA, which is to fully study and analyze all problems
> affecting law enforcement officers in the State of New Jersey, that a
> comprehensive study of the 1967 disturbances be conducted.10

The authorizing resolution delegated appointment of PBA Commission
members to the association's president, John J. Heffernan.11 He
selected seven commissioners, all policemen and all members of the
PBA.

Upon release of the *Report For Action* by the Governor's
Commission, PBA spokesmen rejected the official version of riot events
and *predicted* that their parallel investigation would produce contrary
findings. President Heffernan greeted the official report by saying, "We
are appalled at the findings of the [governor's] riot commission,
especially in the interests of law and order. *The PBA riot study and
investigation committee is certainly going to come up with different
findings.*"12

True to this prediction, three months later the PBA Commission
released an interim report of 28 pages entitled "A Challenge to
Conscience" which includes arguments against most of the Governor's

300

Commission's findings relating to law enforcement agencies. Two areas singled out for condemnation were the findings that "There was no conspiracy involved in the riots," and that "Police used undue force in riot situations or they 'overreacted.' " The interim PBA report contended, to the contrary, that conspirators caused the disorders: "Someone had to pull the [fire] alarm and someone had to place snipers in strategic places beforehand if the plans were to work. This did not just happen. It had to be planned and under the law this sort of planning is called by another name—criminal conspiracy."[13] To the finding that police overreacted, it responded:

> Were any of the commissioners who accuse police of using undue force on the firing line? Do they really know what they are talking about? Use of the term "undue force" is an exercise in tortured semantics that police refuse to accept. Not only is the charge without merit, it is an insult to brave men who risked their lives for the public and equally unacceptable to reasonable people.[14]

A more systematic and thorough attempt to refute the official interpretation of the riot awaited the PBA's final report. This report, entitled *The Road To Anarchy* and released in the summer of 1968, took as its point of departure the findings of official riot commissions. It then marshaled evidence to support its findings, most of which directly contradicted the findings of official commissions. *The Road To Anarchy* was introduced, for example, by the PBA Commission's version of official commission conclusions:

> We Americans have been asked, in recent months, to believe:
> —That white racism causes black riots.
> —That riots are spontaneous explosions, without planning or direction.
> —That a consistent pattern of police brutality is evident in the Negro ghettos of our nation's cities, and is a cause of rioting; and
> —That rioting is directly traceable to poor housing, to substandard education, to joblessness.
> We have been solemnly assured that this is the case by President Johnson's National Advisory Commission on Civil Disorders, and by Governor Hughes' New Jersey Commission.[15]

The PBA Commission assessed the validity of these conclusions by studying three primary questions paralleling the questions adopted by the official study groups: "What happened? Why did it happen? What was the official response?"[16] Not surprisingly, the PBA's conclusions were directly opposed to those advanced by the official commissions:

> The riot Study Committee of the New Jersey State Patrolmen's Benevolent Association categorically and totally rejects these conclusions as unsubstantiated, unfounded and unwarranted. We find instead that our nation is moving toward two societies: One bound by the rule of law and the other exempt from the law. We find instead that the lawlessness on our nation's streets feeds on and is nurtured by the weakness of official response. As the excuses and apologies for lawlessness grow, so does the lawlessness. We charge that a conspiracy exists of radical elements, dedicated to the overthrow of our society—*and that this conspiracy is aided, perhaps unwittingly, by people at the highest levels of government and society.* And, this committee concludes, the future of our free society will be in grave doubt, unless and until all Americans rededicate themselves to the preservation of law and order: for without law, there can be no peace, and without order, there can be no progress.[17]

Ten specific findings are discussed in the report's conclusion, for which 13 recommendations for change are advanced.

By advancing recommendations reflective of police interests and reform proposals contradictory to those offered by the official commission, the PBA Commission provided state and city policy makers with alternative courses of action to those embodied in the official *Report For Action*. The claim to authority asserted by the Governor's Commission was thus partially countered, at least in the law enforcement area, by the competing commission.

Competing assertions of authority characterizes only part of the competition between alternative study commissions in the post-riot investigations. The grounds for claiming authority were based upon legitimating instrumentalities made available through the use of the commission as an investigative device. That is, the PBA Commission used the commission format to enhance the legitimacy of its inquiry in ways similar to its use by the Governor's Commission. It did so less exhaustively than the official commission, but enough to create the impression that its findings were based upon thorough investigation and careful deliberation. Because of its elaborate procedures and symbolic objectivity, neutrality and scholarship, the PBA Commission is an excellent example of how the commission format may be used to legitimate claims to authority in the competition that characterizes the post-riot period.

The New Jersey State PBA employed the commission form of investigation to undermine interpretations advanced by the Governor's Commission and to lend credence to its own. Its formal structure and procedures closely resembled those used by the official commission. Its seven members recruited a six-man staff which conducted interviews, gathered information from throughout New Jersey and compiled an extensive list of exhibits and documents numbering well over 2,000 pages. Members of the PBA Commission began conducting hearings in November 1967 and seven months later had obtained over 2,000 pages of testimony from more than 65 witnesses in four cities. The members also toured ghetto areas. The entire undertaking was financed by the New Jersey State PBA. Through these procedures the PBA Commission claimed, in its final report, to have "conducted a thorough and exhaustive seven month investigation of last summer's civil disorders."[18]

The PBA Commission also challenged explicit claims to legitimacy asserted by the official Governor's Commission. It charged that the official investigation was biased since it lacked a police representative.[19] The interim report acknowledged "that had Governor Hughes named a police representative to his Commission, our own investigation would not have been necessary. It is unfortunate that although every other segment of our population was represented, the police were not."[20] The PBA sought to convey the impression that its investigation insured "adequate representation for all the various points of view so as to guarantee the validity of any later conclusions or recommendations." "Adequate representation" in this case consisted of inviting testimony in public hearings from "patrolmen, superior officers, ghetto spokesmen, local political authorities and others."[21] Virtually no ghetto spokesmen accepted invitations to testify, however, and only those local political authorities in agreement with positions of the New Jersey State PBA appeared to testify.

The PBA indictment of the official inquiry charged that police witnesses were received with hostility during its hearings. The Governor's Commission called Inspector Thomas M. Henry of the Newark Police Department to testify on departmental processing of citizen complaints against police; he tried unsuccessfully to present evidence of brutality against policemen during the riot. Later, in testimony before the PBA Commission, Henry charged that the Governor's Commission was not interested in his materials: "I volunteered information to them about details of the riots, such as being shot at on two occasions and witnessing other incidents, but they didn't appear to be interested. It appeared unusual to me."[22]

The PBA Commission's final report contains additional arguments about unfavorable reception of police spokesmen at the official panel's hearings. The following transcript from the PBA hearings, included in its final report, probes the treatment given a newspaper reporter who testified he had foreknowledge of an impending riot:

Q: Mike, did you ever divulge that information to the Governor's Commission?
A: No, sir.
Q: Did the Governor's Commission ever ask you that information?
A: No, they didn't.
Q: Why?
A: They asked me if I had known that there was going to be a disturbance in Englewood. I said, "Yes." That was the end of the questioning.
Q: They weren't interested in going deeper into that question and if they did, you would have given them the information?
A: Right.
Q: You would have given them that information?
A: Right.
Q: Mike, do you think something is wrong with that type of investigation where they are not interested in the facts?
A: I did get the feeling that they didn't go into it thoroughly. I felt they didn't ask enough questions. I was there for about 15 minutes.[23]

The PBA Commission equally challenged what it considered the political expediency of the official *Report For Action*. It accepted at face value Governor Hughes' vivid characterization of the rioters during the disorder and quoted his statements liberally in its report.[24] It viewed the absence of any mention of the governor's statements in the official report and the failure to bring court action on the basis of those statements as neglect dictated by political pressures: "Why was not a criminal investigation demanded by the Governor? The devious, socially oriented Governor's Commission does not answer the question. Why was not a special Grand Jury investigation initiated? Why did the

Governor fail to follow through on his beliefs? Already, too much time has passed. The NJSPBA demands answers to these questions."[25]

Questions of political expediency also arose when the PBA commented on the official commission's censure of local public officials' role in suppressing the disorder. The PBA Commission drew attention to the disparity between the official commission's treatment of the two levels of authority:

> The Commission merely spewed forth their unfounded charges without mentioning who was the commander-in-chief of the operations [Governor Hughes]. If and when errors are made one would normally turn to the officer in command to seek explanations. The Commission's failure to complement its charges by directing inquiry to the executive authority responsible for the command decisions that were made irresponsibly left local personnel, who were not in the highest echelon of command, to absorb the weight of the Commission's spurious and unqualified allegations.[26]

The PBA Commission thus attempted to invalidate the Governor's Commission's claim to political neutrality by pointing to areas where political expediency may have influenced its report.

The PBA also attacked the factual accuracy of the *Report For Action.* Law enforcement agencies submitted well over half of the documents, reports and exhibits received by the Governor's Commission. These ranged from precise police records on ammunition fired during the disorder to poorly written surveillance reports on suspected Communists, leftists and agitators (including one member of the Governor's Commission). Because the official commission's report did not refer to this information the PBA Commission charged it with neglecting "facts" it had before it.[27] For example, the Newark Police Department submitted a document charting police brutality charges from 1960 through 1967. It contended that over 150,000 arrests were made during this period of time, that only 67 complaints of excessive force were received and that, after thorough investigation, only three of these were substantiated. Yet the Newark Police Department document claimed that during this same period over 1,000 assaults were made on police officers, more than half of which resulted in injuries to the officers. The absence of this information in the *Report For Action* led the PBA to argue "that these statistics were proffered and made available to the Governor's Committee, but they apparently chose to ignore them." The PBA Commission also charged Oliver Lofton, a member of the Governor's Commission and administrator of the Newark Legal Services Project, with failure to substantiate three complaints of brutality he filed for clients against Newark police and with preventing police from questioning alleged witnesses.[28]

Where the official commission equivocated on information before it, the competing commission advanced its point of view. On the conspiracy question, the Governor's Commission neither denied nor affirmed the existence of planning behind the Newark disorder.[29] The PBA Commission took advantage of this equivocation:

> They [the Governor's Commission] did not, however, rule out a conspiracy. Indeed, the question was left for "other authorities, armed with stronger powers and conducting investigations into the matter." The information collected by the Riot Study Committee of the NJSPBA appears to yield a reasonable inference that there was both prior planning and conspiracy leading up to the disorders in Newark as well as organized criminal activity during them.[30]

Thus the competing riot commission questioned the information gathered and the inferences made from that information.

The PBA Commission went beyond challenging the political neutrality and factual accuracy of the official riot commission by attempting to establish its own legitimacy. Besides asserting that its study was representative and thorough, the PBA Commission employed many of the same symbols of legitimacy that characterized the official inquiry. The PBA Commission identified its inquiry with public officials' statements when those statements agreed with positions taken by law enforcement personnel and agencies.[31] It relied on scholarly commentary conforming to its view of contemporary black protest politics.[32] It also invoked symbolic aspects of civic authority: all of its Newark hearings were held in City Hall with the approval of the city administration, which conferred quasi-official status on the PBA probe. This tactic predictably antagonized and aroused those interests it attempted to undermine. Opponents of the PBA condemned the hearings because they "implied municipal sanction."[33] Lofton commented: "the PBA probe is unofficial—'conducted by a fraternal order'—but seems to have taken on an official nature by the fact that the probers have met in City Hall."[34]

The PBA Commission did not confine its work to challenging the official commission and establishing legitimacy for its own inquiry. Like other commissions we have examined, it expressed the interests of its sponsor, most explicitly in its recommendation "that the base salary rate of all law enforcement personnel immediately be raised to a minimum of $10,000 per year."[35] The PBA Commission also recommended legislation protecting police in civil disorders, opposed civilian review of police conduct and supported increased training and equipment for law enforcement personnel. Fraternal organizations representing law enforcement personnel joined the PBA in condemning the Governor's Commission for excusing lawlessness and violence while harshly criticizing police conduct. Support for the PBA's work came from the New Jersey Narcotic Enforcement Officers Association, State Fraternal Order of Police, Newark Association for Community Reform, Fireman's Benevolent Association and the New Jersey State Veterans of Foreign Wars. The VFW claimed, for example, that "the members [of the Governor's Commission] may well state that they are not law enforcement specialists. Neither are they sociologists and yet they piously assumed the mantle of experts on the so-called roots of the problem. The commission's statement that the riots were not planned but were spontaneous is not shared by anyone who was in Newark during the sniping and looting display."[36] Other disaffected law enforcement groups coalesced around the PBA Commission in opposition to the official commission's findings and recommendations.

Whether the PBA Commission had any impact on the degree to which the recommendations of the Governor's Commission were eventually implemented is impossible to assess. If it had not existed, interests opposed to the proposed reforms would probably have become mobilized in legislative councils, executive offices and bureaucratic agencies. The PBA Commission's contribution was to provide a forum for the expression of dissenting views by opposition groups. To the extent that the competing commission successfully used its legitimating symbols it impaired the claims to legitimacy made by the official commission and thus revealed limits to the authoritativeness of the *Report For Action*.

Detroit: The New Detroit Committee

The official riot commission in Detroit was unable to monopolize the field of post-riot investigation and its work generated parallel and competing inquiries. After investigating Detroit's anti-poverty program, for example, the Mayor's Development Team proposed bringing the local poverty agency indirectly under control of the mayor's office in the new "Social Development Agency." A parallel legislative study group, chaired by James Del Rio, a black state legislator from Detroit, examined Detroit's anti-poverty program and alleged that it was already controlled by the mayor: "The Mayor literally runs a one-man TAP [Total Action Against Poverty] program, appointing himself as its chairman, together with an appointed Director and Assistant Director who carry out his bidding without interference or meaningful participation by hardcore poor."[37] Just two months after release of the Development Team's report, the legislative study group recommended that an advisory committee composed of the "hardcore poor" become the governing board of the local poverty program.

The most explicit challenge to the Development Team's efforts came from a second, and more important, parallel study group. The relations between the Mayor's Development Team and the New Detroit Committee graphically illustrate the process by which parallel investigative bodies compete for legitimacy in responding to civil disorders. Appointment of the New Detroit Committee actually preceded by seven days the creation of the Mayor's Development Team. Governor Romney and Mayor Cavanagh sent telegrams to 150 community leaders inviting them to discuss "the City's current and future problems" during the disorder. After this meeting the two political executives appointed Joseph L. Hudson, Jr., president of Detroit's largest department chain store, as the New Detroit Committee's chairman.[38] He in turn selected 38 additional committee members whose work was "intended to show not only that something was being done as a consequence of the riots, but also that there was a recognition that necessary remedial actions would have to be as sweeping as the causes and the dimensions of the disturbances themselves."[39] Originally the New Detroit Committee and the Mayor's Development Team were intended to work in tandem in Detroit's rebuilding effort. But differences between the two study groups eventually disrupted harmonious relations and led to competition over appropriate strategies in rebuilding Detroit.

The New Detroit Committee drew its membership exclusively from representatives of Detroit's private sector, including the chairmen of Ford, Chrysler and General Motors Corporations; the presidents of United Auto Workers, Detroit Edison, Michigan Bell, Michigan Gas and six other business concerns; and six administrators of private social service agencies. The New Detroit Committee took pride in announcing that "many of these members are world-renowned leaders in their own spheres." The committee thus represented the private elite of Detroit. Yet, by its own standards, the committee desired to be "broad enough to be representative of many of the viewpoints in the black and white communities."[40] Nine black residents of Detroit were therefore included among the committee's 39 members.

Two weeks after appointment, the New Detroit Committee was attacked by the New Black Establishment Committee, a group of over 300 Detroit blacks. The militant organization described the committee as "another arm of the white power structure out to impose its notions of what's best for them upon black people."[41] The issue of adequate representation of residents of riot-affected areas created tensions within the committee. It claimed that "three of the nine Negro members proudly acknowledge the label of militant,"[42] but all three had resigned by the time the New Detroit Committee released its progress report.

The New Detroit Committee held 15 meetings in the nine months between its creation and release of the progress report. It relied on a staff of nearly 100 persons on loan from business and labor groups represented on the committee. The committee and its staff divided into five research teams: communications; community services; education and employment; law and finance; and redevelopment and housing. In April of 1968 it released a progress report which dismissed the riffraff interpretation of participants in the Detroit riot and reported that no evidence could be found about any conspiracy or planning prior to the violence. The report also described immediate post-riot efforts to clean up the riot-affected areas. The main body of the report contains a list of 50 individual endeavors undertaken by the committee unassisted by the Development Team and assesses areas of success and failure. The progress report includes the first public admission of a breakdown of expected cordial relations by critically reviewing Mayor Cavanagh's treatment of pressing inner-city problems and listing 12 recommendations for action directed at the mayor and common council.

The initial harmony between the two study groups actually dissipated shortly after their independent investigations began. The previous experience of members of the two study groups may have contributed to the dissolution of harmonious relations. A commissioner from the Development Team commented:

309

The initial response of the New Detroit Committee was fantastic. The members they had could move this city if they wanted to. Industry gave them a talent-loaded staff. So at first we worked with them and had confidence in them. But they all lacked experience in dealing with inner-city problems. They were naive. They did work long and hard, but no progress resulted. Finally liaison between us just broke down.

A staff member of the New Detroit Committee similarly remarked:

The New Detroit Committee had all the resources in the city. But we couldn't get anything done. Partially this was the fault of the committee members. We had to spend a large amount of time just informing them what the problems are. Some learned. Others still don't know what has to be done. But city hall and the Development Team didn't give us any cooperation either. They had very little interest in what we were trying to do.

The two study groups went about the rebuilding effort by different routes. Independent study of different subjects by the two groups led to disinterest in what the other group was doing rather than complementary activity. The coordinator of the Development Team noted: "We had a document after ninety days. The New Detroit Committee had nothing. And yet, they acted just as if our report didn't exist. They were out meeting groups, talking to people, trying to change people by education. We desired immediate action and worked through city agencies to get it."

The primary reason for competition between the two study groups, however, derived from the different interests represented by members. The Development Team, as the official, public study group, concentrated on municipal agency reorganization. To do so it allowed and even encouraged the New Detroit Committee, as the private study group, to absorb community concern and deflect criticism and attention away from its work. But the New Detroit Committee insisted on doing more than public relations. By involving itself in Detroit's public response to the disorders, it threatened to usurp functions normally performed by the mayor's office, agency heads, or, in the immediate post-riot context, by the Mayor's Development Team.

The threatened incursion by a private study group into areas traditionally reserved for public authorities raised the issue of which riot investigation could legitimately give direction to public agencies.[43]

The Development Team claimed exclusive prerogatives in giving directives to public agencies, but the New Detroit Committee's investigation led it to believe that the practices of public agencies were in need of reform and it desired to directly effect those changes. The Development Team member in charge of liaison with the New Detroit Committee recalled the friction:

> We thought the New Detroit Committee would come up with *new* proposals. We hoped they would put new issues before the community. But they insisted on going to city agencies to get their ideas. What this meant was that they were getting *old* ideas that hadn't worked. And they entered agencies not only to get ideas, but also to change practices. We had a devil of a time keeping them from going into city agencies and picking up their old programs.

A staff member of the New Detroit Committee gave a different version of the conflict:

> They didn't tell us what was going on over there and they didn't receive our suggestions favorably. All they really wanted was to secure their own vested interests. They were concerned that we not get out of hand and go in directions they didn't like or that we take over some of their functions. Cavanagh just wanted to be sure that his position wasn't threatened by us. And he did feel threatened! That is why he never once went out of his way to aid us.

Relations between the two riot study groups deteriorated as basic questions of authority were raised in Detroit's rebuilding effort. Each organization claimed legitimacy for engaging in activities considered illegitimate by the other group.

Relations did not improve over time. With each new overture from the New Detroit Committee, the Development Team became more cautious about allowing it access to public agencies. As another staff member from the New Detroit Committee put it: "Their liaison man sat in on all of our sessions, but he just watched us. They didn't offer any help or make any suggestions—all they really did was to watch out that we didn't go too far." As the conflict between the two groups crystallized, coordinator Strichartz of the Development Team, at the fiftieth anniversary meeting of Detroit's United Community Services, attacked private welfare agencies' allocation of publicly gathered resources to middle-class areas at the expense of more pressing needs in low-income black neighborhoods.[44] It was clear from the address that he was also critical of allowing private groups to assume essentially public functions like those attempted by the New Detroit Committee.

Milwaukee: The Little Kerner Commission

Mayor Maier's official program for Milwaukee prompted harsh criticism from black groups not represented in the deliberations producing the 39-point program and from state officials, who bore the brunt of a large share of the recommendations (see Table 7.4). State Senate Republican majority leader Jerris Leonard responded to these demands by spearheading the creation of a state riot commission. In May 1968, as chairman of the Wisconsin Legislative Council, Senator Leonard appointed an "Advisory Committee on the Report of the National Commission on Civil Disorders."

The "Little Kerner Commission," as it came to be known, consisted of two state legislators, two university professors, two businessmen, one labor leader, one clergyman and one state administrator. It conducted 15 hearings over an eight-month period in four Wisconsin cities with significant black populations. It heard 151 witnesses, employed a staff of three researchers and collected 85 documents. A final public report of over 100 pages was released in January of 1969 and it included 74 recommendations for implementing in the state of Wisconsin the proposals of the Kerner Commission.

The stated purpose of this study group was to determine how the findings of the Kerner Commission *Report* could usefully be applied to state government in Wisconsin. Its charge explicitly states this:

> It was the committee's task to determine what, if any, of the findings and conclusions of the [National] Report are applicable to Wisconsin, and to determine what opportunities exist for *state government* to remedy problems which are raised by the Report.[45]

The most significant feature of the Littler Kerner Commission's report is, however, the manner in which it sought to reverse the impression created by the 39-point program that Wisconsin's Republican-controlled state government was the jurisdiction most in need of reform in the area of race relations. Despite its assigned task, the Little Kerner Commission directed fully one-third of its recommendations for change at local governmental jurisdictions, most of which identified Milwaukee's city administration as the target for reform.

312

In addition to these proposals, the Little Kerner Commission adopted a firm position on what it regarded as administrative shortcomings in Milwaukee's municipal agencies. The police department, for example, was described in the following terms:

> In Milwaukee, no person or agency in a position of authority over law enforcement has demonstrated a willingness to discuss police policy with citizens. The consequence is a sense of frustration in the Negro community, a loss of confidence in the police, an increase in tensions and, in general, a deterioration in the relationships between police and ghetto residents. . . .In Milwaukee, it is not clear to the public who has *responsibility* for making important law enforcement decisions (although it seems clear that most important decisions are in fact made by the police chief).[46]

Instead of confining its analysis to aspects of state government, as stated in the charge, the competing commission targeted reforms for local jurisdictions and critically evaluated Milwaukee's city administration.

The attack on Maier's administration provoked a dissent from the lone commissioner from Milwaukee, a Democrat and supporter of Maier. Assemblyman Robert Huber issued a "supplementary statement," included in the final report, that in part reads:

> If there is anything that I disagree with in the report, it is the thinly disguised effort to discredit the sincere efforts of the city of Milwaukee to solve the problems of the inner city. If I were to name any organization dedicated to discrediting the city administration, I would lay the blame with the [state] department of industry, labor and human relations. I am happy to say they seem to have stayed far enough away so we could get to our job. I am disturbed but a little less now about the situation in Milwaukee than I was at the first hearings we held. At these first few hearings, it was painfully obvious, but thinly disguised, that the administration of the city of Milwaukee and the police department were under attack. I felt that this committee was not going to go any place if that was going to be its main objective. While there are always areas to which you can speak for improvement, whether it is the city of Milwaukee or the police department, when you are dealing with a controversial subject, you have to deal not just with the negative part of it, but what is being done positively. The city of Milwaukee is doing things. Everyone will measure what Milwaukee is doing from where they sit.

Some say the city administration is making a constructive effort. The progressive changes which are now taking place in the city of Milwaukee accent positive thinking, and I think they will bring about the communication and unity of purpose that is needed in that city.[47]

This is a familiar pattern. The mayor blamed the state. The state commission blamed the city. Huber, representing Milwaukee on the state panel, dissented from the Littler Kerner Commission, stressing that the locus of blame most appropriately fixes on state agencies. Jurisdictional disputation thus characterized the competition for legitimating reform proposals in Wisconsin. In part this reflected the partisan division between city and state executives. But it was also promoted by the impression conveyed in the 39-point program that Wisconsin's Republican-controlled state government shared major responsibility for correcting racial inequalities in its cities. The Little Kerner Commission's attempt to hold municipal jurisdictions accountable for enacting reforms simply reversed the fixing of blame.

Conclusion

After several false starts, political executives appointed official riot study groups. In each city discontented groups questioned the composition and orientation of the official study panels, or objected to the character of official explanations and recommendations. These misgivings stimulated the creation of parallel riot study panels, which we have labelled competing riot commissions.

The origins of competing commissions can be traced to the incomplete representation of interests on the official study groups. Official study groups tended to explain the violence in ways favorable to the interests represented by their members and to recommend reforms that did not threaten and tended to enhance those interests. Interests excluded from membership on the official investigations tried to deflect blame from themselves and sought reform proposals that benefited them. Competing riot commissions provided such alternatives.

In addition to the contagious aspect—"if they do it, so can we"—adoption of the commission format by excluded interests was a convenient way to combat the adverse effects of the official study groups. It was available and could be created with relative ease. As a temporary, *ad hoc* response to concerns generated by riots it involved

314

none of the heavy costs and commitments that more permanent or structured responses would entail. Also, the appointing group or individual could exercise a measure of control over the outcome of the process. The assignment of tasks, selection of members and provision of supporting resources remain the prerogatives of the competing commissions' creators. Thus competing commissions arise for many of the reasons that official commissions do.[48] Competing riot commissions are created to promote interests their sponsors consider either neglected in the official investigations' final reports, or that they anticipate will be neglected. Sensing that its interests would be slighted, the New Jersey State Patrolmen's Benevolent Association formed a commission when it learned that no law enforcement representatives had been placed on the Governor's Commission. In Milwaukee, the Democratic city administration targeted state government for reform through the 39-point program which led Republican state officials to create a competing riot commission which targeted reform back to the city of Milwaukee. Although not created for this purpose, the representation of Detroit's private elite on the New Detroit Committee led that group to undermine the work of the Mayor's Development Team, which represented that city's official political leadership. Competing commissions may thus be viewed as reflecting their sponsors' desire not to let the official investigations' conclusions and recommendations go uncontested.

Competition For Authority

Contests between official and competing riot commissions take place over claims to authoritative status of the official study groups. Official commissions' claims to authority are always precarious. To some degree the claims rest on the public expectation that public officials who appoint commissions will be bound by the advice that is forthcoming. But as we pointed out in chapter 5, public officials may choose not to receive a commission's advice, particularly if the advice runs counter to their policy agenda. Despite general public expectations, official commissions are *advisory* and *recommendatory* to their sponsors, who need not heed the advice they sought.

Official commissions may claim to be authoritative by virtue of their official position; they are appointed by public officials and receive public funds. But authoritative status is not the same as official status. We return here to our earlier (but no longer hypothetical) discussion of the mutually exclusive claims to authoritative status made by official and competing riot commissions. In Milwaukee an official municipal investigation claimed authoritative status but so too did an official state commission. Both riot study groups claimed authority over the same political questions. In Detroit a competing private commission, appointed by public officials, claimed authority to engage in activities within the jurisdictional domain of the official public commission. And in Newark a private competing riot commission sponsored by a police fraternal organization advanced what it claimed were authoritative law enforcement policy proposals in opposition to a different set of prescriptions offered by the official state riot commission.

Clearly riot commissions possess no monopoly on authority by virtue of their official status; rather they enjoy only as much authority as they can successfully develop or assert. This is consistent with Talcott Parsons' well-known observation that there is another source of authority in modern societies besides Weber's office incumbency.[49] Parsons argued that authority may also be based upon superior skill, technical competence and knowledge.[50] Hence the importance of identifying how official and competing riot commissions manipulate symbols and otherwise try to establish legitimacy for their inquiries in order to enhance acceptance for their work by public officials and the society in general.

Competition For Legitimacy

Official and competing riot commissions lack the necessary requisites to enforce their findings and recommendations. Instead, each attempts to establish legitimacy for its work. Although official study groups initially inherit a degree of legitimacy by virtue of the endorsements by public officials with which they are launched, this does not insure their continued acceptance or even the retention of their original high public regard. They must continually struggle to establish their legitimacy, a task made more complicated by the existence of parallel study groups. Many of the symbols employed by the competing commissions are exactly the same as those developed by official study groups; both types of commissions claim representativeness, promise a thorough inquiry, assemble a research staff, employ consultants, hold formal hearings, take testimony from witnesses and collect documents. Both generally assert political and scientific legitimacy for their work, tailor their reports to ideas currently popular and issue final reports including urgent recommendations for reform.

Variations may be observed among competing commissions in the strategies they adopt in trying to establish the legitimacy of their inquiries. The PBA Commission was concerned mainly with the law enforcement policy area. With this narrow policy focus, especially compared to the broad-ranging Governor's Commission, the PBA could afford to attack in depth and at length the assertions made in this area by the official commission. The PBA Commission could demand attention because the policy focus it selected was in its area of expertise. But the commission also suffered because members were interested parties. The New Detroit Committee sought legitimacy for its activities by maintaining that the private resources it could mobilize for rebuilding Detroit were superior to those available to the public sector, particularly as these were deployed by the official Development Team. The Little Kerner Commission attempted to reverse the impression created by the 39-point program that the state legislative agenda required reordering by articulating an alternative municipal agenda aimed at the city administration in Milwaukee.

One offshoot of the competition for legitimacy that characterized post-riot investigations was to dilute the impact of the nonpolicy functions of the official riot commissions described in chapter 3. Challenges to the validity of official commission explanations undoubtedly perpetuated mass uncertainties about the causes, nature and effects of the racial violence. This was particularly so when competing commissions went beyond questioning the adequacy of interpretations offered by official commissions to provide alternative explanations.

In their final reports the competing commissions predictably arrived at conclusions exonerating their sponsors from blame and issued reform recommendations either protective of or advantageous to their sponsors' interests. Like the official riot commissions, the competing commissions mobilized the political interests of the particular groups they represented.

NOTES, CHAPTER 8

1. David Easton, *The Political System* (New York: Alfred A. Knopf, 1953), p. 132. Although our use of the concept of authority is conventional in one sense, it is not the conventional Weberian usage. We return to this subject in the conclusion of this chapter.

2. Anthony M. Platt, *The Politics of Riot Commissions* (New York: Collier Books, 1971), p. 4.

3. Ibid., emphasis in original.

4. Ibid.

5. Generally, see Easton, *The Political System.*

6. Governor's Select Commission, *Report For Action,* pp. 143, 144, 177.

7. Newark *News,* 16 February 1968; see also Ron Porambo, *No Cause For Indictment: An Autopsy of Newark* (New York: Holt, Rinehart, and Winston, 1971), pp. 28, 29.

8. Newark *News,* 14 February 1968.

9. New Jersey State Patrolmen's Benevolent Association, "A Challenge To Conscience: A Summary of the Report of the Riot Study Commission" (mimeo.; Maplewood, New Jersey; dated May 1968), p. 1.

10. Findings of Riot Study Commission of the New Jersey State Patrolmen's Benevolent Association, Inc., *The Road To Anarchy* (Maplewood, N.J.: New Jersey State Patrolmen's Benevolent Association, 1968), p. 33.

11. Immediately after the Newark disorder, Heffernan displayed an increasingly tough police attitude: "The restraint on police is so great it will finally let go and there will be tremendous fatalities. The situation is increasingly intolerable. Why shouldn't looters carrying away TV sets in open sight be mowed down like anyone else committing a serious felony? You can't play footsy with an animal element"; quoted in the Detroit *News,* 25 July 1967.

12. The greeting followed by one day the release of the official report; see Newark *News,* 12 February 1968, emphasis added.

13. N.J.S.P.B.A., "A Challenge To Conscience," p. 5.

14. Ibid., p. 7.

15. N.J.S.P.B.A., *The Road To Anarchy,* p. 9.

16. Ibid., p. 10.

17. Ibid., p. 9.

18. Ibid., p. 32. For a description of procedures followed by the P.B.A. Commission see ibid.

19. President Heffernan greeted the official commission report by saying, "The governor's commission, weakened in its creation because not a single law enforcement officer was named to it, has rendered a serious disservice to the public in intimating that no conspiracy existed"; quoted in Newark *News,* 26 February 1968.

20. N.J.S.P.B.A., "A Challenge To Conscience," p. 4.

21. N.J.S.P.B.A., *The Road To Anarchy,* p. 36.

22. Quoted in the Newark *News,* 17 February 1968.

23. N.J.S.P.B.A., *The Road To Anarchy,* p. 122.

24. The report of the P.B.A. Commission indicates that, "The Governor declared that the riots were 'plain and simple crime,' 'obvious open rebelling,' and 'criminal insurrection.' He declared that 'we must use force to combat force,' and that 'the provisions of the emergency disaster proclamation are broad enough to permit the shooting of looters if they do not cease their criminal activities.' And Governor Hughes later remarked that, 'Snipers have to be shot down if you can get at them' " (ibid., p. 157).

25. Ibid., p. 55. The anger embodied in the questions posed by the P.B.A. Commission does not make them any less valid. Police irritation at the absence of any follow-up to Governor Hughes's statements about "criminal insurrection" and "obvious open rebelling" is certainly understandable. Elsewhere we have suggested that inflammatory statements like Hughes's create a climate within which citizens operate. No less applies to the police. Hughes's remarks gave license to the police to take the extreme views embodied in his statements. Although we suggest elsewhere that Hughes should never have granted this license, it is equally reasonable for the police to be irritated that, once licensed, the locus of authority did not back them up.

26. Ibid., p. 148.

27. Note the P.B.A. Commission's general indictment: "They either ignored information that they had received, or refused to acknowledge or seek out information readily accessible to them. . . .The failings of the Governor's Commission to fulfill its duty to the people of New Jersey, the questionable validity and/or accuracy of many of the statements and findings made by the Commission, and the careless manner in which it collected and disposed of evidence presented to it have been pointed out previously in this report and will continue to be seen throughout the remainder of it" (ibid., p. 123).

28. Ibid., pp. 41, 48, 49.

29. It said, "The evidence that witnesses or interviewees were able or willing to provide to the Commission would not support a conclusion that there was a conspiracy or plan to organize the disorders" (Governor's Select Commission, *Report for Action*, p. 142).

30. N.J.S.P.B.A., *The Road To Anarchy*, p. 87.

31. See, for example, the references to Governor Hughes and to Mayor Addonizio's claim that outside agitators participated in the Newark disorder in ibid., p. 54.

32. The competing commission's final report refers to "the words of Charles S. Hyneman, former president of the American Political Science Association: 'We have fallen into a mood of acceptance of protest as being good in itself. Because the Negro has a just cause, it is assumed that the disorders he creates should be excused no matter the extent of

COMMISSION POLITICS

disruption to a city or even a nation. Ordinary duties of citizenship are supposed not to apply to him. Obviously this is disastrous' " (ibid., p. 23).

33. The condemnation was given by the biracial Committee of Concern that also said the hearings would lead "to further alienation of the community and the city's government." The committee concluded by calling on "all segments of our community to join in halting holding the hearings at City Hall and the insidious danger they represent" (quoted in the Newark *News*, 23 February 1968).

34. Newark *News*, 31 January 1968.

35. N.J.S.P.B.A., *The Road To Anarchy*, p. 189; see also p. 21 in ibid.

36. Quoted in the Newark *News*, 27 February 1968.

37. Special Committee to Investigate Irregularities in the Total Action Against Poverty Program in the City of Detroit, "Examination of the War On Poverty," Michigan House of Representatives, 74th Session, January 1968, p. 1.

38. We have labeled the New Detroit Committee a "competing" riot investigation for purposes of analysis here. It is clear that the committee was originally created by two public officials: Governor Romney and Mayor Cavanagh. We do not view the New Detroit Committee as an official riot investigation in spite of how it was appointed because only one of its 39 members was selected by public officials and the committee did not receive public financing.

39. The New Detroit Committee, *Progress Report* (Detroit, Michigan: The New Detroit Committee, April 1968), p. 24.

40. Ibid., pp. 4, 23.

41. Quoted in the Detroit *News*, 11 August 1967. The spokesman for the group, the militant black Reverend Albert B. Cleage, commented, "We'll run this town. We'll build the homes and the stores. The white man will have to deal with us" (ibid).

42. The New Detroit Committee, *Progress Report*, p. 22.

43. Frank Joyce notes that the New Detroit Committee desired to operate certain municipal tasks normally thought the province only of public agencies. The logical extension of this type of private group effort "is a new kind of effort on the part of corporations, and a new kind of liberalism, or at least liberalism from a new source. In some places the idea might eventually result in corporate subdivisions that would run things like the Job Corps. Corporations might even be hired to administer cities. . . .The questions become simply, who is going to pick up the garbage, or who is going to see that the police get to work on time, and so on, and these are the kinds of operations best left to corporations, whose primary criterion is efficiency. And this is, in part,

the primary criterion of the New Detroit Committee"; Frank Joyce, "Postscript From Detroit: Death of Liberalism," *The Center Magazine* 1, no. 3 (March 1968):46.

44. On the distribution of money and material perquisites to the poor, Strichartz commented: "Frankly, I think the public agencies were more responsive than the private agencies." Remarks of Richard Strichartz before the 50th Anniversary Session of United Community Services of Metropolitan Detroit (mimeo.; Detroit, Michigan; dated 28 September 1967), p. 8.

45. See Advisory Committee on the Report of the National Commission on Civil Disorders, *Final Report* (Madison, Wisconsin: Wisconsin Legislative Council, January 1969), p. 17, emphasis added.

46. Ibid., p. 30.

47. Ibid., pp. 5, 6.

48. We might conjecture about why the three competing riot commissions discussed in this chapter carried out their investigations, whereas the "false starts" did not. One reason may be that the interests of the sponsors of the competing commissions were more directly and sizably threatened or challenged by the composition and work of the official study groups than the interests of the sponsors of the false starts.

Note also the changes in the ideological character of competing riot commissions over the time span of 1917 through 1943, compared to the more recent period. The early efforts to diminish the impact of official riot commissions through competing commissions were much more problack than competing commissions of the current era. In large part this is explained by the generalized antiblack ideology that characterized so many of the early official riot commissions. The competing commissions in the early period originated from sponsoring groups with problack sentiments that attempted to undermine antiblack expressions in official reports. The 1943 Marshall investigation in Detroit is a good case in point.

In the current era, when antiblack expressions have been less generalized or at least less crudely presented in official commission reports, the competing commissions have tended to be sponsored by groups opposed to the interests of blacks. This latter patterning may explain why recent competing commissions have been sponsored by establishment and elite interests that lack representation on the official commissions.

49. Weber argued that authority in rational-legal-social systems is characterized by an impersonalized order of generalized and universalistic rules and that the exercisers of authority possess legitimacy by virtue of office incumbency. Thus authority for Weber is equated

automatically with official position. See Talcott Parsons, ed., *Max Weber: The Theory of Social and Economic Organization*, trans. A. M. Henderson and Talcott Parsons (New York: Free Press, 1947). Weber's position is found on pages 56-77 and Parsons's critique on pages 58-60 n. 4.

50. Parsons points out that Weber himself saw, but did not recognize analytically, a form of authority other than that based upon office incumbency when the impersonal order in rational-legal systems breaks down. Parsons uses the illustration of the modern physician as an exerciser of authority who does so on the basis of skill, knowledge, and competence rather than by virtue of holding legal office. It is intriguing to note the parallels with Parsons's "technical competence" type of authority that arise if we substitute riot commissions for physicians. Office incumbents (public officials) faced with the breakdown of routines in an impersonalized order (civil disorder) turn to physicians (riot commissions) as possessors of skill, knowledge, and competence for advice. The analogy of riot commissions to Parsons's physician becomes even more clear if we engage in the same substitution using Parsons's statements: "This authority rests, fundamentally, on the belief on the part of the patient [public officials] that the physician [riot commission] has and will employ for his benefit a technical competence adequate to help him in his illness [civil disorder]." And: "His [riot commission] getting his orders [recommendations] obeyed depends entirely on securing the voluntary consent of his patient [public officials] to submit to them" (ibid., p. 59). Thus the kind of authority involved here is quite different from that derived from office incumbency. Perhaps needless to say, this analogy serves nicely to show inherent limits on the authority of riot commissions that have yet to achieve a level of technical competence equivalent to the modern physician.

9

Implementation of Riot Commission Recommendations

Political legitimacy and authority are important to riot commissions because they enhance the likelihood that their recommendations will be adopted as public policy. A commission's concern for the impact of the reforms it proposes has a direct effect upon its procedures and upon its efforts to endow commission reports with scientific validity and political acceptability. Despite riot commissions' emphasis on the importance of implementing their recommendations, however, most observers have failed to consider what happens to these proposals for change after the commission dissolves. The assumption seems to be that the political significance of a commission ends with the release of its reports.[1] Yet it is impossible to evaluate the impact of any political structure, process or recommendation without examining what effect it has on policies adopted by the larger political system.

Riot commissions and other official inquiries represent the most immediate and visible official response to racial violence. To know what becomes of riot commission recommendations is to understand to a considerable degree the ways in which official political institutions reacted to the racial violence.[2] The extent to which the 1960s riots are thought to express political demands depends in important respects on how the putative demands are received. Previously we dealt with the rhetorical and symbolic receptions given rioters' demands and with the processes created to deal with them. In what follows we focus on their substantive reception.

The widely held impression is that few reforms proposed by riot inquiries are ever adopted. Kenneth B. Clark's testimony before the Kerner Commission is often quoted:

> I read that report...of the 1919 riot in Chicago, and it is as if I were reading the report of the investigating committee on the Harlem riot of '35, the report of the investigating committee on the Harlem riot of '43, the report of the McCone Commission on the Watts riot. I must again in candor say to you members of this Commission—it is a kind of Alice in Wonderland—with the same moving picture re-shown over and over again, the same analysis, the same recommendations, and the same inaction.[3]

Judge A. Leon Higginbotham echoed Clark's pessimism in a dissenting opinion written for the National Commission on the Causes and Prevention of Violence:

> Surveying this landscape, littered with the unimplemented recommendations of so many previous commissions, I am compelled to propose a national moratorium on any additional temporary study commissions to probe the causes of racism or poverty, or crime, or the urban crisis. The rational response to the work of the great commissions of recent years is not the appointment of still more commissions to study the same problems—but rather the prompt implementation of their many valuable recommendations.[4]

Others have similarly concluded that, during the year after its report, the Kerner Commission's recommendations were virtually ignored.[5]

In this chapter we will assess the degree to which recommendations made by riot inquiries in Newark, Detroit and Milwaukee were adopted as public policy by focusing on the three "official" inquiries conducted in these cities and on two other "competing" inquiries which were initiated with official blessings (the New Detroit Committee) or by other governmental jurisdictions (the Little Kerner Commission). By determining the frequency with which recommendations were implemented, we will be able to confirm or reject the widely held belief that a commission's reform proposals usually are never enacted. In Chapter 10 we will concentrate on the *political* aspects of attempts to implement the reform proposals, thus identifying the most salient factors in a recommendation's implementation. Rather than viewing riot inquiries as existing in a political vacuum, our research strategy places the work of riot commissions in the context of the larger political system where the fate of their recommendations is ultimately determined.

Newark: The Governor's Commission

The Governor's Select Commission on Civil Disorder released its 200-page *Report for Action* after just over six months of investigation and deliberation. The *Report* is devoted primarily to an analysis of the causes of and remedies for racial violence in Newark with cursory attention to Englewood and Plainfield, New Jersey. It concludes with a 16-page section listing 99 recommendations, many of which call for reform of political, social and economic programs affecting Newark's black community.

Periodically the Governor's Commission expressed concern about seeing its recommendations implemented as public policy. In writing the *Report* itself, the commission adopted language intended to assuage the concerns of those groups and public officials, particularly the governor, upon whom it perceived its recommendations to be dependent for enactment. Just prior to releasing the *Report*, Commission Chairman Lilley unsuccessfully appealed to Governor Hughes to extend the life of the commission due to "a strong feeling on the part of the Commissioners that the great amount of time and effort that they have expended would have no results unless some body was concerned about implementation."[6] Later, individual commissioners lobbied for adoption of the proposed reforms. Consistent with the title of its final document, *Report for Action*, the commission presented its reform proposals with considerable urgency:

> The mood in our cities clearly indicates that commissions like ours will have outlived their usefulness unless action is forthcoming from their recommendations. Our disadvantaged communities must see far more tangible evidence of a commitment to change than has emerged so far, or the summer of 1967 is likely to become a prologue to tragedy, and the time for study and planning will have run out.[7]

The Governor's Commission sought to create the public impression that most of its recommendations could be implemented relatively easily, without substantially increased expenditures. At a press conference called to release the *Report*, Lilley expressed confidence that the proposed reforms would be complied with because, he said, no additional funds would be required to implement over half of the recommendations, some recommendations were already in the process of being carried out and still other proposals "should be accepted wholeheartedly."[8] This initial optimism proved unrealistic; the recommendations engendered considerable controversy and met with strong, generally effective, opposition.

Despite controversy generated by the commission's proposed reforms and subsequent opposition to them, some recommendations were implemented. Table 9.1 presents the number and percent of recommendations targeted for each of the seven governmental jurisdictions singled out for reform and the number and percent of the recommendations receiving favorable action from those jurisdictions.[9] Just over one-fourth of all of the reform proposals received favorable action, in contrast to popular impressions that few, if any, recommendations are ever enacted as public policy. On the other hand, the one-fourth adoption ratio also calls into question the unqualified optimism of spokesmen from the Governor's Commission.

Important differences in the rates of implementation emerge from the data presented in Table 9.1. The various governmental jurisdictions targeted for change varied considerably in the degree to which they adopted proposed reforms. The state of New Jersey acted favorably upon nearly half of the recommendations aimed in its direction (14 of 29); and over half of all successfully implemented recommendations (14 of 26) received favorable action from this jurisdiction. Newark proved much less receptive to reforms proposed by the Governor's Commission, acting favorably on only one-fifth of the recommendations aimed in its direction.

We have labeled the state of New Jersey the *primary jurisdiction* because it was the governmental unit presided over by the executive originally appointing the (Governor's) Commission. The relatively high rate of enacting reforms within this primary jurisdiction may be explained by several factors. Members of the commission were originally selected by Governor Hughes and their views on which policies should be initiated reflected his policy agenda to a greater extent than the agendas of public officials in other jurisdictions. More explicitly, the commissioners "tailored" their recommendations aimed at the state to fit the needs of the appointing executive with the intent

TABLE 9.1

Governor's Commission's Recommendations: By Jurisdiction Targeted for Reform and Number Receiving Favorable Action

Governmental Jurisdiction Targeted for Reform	Number of Recommendations	Percent of Recommendations	Number Receiving Favorable Action	Percent Recommendations Receiving Favorable Action
Newark	33	33	7	21
Essex County	6	6	1	16.6
State of New Jersey (*Primary Jurisdiction*)	29	29	14	48.2
Federal Government	4	4	1	25
Combined or no jurisdiction specified	22	22	3	13.6
Englewood	2	2	n.a.	–
Plainfield	3	3	n.a.	–
TOTALS	99		26	26

of gaining a favorable reception. Later, individual commissioners lobbied the governor for enactment of their suggested reforms.

Contrast this favorable posture of the commission toward its primary jurisdiction with its highly critical review of the Addonizio administration, its thorough cataloguing of deficiencies in Newark's municipal services and its charge that blacks were systematically denied access to political structures in Newark. The recommendations directed toward Newark, which lacked any representation on the commission, were much more specific and costly and slightly more numerous than those targeted for the primary jurisdiction.

The lowest frequency of successful implementation occurred in the category of "combined or no jurisdiction specified" (see Table 9.1). Here attributions of joint responsibility among multiple governmental jurisdictions or the absence of attributions of responsibility altogether appear to have led to failures to adopt commission recommendations. These observations will be elaborated in chapter 10 where close attention is given to each recommendation and the political response it elicited.

Detroit: The Mayor's Development Team

Toward the end of Detroit's civil disorder, Mayor Cavanagh charged the Mayor's Development Team with three tasks: to alleviate riot-caused hardship by restoring public and community services; to formulate a blueprint to guide city agency plans aimed at the social and physical redevelopment of Detroit; and to act in liaison with the New Detroit Committee and city agencies in carrying out agreed-upon plans. The Development Team wholly failed to accomplish its third task, but fulfilled the first and second tasks to a significant degree—in the process accomplishing more than any other riot inquiry reviewed here.

The First Task: Restoration of Services

In carrying out its first assignment—"to coordinate city departmental activities to assure that the appropriate measures are taken to restore public and community services and alleviate hardship"[10]—the Development Team directly intervened in city agency operations to provide emergency relief and restoration of services. Few riot commissions have been mandated with such a directly interventionist role, yet commissions may function as well and perhaps even better in this capacity than in their more traditional tasks. The Kerner Commission, for example, achieved its sole legislative enactment by directly intervening on behalf of the insurance bill.[11] Similarly, the Development Team justifiably claimed to have essentially fulfilled its first task.[12] Consideration of the tactics it used to provide emergency relief may illuminate an area rarely assigned to commissions, but one uniquely within the realm of their capabilities.

One of the Development Team's five operating divisions, "Emergency Plans" (see Table 7.3), assumed primary responsibility for implementing the first task. It began by absorbing the personnel, resources and functions of the existing Mayor's Summer Task Force, created by Cavanagh the prior summer in response to minor racial hostilities in Detroit's Kercheval section. Before the 1967 riots, the Summer Task Force had monitored tense racial situations, worked with the Mayor's Council on Youth Opportunities and channeled available resources to poverty-stricken neighborhoods. During the 1967 Detroit disorder, it continued to monitor and report rumors about the instances of burning, looting and shooting. It performed these same services under the auspices of the Development Team, also providing 24-hour coverage of rumors, determining their accuracy and either transmitting valid rumors to appropriate city agencies or reporting false rumors to community leaders. The rumor-monitoring service continued for one month under Development Team sponsorship; thereafter it became a permanent program incorporated into Detroit's Commission on Community Relations.

Immediately after the violence, many Detroit residents were unable to determine the whereabouts of relatives and friends. Thirty-three persons were killed, another 300 injured and nearly 7,000 were arrested. To locate persons unaccounted for, the Development Team initiated "Project Find," consisting primarily of a roster of arrestees in custody and the injured in local hospitals. The missing persons roster was maintained for over two months and at its peak listed the names and locations of several thousand citizens. The Development Team enlisted the assistance of municipal courts, the police department, the sheriff's office and the city health department in assembling and maintaining the roster.

The Development Team also intervened to provide an emergency food-distribution system in neighborhoods affected by the riot. Burning and looting effectively closed most retail food outlets in several areas of the city and foodstuffs remained unavailable or merchants refused to reopen their stores in the wake of the riot. The Development Team coordinated the provision of food to these neighborhoods with the assistance of Detroit's Office of Economic Opportunity and Office of Civil Defense and prodded the release of additional resources from the Department of Agriculture and the American Red Cross.

Food scarcity in riot neighborhoods created a phenomenal increase in the prices of available food, with some items more than doubling. To alleviate this problem, the Development Team intervened to guide an ordinance through the city council which prohibited price gouging and coordinated the enforcement of the ordinance with the City Health Department. The Development Team also made referrals for replacement of damaged or lost clothing and furniture to social service agencies, prompted the Sanitation Division and Health Department to assign added personnel for rodent and pest control, helped citizens obtain emergency, long-term, interest-free loans from Detroit's Office of Economic Opportunity and extended similar considerations to riot-damaged small businesses.

An immediate, pressing problem was shelter for residents whose housing had been burned out. The Development Team provided temporary housing in devastated areas through the Office of Civil Defense and the Wayne County Department of Social Services. After exhausting temporary facilities, the Detroit Housing Commission allowed displaced families to move into available public housing, made similar arrangements for FHA and VA housing and provided housing for large families in nearby Fort Wayne. The Fort Wayne facilities later became permanent residences for these and other large families.

Probably the most obvious area in which Detroit's recovery differed from that of other riot-torn cities was the degree to which city officials, acting through the Development Team, removed the scars of the riot. Firegutted buildings along Springfield Avenue in Newark and Third Street in Milwaukee are still untouched as of this writing. In 1969, when President Richard M. Nixon toured Seventh Street in the District of Columbia, he termed the stark ruins of civil disorder a highly visible sign of the city government's inability to cope with immediate problems; those ruins remain virtually the same in 1974. In contrast, Detroit demolished burned-out buildings in riot-torn neighborhoods through the direct intervention of the Development Team. The status of 211 buildings which were destroyed or damaged during the Detroit riot is reported in Table 9.2. Only three months after their destruction by fire, most had been razed, a record which generated stories about how the riots were Detroit's "instant urban renewal program." The vacated land on which burned structures had stood was replaced with

TABLE 9.2

Progress Report on Building-
Demolition in Detroit–16 October 1967

Status of Building Demolition	Number of Buildings
Buildings removed by owner	119
Buildings removed by Department of Public Works	6
Buildings scheduled for demolition by Department of Public Works	31
Buildings awaiting council hearing to confirm demolition order	8
Buildings under investigation and processing in Buildings and Safety Department	47
TOTAL	211

Source: Mayor's Development Team, *Report,* p. 158

grass-filled lots and mini-parks under the direction of the Development Team.

The process by which burned structures were demolished reveals the central role played by the Development Team in alleviating emergency conditions. Privately owned burned-out buildings could not simply be demolished by the city; enabling legislation was necessary. The mayor's office, Development Team and Public Works Department drew up and supported an ordinance before the city council authorizing demolition of riot-damaged and -destroyed buildings upon recommendation by the Fire Marshal's Office and the Department of Buildings and Safety Engineering. The ordinance unanimously passed the city council along with a companion resolution requiring a lien to be placed on properties with burned buildings. This induced some property owners, especially those partially or fully covered by insurance, to demolish damaged buildings on their own. This accounts, in part, for the 119 buildings reported removed by owners. Without such legislative prodding, building owners would probably have done nothing in the well-founded hope that an urban renewal or model cities program would increase returns on their property. Besides prodding property owners, the Development Team pressured city agencies to speed up demolition activities.[13]

Finally, the Development Team helped formulate emergency plans for relief in future disorders, should they occur. It drew up a plan to guide city agencies in providing immediate relief services for neighborhoods affected by looting, fires and the kind of interruption of services experienced during and immediately after the 1967 violence. The plan drew heavily on procedures used by the Development Team after the 1967 disorder. After future disorders, however, these recovery tasks would be assigned to and provided by city agencies rather than by an *ad hoc* organization like the Development Team. To insure the plan's workability, the Development Team scheduled several "dry-runs" employing city agencies. The plan included emergency provisions for the Detroit police and fire departments to make a prompt and orderly response in the event of future disorders. The emergency provisions were not made public, but assurances that adequate steps had been taken are contained in the Development Team's final *Report*.[14]

The Second Task: Blueprinting the Future

The second task assigned to the Development Team by the mayor was: "to coordinate long-range planning by city departments in creating a blueprint for the social and physical redevelopment of the city."[15] The Development Team exhaustively reviewed the past performances of all city agencies, evaluated the quality of services they rendered and made numerous recommendations for change for *each city agency* with the objective of improving the service delivery capacity of the municipal bureaucracy. Its recommendations number in the hundreds. Well over half of its 822-page final *Report* is devoted to reviewing the performance of city agencies and recommending changes affecting the agencies' personnel, budgets, structures and functions.

Besides detailing specific reforms for each agency, the Development Team provided a "blueprint" for Detroit's social and physical redevelopment, consisting of three fundamental proposals intended to encompass

332

the hundreds of specific recommendations targeted for city agencies. The proposals included: (1) consolidation of all social service agencies under a superagency indirectly responsible to the mayor's office (see Table 9.3); (2) consolidation of all physical development agencies under a superagency likewise indirectly responsible to the mayor's office (see Table 9.4); and (3) creation of a "Community Renewal Program" in the mayor's office responsible for all research and evaluation (see Table 9.5).

The Third Task: Carrying Out the Blueprint

Mayor Cavanagh assigned the Development Team a final task: "to act in a liaison capacity with the 'New Detroit Committee' and to coordinate all city agencies in their relationship with other governmental and private entities as they affect the carrying out of the Mayor's Development Team assignments."[16] This charge requested the Development Team to oversee the implementation of its own recommendations. Initially Cavanagh had envisioned that the New Detroit Committee would be the vehicle for carrying out the proposed reforms, but the expected harmony between Development Team and New Detroit Committee members failed to materialize. As shown in chapter 7, the two study groups evolved into competitive bodies and the Development Team ignored the New Detroit Committee, turning its attention to implementing the recommended city agency reforms.

In contrast to its marked accomplishments in restoring vital public services and charting a blueprint for Detroit's future, the Development Team wholly failed in the much more difficult task of putting into practice the change measures stipulated in the blueprint. City agencies effectively resisted specific reforms aimed in their direction and prevented the adoption of the three comprehensive recommendations. A preliminary explanation for this uneven success pattern, elaborated more fully in chapter 10, focuses on the response to Development Team activities by the municipal bureaucracy in Detroit, one of the most reformed city bureaucracies in the nation.[17]

The Development Team paid little attention to studying riot causes and disdained fixing blame. Instead it concentrated on deficiencies in the provision of municipal services that it viewed as remediable. Acting as an "arm of the mayor," it provided emergency relief and restored vital public services in the crisis-charged atmosphere following the riot. City agencies made this task possible by breaking with established routines to supply the required resources, personnel and services. Their unqualified cooperation allowed the Development Team to deliver

TABLE 9.3

Proposed Organization Chart for the Social Development Agency

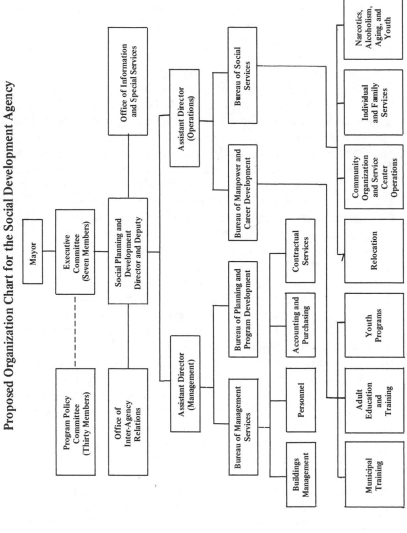

Source: M.D.T. *Report*, p. 228

TABLE 9.4

Organization Chart: Proposed City Development Agency*

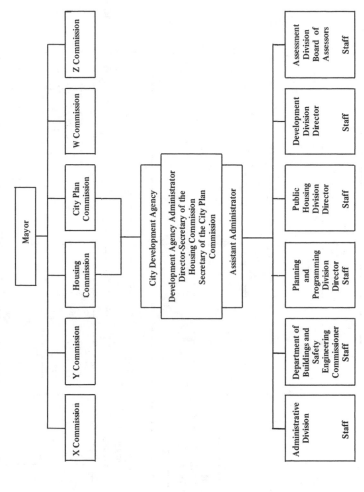

*Dotted lines indicate agencies that should be included in an administrative study to determine the feasibility of their being merged into the new proposed organization.

Source: M.D.T. *Report*, p. 58

TABLE 9.5
Proposed Organization of Community Renewal Program

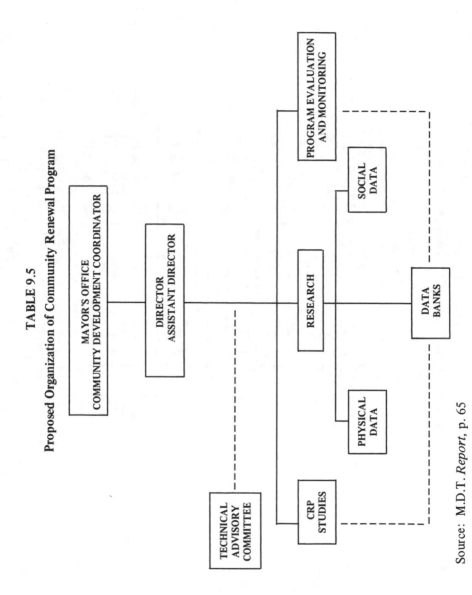

Source: M.D.T. *Report*, p. 65

emergency services to riot-scarred, predominantly black neighborhoods without detracting from services provided to other neighborhoods. The recovery effort was thus not encumbered by resistance from anti-black groups. City agencies were rallied and directed in the recovery effort after the Development Team assured the agencies that the break with routine functions was for a specific, emergency task of limited duration. The municipal bureaucracy proved responsive and instrumental in assisting the Development Team to accomplish its second task by unreservedly providing the personnel and resources necessary to formulate the blueprint for Detroit's future.

But city agencies refused to cooperate with the Development Team in its third task, actively resisting implementing the blueprint. They did so, as will be shown in chapter 10, because the blueprint had long-range implications that threatened the agencies' existing autonomy, professionalism and control. In their opposition, city agencies were supported by primarily white clientele groups which perceived an advantage to blacks in the distribution of resources outlined in the blueprint.

Detroit: The New Detroit Committee and the Limits of Private, Volunteer Intervention

Severe rioting not only prompts public elites to respond in some manner, it also elicits statements of concern from private sector elites. As shown in chapter 2, racial violence traditionally produces a call for reform from businessmen and business groups. After the 1960s riots, private elites expressed concern and made rhetorical commitments to marshal their resources to solve ghetto problems. Specific proposals ranged from the application to ghetto problems of newly discovered space technologies to the National Alliance of Business's goal of yearly hiring hundreds of thousands of unemployed and "unemployable" ghetto residents.

Nowhere in the nation did private elites respond with as significant a rhetorical commitment to easing racial problems as in Detroit. As its name implied, the New Detroit Committee promised no less than a municipal renaissance. It vowed to revitalize the city and to alter the status of black residents by channeling sizeable resources from prestigious commercial, corporate and trade union institutions to the city's disadvantaged black population.

The pledge was taken seriously locally and attracted national attention because Detroit's private elite is concentrated in a commercial-industrial-labor hierarchy and all of these interests were substantially represented on the New Detroit Committee. This same private elite created and controls one of the largest manufacturing complexes in the world. It has a long history and a well-deserved reputation for getting things done. During World War II, for example, it changed Detroit into the nation's arsenal overnight and it repeatedly conducts the most successful United Fund charity campaigns in the nation.

The impact of the New Detroit Committee on Detroit's rebuilding effort provides insight into the sufficiency of private elite responses to racial violence. Our extensive review of New Detroit Committee activities also illuminates the nature of voluntary group intervention into municipal affairs during racial crisis. Volunteers approach crisis settings with outlooks and strategies fundamentally different from those of public officials. They lack the constraints public officials so often claim to operate under, but they may experience restraints of a different order in racially troubled settings.

In its unsuccessful attempt to alter the structure of Detroit's municipal bureaucracy, the Mayor's Development Team received virtually no assistance from the New Detroit Committee. Relations between the two riot inquiries deteriorated to competitive exchanges and eventually outright hostility. Both groups, however, continued to affirm the goal of upgrading the status of blacks in Detroit. In contrast to the Development Team's use of city agency resources and personnel, the New Detroit Committee relied upon personnel and funds supplied by industry and trade union representatives. Through its first two years of existence, the committee repeatedly claimed success in achieving its goals; even when its efforts demonstrably fell short of stated objectives, it reassured concerned residents that corrective measures had been adopted.

The New Detroit Committee published a *Progress Report* charting areas of success and failure after the first nine months of its existence. More than 50 different projects intended to redress black grievances and rebuild Detroit were undertaken during this period. The *Progress Report* stressed the substantial accomplishments of the projects:

> No one is more aware of the success of the New Detroit Committee than its own members. . . .Though we have no statistics to verify our view, we have seen people change from apathy and indifference to fervent concern for the well-being of the less fortunate. We have

observed easing of previously inflexible views on housing and employment. We have noted the growing legislative success of open occupancy housing measures in the Detroit area and throughout the state of Michigan, with all of its symbolism of interracial goodwill. Often, there are intangible successes and few of them will show up on the pages of this document. But they are important successes— such as the changed attitudes and, hence, changed lives of many young executives who have served on the New Detroit task force. These men and women have great ability to influence the future direction of their own businesses and institutions, and in them, a great new hope is represented.

The *Progress Report* acknowledged shortcomings on some of the projects, but also emphasized its continuing commitment to action:

In this accounting of our progress, and our lack of it, the Committee wishes to make it clear that this is not a final report. We do not think that a final report can be written in the foreseeable future. Perhaps it can never be written. The problems confronting all of us in the Detroit metropolitan area are far too complex and hardened into our nation's character and personality by centuries of tradition and neglect for ready resolution.[18]

The *Progress Report* was, however, the last public report and the actual performance of the New Detroit Committee did not bear out its projection of a "great new hope" for Detroit.

The New Detroit Committee's claim of substantial success was misleading. The five most important areas on which it chose to concentrate were:(1) attempts to secure state legislation favorable to blacks in Detroit, (2) a program of industrial assistance to public schools, (3) applications for federal funds, (4) attempts to negotiate harmonious relationships with Detroit's black community and (5) a widely heralded employment program for jobless residents. The New Detroit Committee failed to achieve its objectives in the first, third and fourth areas. Its successful activities in the second area generated considerable controversy. Its claims to success in the final area are questionable.

The N.D.C. and the Michigan State Legislature

The New Detroit Committee initially concentrated its efforts on a special session of the Michigan legislature convened by Governor

Romney two months after the Detroit riot. The committee supported a package of bills before the special session and prestigious members appeared before the legislature on its behalf. The sizeable lobbying campaign undertaken for a bill on open occupancy is described in the committee's *Progress Report*:

> The New Detroit Committee urged the Governor to include on the agenda of the 1967 Special Session of the State Legislature an appeal for a meaningful open occupancy law. It was also for this reason that every one of the members worked hard and long to assure passage of an open occupancy bill in the Fall of 1967. There were several trips to Lansing, there were numerous speeches and communications. Acting as individuals and as representatives of the organizations which they head or for which they speak, rather than as the New Detroit Committee, these men and women brought tremendous pressure to bear in support of this measure.[19]

The special legislative session provided an immediate test of the committee's persuasive power and the amount of influence its prestigious members could and would apply. Despite the direct access of many well-known New Detroit Committee members to influential members of the Republican-controlled state legislature and the office of Republican Governor Romney, none of the bills it proposed or lobbied for were enacted.

Open housing legislation received more attention from the committee than any other single measure. Written by the New Detroit Committee, the legislation received strong backing from Governor Romney after many committee members petitioned for his support. Representatives from many of Michigan's most important commercial and industrial institutions contributed funds and their own time to lobby on behalf of the bill. But the measure failed to pass either house of the state legislature.

The committee's unsuccessful campaign for open occupancy legislation tempered committee members' initial optimism about what they could do to promote change in race relations at the state level. It was the first time many committee members had engaged in open conflict with other powerful interests on a pressing *social* issue. Industrial executives from Chrysler, Ford and General Motors; the heads of all utility corporations in metropolitan Detroit; and leaders of numerous businesses had taken a strong stand and had encountered defeat.

One unanticipated consequence of the committee's highly visible activity, as world-renowned business leaders paraded to Lansing on behalf of the open housing bill, was that various white groups turned against the committee and opposed other bills pending in the special legislative session.[20] The New Detroit Committee strongly supported a bill that would have redefined the legal relationship between landlords and tenants by giving additional judicial recourse to low-income tenants, but the legislature defeated the bill. Similarly, a bill drafted by the committee, acting on behalf of the Detroit Board of Education, providing for $5.3 million in supplemental education aids for inner-city schools, failed to be released from committee in the special session. Although the legislative session was specifically called to consider post-riot measures for Detroit, it failed to enact those bills to which the New Detroit Committee gave highest priority, despite a massive campaign on their behalf.

Industrial Assistance to Detroit's Public Schools

The New Detroit Committee sponsored a program whereby private industry "adopted" inner-city schools with full approval from the Detroit Board of Education. The partnership between private industry and school administrators was viewed as an alternative to the defeated legislation to upgrade inner-city schools. If successful, it would provide a model for private assumption of what traditionally have been considered public functions.

After being prodded by the New Detroit Committee, Michigan Bell Telephone Company adopted Northern High School in Detroit. The private company provided administrative and teaching assistance, special equipment and new course materials. It also helped to write a new curriculum, ran job-training classes and hired qualified graduates from the school. Under New Detroit Committee auspices, the Chrysler Corporation undertook a similar partnership with Northwestern High School in Detroit.

The school adoption program received national attention as an innovative approach to supplement facilities and resources for inner-city schools. Educators praised the partnership as a unique experiment in upgrading the quality of educational services. But controversy plagued the program. Critics pointed out that private industries altered the educational programs in the adopted schools by including measures

341

explicitly designed to meet the sponsoring corporations' needs. Confirming the critics charge, the committee's *Progress Report* describes some of the educational changes introduced by the Chrysler Corporation at Northwestern High School:

> The corporation has hired some graduates, has helped others who failed initial skills tests, and has placed some students in a pre-apprenticeship training class. One of its major efforts has been the creation of a complete auto mechanic shop and course for the school. It also has donated a variety of equipment important to the development of automative skills.[21]

As the program continued, critics charged that the New Detroit Committee had gone beyond paternalism to create a training system through the public schools, thus insuring large corporations a ready supply of marginally skilled employees. Critics viewed corporate assistance as a ploy to exploit black schools as a future labor supply. Illustrative of this criticism was the charge that the Detroit school system abdicated its responsibilities by approving the school partnership program:

> This is a tacit admission by the Detroit school system, which exists separately from the city government, is autonomous, and has its own tax base, that it is either incapable or unwilling to carry out a real educational program in the ghetto. In effect, they have sold one of the public high schools of the city to private enterprise, which has promised to put resources into the school system that the public realm cannot itself do, such as a redesign of the curriculum, the hiring of additional teachers, the setting-up of extra courses, and so on.[22]

Whether critics' aimed their charges at the Detroit Board of Education or the New Detroit Committee, the school adoption program remained in the foreground of public concern about appropriate methods for upgrading the deteriorating inner-city school system.

Applying for Federal Funds

The issues posed by the school partnership program had wider implications. The committee desired to obtain funding for several programs from public sources. Its *Progress Report* revealed publicly the committee's decision to initiate several major programs requiring extensive federal funding. The report announced that the committee would apply for $750,000 from the federal government to recruit, train and employ over 1,000 inner-city youths in a summer recreation program. It applied for a $500,000 grant from the federal government for a performing and fine arts program to be administered by a neighborhood agency of the committee's choosing. And it would seek $500,000 from the federal government to help neighborhood associations in deprived areas to construct tot lots, postage-stamp parks, playfields and closed-street recreation programs.

The committee's projected programs gave additional ammunition to critics who claimed that applying for federal funds, determining recipient groups and specifying program objectives were essentially decisions about the use of public funds over which public review and accountability should be provided. The critics also noted that none of the committee members had been publicly elected, all the staff came from private industry and the committee remained unaccountable to any constituency except itself.[23] The committee's response to this challenge was inconsistent. At times it claimed to be a democratic group: "The citizenry has at times forgotten the democratic nature of our society and of the Committee." At other times it appealed for unquestioning support: "The New Detroit Committee can never do more than what it is allowed to do by the people it represents. It can give leadership. But leaders must have followers or their work, however progressive or right or noble, is ineffective."[24]

The dilemma of being a private group applying for public funds plagued the New Detroit Committee throughout its existence and proved impossible to resolve satisfactorily. The committee viewed its private status as a strength because it allowed members to take firm positions on controversial and often unpopular issues without regard to public opinion. Yet this also meant that the committee could not be held responsible for its expenditure of public funds. The committee attempted to dispel critics' fears:

It is necessary to add a concluding admonition that any projection of the future of the New Detroit Committee must include an understanding of the basic premises upon which the Committee has operated since its inception. Important among these is the determination on the part of the New Detroit Committee not to duplicate or supersede existing private or public agencies and institutions, but rather to help redirect or motivate such institutions toward more prompt and effective solutions to the social problems of today. Therefore, the Committee must be certain to effectively interrelate with the private and public institutions in order that it can help research, innovate and audit, and not be looked upon as a "super agency."25

Such efforts to reassure critics failed and they continued to hammer on the accountability issue until the New Detroit Committee finally abandoned its ambitious plans to apply for federal funds.

Relations Between N.D.C. and Detroit's Black Community

The preceding controversy took a unique form in the committee's relationship with Detroit blacks. In selecting 39 committee members, the appointing executives and committee Chairman Hudson tried to obtain adequate representation from various factions of Detroit's black community. Hudson appointed nine blacks to the committee, three of whom had strong ties with militant black community organizations. This apparent resolution of the representation issue proved unsatisfactory as black groups with varying degrees of militancy vied for support from and positions on the New Detroit Committee.

The representation dispute was intrinsically interwoven with conflicts over the distribution of patronage. The New Detroit Committee sponsored and funded several projects that it wanted community-based black organizations to administer. Decisions about which black organizations would receive project funds forced the committee to choose from among different ideologically oriented black groups.

The promise of significant increases in funds, programs and recognition for inner-city groups from the New Detroit Committee, the city agency reshuffling and reorientation under the Development Team plan and several state and national program developments after the riot had an important impact on group politics in Detroit's black community. Shortly after the 1967 riot, two black organizations were formed by consolidating pre-existing groups. The Reverend Roy A. Allen brought together several moderate black groups to form the Detroit Council of Organizations in August 1967. A month later the Reverend Albert Cleage, Jr. formed a more militant group, the Federation for Self-Determination, from a number of Detroit-based, black nationalist organizations. Competition between the two organizations centered around which would control the promised perquisites following the riot. Both groups enjoyed sufficient support in the black community to force the New Detroit Committee to consider funding them in community-based projects.

Because of its elitist composition, the New Detroit Committee was vulnerable to criticism from both groups, which it attempted to avoid by seeking harmonious relations with each. Harmony with the moderate Council posed few problems, but the militant Federation repeatedly questioned whether the committee's white, establishment members could seriously address black problems. New Detroit Committee members made repeated, unsuccessful attempts to satisfy the Federation's militant demands. Locke describes the overtures prestigious committee members made to Cleage:

> It was not long, however, before a series of closed-doors meetings between Cleage and the captains of Detroit industry began to receive widespread, and in the minds of many, well-planned publicity. National publications carried stories of Henry Ford II's making a pilgrimage to Cleage's church in the heart of the riot area for a lengthy meeting, with top aides of both men present. Joseph L. Hudson, Jr., chairman of the New Detroit Committee, made repeated public statements after private meetings with Cleage that led the community to anticipate that a truce, if not a potential working agreement, was in the making.

The personal negotiations between Cleage and elite committee members led to the promise of sizeable funds for the Federation:

> That more than a truce was in the offing became evident as Cleage began to submit a series of requests for funds to the New Detroit Committee. When Committee members initially balked at the requested $137,000 grant, Hudson and Ford personally pledged to raise 25 per cent of the funds. A larger request of $750,000 from the Ford Foundation gained the personal endorsement of many New Detroit Committee members.[26]

The New Detroit Committee's standing among militant blacks deteriorated, however, when Ford Foundation and New Detroit Committee funds did not materialize and personal pledges by Hudson and Ford went unfulfilled.

To make amends for unmet promises and to satisfy the increasingly harsh demands of both moderate and militant black groups, the New Detroit Committee granted $100,000 to Reverend Allen's Council and an equal amount to Reverend Cleage's Federation. The Council received a year's funds to establish three neighborhood offices to help inner-city residents obtain social services. The Federation-sponsored program, also funded for one year, promised to be much more ambitious. It would set up an applied research center to identify the most important problems and propose solutions; begin a training program for community organizers, advocacy planners and citizen-grievance personnel; and publish a biweekly Federation newsletter.

The Council accepted its grant without reservation, but the Federation rejected the funds awarded by the New Detroit Committee on the grounds that too many conditions were attached to the grant. The Federation maintained that the committee had placed such severe restrictions on the use of the funds that acceptance of the money would seriously compromise the black nationalist principle of self-determination. The New Detroit Committee later explained the rejection:

> Stipulations relating to this grant were to have been negotiated by staff of the Committee and the FSD in the days following. However, for reasons which are unclear, FSD announced withdrawal of its application and severance of all relations with the New Detroit Committee on grounds that the offer of funds had "strings attached" and was "in conflict" with the goal of self-determination. . . .Committee staff representatives were unsuccessful in efforts to repair the break.[27]

After Reverend Cleage terminated all relations with the New Detroit Committee, two militant black members of the committee followed suit by immediately resigning. Shortly thereafter, the third and only remaining black militant New Detroit Committee member also resigned. The committee thus failed to achieve a balance between factional divisions in representation and patronage distribution.

Employing the Jobless

The New Detroit Committee claimed its most substantial success in formulating employment programs to hire the "hard-core unemployed." Acting upon the belief that jobs held the key to solving racial problems, the committee gave employment programs a high priority. It formed a working partnership with the Greater Detroit Board of

346

Commerce's Manpower Development Committee which previously had engaged in several employment programs. The two organizations jointly initiated and coordinated over 175 separate job training and placement programs.

The short-term results of the efforts by the two groups are impressive. In one referral center alone, over 1,700 persons from the inner-city were placed on jobs in the first eight months after the Detroit riot. Automobile corporations were prevailed upon to accept referrals from agencies established by the two groups. By April 1968, Chrysler had hired 645 inner-city residents, Ford had used a crash program to hire 4,600 jobless persons, and General Motors had initiated "operation opportunity" to recruit previously unemployed persons.[28]

Although the automobile industry received most of the attention, other commercial and industrial firms also cooperated with the New Detroit Committee in providing employment opportunities for inner-city residents. After eight months the committee reported:

The "unemployables" have been performing as well as or better than the regular employees and their retention rate has been as high or higher. However, the more recent reports, based on such factors as addresses, education and similar criteria of persons being hired, allow an estimate that 12,000 "hard-core unemployable" inner-city residents have been hired between the time that the new recruiting policies were installed and the time of the preparation of this report.[29]

Success during the first eight months of work continued over the subsequent eight months.

However impressive the record of jobs provided during the first 16 months after the 1967 riot, the achievements in employment may not be exclusively attributable to the New Detroit Committee's work. General prosperity contributed to the hiring of "hard-core unemployables" as did an actual labor shortage in Detroit. During this same period, Detroit's unemployment rate dropped to a 15-year low, bottoming out in 1968 at 3.8 percent as is shown in Table 9.6. The New Detroit Committee was most actively engaged in its hiring program in 1968. An expansionary economy and favorable employment conditions in the automobile industry facilitated the hiring program.

347

Table 9.6

Annual Average Unemployment Rates in Detroit
S.M.S.A. and Central City Areas–1967-1971

Detroit	Percent Annual Unemployment				
	1967	1968	1969	1970	1971
Standard Metropolitan Statistical Area (SMSA)	4.5	3.8	4.1	7.0	8.4
Central City	5.2	5.1	5.5	8.2	10.0

Source: U.S. Department of Labor, *Manpower Report of the President* (transmitted to Congress March 1972), p. 246

These favorable economic conditions in Detroit could not guarantee how long the jobs would last, however. Inner-city residents were hired on the time-honored principle of "last-hired, first-fired." With a subsequent decline in Detroit's economic picture, black unemployment rates nearly doubled in the three years following 1968, as depicted in Table 9.7.[30] Those employed in the 16 months after the 1967 riot were thereby the first to be laid off, undoubtedly contributing to the rapid rise in unemployment among minority group persons. The recessionary trend beginning in 1969 and continuing through the early 1970s had a particularly strong impact on the automobile industry which experienced severe employment dislocation from 1969 through 1971.

The New Detroit Committee's efforts to rebuild Detroit after the 1967 racial violence thus achieved mixed results. It was rebuffed in lobbying legislative bodies and other public agencies for measures it favored. Its relationship with organizations in the black community remained precarious, at best, throughout its existence. It created hostility when it attempted to perform functions traditionally reserved to public agencies. In the end the committee performed best in areas where its members held powerful private positions bearing upon the tasks undertaken. Regardless of critics' reservations, the New Detroit

348

Table 9.7

**Annual Average Central City Unemployment
Rates in Detroit: By Race—1968-1971**

Race	Percent Annual Unemployment			
	1968	1969	1970	1971
White	3.9	3.9	6.1	7.5
Negro and Other Races	7.3	8.5	11.9	14.2

Source: U.S. Department of Labor, *Manpower Report of the President* (transmitted to Congress March 1972), pp. 247-50

Committee could point to significant contributions in the public schools and in finding work for the unemployed. The success and lack of success in these five areas in turn had important consequences for the committee's organizational structure and its method of operation.

From ad hoc Voluntarism to Bureaucratic Permanence

In its first year the New Detroit Committee experienced a variety of important organizational transformations. It was initially conceived as an *ad hoc* organization to commit volunteer commercial, industrial and trade union resources to help rebuild Detroit. Its original composition and goals gave the committee a reformist identity but, unlike traditional, upper-middle-class reform movements,[31] the committee included *the economic and social elite of Detroit.* This identity exposed the committee to the charge that it was a white-dominated, establishment-oriented organization whose paternalistic concern for Detroit's black population only masked a deeper commitment to maintaining existing economic and political relationships. To avoid this appearance, the committee appointed three militant blacks as members and allocated funds to a militant black organization. When the three black members resigned and the militant black group rejected the funds, the organization again became vulnerable to the white-establishment charge.

349

Undaunted, the committee continued to pursue its original goals. It achieved some success when members directly intervened to draw upon the resources of the powerful private institutions they headed, most notably in the school adoption and jobs programs. With the passage of time, however, its reformist zeal waned. Members' commitment and involvement declined within a matter of months. Although their names remained on the mastheads of committee publications, Henry Ford II, James M. Roche, Lynn A. Townsend and other prestigious members no longer attended the organization's meetings, sending instead less prominent representatives from their institutions.[32] The absence of these prestigious figures precluded a strategy of direct intervention by elite members that had produced some successful developments. The New Detroit Committee originally envisioned a crash program for rebuilding the city that would take no more than six months to accomplish. After that, the committee expected to turn various projects over to public officials and agencies and dissolve itself. Detroit's problems, particularly those dealing with race, proved to be vastly more complex and difficult to solve than originally expected. The dissolution of the committee after six months would have signalled defeat; so the New Detroit Committee decided to remain involved as a permanent organization.

The transformation of the New Detroit Committee from a voluntary group to a permanent organization indicated the defeat of its original objectives and strategies. The permanent organization only faintly resembed the voluntary group. When it became a permanent organization, personnel donated by private industry were replaced by personnel hired directly by the committee. An administrative structure was developed to direct and supervise the new employees. A permanent research and administrative staff guided various employee task forces in what promised to be a sustained attack on Detroit's problems. The New Detroit Committee thus evolved from a voluntary team of Detroit's elite directly intervening in municipal affairs to a bureaucratically organized private group attempting to stimulate reform.

These altered structures and strategies subsequently led to a different set of goals. Instead of undertaking projects of its own and intervening directly to pressure public agencies, the New Detroit Committee became primarily a funding agency.[33] It was incorporated within the Metropolitan Fund, an established, private, non-profit agency funding urban projects in the six-county southeastern Michigan region.

The new goal of providing funds was confirmed when, one year after creation, the committee's chairmanship changed hands from Joseph L. Hudson to Max M. Fisher. Fisher, a Detroit civic leader and philanthropist, had gained international renown for his success in raising funds for the United Jewish Appeal, of which he was president. Upon assuming the position, Fisher immediately set a goal of raising $10 million for distribution among groups working to improve race relations in Detroit. The ambitious agenda announced at the time of the committee's creation was thus modified to funding community-based groups from behind the scenes.

If the Development Team experience illustrates limitations on public officials' ability to stimulate comprehensive reform in the public sector, the experience of the New Detroit Committee reveals the inability or unwillingness of a resource-laden private elite to evoke major and lasting change in a city's race relations through voluntary action. Although the committee drew representatives from Detroit's commercial-industrial-labor complex, it did not directly commit those institutions to an attack on race problems in Detroit. The powerful and personally affluent elite representatives initially joined the committee with righteous zeal for reform, but their involvement ebbed in the face of controversy about its work and the declining visibility of racial problems. With the passage of time, the structures, activities and goals evolved from those of a volunteer group engaged in direct confrontation and seeking immediate changes to a permanent organization with paid employees who funded various groups involved in improving race relations.

This transformation of the New Detroit Committee from a volunteer group to a bureaucratically organized funding agency illustrates the inadequacy of voluntarism as a way of easing a municipal crisis like that experienced by Detroit. With the passage of time and the erosion of reformers' promises of significant change, the committee became yet another private service agency on the urban landscape.

The problem of voluntarism is probably best illustrated by the committee's accomplishments in hiring the previously unemployed and in the school adoption program. Both areas served the interests of the private institutions represented on the New Detroit Committee. Given the labor shortage, the institutions represented on the committee were not impaired and may have benefited from an employment program for ghetto residents, since no assurances were given that the recruits would be retained in less prosperous times. Similarly, in the adoption of

351

ghetto schools, provisions were included for upgrading educational facilities and training, but in terms of the manpower needs of these potential employers. Where the committee claimed success, the programs served—or at least were not obviously incompatible with—the interests of private institutions represented on the committee. Where these private institutions' interests did not stand to benefit, or other group interests were threatened, the New Detroit Committee failed to achieve its goals.

Milwaukee: The 39 Points

In the midst of Milwaukee's riot, Mayor Maier offered a 39-point program developed from programs he had previously proposed without success. Maier repeatedly relied upon this program when subsequently challenged to respond to the riots, thereby transforming that set of proposals from a mere restatement of previous position papers into Milwaukee's official program. The status the program came to assume was described by Maier in testimony before the Kerner Commission two months after the riot:

> We worked out what we might call "Milwaukee's Little Marshall Plan"—a 39 point program for action to build that "Greater City of Trust and Confidence and Hope for All." It was a "Statement of How." It was prefaced with the statement that "it is simple to lay out objectives and describe what should be done. The trick is how."[34]

In speeches before business groups, labor unions and civic organizations, Maier frequently advanced the 39-point program as the city administration's official response to the violence.[35] He also issued periodic "status reports" charting progress in implementing the recommendations.

Despite the visibility Maier created for the 39 points and the support he attempted to develop for it, the program fared more poorly in the implementation process than did official recommendations in either Newark or Detroit. Table 9.8 presents the number of recommendations and the percent targeted for each of the five governmental jurisdictions identified for reform, as well as the number and percent of the recommendations actually implemented within those jurisdictions. Relatively few measures received favorable action. Only seven of the 39 points, less than one-fifth, were implemented.

352

TABLE 9.8

Milwaukee's 39-Point Program: By Jurisdiction Targeted
for Reform and Number Receiving Favorable Action

Governmental Jurisdiction Targeted for Reform	Number of Recommendations	Percent of Recommendations	Number Receiving Favorable Action	Percent Recommendations Receiving Favorable Action
Federal	13	33.3	1	7.6
State	14	35.8	2	14.2
Federal and State	2	5.1	1	50.0
County	3	7.6	0	0
City of Milwaukee (*Primary Jurisdiction*)	7	17.9	3	42.8
TOTAL	39	17.9	7	17.9

As in the New Jersey case, governmental jurisdictions appear to have an important bearing on implementation patterns. The *primary jurisdiction* of Milwaukee, where the 39 points originated, achieved the highest rate of successful implementation; nearly half of these reforms were adopted. Indeed, nearly half of all of the implemented 39 points were favorably acted upon by the city. State and federal governments were much less favorably inclined to adopt the recommendations targeted for their jurisdictions.

Significantly, the 39 points allowed the mayor to target recommendations for change away from Milwaukee, thus drawing attention to other governmental jurisdictions during the post-riot period. Three of the 39 points targeted Milwaukee County as the jurisdiction for change, as is shown in Table 9.8. The first urged "That the county furnish aid for urban renewal and establish a county relocation agency."[36] The other measures called for the county to share the costs of services previously borne only by the city and for the county to bring welfare clients "into full partnership in our society." These recommendations received relatively little attention and the county did not adopt any of these proposals.

Only seven of the 39 points were aimed at the city itself and even within this jurisdiction only two of the seven proposals were aimed directly at the mayor's office. One urged increased employment opportunities and the second called for a crash program to improve park and recreational facilities in Milwaukee's Inner Core (the city's black section). Mayor Maier referred the employment measure to the Milwaukee Voluntary Equal Employment Opportunity Council and the park and recreation proposal to the County Park Department. Neither recommendation was adopted and Maier declined to intervene further on their behalf.

The implementation of two additional proposals aimed at Milwaukee hinged on the creation of a "biracial council," which Maier and the Milwaukee Council on Religion and Race promised to appoint shortly after the riot. The council was to be responsible for reviewing hiring and promotion practices within the police department, processing citizen complaints against the police, and working with teenagers for possible later appointment to positions in the police department. These measures failed to be adopted, however, and the Council on Religion and Race and Maier decided later not to form the promised biracial council. Mayor Maier was thus directly involved in the failure to implement these four recommendations, even though they originated

354

with the riot inquiry he sponsored and were aimed at the jurisdiction over which he presided.

The three recommendations reported in Table 9.8.to have received favorable action from the Milwaukee jurisdiction were all aimed at the common [city] council. They proposed that the common council approve a Model Cities grant application, fund two additional staff members for the Milwaukee Commission on Community Relations and provide an additional assistant in the mayor's office who "shall be a Negro, to keep open lines of communication with minority groups." All three recommendations were implemented in early 1968 when the common council approved the Model Cities application and funded the manpower requests.

One-third of the 39 points were aimed at the federal government. These 13 recommendations included requests for increased antipoverty funds for Milwaukee, assurances that antipoverty funds actually reach the poor, use of antipoverty funds for teacher aides, funding of the Model Cities program, speeding up redevelopment programs, and construction funds for neighborhood facilities and service centers. They also urged adoption of a federal rat control program, massive federal programs to abate air and water pollution, adoption of federal programs for open spaces in urban centers, sharing of low- and middle-income housing by all municipalities including suburbs, conditional withdrawal of federal grants for community facilities until low- and middle-income housing was included in suburban zoning codes, conditional withdrawal of federal aids to education until pupils were exchanged between suburbs and cities and other measures designed to reduce social and economic stratification throughout metropolitan areas. Several groups within the black community raised strong objections to these 13 proposals as nonresponsive to black needs. In part they viewed the recommendations as irrelevant to racial tensions in Milwaukee, repeatedly citing the proposed abatement of air and water pollution as a case in point. A more frequent complaint from black groups was that Maier should have formulated feasible proposals dealing with his own jurisdiction in Milwaukee rather than turning to distant federal sources for solutions.

Responding to local criticism, Maier engaged in a series of activities designed to pressure federal sources and convince his constituents that federal reforms were attainable. He ran an advertisement in the *New York Times*,[37] wrote and made public a 12-page, single-spaced letter to President Johnson urging his support for the 13 measures and gave frequent speeches arguing that the real solutions must come from Washington, not Milwaukee. Three of the 13 recommendations aimed at the federal government and Maier's efforts to implement them were:

Point 13. That federal programming be expanded for job training, improved education, and housing opportunities throughout metropolitan areas.

The Mayor advocated this in his letter to the President on August 19th, and has repeatedly tried to alert the public to the overriding importance of these programs.

Point 14. That the Model Cities program be funded by the federal government at realistic levels.

The Mayor repeatedly, in the letter to the President, in national meetings, and in many other forums, has backed realistic funding of the Model Cities program.

Point 15. That there be a commitment to speeded-up redevelopment programs.

In letter to [the] President, the Mayor cited the general need to speed up the urban renewal process to prevent hardships. He specifically asked approval of Associated Hospitals Project, Halyard Park project, Civic Center North project. As a result of the letter, Secretary Weaver informed the Mayor that Halyard Park has been advanced substantially in federal priorities.[38]

On only one of the 13 measures aimed at the federal government did the city administration go beyond writing letters, making speeches, urging approval or running advertisements. It applied for $2 million for federal rat control funds and received $50,000 for this purpose from the Public Health Service. Otherwise, however, the 13 points were largely ignored by the federal government.

As reported in Table 9.8, two points were directed at both the federal and the state governments. These measures proposed obtaining federal and state funds to attract private enterprise to locate in Milwaukee's nearly all-black Inner Core. The Federal Economic Development Administration granted $90,000 for this purpose to the Mayor's Division of Economic Development in early 1968. The state of Wisconsin refused a similar request for $150,000, even though it established a $1 million fund for the Inner Core. The state's refusal to comply with Maier's request gave an early indication of post-riot hostilities between the two jurisdictions.

Fourteen of the 39 points were aimed at the state government in Wisconsin, the largest bloc of recommendations targeted for any jurisdiction. In contrast to reform measures addressed to the federal government, the state recommendations were specific:

1) enabling legislation for a county-wide open housing law;
2) revision of the formula applying to state aid and shared taxes;
3) creation of a state urban renewal agency;
4) state grants-in-aid for urban renewal to all participating municipalities;
5) creation of a housing board to aid municipalities in slum clearance and low-rent housing with specific provisions for payment of relocation costs;
6) establishment of a mortgage insurance agency to lend funds directly to high-risk areas where loans are difficult to obtain;
7) revision of zoning ordinances to permit all classes of housing in all municipalities;
8) revision of state insurance laws;
9) state-initiated programs for aiding minorities in obtaining positions in commercial enterprises;
10) review of state property tax exemptions;
11) state authorization for merging redevelopment and housing authorities;
12) state grants-in-aid to provide for fifty per cent of all police costs above normal;
13) property tax load equalization among local governments;
14) a special session of the legislature called by the governor to consider each of these proposals.

Although most of these measures had been advocated previously by Maier, they generated intense controversy over subsequent months as the state and city administrations tried to shift responsibility for easing Milwaukee's racial tensions to each other.

Governor Warren P. Knowles, a Republican unsympathetic to past initiatives from the Democrat Maier, precluded immediate consideration of the 14 measures by refusing to call a special session of the state legislature. Thus Knowles effectively defused Maier's momentary support and insured that these state-targeted recommendations would have to compete for a place on the legislative agenda with a host of other bills during a regular session. At the regular legislative session, Maier presented nine of the 14 measures drafted in bill form and estimated the cost of implementing them at $134 million. As reported

357

in Table 9.8, only two of the bills passed; significantly, neither required any expenditure of state funds. The first was a relatively innocuous bill authorizing the administrative merger of the redevelopment and public housing authorities in Milwaukee. Another, equally inexpensive, was the passage of enabling legislation authorizing counties to enact open housing laws, provided that all municipalities within the county agreed to grant it enforcement powers.

Exploiting Milwaukee's racial crisis by seeking increased municipal resources from jurisdictions outside the city reinforced Maier's claim that solutions to problems in housing, employment, education and poverty were beyond local capabilities and therefore required action from national, state and county jurisdictions. Over four-fifths of the 39 points were targeted at jurisdictions other than the city of Milwaukee, generally without much impact. Milwaukee County gave scant attention to the recommendations aimed in its direction and implemented none. Federal agencies provided funds for a rat control program and granted economic-development-assistance money, but otherwise proved unresponsive to proposals for additional funds. The Republican-controlled Wisconsin state administration and legislature were even less responsive to requests for assistance from the Democratic city administration, enacting only two recommendations—both of which allowed lesser jurisdictional units to adopt administrative reforms at no cost to the state.

The disposition of the seven recommendations aimed at the city of Milwaukee illustrates the tendency of political executives to exploit racial crises to further their own ends at no cost to themselves. Maier was directly responsible for the nonadoption of four recommendations in the Milwaukee jurisdiction. He simply referred two of the proposals to city and county agencies for their inaction, as it turned out, and dealt a death blow to two others by failing to appoint the promised biracial council.

Executive aggrandizement in the midst of crisis is even better illustrated by the three municipal recommendations that were implemented. Significantly, all three were adopted through common council action. Prior to the 1967 riot, the common council refused to approve Maier's Model Cities application on grounds that he was attempting a "power grab," "patronage ploy" and "complete control of jobs" in the program.[39] Armed with the Model Cities recommendation in the 39-point program after the riot, Maier deftly prodded the council into approving the grant application.[40] After obtaining council approval of the remaining two recommendations for increased personnel in the mayor's office, Maier appointed an additional staff assistant for the mayor's office, John Givens, founder of Milwaukee's original chapter of the Congress of Racial Equality, and thereby partially mollified some black groups. Obtaining council consent for additional executive personnel was no trifling task. As in the prior rejection of Model Cities applications, Milwaukee's nonpartisan city councilmen jealously guarded the limited patronage positions and viewed with suspicion any mayoral attempt to increase appointive personnel as a threat to the city's strong civil service system.[41] Yet in the riot's aftermath Maier, occupying a formally "weak" mayor's office, was able to obtain council approval for measures he previously had been denied.

Milwaukee: The Little Kerner Commission

The unfavorable reception given by the Republican-controlled state administration and legislature to recommendations aimed at the state was closely tied to the activities of the Republican-created and -dominated "Little Kerner Commission." Demonstrating that more than one jurisdiction could play the game of scattering recommendations, this commission aimed one-third of its reform proposals at local governments, most of which dealt directly with the city administration in Milwaukee. None of these recommendations was implemented nor did attempts to carry them out consist of more than rhetoric. But the rhetoric did serve to express the Republican state officials' conviction that the causes of the riot resided in Milwaukee and remedies would have to be forthcoming from the Democratic-controlled city administration.

The major thrust of the Little Kerner Commission's recommendations was, nevertheless, aimed at Wisconsin's state government. These fared little better than the reforms directed at local jurisdictions: nine bills were eventually drafted and introduced in the 1969 state legislative session at the request of the commission, but they covered less than half of the recommendations aimed at state government. Only two eventually passed.

The record of implementing recommendations following Milwaukee's racial violence is bleak. The proposed reforms served primarily to extend partisan divisions pre-dating the 1967 riot. Within the primary jurisdiction of Milwaukee, Maier was able to obtain approval for one program and personnel requests that previously had been denied, but other reform measures were less successful. The Little Kerner Commission's recommendations failed to alter policy directions at the state and municipal levels. Each reform program embodied the selected interests of its sponsor. Not surprisingly, opposing interests dominant in other jurisdictions precluded the adoption of their policy advice.

Accounting For Implementation Patterns

The material reviewed in this chapter shows certain patterns of targeting recommendations and program implementation following riots. These and other themes are advanced in chapter 10, which more explicitly considers the riot inquiries and their policy advice in the context of the larger political system.

We introduced this chapter by suggesting that it is of intrinsic interest to know what happens to recommendations from riot inquiries after they are issued. Our findings support the widespread popular belief that most recommendations are not adopted, yet a *sizeable minority* of proposed reforms were implemented. In Milwaukee slightly more than one-fifth of the 39 points were adopted; in Detroit the Development Team successfully pursued two of the three major tasks assigned to it; and in Newark more than one-fourth of the Governor's Commission's 99 recommendations received favorable action.

The failure to implement a majority of the recommendations may be explained, in part, by the reassurance functions performed by riot inquiries. In chapter 4 we suggested that riot commissions reassure anxious citizens that racial problems are being addressed. But to the extent that commissions do assure citizens that issues of racial conflict are in hand, they may diminish the likelihood that reforms they propose will be implemented. By reducing citizen demands for action, riot commissions may remove the necessary condition of mass support for effective policy changes, including costly and innovative reforms.

Another reason for the relative failure to implement recommendations is that a *stalemate between governmental jurisdictions* may result from the tendency of riot commissions to propose a large number of reforms for jurisdictions other than the one within which they are appointed. We noted this tendency in chapter 7 where the jurisdiction targeted for reform by a commission was usually not the same jurisdiction within which the commission had been created. The potential for stalemate arises because an *ad hoc* group in one governmental jurisdiction calls upon public officials in another governmental jurisdiction to adopt reforms. Our evidence indicates that reforms recommended for adoption reflect political executives' interest in deflecting responsibility for ameliorating riot-induced crises onto other jurisdictions.

One important consequence of commissions deflecting the target for reform is to reduce the likelihood that their recommendations will be successfully implemented. The adoption of official recommendations in the three cities is presented in bar-graph form in Table 9.9, by governmental jurisdiction.

In each case, the *primary jurisdiction* is the governmental jurisdiction within which the official riot commission or study group was appointed while the *secondary jurisdiction* is an alternative jurisdiction which happened, except in Detroit, to be the target for reform in the largest number of recommendations. Thus the primary jurisdictional units for the Milwaukee and Detroit cases are the cities of Milwaukee and Detroit. In the Newark case, however, the official Governor's Commission was created at the state level and thus the primary jurisdiction is the state of New Jersey. Secondary jurisdictional units targeted for the largest number of recommendations in the Milwaukee and Newark cases were, respectively, the state of Wisconsin and the city of Newark. Table 9.9 suggests that the jurisdictional units within which riot commissions and study groups were created adopted commission recommendations at a much higher rate than did alternative governmental jurisdictions. The notable success of the Mayor's Development Team in Detroit supports this observation: in formulating recommendations it ignored federal and state jurisdictions, instead concentrating on municipal reforms where it achieved two-thirds of its objectives. The more general tendency of riot commissions to target most of their recommendations for secondary jurisdictions thus reduces the chances that they will be implemented.

The pattern of implementation displayed in Table 9.9 additionally suggests that jurisdictional boundaries circumscribe the authoritativeness of riot commissions. The authority of official inquiries is tenuous at best because of their advisory status and because of the separation of powers within jurisdictions. But their authority is non-existent and their legitimacy is even more tenuous in prescribing reforms outside of their governmental jurisdiction. The relatively few recommendations implemented by secondary jurisdictions confirms the fact that riot commissions lack widespread authority to formulate acceptable change proposals.

The relatively high degree of success within primary jurisdictions stems from at least three factors. First, participants in riot inquiries

TABLE 9.9

Implementation of Official Riot Inquiry Recommendations by Jurisdiction

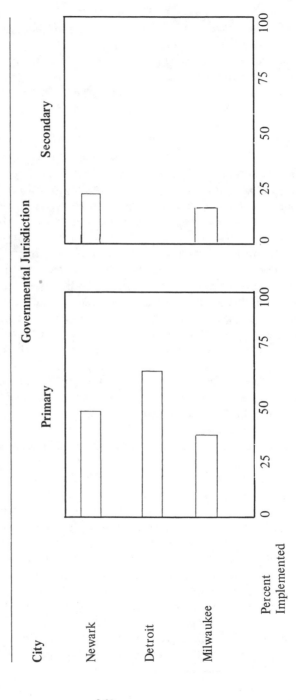

reflect the dominant interests in the primary jurisdiction and these "representatives" tend to formulate programmatic recommendations coincident with the aims of public officials in that jurisdiction. Second, the tendency of riot commissions to direct relatively few reform recommendations, and the least controversial ones at that, at the primary jurisdiction improves the chances of implementation at that level. Third, the predilection of public officials to use riot commission recommendations for their own ends further affects success rates in the primary jurisdiction.

NOTES, CHAPTER 9

1. To our knowledge, none of the numerous existing studies on riot commissions is concerned with tracing the eventual outcome of commission recommendations.

2. Our research strategy assuredly does not provide an exhaustive account of all political responses to the riots. Among the more important areas not given treatment in our approach are: policy developments independent of riot-commission deliberations and recommendations, the consequences of the racial violence for increasing black self-consciousness, and relatedly the marked increase of black electoral mobilization in riot and nonriot cities.

3. National Advisory Commission on Civil Disorders, *Report* (New York: Bantam, 1968), p. 483.

4. National Commission on the Causes and Prevention of Violence, *To Establish Justice, To Insure Domestic Tranquility* (New York: Awards Books, 1969), pp. 119-20. Higginbotham, vice-chairman of the commission, also remarked, "I must confess to a personal sense of increasing 'commission frustration'. . . .There is too little implementation of the rational solutions proposed, and too often the follow-up is only additional studies" (ibid., p. 119).

5. See the discussion in ch. 4 of this volume.

6. Letter from Robert D. Lilley to Governor Richard J. Hughes dated 7 February 1968, in the files of the Governor's Select Commission on Civil Disorder on deposit in the Governor's Office, Trenton.

7. Governor's Select Commission on Civil Disorder, *Report For Action* (State of New Jersey: February 1968), p. 10.

8. Newark *News*, 11 February 1968.

9. As in Detroit and Milwaukee, we determined "favorable action" by tracing each of the commission recommendations to ascertain how it was received and disposed of by the most relevant public officials and

agencies over a two-year span. Our determination of whether a recommendation received "favorable action" is based upon reports to the official commission, public documents, news accounts, and interviews with appropriate public officials and personnel in public agencies. The data for these decisions, especially in the Newark case, are more fully reported in chapter 10.

10. Executive Order Number 17, files of the Mayor's Office, Detroit, Michigan; dated 3 August 1967.

11. See chapter 4 in this volume.

12. The claim reads: "The Mayor's Development Team was able to achieve a high degree of success in meeting post-riot emergency needs." See Mayor's Development Team, *Report To Mayor Jerome P. Cavanagh* (Detroit: City of Detroit, October 1967), p. 143.

13. The Development Team's assessment of Detroit's immediate riot-recovery effort is supported by Locke: "The response to the riot by public and private social agencies was one of the high points of the riot and the post-riot period. Generally it was upon these agencies that the bulk of the relief work fell, along with the task of helping the city to return to some degree of normalcy. Under the constant prodding of the mayor's office, the public works and sanitation departments dealt with the physical scars of the riot in a highly efficient manner. By four months after the riot, many of the damaged buildings had been razed and the ground leveled." See Hubert G. Locke, *The Detroit Riot of 1967* (Detroit: Wayne State University Press, 1969), p. 101.

14. Mayor's Development Team, *Report To Mayor Jerome P. Cavanagh*, pp. 149-53.

15. Executive Order Number 17, files of the Mayor's Office, Detroit.

16. Ibid.

17. Detroit has one of the most completely reformed civil service systems in the nation, providing broad coverage for municipal employees and city departments. City agencies are in reality governed by an impressively strong Civil Service Commission, which is politically constrained only by budgetary allocations from a nonpartisan and at-large elected city council.

18. New Detroit Committee, *Progress Report*, pp. 4, 2, 3.

19. Ibid., p. 38.

20. The New Detroit Committee finally expressed its reactions to these developments in its *Progress Report*: "No one is more painfully aware of the failures of the New Detroit Committee than the members of the New Detroit Committee itself. Seldom have we risen to our own defense. To take such time would mean lost time in the face of a most fantastic challenge. Yet, we have admittedly been disappointed to think

that the criticisms aimed at the Committee could possibly weaken its credibility and its effectiveness" (ibid., pp. 3, 4).

21. Ibid., p. 49.

22. Frank Joyce, "Postscript from Detroit: Death of Liberalism," *The Center Magazine* 1, no. 3 (March 1968): 45.

23. Critics were particularly incensed about the committee's decision not to allow even local news media to attend its meetings. This decision was made during the committee's first meeting, and recounted in the *Progress Report*:

> It was also announced that, although a Detroit newspaper had already accused the New Detroit Committee of operating in secrecy, the meetings would be closed to the press and to all persons not directly associated with the Committee's operations. While it was recognized both that "the news media intend to print something . . .and we have nothing to hide," Mr. Hudson said that he felt "very strongly" that the presence of reporters at Committee and subcommittee meetings "would disrupt, rather than help, what we have to do." The Committee fully agreed.

(New Detroit Committee, *Progress Report*, p. 25.)

24. Ibid., pp. 4, 5.

25. Ibid., p. 151.

26. Hubert G. Locke, *The Detroit Riot of 1967*, p. 115.

27. New Detroit Committee, *Progress Report*, p. 69.

28. These figures are reported in ibid., p. 56.

29. Ibid., p. 57.

30. Statistics on unemployment in central-city areas obtained and distributed by the Department of Labor from the mid-1960s through 1971 provided the data reported in Table 9.7. Comparable data for later years is not available because, in December 1971, the gathering of central-city unemployment statistics was discontinued by the federal government. In 1971, unemployment rates in central cities had averaged 12.4 percent and, perhaps providing evidence of the effectiveness of the Nixon administration's "benign-neglect policy" one year prior to national elections, they were thereafter discontinued. For a discussion of this particular issue and the more general practice of governmental manipulation of supposedly "objective" statistics, see Eugene Keller, "Politicizing Statistics," *Dissent* 20, no. 2 (Spring 1973): 142-45.

31. For an excellent discussion of the motivations, activities, and goals of traditional upper-middle-class reformers and reform groups, see Edward C. Banfield and James Q. Wilson, *City Politics* (Cambridge, Mass.: Harvard University Press and the M.I.T. Press, 1963), pp. 138-50;

and James Q. Wilson, *The Amateur Democrat* (Chicago: University of Chicago Press, 1962).

32. Contrast these absences with attendance requirements imposed at the committee's first meeting: "To ensure top-level continuity and involvement, Mr. Hudson declared that except for a few members whose organizational responsibilities were international, he would not permit substitutes to attend the full meetings" (New Detroit Committee, *Progress Report*, pp. 24, 25).

33. At its first meeting, the committee had disavowed any intention of becoming a fund-raising organization: "There were only two 'clear' restrictions on New Detroit's activities. First, that the Committee's responsibility was to 'look forward; not backward'. . . .Second, that the Committee was not a fund-raising organization, although it might choose to evaluate the needs for funds, to identify sources of funding and priorities, and, possibly, to encourage contributions" (ibid., p. 25).

34. Mayor Henry W. Maier, "Statement to President's Commission on Civil Disorders," (mimeo., dated 5 October 1967), p. 5.

35. A representative selection from one such presentation reads:

Some of you will recall that in the wake of the civil disorders in Milwaukee last August, a 39 point program was drawn up by the Interdenominational Ministerial Alliance and the Mayor's Office after a number of meetings with representatives of the inner city community. On one of the charts in this room, you will find those points delineated in terms of their relationship with various levels of government and private sectors affecting Milwaukee. There is also included in the packet at your table a status report on the 39 points. You will note that a number of the recommendations in that report, such as the passing of a Federal rat control program, have now become fact. . . .You will note that with some items—such as some of the bills we had introduced in the state legislature—we have gone about as far as we can go at the moment. Other items are still in process.

("Mayor's Civic Report Breakfast" [mimeo., dated 24 January 1968], pp. 3, 4).

36. The statement of particular measures from the 39 points is taken here, and will be in what follows, from "Status Report on 39 Points" (mimeo., prepared by the Mayor's Office of Milwaukee, dated August 1968).

37. When asked why the advertisement was placed in the New York *Times*, the mayor's chief assistant replied, "It's a toss-up between the *Times* and the Washington *Post*. Congress is what you have to affect" (quoted by H. R. Wilde, "Milwaukee's National Media Riot," in *Urban*

Government, 2nd ed., ed. Edward C. Banfield [New York: The Free Press, 1969], p. 686).

38. "Status Report on 39 Points."

39. Councilmen's skepticism about the draft application submitted by Maier was later vindicated by the events Whitehead reports:

> Later, after Milwaukee did secure some Washington money, it was cut off briefly by HUD because the city's provisions for citizen participation were weak—too many members of the model cities policy board were to be named by the mayor. After Maier agreed to have a majority of the board elected, his supporters won the elections. The top staffers of the model cities agency are strong Maier men. As open and closed administrative styles alternate here (and the closed style seems to come up more than the open one), the program, HUD regional officials insist, fails to make any progress.

(Ralph Whitehead, Jr., "Milwaukee's Mercurial Henry Maier," *City* 6, no. 2 [March-April 1972]: 18).

40. Opposition remained to the Model Cities program, but that opposition now took a different form. The main aldermanic opponent of Model Cities now stated his opposition in these terms: "I think the one overall point that just has to be made is that as long as we give rewards for riots, we are going to have more riots. I would oppose anything that would appear to be a reward to the people of the inner core. To adopt Model Cities on an emergency basis would obviously be a reward for rioting" (Milwaukee *Sentinel*, 7 August 1967).

41. Whitehead gives this account of Milwaukee's patronageless status:

> Power is scarce around the mayor's office. Legally the post carries little clout. Its patronage is virtually nil. Of Milwaukee's roughly 11,500 city employees the mayor names only 450 to their jobs. Only a handful of those posts are full-time and salaried, and even they can be filled only if the 19-member common council consents to the mayor's appointments.

(Ralph Whitehead, Jr., "Milwaukee's Mercurial Henry Maier," p. 13).

10

The Politics
of Implementation

If, as we have maintained throughout this volume, the meaning ascribed to riots is as inseparable from the processing of riot events as from the behavior of the rioters themselves, then the reception given to the proposals of official riot inquiries is most important. In this chapter we trace the fate of such recommendations and seek to account for the low implementation rates observed in the previous chapter. We hope to shed light on two related questions: to what extent does the policy process contribute to perceptions that the riots express political demands and to what extent did the riots successfully change existing political relationships. We assess the meaning the riots came to have and the changes they fostered by analyzing the politics surrounding efforts to implement the reforms proposed by riot inquiries in the three cities. In so doing, we hope to identify the primary political factors accounting for the degree of recommendation implementation and to explain the eventual outcome by observing patterns of opposition and support that developed for the reform proposals.

Through their recommendations, recent riot commissions have urged major adjustments in public policy, alterations of priorities and redistribution of resources. The proposed reforms have elicited support from some sources and opposition from others. Often the acceptance or rejection of reform measures mirrors the conflict between different governmental jurisdictions or between branches of government within a single jurisdiction; but ultimately the recommended changes are disposed of by the political system. Understanding the process and the direction of that disposition is the purpose of this chapter.

The New Jersey Governor's Commission: Uncertain Reform

In chapter 9, we indicated that slightly over one-fourth of the Governor's Commission's recommendations were implemented in New Jersey. Yet simply listing the number, jurisdictional target and frequency of implementation does not adequately convey the impact the reform proposals had on political relationships in Newark and in the state at large. The success or failure of commission recommendations hinged upon how they were received by the larger political system, of which the commission was a part. The following examination considers the most important reforms aimed at Newark and the responses they elicited and then discusses those directed at the state.

The Governor's Commission characterized city hall in Newark as unresponsive to blacks and described blacks as generally distrustful of Mayor Addonizio's administration. More specifically, the commission charged that the city administration failed to appoint blacks to responsible positions and was hostile to the local antipoverty agency, and that Addonizio had reneged on campaign promises to blacks.

The commission also faulted Addonizio for failing to develop structures to hear citizen grievances, for political interference in the police department, for too heavy reliance on patronage appointments resulting in high staff turnover, for lax enforcement of gambling laws, for inadequate preparation for civil disorder and for practices that resulted in "a widespread belief that Newark's city government is corrupt."[1] To correct these deficiencies, one-third of the commission's recommendations were aimed at Newark's city administration. The proposals are specific and detailed. They range from a plea to remove Newark's antipoverty program from city administration control to a call for a grand jury investigation of alleged official corruption in city hall.

The Newark Response

Most public officials in Newark reacted to the *Report for Action* with predictable hostility. After the *Report* was released, the Newark City Council went on record as being "indignant" because none of its members had been asked to testify before the commission. The council adopted a resolution stating it "deplores that the report fails to mention one word in criticism or condemnation of the riots themselves, and the indiscriminate looting."[2]

Other prominent public officials in Newark had similar reactions. Deputy Mayor Paul Reilly, Corporation Counsel Norman Schiff, Health and Welfare Director Mrs. Larrie Stalks, Police Director Dominick A. Spina, and Human Rights Commissioner James Threatt were all reported by Donald Malafronte, head of Newark's model cities agency, as "shocked" that the Governor's Commission had "fudged the real issues" by urging a grand jury investigation of corruption in City Hall instead of giving greater emphasis to upgrading education, employment and housing programs. Police Director Spina's reaction to the *Report* illustrates the generally hostile response:

> [The commission has gone to] great lengths to discredit the Newark Police Department in every possible way. [I read the report] with a sense of disbelief, frustration and concern. The inevitable feeling that the Newark police were the proximate cause of the disorder pervaded the entire document. At no single place in the report were there any kind words concerning the dedication, the courage and loyalty of the men in blue who worked inhuman hours of duty to help establish order in this troubled city. Nothing in this report alludes to the racists, bigots and subversives who laid the climate for the disorder starting in the summer of 1965.[3]

At least three fraternal police organizations joined the protest.

Mayor Addonizio surprised his subordinates and other Newark officials by announcing that he "embraced" the *Report's* findings and proposals. The day after release of the *Report* he praised the commission's efforts: "The report appears, at first glance, to represent a lot of honest, hard work, with some of it off the mark but most of it reasonable and accurate, considering the confusion and complexity of the issues."[4]

Addonizio even praised recommendations that appeared to threaten directly his administration. He indicated he intended to take affirmative action on all recommendations within the municipal jurisdiction. If any recommendations were modified or deemed impossible, he promised to announce the reasons to the commission at a later date. At a press conference five days after release of the *Report*, Addonizio said: "We intend to act fast. I want action on all matters pertaining to Newark by the end of next month and I will ask the commission to reconvene at that time to accept our action report."[5] By the end of the month, however, the commission no longer existed; no "action report" was forthcoming.

Addonizio responded to the commission's *Report* with more than mere verbal acceptance, praise and promises. In the weeks following release of the *Report* he engaged in a series of activities intended to counter charges of shortcomings in his administration. The mayor and his staff, adopting measures taken directly from the *Report*, attempted to show the city administration's full compliance with commission recommendations. The degree to which Addonizio's initial acceptance and apparent commitment to implementing recommendations were fulfilled may be assessed by a detailed consideration of responses to the measures.

Reforming the Newark Police

The Governor's Commission devoted several recommendations to controversies about the police which were current in Newark at the time of its deliberations. Addonizio had equivocated on each of these issues, but his public posture changed substantially after release of the *Report*.

For example, a proposal before the City Council to provide the Newark Police Department with a canine corps had drawn strong support from the North Ward Citizens' Committee, a white vigilante group headed by Anthony Imperiale, and had provoked equally strong opposition from blacks. Imperiale had placed the proposal before the City Council at every council session over a four-month period. With Addonizio stating no clear preference, the City Council defeated the proposal, then approved it, reversed itself again and defeated it, and then sent it to a study committee. After the Governor's Commission recommended that the "canine corps should be abandoned on the ground that the technical benefits such a corps might yield are far outweighed by the hostile response this proposal has evoked in a large sector of the community,"[6] the study committee and Addonizio urged its rejection. With the mayor's backing, the City Council defeated the measure by a seven-to-two margin.

An equally controversial issue concerned the assignment of black police officers to Newark's predominantly black Central Ward. Residents there had long demanded black police officers in command positions for their neighborhoods. Shortly after the 1967 disorder (but prior to the commission's report) Addonizio elevated Lieutenant

Edward Williams to captain, a rank carrying with it command status. Williams was the first black officer to hold such a position in Newark. His promotion provoked strong protest from two white police fraternal organizations, the Policemen's Benevolent Association and the Fraternal Order of Police, on grounds that five white officers with greater seniority had been bypassed. Instead of placing Williams in command of the fourth precinct, which encompassed the black Central Ward, Addonizio catered to the protests by assigning Williams to head the community relations bureau, a division lacking enforcement powers.

In the months following Williams's promotion, numerous black organizations, including the local NAACP, CORE, Urban League, and United Afro-American Association, petitioned the mayor to transfer Williams to command of the fourth precinct. Addonizio did not honor these requests because of intense opposition by the police fraternal organizations, which warned him that such a transfer of Captain Williams would prompt a virtual rebellion among rank-and-file police officers. But two days after the Governor's Commission recommended the transfer, Addonizio made the assignment anyway, using the commission's recommendation to justify the move. Within hours, the fraternal organizations made good on their promise. Over 100 rank-and-file police officers picketed city hall with signs stating "Keep [former Commander] Zizza at 4th" and "Mayor Cops Out."[7] The Fraternal Order of Police also filed an unsuccessful petition with the New Jersey Civil Rights Commission claiming the transfer violated former Commander Zizza's civil rights because it was based exclusively on considerations of race.

Another recommendation prompted equally strong opposition from the two policemen's organizations. The commission urgently requested Addonizio to name a five-member civilian review board independent of the Police Department to receive and rule on citizen complaints about police misconduct. The commission proposal was not new. The Addonizio administration had rejected demands for a citizen review panel twice before—in 1963 shortly after Addonizio had been elected with strong support from blacks, and again in 1965 after a black man had been fatally shot by a police officer. In 1963 and 1965, city hall was picketed by civil rights groups and police officers. But Addonizio rejected the proposed board in favor of a compromise: complaints about police brutality would be forwarded to the Federal Bureau of Investigation. In its *Report*, the Governor's Commission took exception to this plan because it felt the FBI's investigation of complaints from 1965 to 1967 had been inadequate.

When Addonizio announced Captain Williams's transfer he also revealed that the proposed civilian review board would be reconsidered. Addonizio said that, if such a panel was appointed, the first member he would name would be Robert D. Lilley, chairman of the Governor's Commission. He reasoned that a large burden had been placed on his administration for implementing the commission's recommendations and that individual commissioners should share in that burden: "They have a responsibility. They can't write a report and just walk away."[8]

The mayor's disclosure provoked an intensive campaign by police fraternal organizations against interference with police affairs. The fraternal orders made known their intention to file court action against any form of civilian review. Addonizio received pressure in the opposite direction from civil rights groups. Willie Wright, president of the United Afro-American Association, declared that failure by the mayor to adhere to the commission's recommendation would produce "one of the largest demonstrations this city has ever seen."[9]

Addonizio resolved the dilemma by developing another compromise measure. He rejected the commission's proposal for a civilian review board in favor of sending an "ombudsman" plan to a study committee for 45 days. The "ombudsman" plan consisted of appointing a single individual to monitor the conduct of all city agencies, including the police department. Norman N. Schiff, Newark's corporation counsel, conducted the study and released a 31-page report recommending adoption of the plan:

> An ombudsman is a worthwhile experiment in Newark and other large cities. With the proper direction it can be a source of impartial and effective review of citizens' grievances. It can be an effective instrumentality for constructive criticism of existing administrative functions and actions. It can provide an atmosphere where a citizen can lodge a complaint without fear of retaliation or reprisal. The need for an effective mechanism to close the widening gap between the average citizen and his local government has never been greater nor more urgent.[10]

The Schiff report recommended that either the chief justice of the State Supreme Court or the mayor select the ombudsman with the approval of the City Council. The "ombudsman" would be given subpoena power and would review complaints against all city agencies. By the time the Schiff report came out, nearly three months had elapsed since the Governor's Commission made its recommendation. Interest in the proposal had waned and the Schiff report received little attention. In the subsequent months, neither the mayor nor the chief justice of the State Supreme Court appointed the recommended "ombudsman." No review agency was ever created. Thus Addonizio managed to postpone action until the controversy had subsided and pressures for action had dissipated.

Not all of the recommendations criticized the Newark Police Department. Nor were Newark policemen blind to opportunities offered by some aspects of the *Report.* The commission proposed salary increases for patrolmen from the entering minimum of $6,951 to $7,800 and, after five years service, from the maximum $8,002 to $10,000. Addonizio opposed this plan as too costly, proposing instead an auxiliary police force of 1,500 volunteers under civil defense auspices. Central ward businessmen strongly endorsed the plan, while police fraternal organizations successfully opposed it.[11] After defeating the mayor's alternative plan, the police organizations engaged in a nine-month campaign to increase salaries for rank-and-file police officers. The fraternal orders demanded a base pay of $10,500 and presented their demands at city hall and the state house. They were joined in these demonstrations by Newark firemen and two firemen's fraternal organizations which, like the police representatives, justified the salary demands by emphasizing the Governor's Commission's recommendations.

The police-salary controversy eventually led to a "sick call" or "blue flu" strike on November 29, 1968, that forced Addonizio to proclaim a state of emergency, apply a curfew and call in county sheriff's officers. Over 1,000 of the 1,350-man Newark police force called in sick. The salary issue revealed publicly a growing split within rank-and-file policemen as black police officers refused to join the strike and made known their displeasure at the tactics of the white police fraternal organizations. Several months earlier black officers had formed their own fraternal organization, the "Black Shield."[12] Regarded with suspicion by the white fraternal organizations, the Black Shield remained discreetly silent on divisive racial issues affecting the police department, such as Captain Williams's transfer and the civilian review board proposal.[13] The strike provided an opportunity for the organization to break with existing ethnic fraternal groups on an issue other than race.[14] During the strike black policemen and county sheriff's officers maintained order in the city until Addonizio obtained a court injuction forcing white officers to end the strike. Police officers did not receive the salary increases they wanted, but they did get an across-the-board $600 raise.

The Poverty Program and Medical School Controversies

In its final *Report*, the Governor's Commission issued eight recommendations dealing with Newark's antipoverty agency, the United Community Corporation (UCC). Its first and most important recommendation was that UCC remain independent of city adminis- tration control. The commission feared Addonizio's adoption, shortly after the 1967 disorder, of measures intended to establish control of UCC in conformity with recent federal legislation. The Addonizio administration had often come in conflict with UCC during the antipoverty agency's first three years, and the mayor was expected to seek control of the program. But a week after the Governor's Commission urged continued independence for UCC, Addonizio announced he would abide by the commission's wishes: "I have no intention of interfering with the operation of the United Community Corporation in any way. We are anxious to work together for the betterment of the community action agency."[15] Despite his announced intentions, over the next six months Addonizio's administration established virtually complete control of the UCC.[16]

This controversy constituted only a small part of an even more hotly contested issue: whether the $71 million New Jersey College of Medicine and Dentistry would be built in Newark's central ward and, if so, whether black residents there would have a say about the conditions under which the facility would be built. Both the Kerner Commission and the Governor's Commission described the medical college dispute as a major precipitant of the 1967 riot and, in the months following the violence, the controversy remained unresolved. Medical professionals from the college continued to prefer a suburban location while public officials from city, state and federal jurisdictions insisted on building the medical college in Newark's Central Ward. Spokesmen from Newark's black community did not object to placing the medical college in Newark, but they took strong exception to the terms under which public officials sought its relocation. These terms included alloting as many as 150 acres of land for the college, relocating over 22,000 site residents, the college's unwillingness to provide health services to neighborhoods surrounding the facility, the absence of guarantees on minority group hiring during the construction phase and the lack of suitable housing for relocation.

The Governor's Commission issued six recommendations about the medical college at a critical stage of the controversy. It urged a Newark location for the medical college, but on terms substantially the same as those demanded by Newark's blacks. Specifically, it recommended reduced land allocation; medical college ownership, administration and improvement of Newark's City Hospital; provision of community health services by the college; and assurances that blacks would have meaningful participation in all decisions pertaining to the medical college's relocation.

One month after release of the commission's report, an *ad hoc* negotiating committee composed of public officials from city, state and federal jurisdictions, medical professionals from the college, and representatives from Newark's black community reached agreement on all provisions for building the medical college in Newark. Following closely the guidelines laid down by the Governor's Commission, the agreement held that the size of the site would be limited to 56 acres, a health services program would be initiated, site residents would be satisfactorily relocated, minority group members would be employed in building the college, a broad-based community group would share in major decisions and community-based corporations would build new housing for residents. All parties to the dispute hailed the agreement as a major breakthrough in solving the medical college dispute and related issues. However, over the following two years, all provisions of the agreement were systematically violated, except the size of the land parcel allotted to the college.[17]

Official Corruption: Uncertain Beginnings and Final Convictions

Of the 99 recommendations made by the Governor's Commission, the proposal for a grand jury investigation into alleged official corruption in Newark received more attention and created greater controversy than any other single recommendation. The commission observed: "There is a widespread belief that Newark's government is corrupt." It recommended "that a special grand jury be called to investigate allegations of corruption in Newark."[18]

For evidence of corruption in Newark, the commission relied primarily on two sources. The first consisted of presentments made by four grand juries in the early 1960s: one in 1961, one in 1964 and two in 1965. What disturbed the commission about the previous grand juries was the absence of any follow-up action on the presentments, all of which came to similar conclusions on the extent of corruption in Newark and the degree to which public officials interfered in police department affairs to conceal official corruption.[19]

Testimony from Deputy Police Chief John Redden, widely regarded as Newark's "cleanest cop," provided the commission with a second source of information. The commission relied heavily on Redden's testimony that public officials and police officers openly tolerated gambling in Newark, quoting him 30 different times in its *Report*. For example:

> When Deputy Police Chief John Redden was asked about the prevalence of bookmaking and numbers playing in Newark, he told this Commission: "Based on my own experience, based on previous Grand Jury investigations, based on the statement—the public statement—of a man such as former Assistant Attorney General Bergin, I would say that it was very prevalent. It is very large business." Mr. Redden also cited that presentment as evidence that assignment of police personnel was made for political reasons.[20]

The commission's investigation and recommendations about corruption in Newark led to three important developments: creation of a special gambling unit by the Newark Police Department, empaneling of an Essex County grand jury to investigate official corruption and convening of three federal grand juries to investigate official corruption, gambling and income tax evasion.

The Special Gambling Unit. Addonizio and Police Director Spina quickly reacted to the commission's allegation that gambling laws were leniently enforced in Newark. Three days after the commission's *Report* appeared, they jointly announced creation of a special nine-man "gambling squad" within the Newark Police Department. As if to challenge the Governor's Commission and its principle witness, Addonizio and Spina named Deputy Chief Redden to head the special unit and encouraged him to verify by effective action his commission testimony. Redden was on the spot, for if he failed to reveal the widespread gambling he had described, he would discredit his testimony, undercut the commission's findings and exonerate the city administration and the police department. By naming Redden, a police officer who was immune to charges of a whitewash, the two city officials also created the impression that they were serious about unveiling corruption.

From its appointment to its dissolution, the special gambling unit provides a microcosm of the way public officials create *ad hoc* devices while under fire and later undermine their own creations. The unit existed for eight weeks before Police Director Spina dissolved it. Redden spent the first two weeks selecting officers of his choice and organizing the gambling squad. Difficulties in obtaining search warrants initially impaired the unit's effectiveness and some weeks later Redden's officers were assigned emergency patrol duty to assist in quelling disturbances following the assassination of Dr. Martin Luther King. Then, on April 15, 1968, Police Director Spina disbanded the gambling unit. Thus after two months, but in reality only five working weeks because of delays and interruptions, the widely heralded drive to enforce gambling laws ended. Spina explained that his directive to dissolve the unit became necessary due to a shortage of manpower. A member of the gambling squad gave a different reason: "Several 'good' raids were set for the end of this week. We were getting close to the big people."[21]

After abolishing the gambling squad, Spina assigned Deputy Chief Redden to "planning and research" work within the department and placed most other members of the squad on foot-patrol duty. Redden reacted by observing: "These men [of the special unit] have proven that gambling is pretty prevalent and is a big business. I'm sorry we are being disbanded, the men really worked at this and were developing a lot of information."[22] Mayor Addonizio, vacationing in Florida at the time, expressed surprise at the gambling squad's dissolution, but supported Spina's action: "When I formed the squad I said if Redden had knowledge of what he testified to he should be put in charge... what he's made is perfunctory arrests—the rest of the department has done almost as well."[23] The local press disputed how perfunctory the special gambling unit's performance actually was. In its five weeks of field operation, the Redden unit made 22 arrests, confiscated $16,388.77 in cash and $15,369.52 in numbers play. It also seized two shotguns, six pistols and $10,000 in stolen merchandise and uncovered extensive loan-sharking operations.[24]

The County Grand Jury. Essex County Prosecutor Joseph P. Lordi, perhaps due to his different constitutional and constituent base, pursued commission allegations much more vigorously than did Newark public officials. In what was interpreted at the time as a rebuff of city officials, Lordi announced his intention to convene a county grand jury to investigate official corruption, lax gambling-law enforcement and extortion just two days after the dissolution of the municipal gambling squad. He made good on his promise by empaneling the grand jury on May 27, 1968.

Two months later the grand jury returned an indictment against Police Director Spina on four counts of nonfeasance for "willfully" refusing to enforce New Jersey gambling laws. The indictment alleged that Spina failed to perform his public duty to curb lotteries, gambling and bookmaking and censured the police director for disbanding the special gambling squad. In all four counts of the indictment, the dissolution of the gambling squad was given as evidence of Spina's willful neglect of duty. With more than passing coincidence, at the same time that it indicted Spina, the grand jury handed up 28 additional indictments naming 17 persons, all resulting from the work of the short-lived gambling squad under Deputy Chief Redden.

Spina pleaded innocent to the indictment, but nevertheless submitted his resignation. Addonizio refused to accept it and instead released a four-page statement vigorously defending Spina. Addonizio relied, in part, on the Kerner Commission's praise of Spina: "The Kerner Commission used Director Spina as an example of bravery under fire and coolness under the kind of pressure which panicked lesser men all around. I can't consider this to have been a failure to perform his duty."[25] He also labeled the gambling laws used in Spina's indictment as "hypocritical" for prohibiting certain types of gaming while allowing others. What particularly galled Addonizio was the grand jury's unwillingness to call Spina as a witness while it took extensive testimony from rank-and-file police officers, including Deputy Chief Redden.

The prosecution's case against the police director proved particularly weak because it relied for evidence primarily on the decline in arrests for gambling after the grand jury presentments in 1965. The prosecution listed over 100 addresses where gambling allegedly took place and charged that Spina either knew or should have known about such operations but deliberately failed to act. The defense argued that Spina had no knowledge of illegal activities at the addresses listed and if other law enforcement jurisdictions had such knowledge they should be on trial for not acting. Spina won acquittal on all counts. Superior Judge Samuel A. Larner directed a verdict of acquittal because the state failed to prove he had any direct connection with gambling activities in Newark, although the judge acknowledged that "a substantial picture of laxity and inefficiency in the enforcement of gambling laws" had been presented by the state.[26]

Three months following Spina's acquittal, in January 1969, the same Essex County grand jury issued a 12-page presentment calling for his removal as police director. The grand jury demanded Spina's replacement for failure to enforce gambling laws and denounced Addonizio for terming gambling laws "hypocritical." The presentment's findings again emphasized lax gambling-law enforcement in Newark[27] and reiterated the grand jury's praise of Redden's gambling squad and called for its reinstatement.

Two days prior to the presentment's release, however, Spina averted the grand jury's proposal by reactivating the gambling squad, this time without Deputy Chief Redden. He also attempted to outflank the grand jury by requiring all police officers to submit a report each week detailing any knowledge they had of gambling in Newark. Director Spina reacted to the presentment by labeling it "harassment" and "venomous." He charged:

> Such action is absolutely amazing because the presentment is simply a parroting of the worthless testimony presented in New Jersey Superior Court less than two short months ago. The case was thrown out because these allegations made against me then, in the form of an indictment and now in the form of this presentment, completely failed to indicate any dereliction of duty on my part. Such charges can never succeed because I have not been derelict in my duty.[28]

Police fraternal organizations strongly supported Spina and opposed the grand jury presentment as "outside interference" in departmental affairs. The grand jury's findings had virtually no impact and Spina's removal was not seriously considered.

The Essex County grand jury then turned to the Addonizio administration and Newark's City Council to determine the extent of official corruption, kickbacks, bribery and extortion. Although it issued no additional indictments or presentments, the importance of its work cannot be underestimated in view of subsequent developments. In December 1969 the grand jury recessed, after meeting for 19 continuous months, hearing 228 witnesses and developing over 5,000 pages of testimony.

The Three Federal Grand Juries. The recess of the Essex County grand jury was prompted by the empaneling of three separate federal grand juries to investigate corruption within the New Jersey field offices of the Internal Revenue Service, Mafia-controlled gambling operations in New Jersey and official corruption in Newark. Frederick B. Lacey, United States attorney for New Jersey, convened the three federal grand juries after local and state investigations proved unproductive. By mutual agreement, Essex County Prosecutor Joseph P. Lordi gave Lacey all information gathered by the Essex County grand jury and prospective witness lists. In addition, Lordi's two top assistants obtained leaves of absence to work for Lacey. Each of the three federal grand juries obtained indictments and convictions where prior local and state efforts had failed.

The first federal grand jury found substantial misconduct by field agents of the Internal Revenue Service. One high-ranking revenue agent was dismissed and two IRS employees were indicted and convicted for falsifying tax information of reputed Mafia organization members. The second federal grand jury found a network of Mafia-linked persons operating an interstate gambling operation, with headquarters in New Jersey, that grossed over $20 million each year. The investigation received considerable national publicity when Attorney General John N. Mitchell predicted:

> In this state [New Jersey] within the next week to 10 days there is going to be a massive indictment of public officials on the local level, and also in this state, through the activities that we have carried on, we're going to break the largest gambling syndicate that's ever been broken up in this country.[29]

Six days later the federal grand jury indicted 55 persons, including Simone Rizzo [Sam the Plumber] Decavalcante,[30] for conspiring to operate an interstate lottery or numbers racket. One hundred Federal Bureau of Investigation agents arrested 42 of the 55 persons within the first three hours after their indictment in what J. Edgar Hoover called "the largest series of Federal Gambling arrests in this area."[31]

Of the three federal grand juries, the investigation of official corruption in Newark eventually became the most publicized. The inquiry began where the recessed Essex County grand jury left off by concentrating on bribery, kickbacks and extortion in Newark. Mayor Addonizio, Chief Municipal Judge James Del Mauro and numerous other Newark public officials refused to testify and only reluctantly supplied the grand jury with subpoened information. The chief justice of the New Jersey Supreme Court suspended Judge Del Mauro for invoking the Fifth Amendment when asked by the grand jury about discrepancies in his individual income tax returns and for refusing to produce income tax information. Judge Del Mauro then resigned from the municipal court.

Mayor Addonizio's refusal to testify before the grand jury prompted demands for his ouster by newspapers, civic and business groups and several black organizations. State Attorney General Arthur Sills gave the demands an unsympathetic hearing, ostensibly because of possible interference with the grand jury's investigation, even though U.S. Attorney Lacey had assured him that no such interference would occur. The corruption controversy attracted even wider attention when Philip W. Gordon resigned as Newark's corporation counsel after admitting to the grand jury that he had accepted cash payments from a businessman who had contracts with the city and shared them with a city councilman.

On December 17, 1969, the federal grand jury indicted Addonizio and nine incumbent or former city officials on 64 counts of extortion, conspiracy and income tax evasion going back to January 1, 1965.[32] Five persons not holding public office were also indicted, including Anthony (Tony Boy) Boiardo who reputedly held a high position in the Mafia. The federal grand jury relied primarily on information developed by the Essex County grand jury as the basis for the indictments.

The indictment of Addonizio contributed substantially to his failure to be reelected. Black candidate Kenneth Gibson, who defeated him in June 1970, announced that one of his first acts as mayor would be to appoint John Redden as police director. One month later, Addonizio and four other defendants were found guilty of conspiring to extort more than $1.4 million and actually extorting $253,000 from contractors doing business with the city over a five-year period. The press, prosecuting attorneys and defendants attributed the original impetus for legal action against official corruption to the investigation and recommendation of the Governor's Commission.

Investigating Official Violence

The Governor's Commission also urged an investigation into the circumstances surrounding the 26 deaths recorded during the Newark riot and expressed concern about the insufficiency of an inquiry into the subject by a local grand jury:

383

The location of death, the number of wounds, the manner in which the wounds were afflicted all raise grave doubts about the circumstances under which many of these people [riot casualties] died. . . .The Commission views with concern the fact that such action [grand jury investigation of death causes] has not yet been completed. These homicides are matters of grave concern and should be quickly and exhaustively investigated and resolved by the appropriate grand jury.[33]

The commission recommended a complete public disclosure of the grand jury's findings, especially for cases where no indictments were returned, and urged the governor to review the findings to see that justice had been done.

An Essex County grand jury investigated the 26 deaths, taking testimony from over 100 witnesses and issuing a 27-page presentment two months after the Governor's Commission released its *Report.* The grand jury commended state and local police for acting with "courage and restraint," supported police demands for additional armaments and concluded that it found no evidence to justify any indictments. Most of the witnesses were law enforcement personnel and their views were substantially represented in the final presentment. The grand jury virtually excluded the possibility that state and local police could be held accountable for the deaths:

In the final analysis, the responsibility for the loss of life and property that is the inevitable product of rioting and mass lawlessness cannot be placed upon those whose duty it is to enforce law and protect the freedom of society. It rests squarely upon the shoulders of those who, for whatever purpose, incite and participate in riots and the flouting of law and order in complete disregard of the rights and well-being of the vast majority of our citizens.[34]

The presentment justified the grand jury's near exclusive reliance on testimony from local and state police because of what it termed the "uncooperative attitude" of the Newark Legal Services Project (NLSP). As an agency of Newark's antipoverty program providing legal aid to the poor, NLSP gathered volumes of testimony immediately after the 1967 disorder from eyewitnesses to the 26 deaths and submitted the information to the Kerner and Governor's Commission. Oliver Lofton, a member of the Governor's Commission and head of NLSP, initially withheld this information from the grand jury because of "open antagonism" to the antipoverty agency's work expressed by the prosecutor's office. The grand jury presentment declared that NLSP helped inflame the black community by releasing testimony on riot deaths and by distributing pictures of riot victims to the press. It also questioned the validity of the testimony gathered by NLSP:

> It was apparent that little or no investigation was undertaken of the background of many workers and volunteers (in NLSP). The jury could only conclude that during the excitement many of those taking statements from persons involved in the riots either deliberately or unconsciously distorted these statements and in many ways conducted themselves so as to create in the minds of the public a biased and inaccurate impression of many events connected with the disturbances.[35]

The grand jury's failure to present indictments or criticize police conduct drew varied reactions. Newark's Committee of Concern, cochaired by Lofton, labeled the presentment a "whitewash" of police misconduct. Police Director Spina said the report confirmed his view that Lofton never should have been on the Governor's Commission in the first place. Spina praised the document and used its findings to question the work of the Governor's Commission:

> My primary feeling is that the grand jury is truly representative of Americanism; they made a thorough analysis of the facts and their recommendations are good. I can't praise the report too much; they did an outstanding job. If this grand jury had worked on the Governor's Commission on Civil Disorder, which issued a riot report earlier, that report would have been a finer job.[36]

The grand jury's presentment was strongly criticized by two members of the Governor's Commission. Lofton and John J. Gibbons described the grand jury's investigation as inadequate because of the dependence on one-sided evidence collected from local and state police.[37] They also defended NLSP's activities, citing favorable evaluations of the agency made by the Kerner and Governor's commissions. Gibbons singled out the prosecutor's office for conducting a superficial inquiry and for not providing the grand jury with thorough evidence.[38] Governor Hughes did not review the grand jury's findings, as requested by his commission, and issued only one public statement on the matter: "I want to assure the people that the State police are not in the business of doing anything but protecting citizens."[39]

A final investigation arising out of the Governor's Commission's recommendations involved Governor Hughes more directly. Immediately following the July disorder numerous charges of wanton shooting, beating and destruction of property were made by civil rights groups, clergymen and black businessmen against local and state police officers. State police were repeatedly accused of uncontrolled violence against black residents and black-owned property.[40] The Governor's Commission's investigation substantiated the accusations and the *Report for Action* charged law enforcement personnel with engaging in "a good deal of indiscriminate shooting." It asserted: "the amount of ammunition expended by police forces was out of all proportion to the mission assigned to them."[41] The commission was dismayed when it discovered that members of the state police intentionally and systematically fired into stores marked with "Soul Brother" signs. It recommended an immediate and exhaustive investigation into police misconduct with discipline for those responsible and state compensation for those who suffered property losses. The recommendation fell primarily upon Governor Hughes for action.

Five days after release of the *Report for Action*, State Attorney General Arthur J. Sills, responding to the commission on behalf of the governor, announced that an "exhaustive" investigation into charges of misconduct by state police personnel revealed that such claims could not be validated. When pressed by newsmen to explain differences between his report and the commission's findings, Sills replied, "I'm not in a position to line up 600 men and ask each one of them if they did it. We can't just line up all the policemen and pick out every fifth one and say 'you're guilty.' "[42] Sills concluded his report by saying that all information would be turned over to the Essex County grand jury; it later returned no indictments.

The "exhaustive" investigation Sills reported actually began shortly after the 1967 disorder ended. Governor Hughes asked Colonel David B. Kelly, superintendent of the New Jersey State Police, to look into possible misconduct by state police personnel. With the Governor's Commission's investigation at mid-point, Colonel Kelly made public the fact that state police officers had spent over 150,000 man-hours checking reports of police misconduct. On the same occasion he announced the inquiry's preliminary findings: "There was no need to take any disciplinary action. We found nothing to substantiate the charges. Just remember one thing: the police didn't start the riots."43 This same state police investigation of itself later provided the sole basis for Sills's "exhaustive" investigation. Nothing further came of the investigations into state police culpability.

The State Response

The Governor's Commission's request that Hughes investigate police misconduct was but one of 29 recommendations directed explicitly at the state of New Jersey. In contrast to reforms proposed for Newark, the state recommendations were considerably less specific and detailed.44

Public officials in Newark made vigorous efforts to draw attention to the reforms aimed at the state, arguing that they appropriately identified a possible source of increased municipal revenues and calling for their immediate implementation. Addonizio, for example, applauded proposals for funds and program support from state sources that he had consistently urged during his six-year tenure as mayor. He particularly approved the commission's statement that "the resources of Newark and urban centers are no longer adequate to cope with the recurrent crises that afflict them."45 Addonizio similarly welcomed demands that the state judiciary absorb Newark's municipal courts, that a single state agency centralize funding of all public welfare and that a broad-based revenue measure relieve Newark's dependence on local property taxes. Besides focusing attention on the capacity of the state to absorb costly municipal programs, emphasizing recommendations aimed at the state drew attention away from shortcomings in the city administration and minimized the importance of reforms targeted for the city.

Mayor Addonizio saw in some commission recommendations an opportunity to rid his administration of public services that had become extremely costly and virtually unmanageable. The *Report for Action*, for example, proposed that the State Education Commission take over all administrative functions for Newark's public school system and channel special aid to it. Addonizio embraced these proposed reforms and invited advocates of the state takeover plan to "come and get it." In a letter to Governor Hughes and State Education Commissioner Carl Marberger, Addonizio made known his city's willingness to cooperate "in making the transfer quickly and efficiently."46

The target of Addonizio's campaign to draw attention away from Newark was Governor Hughes. The day after release of the *Report*, Hughes held a press conference generally praising his commission's document and its work. He refused, however, to comment on how recommendations aimed at the state might be implemented. Two days later, Hughes presented his annual budget message to the legislature in which he urged acceptance of a balanced budget calling for $1,064 billion in expenditures. To secure a promised "no-new-taxation" fiscal year, Hughes cut the Department of Community Affairs' budget request from $24 million to $13.1 million. Addonizio charged Hughes with ignoring proposals from his own riot commission:

> Newark is moving on the report and moving fast and I hope that the state will join us as we move. I must confess, however, that the state budget introduced †his week reflects none of the urgency found in the commission report nor do the speeches of state officials. Not only has there been an incredible failure to substantially increase state aid, but the budget of Commissioner [Paul N.] Ylvisaker's new Department of Community Affairs was cut by $11 million even before it was presented to the legislature.[47]

Hughes responded to the criticism by restating his confidence in the Department of Community Affairs and its ability to function effectively under the proposed budget. He then departed New Jersey for a two-week vacation in Florida.

Upon returning from Florida, Hughes' equivocation on the commission's *Report* continued in the face of mounting criticism. Addonizio continued to call for state action, as did the Newark City Council. Democratic state assemblymen from Essex County urged the governor to act favorably on the *Report*, and the Republican legislative leadership appointed a six-member committee to study ways the state might implement the commission's recommendations. A confederation of 40 black and Puerto Rican civil rights groups, known as the Statewide Conference on Minority Problems, petitioned Hughes to take immediate action on the commission's proposals.

Hughes responded to these demands by reiterating his opposition to increasing taxes. He did suggest, however, that he might submit a supplemental message to the state legislature urging adoption of commission recommendations not requiring additional expenditures and therefore not threatening his balanced budget. At other times, the governor was overtly hostile to the commission's *Report*. After returning from vacation, for example, Hughes released information showing his mail running four-to-one against the *Report* and its recommendations.[48]

In response to Hughes' unyielding stand against any new programs that might unbalance his budget, Addonizio adopted another ploy. The mayor sought to place responsibility for implementing the recommendations directly on members of the Governor's Commission. He challenged commission members at a press conference:

> Now let them [commission members] join me in an effort to get the state budget revised so it will reflect some of the recommendations in the report. I don't believe the commission can write a report and then just walk away. I hope the state, which was severely criticized by the commission for failure to support local municipalities, will join us as we move.[49]

Addonizio revealed that he envisioned asking commission members to join him in seeking a meeting with Hughes and state legislative leaders to obtain a revised state budget so that recommendations could be carried out.

The Governor's Commission Intervenes

The crisis generated by the assassination of Dr. Martin Luther King, Jr., on April 4, 1968, changed the dimensions of the dispute. The governor was widely criticized for failure to act on the commission *Report*, and demands for immediate, visible and meaningful action came from several sources. Several members of the commission directly intervened, privately indicating to Hughes that unless prompt action was forthcoming they would publicly denounce his silence.

On April 8, Hughes convened a joint session of the state legislature to deliver a special message on the need to adopt measures to meet urban and racial problems. State legislators received the address as an eloquent and compassionate plea for assistance to urban communities, but also pointed out that it did not go beyond vague generalities.

After the special message, Hughes called all 10 members of the Governor's Commission and its eight top staff members to his residence to formulate a set of programs in response to urban needs and to establish funding levels for the programs. The meeting reversed Hughes' previous position on a balanced budget. Commission members persuaded him to adopt recommendations from the *Report for Action* and to urge the legislature to fully fund the programs. Three weeks after the assassination of King, Hughes submitted a supplemental appropriation request to the state legislature calling for $126.1 million additional expenditures for programs taken almost verbatim from the *Report*. Table 10.1 reports the programs advocated and the funding level for each measure as transmitted by Hughes to the legislature. In submitting the supplemental appropriation request, Hughes acknowledged the forces influencing his decision:

> This might be the most important work that any New Jersey Legislature was ever called upon to do. This work, the urgency of this mission, has been impressed upon all of us from many quarters—by the Lilley [Governor's] Commission, by educators, and by parents, and law enforcement authorities, and the press, and citizens of every interest and every circumstance—but most importantly of all, by out own intelligence and our own conscience. It is as though an alarm had sounded, awakening us from a long neglect to a present duty. The work before us is not easy—but it is about that work, about the unmistakable need for immediate action, that I wish to speak to you today.[50]

TABLE 10.1

Supplemental Appropriation Expenditures Requested In Response to Governor's Commission Recommendations

Program Area	Funding Level
I. ASSUMPTION OF 75 PERCENT OF WELFARE COSTS	$ 54,500,000
Work Incentive Program and Day Care	1,438,000
Subtotal	55,938,000
II. URBAN PROGRAMS AND LAW ENFORCEMENT –	
School Construction	2,000,000
Urban Education Corps	500,000
Educational Opportunity Fund	2,500,000
Neighborhood Education Centers	480,000
Head Start Supplement	100,000
Skills Center Expansion	1,547,000
School Lunch Program	3,000,000
Employment	3,500,000

Law Enforcement –
(a) Police training –

1. Scholarships	75,000
2. Operation Combine	185,000
3. Attitudinal testing	50,000

(b) Police Cadet Program 300,000
(c) Sixty additional State Police 500,000
(d) Police effectiveness –

1. Communications	400,000
2. Police Laboratory	475,000
3. Regionalization	50,000
4. Special agents	no cost
5. Civilians	no cost
6. Recruitment	no cost

(e) Unified Court System .... no cost
(f) Recording for municipal courts 105,000
(g) Summons in lieu of arrest .... no cost
(h) Release on recognizance .... no cost
(i) Study by Administrative Director 25,000
(j) Probation Aides 350,000
(k) Civil Rights Division 275,000
(l) Consumer Protection 100,000

Narcotics Control 2,320,000
Community Health Centers 720,000
Summer Recreation 650,000
            Subtotal 20,207,000
III. EMERGENCY SCHOOL AID 25,000,000
IV. HOUSING –
(a) Housing Assistance Fund 12,500,000
        rent supplements
        interest subsidies
        in lieu payments
(b) Mortgage guarantee 5,000,000
(c) Rehabilitation loans 5,000,000
(d) Expansion of revolving demonstration
        fund 2,500,000
        Subtotal 25,000,000
            TOTAL $126,145,000

Source: Special Message of Richard J. Hughes to the Legislature, 25 April 1968, p. 52

Hughes also proposed that the state legislature place on the ballot, for referenda, four bond issues totalling $1.75 billion for future capital needs. The bond issues and the urban aid package were to be financed by a 1 to 5 percent graduated state income tax.

Opposition to these measures developed immediately. Republicans, who controlled the state legislature by a 4-to-1 margin, drew up a counterproposal calling for a $58.4 million urban aid package and a $890 million bond issue to be financed by excise taxes and possibly a 1 percent increase in the state sales tax. In the Republican program, the prime beneficiaries would be rural areas and suburbs. Table 10.2 provides a comparison of the two urban assistance measures.

TABLE 10.2

Comparison of Special Urban Aid Plans and Revenue Measures

EXECUTIVE PROPOSALS

Governor Hughes	Republican Legislators
1. $55.9 million for the state to assume all non-federally aided welfare costs, including work incentive and day-care programs to break relief cycle.	1. $35 million for the state to assume 75 percent of all non-federally aided welfare costs for five categories of welfare aid but not for general welfare assistance.
2. $20.2 million for more urban and law enforcement programs, including more school construction, an educational opportunities fund, and a narcotics control program.	2. $25 million a year in state sales tax funds remitted to the municipalities on an unrestricted-use basis and on a formula that would give big cities a larger share of the funds.
3. $25 million in emergency state school aid to the cities to help them meet their educational problems.	3. $17 million to increase the minimum state aid per school pupil from $75 to $100 per pupil. Most large cities are maximum or near maximum school-aid districts and would get little or nothing from these funds.

4. $25 million to stimulate re-
habilitation and new construction of low-income housing in
slum areas.

4. No housing recommendation.

5. No recommendation.

5. $5 million for law enforce-
ment and anticrime measures,
including a permanent state
crime investigating committee.

6. No recommendation.

6. $10 million for partial first-
year funding of a Medicaid program of hospital, doctor and
health care for poor persons.

REVENUE PROPOSALS

Governor Hughes

Republican Legislators

1. Recommends a one- to five-
percent state income tax.

1. Recommends a five cents per
pack on cigarettes and extension
of excise taxation to pipe tobac-
co and cigars, and a one-percent
increase in the state corporation
income tax, a ten-percent rise in
auto registration and driver's
license fees, and a new highway-
use tax on heavy trucks.

With the governor's special urban aid program in jeopardy, members
of the Governor's Commission regrouped in a rescue attempt. They
formed a "Majority Response Rally" and scheduled May 27, 1968, for
a massive turnout of middle-class whites to show support for the
governor's program. Thirty-eight prominent groups, including civic,
religious, veterans, women, students, education, business, labor and
finance organizations sponsored the rally. But the group clearly carried
the imprint of the Governor's Commission. Seven of the 10 members of
the Governor's Commission and its staff director cosponsored the group
and former governors Robert B. Meyner and Alfred E. Driscoll, also
commissioners, acted as the group's cochairmen.

Some 1,500 persons, mainly suburban housewives, turned out for the rally. Speakers urged adoption of the governor's urban-aid program and a broad-based tax. Literature distributed prior to the rally urged attendance to further the riot commission's recommendations:

"Suburban residents must understand that the future of their communities is inextricably linked to the fate of the city instead of harboring the illusion that they can maintain invisible walls or continue to run away." The above quotation comes from the report by the N.J. Civil Disorder Study Commission, named by the Governor to examine their causes, incidents, and remedies. This distinguished biracial panel of two former governors and other leaders from the state's business, professional and religious communities reported in February. Many of its most urgent recommendations require state implementation, and the Legislature has indicated a willingness to hear what the public thinks while the decisions hang in balance.[51]

The response of the Republican-controlled legislature became evident when the majority leader of the state senate, Frank X. McDermott, told the group: "You haven't come down with the force you should have if the people were with you."[52]

The urban aid package submitted by Hughes failed to pass the state legislature. Instead Republicans adopted their version of an urban aid program, passing a $83.5 million special appropriation that would divide state sales tax revenue evenly among the affluent suburbs and the larger cities. Hughes vetoed the appropriation. The Governor's Commission's attempt to change state-wide policies and to have an impact on upgrading cities like Newark through state legislative assistance thus failed under the weight of prior political cleavages.

This review of the fate of the Governor's Commission's recommendations suggests how reform measures proposed by riot commissions become part of the continuing controversy among competing political interests. Recommendations that required increased appropriations became entangled in a partisan battle between the Democratic governor and the Republican state legislature. Other recommendations became engulfed in jurisdictional conflict between municipal and state executives of the same party. Addonizio embraced recommendations targeted for the state almost as if they were his own and called for immediate eradication of municipal problems through the use of state resources. Governor Hughes' initial reaction to his commission's *Report* was

394

equivocation at best and opposition at worst. After the assassination of King and after being pressured by his own appointees to the commission, Hughes formulated an urban assistance package, but it was defeated by a Republican majority in the legislature.

City officials in Newark adopted a much more complex posture toward the commission proposals than simply using them to deflect attention away from municipal shortcomings. Mayor Addonizio initially responded enthusiastically to reform measures and promised to implement recommendations intended for his jurisdiction. In some cases, like the transfer of Captain Williams and the defeat of the canine corps proposal, he kept his promise. The commission reform proposals allowed Addonizio to take affirmative action in sensitive areas where powerful and divergent political forces had stalemated. This initial affirmative action proved impossible on other, often more important, recommendations. The proposed civilian review board over police activities, for example, was not adopted after fraternal police organizations generated forceful opposition to it. Still other measures were not carried out as time passed and concern dissipated.

With the passage of time the city administration became reluctant to carry through on promised reforms in other ways. Some reform measures went unheeded. Despite initial verbal support for commission recommendations regarding the medical college, the city administration later successfully undermined these same reforms. The city administration adopted some commission recommendations then, later, quietly terminated efforts at reform. This strategy was adopted with the gambling unit, formed immediately after release of the commission's report, quietly dissolved some eight weeks later and reactivated with less ambitious personnel when Police Director Spina was indicted for nonfeasance by a grand jury.

The Governor's Commission had its most impressive impact in the investigation of official corruption by various grand juries. The inquiries led to the indictment and conviction of several prominent public officials in Newark, including the mayor. Yet, at the time, corruption appeared to have only marginal connection to the riot and, prior to the indictments, commission members themselves expressed regret about giving it the emphasis they did. The commission's recommendations resulted in the immediate indictment and conviction of leading Newark officials; even more important, they made a substantial contribution to the succession to power of blacks in Newark.[53]

The Mayor's Development Team in Detroit:
Reform Mayor Versus Reformed Municipal Bureaucracy

In contrast to the Newark and Milwaukee cases where a disproportionately large number of official commission recommendations targeted secondary jurisdictions for reform, the Detroit investigation devoted nearly all of its attention to reforming city agencies in the primary jurisdiction of Detroit. The lengthy Development Team *Report* included literally hundreds of recommendations aimed at the municipal bureaucracy, ranging from detailed proposals for changing agency programs, structures and personnel practices, to comprehensive reorganization reforms that would create three superagencies indirectly responsible to the mayor. Contrasted with its success in fulfilling its first two tasks of providing emergency relief and formulating the recommended changes, the Development Team wholly failed to implement these reforms, and efforts to do so produced intense conflict between one of the most reform-minded mayors in American cities and one of the most extensively reformed municipal bureaucracies in American cities.[54]

Several factors account for the Development Team's decision to focus its recommendations on city agencies. In important respects this focus had been engineered by Mayor Cavanagh. Together with Governor Romney, he insured that the Development Team could ignore the private sector by creating the New Detroit Committee to stimulate reform in nongovernmental areas. In his charge to the Development Team, Cavanagh specified city departments as the governmental units requiring change. Moreover, all of the team members had prior experience in and knowledge about agency operations; some members were even serving as Cavanagh's appointed heads of important departments. They were familiar with bureaucratic personnel, structures and performances and had strong convictions about past agency shortcomings.

Targeting reforms for city agencies also coincided with the Cavanagh administration's disenchantment with Detroit's reformed bureaucracy. Development Team deliberations took place midway through Cavanagh's second term of office, by which time the mayor and his closest associates had come to view city departments as obstacles to be overcome if the city administration's programs were to be carried out.[55]

The conflict between the Cavanagh administration and city agencies had its origins in institutional changes resulting from reforms in Detroit.

Since the enactment of its present city charter in 1918, Detroit has established a set of reformed municipal structures without parallel among large cities. By the 1960s, the city departments had achieved such a degree of autonomy that they functioned largely independent from electoral influences, other political forces and directives from the mayor's office. An ambitious Civil Service Commission, itself isolated from mayoral control, enforced a comprehensive civil service system providing city employees protection from "outside" political intervention.[56] The mayor has fewer than 50 appointees among more than 25,000 departmental employees. He can name, at most, the department director and deputy director in each of the 25 major city agencies. The remaining agency personnel are formally and informally protected from executive interference by the Civil Service Commission, Detroit's two leading newspapers (which periodically launch crusades on behalf of "good government" principles), and agency clientele groups which have been fostered and supported by city departments. Various other nonbureaucratic reform structures also contribute to the relatively autonomous status of city agencies.[57]

During both of his terms of office as mayor, Cavanagh advocated programs that were delayed, blocked or modified by administrative agencies. A political novice who had held no other elective office, Cavanagh defeated incumbent Mayor Louis C. Miriani in 1961 despite Miriani's endorsement by the two leading Detroit newspapers and most important business and labor organizations. In his first term (1962-1966), Cavanagh initiated several reform programs responsive to the constituency that had elected him—liberals, rank-and-file United Automobile Workers members and blacks. When city agencies resisted carrying out these programs, particularly with the emphasis the mayor desired, Cavanagh avoided a direct confrontation by capitalizing on federal funds and programs available under the Kennedy and Johnson administrations.[58] Though he could circumvent city departments beyond his control, he substantially failed to insure that his program emphasis would be adhered to by agency personnel. Re-elected in 1965 with the renewed support of his coalition, Cavanagh again attempted to secure compliance with his programs. After the 1967 riot, the mayor finally encouraged a direct and thorough review of agency performances by singling out city departments as the governmental units that the Development Team should investigate.

The Development Team inquired in depth into the general adequacy of services delivered by city agencies, particularly to blacks, and targeted hundreds of reform recommendations for the departments. It portrayed the riot-induced crisis as susceptible to amelioration if city agency operations could be made more responsive to citizen needs.[59] After recalling the devastating impact of the riot and its depressing effect on the community, the Development Team emphasized that citizens' grievances expressed in the rioting were in important respects a consequence of inept bureaucratic performances and improper agency structures.[60]

Upon release of the final *Report*, Development Team members sought and received Mayor Cavanagh's commitment to persuade city agencies to adopt the reform proposals. Cavanagh circulated a memorandum to all city agencies requiring them to review the Development Team *Report* and to submit responses to his office. The memorandum specifically asked agencies to comment on recommendations affecting their programs and to suggest how they might carry out the reforms. All but one of the 25 city agencies complied with the memorandum.[61] With few exceptions the agencies applauded the Development Team's work in *general* terms, but uniformly rejected as unwise and unworkable the *specific* reforms aimed at programs they administered. Because the recommendations included significant reorganization of bureaucratic structures and the incorporation of hundreds of specific personnel and program changes, the city agencies' unequivocal opposition posed a quandary for Cavanagh.

The Dilemma of a Reform Mayor

Cavanagh had good reason to force reform recommendations on city agencies but, as will be shown, equally strong influences constrained his ability and willingness to do so. Foremost among his reasons for implementing the reform proposals was that they had been formulated by his riot study panel, he had promised to be responsive to its findings and recommendations and the proposed reforms coincided with his prior agenda. In appointing the Development Team, Cavanagh had selected his most trusted advisors as members. To ignore their recommendations would not only be understood as discrediting an executive instrument of his creation, but also as a sign of bad faith with his closest associates. When the Development Team released its *Report*, moreover, Cavanagh had embraced its work and committed himself to using the proposed reforms as a blueprint for rebuilding Detroit.

Cavanagh's implementation of the reforms also held out the promise of resolving the conflict between his administration and Detroit's reformed city agencies. Cavanagh, himself a reformer, shared important values accompanying bureaucratic reform, but he was frustrated and appalled at some characteristics of Detroit's reformed bureaucracy. Like other reform mayors who advance ambitious civic agendas, Cavanagh had been frustrated throughout his first term of office by the unwieldy, impersonal and unresponsive nature of autonomous agencies. The more he had sought decisive program developments, the greater his frustrations became with established traditions, an unwillingness to innovate and an isolated administrative apparatus beyond mayoral control so characteristic of reformed bureaucracies. These were common complaints about autonomous agencies, but Cavanagh's reservations appeared to be even more complex.

Extensive reform of Detroit's municipal bureaucracy had taken place a generation before Cavanagh was elected to office. The mayor viewed city agencies as efficient and professional in delivering municipal services, but unresponsive to changing demographic characteristics of the city. Detroit's population was rapidly becoming 50 percent black, yet the municipal bureaucracy continued to define its service functions predominantly in terms of the needs and demands of whites. In part this was because entrenched agency personnel were almost all white and partially because agencies received support from white clientele groups.[62] Together, these two attributes provided the ingredients for classic bureaucratic inertia. Reform a generation earlier had inadvertently created a municipal bureaucracy incapable of delivering services to a sizable and racially distinct portion of the city's population.

Cavanagh's campaigns for mayor in 1961 and 1965 were successful in part because of the overwhelming support received from blacks. When racial violence erupted in 1967, he forecast a critical review of city departments by appointing experienced agency hands loyal to him to the Development Team and by charging them with assessing the adequacy of city services, particularly in black neighborhoods. His prior feelings about bureaucratic inertia were confirmed and renewed when the study panel described agencies as "self-serving," "in-bred," and "out-moded." The hundreds of recommendations aimed at agency structures, personnel policies and practices, and particularly the proposals to create three superagencies responsible to the mayor, provided Cavanagh with the opportunity to finally establish control over the municipal bureaucracy. Cavanagh's intent was not to disperse patronage, but rather to insure that his programs would be effectively carried through by bureaucratic agents. It was expected that the Development

Team's findings and recommendations would receive Cavanagh's strong support, because they were so congruent with his needs and consistent with his prior agenda.[63]

Despite these expectations, the mayor was constrained from imposing the recommendations upon city agencies. At least three factors directly attributable to the structure of Detroit's reformed municipal bureaucracy provided the constraints: agencies' legal/ structural autonomy, the strength of independent agency constituencies vis-á-vis the mayor and agencies' capacity to build and sustain those constituencies through independent sources of and claims to legitimacy. All had a significant impact on Cavanagh's inability to implement Development Team recommendations. They also illustrate dilemmas of a reform mayor pitted against a reformed bureaucracy and suggest the paradox of having good government with its accompanying reformed institutions resisting additional reform measures.

From a legal and structural position, the Cavanagh administration was particularly dependent upon cooperative relations with city agencies. The extensive autonomy legally accorded agencies and the structural protection provided by a strong Civil Service Commission allowed city departments to comply to a greater or lesser extent with mayoral directives. Lacking the prerogative to appoint agency personnel, Cavanagh had previously relied upon persuasion and the prestige of his office to obtain agency cooperation.[64] To exercise coercion now by imposing the recommendations would likely result in the deterioration of the limited cooperation agencies had given him in prior years. Even worse, city departments possessed sufficient formal and informal resources to undermine the objectives he had charted for his second term of office.[65] An existing degree of autonomy largely insulated them from external political pressure. Moreover, if Cavanagh forced the proposed reforms upon agencies they could later neutralize them and even impair the overall performance of his administration by ignoring programs he assigned priority.

The significant political power available to independent city agencies contributed to the dilemma. If Cavanagh consolidated city departments under the recommended superagencies, he risked alienating three important power blocs within Detroit. The first, of course, was personnel within the agencies themselves who constituted a sizable voting constituency for the mayor. City employees owed no particular loyalty to Cavanagh, having obtained their jobs through merit examination rather than patronage favors. The regard with which agency personnel held the mayor very much depended upon his behavior toward them. In addition to the more than 25,000 city employees, their immediate families and close friends might also withdraw support from Cavanagh if the reforms were implemented. Second, Cavanagh's relationship with common council members could be jeopardized if he followed the Development Team's advice. In Detroit's nonpartisan politics council members frequently establish strong ties with municipal agencies for assistance in furthering pet projects and the agencies reciprocate to enhance their budgetary prospects. The consolidation plan threatened to disrupt these informal relations between councilmen and agencies and promised to give the mayor increased control over city agencies. A third center of power potentially alienated by imposed consolidation was agency-clientele groups. Though Detroit's reformed bureaucracy is autonomous it is not absolutely isolated from external political forces. Rather, its autonomy is preserved by support from specialized-interest groups served by the agencies. These groups (and the agencies themselves) feared that departmental consolidation might endanger the unique agency-clientele relationships.

City agencies further constrained Cavanagh's ability to implement the Development Team's recommendations by making forceful appeals to independent sources of legitimacy to preserve their autonomy. Faced with the prospect of a major overhaul of the municipal bureaucracy, the agencies formulated various arguments designed to undermine the recommendations and to retain their autonomous structures and relationships. These appeals, initially revealed in responses to Cavanagh's memorandum soliciting agency reactions to the Development Team recommendations, took four forms: challenging the validity of assertions underlying Development Team reform proposals; defending past agency performances; using criticism of present operations as justification for increased agency resources; and justifying continued autonomy on grounds of efficiency and professionalism. Agencies articulated these appeals with varying degrees of consistency, but nearly uniformly attributed legitimacy to existing bureaucratic arrangements in Detroit.[66]

Challenging the report's analysis. An initial city agency response to the mayor's memorandum was to challenge the validity of the Development Team's inferences and its claims to expertise. City agencies attempted to discredit the basis upon which the Development

Team made its recommendations and hence its legitimacy. This was made explicit in the Civil Service Commission's response to the reform proposals:

> Contrary to the assumption of a conclusion in the report, the basic distribution of responsibility among the departments of Housing, City Plan, Buildings and Safety, Streets and Traffic, and Health does not constitute an impediment to progress. Rather, the departmental distribution can provide a sound and effective basis for progress because it is based on logic, careful analysis and considered judgment rather than frenetic and hasty eclectic perusal of articles and monographs.[67]

The Office of Civil Defense used much the same logic when it objected to the Development Team's reliance on social scientific analysis:

> As a document reflecting an extensive and comprehensive study of the sociological difficulties that beset the city, it certainly represents a deep and highly professional examination of the problems. But the fact that the report is heavily influenced by the social sciences should be recognized. Otherwise, the reader might tend to accept some of the recommendations in the report without realizing that there are considerations other than sociological that should be examined before the recommendation is accepted.[68]

The Office of Civil Defense strongly objected to the use of social-scientific analyses as the basis for formulating recommendations, arguing that social scientists were not qualified to analyze departmental operations, even if the agency in question (in this case, the Department of Recreation) was quite distant from traditional civil defense concerns:

> If this were a report that embraced professional evaluation of recreational organizations, considerable substance could be attached to the criticism of this department. But, this report is heavily oriented toward the social sciences rather than recreation and one that represents the viewpoint of persons in the field of sociology and psychology rather than those whose professional interests are in the

field of public recreation. Recommendations concerning major changes in this department should be examined more extensively before being accepted.[69]

City agencies repeatedly voiced the opinion that only agency personnel, as experts familiar with departmental practices, were competent to evaluate agency activities.

The Development Team threatened the existing autonomy of the City Plan Commission by recommending that it be consolidated under a superagency responsible to the mayor. The proposal was based on a survey of housing and planning programs in other major cities. The survey was not begun, however, until October 3, 1967, some three weeks before the final *Report* was released, and only six cities had responded to the survey. The City Plan Commission questioned the adequacy of the survey's coverage and took even stronger exception to the Development Team's analysis of the information it had obtained. The Development Team claimed agency consolidation could be the most efficient organizational approach to accomplishing housing, renewal and planning goals, but the plan commission pointed out:

> Of the six replies received, five of them. . .reported that they have an independent planning commission, and none reported delays or lack of efficiency or coordination because of this fact. None of these cities indicated that they have plans to change the present organization for renewal, although the Team states that "all similar proposals in other major cities for reorganization recommend that a single agency be made responsible" (which in itself is circular reasoning).[70]

In fact, the City Plan Commission went on to argue that its re-analysis of the survey information led it to a conclusion opposite that reached by the Development Team.[71]

Another approach agencies used to discredit the recommendations was to call attention to the inadequacy of resources available to the riot study panel. The agencies pointed out that they were formulated in a hurry by panel members who lacked experience and qualifications in the subject areas under investigation and who relied upon outdated information. Part of the Housing Commission's attack on Development Team recommendations stressed these limitations:

Perhaps because the MDT report was prepared during a very limited period of time in terms of its extremely broad scope, it contains much repetition as well as usage of old, outdated reports and studies. Also, while we hesitate to be critical, we could not help noting that a major weakness in the report results from the fact that few, if any, persons with administrative and/or operational experience in the various programs discussed had any significant part in its preparation.[72]

By focusing on the Development Team's time limitations, questioning its expertise and labeling its information outdated, the agency challenged the scientific legitimacy underlying the reform proposals.[73]

Defending past agency performances. The major justification for the Development Team's recommended reorganization of agency structures was the inadequacy of past bureaucratic performances. The study panel attempted to point out delays in program implementation, lack of coordination between departments and less-than-satisfactory delivery of services to black neighborhoods.

City agencies responded by assuming a defensive stance about their past performances. The Development Team observed that the Department of Buildings and Safety Engineering had not encouraged the use of new construction materials and had enforced building code violations in the inner city with little enthusiasm. The department defended itself by claiming that its experimentation and innovation with new building materials ranked it first in the nation, and responded: "Regarding code enforcement activities, I sensed the Mayor's Development Team seems to feel that penalties are important. The Department objective is to obtain compliance hence our Bureau Chiefs do use judgment in granting extensions if it will aid compliance."[74]

The City Plan Commission similarly formulated a positive review of its past record after the Development Team had recommended its consolidation under a new superagency accountable to the mayor. The Development Team faulted the department for extensive delays in executing public housing and urban renewal programs. The City Plan Commission responded:

A significant portion of Detroit's urban renewal projects have had land cleared and available for development for 3 or 4 years. This has been true basically because of inability on the City's part to find developers, and inability on the developers' part to obtain necessary

404

> equity and mortgage financing. . . .On these and other projects where land has been cleared and waiting development for several years, it is conclusively evident that the real cause for delay is the failure to obtain developers who have the money and the tenant commitments to allow them to proceed.[75]

The commission then estimated that the average time required for planning operations represented no more than from 10 to 15 percent of the total time for project development. It denied interdepartmental friction in planning activities, as alleged by the Development Team, and claimed its past record of planning for renewal projects was the best in the nation.[76] It also asserted that successful planning depended upon retention of existing departmental structures that had allowed it to be so successful in the past.

This defense of past agency performances often helped to discredit the validity of the Development Team's analysis and to legitimate existing agency autonomy. Of crucial importance in this regard was the central role played by the Civil Service Commission in governing agency personnel policies. When the Development Team criticized the Detroit Fire Department for inadequate recruitment of black firemen the department relied upon established civil service entrance procedures for its defense:

> The Fire Commission has in recent years worked with the Civil Service Commission to attempt to ease the entrance standards for the Fire Department applicants, and has made progress in this regard. A most recent check with Civil Service indicates that approximately 15 to 20 persons who are given applications for the Department out of every 100 pass the entrance tests and become eligible for placement. The fact of whether a man is colored or not is of no consequence in any way to his entrance to the Department's Training Academy.[77]

Other agencies similarly based their defense of past activities on established procedures and regulations inherent to reformed bureaucracies.

Turning criticism into justification for more resources. When city agencies did acknowledge shortcomings in their operations, they used the study panel's critique as a basis for requesting increased appropriations and manpower. Although admitting past failures, the agencies argued that their inadequacies were attributable to insufficient funds and personnel. The Development Team strongly criticized the Department of Health, for example, for not providing sufficient medical information to inner-city residents, and proposed to transfer this function to one of the new superagencies. The Health Department used the Development Team critique to petition for increased pay for personnel it employed. It argued that the agency's inability to attract qualified personnel accounted for past deficiencies and that increased appropriations would ease such problems.[78]

When the Development Team proposed the creation of a super-agency to deal with social development policies, it recommended that the powerful Civil Service Commission be included under the new unit. The Civil Service Commission proposed instead that its autonomy be preserved and that it could accomplish the objectives of the Development Team if additional staff were made available.[79] The Detroit Public Lighting Commission similarly used a recommendation urging improved street lighting in the inner city as the basis for requesting a complete overhaul of existing lighting facilities that would require additional manpower and funds.[80]

Efficiency and professionalism as sources of legitimacy. Finally, city agencies opposed the Development Team recommendations by indicating that the consolidation measures threatened to erode their efficiency and professionalism, two of the most valued characteristics attributed to reformed bureaucracies. This warning carried considerable weight to city council members, agency personnel themselves, agency-clientele groups and other participants in Detroit's reformed politics. Cavanagh himself was a reform-oriented mayor who had espoused the values of "good government," "efficiency" and "professionalism" that appeared time and again in agency opposition to the recommendations. When agency directors petitioned the mayor to reject the proposed reforms, they framed their arguments in terms appealing directly to Cavanagh's well-known views on the desirability of an impartial, neutral and competent civil service.

Because of its central position in guarding agency autonomy, the Civil Service Commission resisted being included under the proposed superagency dealing with social development. It felt this would threaten its managerial efficiency. The Civil Service Commission claimed:

The proposed organization, as charted, of the suggested social development agency would not be effective or make the task of the Mayor any easier or provide any significant improvements in service to the people of Detroit. This is not said because of any resistance to change, but rather because the proposal does not recognize nor provide for the handling of administrative and management problems in a workable manner.[81]

The Mayor's Committee for Industrial and Commercial Development opposed the recommended superagencies on similar grounds:

If problems of communications exist in City government because of poor coordination between and within departments, and if inefficient administration is the result of poor coordination, it would seem that the superimposing of additional agencies on top of but between the Mayor's staff and the operating departments, would tend to increase rather than eliminate inefficiency.[82]

Existing autonomy, from the agencies' perspective, provided superior coordination within departments and efficiency became the legitimating principle in agency arguments.

Appealing to norms of professionalism provided another source of legitimacy as agencies invoked professional standards in two ways: to question the qualifications of Development Team members and their analysis, and to reject consolidation reforms. The agencies frequently argued that only agency personnel, as professionals familiar with departmental operations, were competent to evaluate departmental structures and activities. The Department of Health suggested that agency personnel with expertise in subject matters of concern to it could provide more appropriate (and acceptable) analyses:

In the health related fields of housing inspection, alcoholism, narcotic addiction, mortality and morbidity statistics, community centers needing health services, manpower development and in the lattice concept as it relates to the health field the report shows need for consultation from experienced health professionals who are working at resolving the problems day by day.[83]

In response to the Development Team's suggestion that departmental organization be subject to review by nationally prominent consultants, one agency asked: "What makes someone away from Detroit an authority? It's a sad comment if we must admit that no one in Detroit knows what is going on and why."[84]

City agencies also indicated that adoption of the Development

Team's recommendations would threaten and even destroy the professionalism that independent departmental status made possible. The
Department of Streets and Traffic claimed that the proposal to include
it under a superagency dealing with physical development would be
disastrous:

> The creation of a huge new department is no guarantee of better
> service, and the relegation of top-flight professional engineers and
> planners to the third or fourth level of such a department with a
> resultant loss of identity can result in less creative effort on their
> part.[85]

The Department of Buildings and Safety Engineering viewed the
proposed incorporation of its operations under the same superagency as
an assault on its professional personnel and cited a national engineering
code to support its position:

> The Engineering Professional Registration Act is quite clear that all
> officers of an engineering firm must be professional engineers. This
> may seem strange to accountants for example. However, the purpose
> is to help place engineering above the almighty dollar. Also, we need
> to guard against our codes being circumvented in a matter of
> expedience. In our department, the end does not justify the
> means.[86]

Appeals to professionalism were thus made in order to defend existing
departmental autonomy.

The consolidation recommendations and the detailed reforms
proposed by the Development Team were viewed by Detroit's
municipal bureaucracy as a threat to established agency structures and
relationships. To preserve the *status quo*, city agencies presented
alternative information and interpretations contradicting the Development Team's analysis, offered some credible explanations for past
departmental performances, blamed past shortcomings on inadequate
resources and justified agency autonomy by the need to maintain
efficiency and protect their professional status. The first three defensive
positions effectively neutralized the Development Team critique by
appealing to legitimating sources supportive of existing arrangements.
The final position invoked the highly esteemed norms of efficiency and
professionalism to preserve and even extend agency autonomy. The
agencies directed these appeals to Cavanagh. His enthusiasm for

engaging in a bitter and prolonged battle to implement the reforms was undoubtedly influenced by these additional constraints, particularly since there was no automatic assurance that he would prevail in what promised to be a bruising fight.

The dilemma posed by bureaucratic opposition to the recommendations and Cavanagh's desire to control program developments placed the Development Team reform proposals in jeopardy. The chairman of the Development Team described Cavanagh's plight:

> The major problem we faced in implementing the report was the presence of in-bred agencies that just wouldn't move. For the simple movement of fifty city planners into the Housing Bureau, we had to try three different times before we were successful. These in-grown agencies opposed us at every turn. I think that Mayor Cavanagh could have implemented the whole damn report in an executive order. But can you imagine what that would do to those agencies in this city? We would have had a riot on our hands!

Cavanagh declined to issue an executive order and chose instead to delay resolving the problem he faced by creating an "executive committee" to implement the Development Team's recommendations. It consisted of seven members: two from the mayor's office, four from city agencies, and Cavanagh.

The executive committee met several times over the following months, but made no visible progress. It encountered persistent opposition from city agencies. After one year, the executive committee ceased to exist and the Development Team's recommendations were never carried out. The chairman of the executive committee explained the status of the reforms 14 months after their release:

> As a working document, I'd have to say the MDT Report is not at this point in time currently being used. It's probably background for a lot of our thinking, but as far as a lot of the proposals, they're being considered on their individual merits rather than as the MDT Report.[87]

The chairman of the Development Team gave a similar assessment:

> One of the main thrusts [of the MDT Report] was to try to increase the awareness on the part of city government of the need to give more attention to services that were or were not being given. Much

409

more needs to be done in meeting housing needs. It [the Report] deals with a number of empires.[88]

The reformed bureaucratic "empires" proved sufficiently resourceful to preclude interference by the executive committee.

The three comprehensive reorganization proposals from the Mayor's Development Team did not advance beyond the study panel's *Report*. The City Plan Commission and the Housing Commission effectively resisted consolidation under the proposed superagency dealing with physical development. City departments providing social services similarly were able to oppose the social development superagency. The third superagency, dealing with research and development, also failed. One member of the executive committee explained:

> I regret to say that there have been no follow-up reports emanating from it [the MDT]. There have been several meetings in the earlier days regarding the implementation of some of the recommendations. Some of the minor ones have been implemented while some of the major ones have not. If I were to seek out the best contribution that the MDT made following the riots of 1967, I would say its status as a catalytic agent forcing a bit of rethinking on the part of traditional city government.[89]

Two minor reforms were implemented, the transfer of 50 city planners to the Housing Commission and the securing of an advocate planner for the Virginia-Park Corporation, a neighborhood self-improvement association. An executive committee member explained:

> We were successful in implementing some of the minor recommendations, those that the mayor could go ahead with without burning the senses of agency people. On the major ones we did not do a good job. This was more of a think piece. It got the agencies and people in the city to think about changes that needed to be made.

Bureaucratic Processing of Crisis

A varied pattern characterized the Development Team's implementation of its three charges: the first and second charges were carried out with considerable success, as shown in chapter 9, but not the third charge. The Mayor's Development Team successfully fulfilled its mandate in areas where the municipal bureaucracy provided unreserved assistance. It failed to achieve its goals when city agencies actively resisted its proposals.

In fulfilling its first charge by providing emergency relief and restoring vital public services, the Development Team had acted as an arm of the municipal executive. City agencies were responsive to the prevailing crisis conditions and complied with directives without delay or timidity. Administrators bent rules, modified regulations and altered procedures in order to assist in the clean-up effort and deliver needed goods and services, seeing the situation as a temporary adjustment to meet specific needs.

In accomplishing its second charge, to recommend ways to reorganize and improve Detroit's municipal bureaucracy, the Development Team received substantial resources and personnel from city agencies. Cavanagh's request for information, facilities and manpower received immediate and unquestioning compliance. City agencies materially helped the Development Team establish an organization, formulate recommendations, and write the 800-page *Report* in less than 90 days, while emergency conditions persisted. Successful fulfillment of the second charge, like the first, depended on the cooperation and compliance of city agencies—agency resources and personnel were loaned to the Development Team for a *specific purpose of limited duration.*

The Development Team failed in its third task. Its recommendations for reorganizing Detroit's municipal bureaucracy were not implemented; the blueprint did not advance beyond the drawing boards. The Development Team, its successor executive committee and Cavanagh were unable to overcome the unyielding opposition of city agencies which mobilized their considerable resources in opposition to the proposed reforms.

Why did the agencies cooperate with the Development Team in pursuing the first and second tasks, but resist it on the third? Immediately after the riot, the Development Team effectively neutralized bureaucratic intransigence and inertia to produce cooperative action with little regard for past performances, inadequate resources, professional norms or autonomous relationships. It did so by portraying the post-riot period as an emergency and calling for assistance to meet the crisis. City agencies complied with these specific and limited requests. The Development Team failed, however, to achieve similar bureaucratic cooperation and compliance in implementing its recommendations even though it pressed claims of an uninterrupted crisis.

411

City agencies rejected the latter appeals and opposed the reform measures because, unlike the first two tasks, the consolidation recommendations involved *general questions of an enduring nature*, concerning fundamental issues of how executive branch power was to be distributed.[90]

The Development Team experience illustrates the ability of public officials and *ad hoc* riot inquiries to break rapidly and effectively with normal routines during emergency periods. It also suggests that public officials and riot inquiries are unable to direct municipal bureaucracies in a sustained attack on conditions that allegedly contributed to rioting. After successfully blocking the executive committee and Cavanagh's attempts to implement consolidation recommendations, the municipal bureaucracy resumed the *status quo ante* and reasserted its autonomy by deciding which agency services would be delivered where and under what conditions.

The behavior and resources of Detroit's reformed bureaucracy thus account in large part for the failure of the Development Team to implement its comprehensive reorganization. This is particularly significant since the mayor had specifically nominated high-level members of his administration for the Development Team who might induce compliance with its findings. The capacity of city agencies to prevail in opposing reform measures supported by the mayor and his staff suggests the extraordinary decentralization of power in American cities. These developments present a bleak picture of the potential for major reform, even when executive influence is mobilized for change, and when events conspire to produce a greater rationale for the need for change than is ordinarily encountered in day-to-day civic affairs.

Milwaukee's 39-Points:
Partisan and Jurisdictional Stalemate

Fully one year before Milwaukee's riot, Mayor Maier and Governor Knowles formulated a joint-emergency plan to suppress civil disorder. When violence erupted, the prearranged plan was implemented without delay or dispute: a "hot-line" between the two offices was activated, a 24-hour curfew covering all of Milwaukee was applied and National Guard troops were summoned. While harmony prevailed in intergovernmental steps designed to suppress violence, the uneasy truce between state and city officials soon dissipated. As the disorder continued, political differences between the two jurisdictions surfaced. The 39-point program failed to overcome partisan and jurisdictional conflicts that characterized relations among various governmental units toward which it was addressed.

Democratic Mayor versus Republican Governor

Initial signs of city-state antagonisms surfaced before the riot ended. A major incident arose concerning letters of identification issued to a dozen Milwaukee civil rights leaders by Joseph C. Fagan, chairman of the State Industrial Commission and the governor's chief civil rights trouble-shooter during the riot.[91] As the official charged with enforcing state laws on equal employment opportunities and open housing, Fagan had previously developed liaison with civil rights workers and other leaders of black groups, most of whom were openly hostile toward Maier's administration. Whether intended for this purpose or not, civil rights workers tried to use the identification letters for free passage through police lines during the riot. Milwaukee police refused to honor the letters and a number of civil rights workers were arrested for curfew violations. The civil rights workers claimed the letters guaranteed them immunity from curfew constraints, but Mayor Maier rejected state officials' authority in the local jurisdiction, threatened legal action against state officials and likened Fagan's behavior to that of a "curbstone commissar."[92] Later he sent a formal letter of protest to the city attorney, the governor's office and the attorney general.

The Maier-Fagan dispute was only a prelude to subsequent hostilities between city and state public officials. The conflict featured not only jurisdictional clashes, but partisan differences between the Democratic-controlled city administration and the Republican-controlled state administration and legislature. The 14 measures in the 39 points dealing with state government were central to the dispute.

Maier initiated the controversy in the post-riot period by making his 14 demands upon the state. He continually hammered at state responsibilities and the necessity for a special legislative session to consider his reform package. But Republican Governor Warren Knowles' immediate reaction was to locate the problem at the local level: "I would urge all community leaders now take prompt action to assess the causes of the disturbances and develop programs to assure that incidents of this kind will not occur again in the great city of Milwaukee."[93]

Black leaders regarded the mayor's insistence on a special legislative session as diversionary. They called attention to the relative absence of proposals directly affecting Milwaukee officials. They argued that Maier was trying to place himself in good standing by turning over the problem to other public officials without doing anything concrete himself. As Lloyd A. Barber, Milwaukee's only black state legislator, argued: "Maier has shown he has no leadership to offer by concentrating on things that require action by state and federal governments."[94] With the exception of black leaders, public officials responded to the proposed special legislative session along partisan lines.[95]

The ensuing weeks witnessed partisan jockeying between city and state officials over who should take action responsive to the riot. Governor Knowles waited a week after Maier's plea for a special legislative session before arranging a high-level meeting of prominent city and state officials to consider the proposal. State legislative leaders and the mayor attended, but Knowles did not, and his absence intensified partisan and jurisdictional divisions. After the meeting the Republican assembly majority leader estimated the total cost of the 14 measures at $25 million annually and commented:

> To call such a session would be precipitous because no one, including Mayor Maier, knows exactly what we want to do. None of these proposals are directly addressed to the problem. I do not believe that the legislature, through transmitted hysteria, should go into session without a well considered program.[96]

Democratic legislators, in the minority at the state level, supported the call for a special session.

When it became apparent that Knowles did not intend to call a special legislative session, the governor was criticized by Maier for weak leadership:

> It appears that the governor is not going to take the leadership. The governor is pretending that the mayor of Milwaukee has the resources of a governor. If they want me to accept the assignment of governor for the next couple of months, I'll be glad to in the absence of an urban governor.[97]

Knowles disputed the substantive merits of Maier's 14 measures that would have redistributed sizeable state resources from suburban communities to Milwaukee. Instead, Knowles placed his faith in jobs for Inner Core residents:

414

The real hope for progress lies in jobs, in preparing people for those jobs, and in understanding. That is why I devote so much effort toward promoting and encouraging industry and business to locate and grow in Wisconsin. No amount of money from federal, state, or local units of government fired in a shotgun approach into Milwaukee will effectively reach the root causes of civil disorder or social problems that breed in cultural and economic poverty.[98]

In response, Maier called a press conference. He charged Knowles with "laying down a pious smokescreen of generalities in suggesting that more jobs would resolve Milwaukee's inner core problems," and went on to ask: "What we need to know, Warren, is how?"[99] Partisan lines had clearly been drawn.

By this time, some four weeks after the violence ended, it was clear that Maier had captured the initiative. His package of legislative bills and call for a special legislative session placed the burden of response at the doorstep of state officials. When community groups or federal officials inquired about what the mayor had done about the riot, Maier repeatedly pointed to his 14 measures lying unattended because the governor refused to call a special legislative session. Maier had "built a case" that effectively removed claims for action from his administration to the state administration.

In classic counter-point, Knowles attempted to defuse Maier's case by releasing a 19-page statement entitled *Urban Problems and State Action*.[100] The gubernatorial position paper reassured concerned parties that the state administration knew of Milwaukee's problems and was planning to resolve them. More importantly, it announced 30 state actions and recommendations "to direct an attack upon the root causes of economic and cultural poverty."[101] A partial list of the recommendations includes: employment of teacher aides in Inner Core schools, consumer protection and education, voluntary organizations used for block clean-up units, strict enforcement of building codes, a rent-receivership program for the Inner Core; day care center for the children of working women; investigation of health, sanitation and rat control programs; and improved garbage and rubbish removal programs by municipalities. Milwaukee officials immediately perceived the distinctly local nature of most of the governor's program. Building code enforcement, garbage services, rent-receivership offices and others in the above listing traditionally had been functions reserved for city governments. The jockeying thus continued as Knowles attempted to blunt Maier's demand for state action by calling for improved municipal services.

The partisan underpinnings of Knowles' program was confirmed for Milwaukee officials when Knowles named the State Department of Industry, Labor and Human Relations as the agency to carry out the recommendations. The department was headed by Fagan who at the same time indicated an interest in running against Maier in the future: "I am very much interested in running for mayor of Milwaukee because I do not believe that the job is being done there that could be done in this area. Despite the fact that Maier had clamped a lid on the riots, he has not dealt with the underlying problems that caused the riots."[102] Maier dismissed Fagan's potential candidacy as an idle threat and the governor's recommendations as a public relations scheme. He continued to call upon Republican state officials for a special legislative session.

Intervention by the Youth Council

Maier's proposals and Knowles' counter-proposals set the stage for an extended partisan battle between state and city administrations over who was or was not responsible for and appropriately responding to the Milwaukee riot. The stage was upset, however, by a series of events having far-reaching consequences for post-riot politics in Milwaukee. The events centered around the Milwaukee NAACP Youth Council and its advisor, Father James E. Groppi.

Over the summer months preceding the violence, the Youth Council had conducted marches on homes of aldermen opposed to open housing legislation, but had remained inactive during the first month after the civil disorder. This dormancy ended abruptly on the evening of August 28 when Father Groppi led 200 Youth Council members on a march to Milwaukee's south side to protest the city's refusal to adopt an open housing ordinance. The uneasy truce between blacks and whites was broken when 3,000 whites greeted the marchers with bottles, stones and chunks of wood as they entered the south side. Another 5,000 whites, by police estimate, surrounded Youth Council members at the march destination, Kosciuszko Park. Black demonstrators raised signs saying "Fair Housing," "Black Power," and "We South Siders Welcome Negroes." Whites responded by shouting at the demonstrators and holding up a large Confederate flag. The demonstrators' departure from the park drew even more hostile reactions:

416

When the marchers got out of the area of the park, the crowd thinned. But a hard core mob of about 600 white youths still trailed along, shouting obscenities and chanting, "We want slaves" and "Get yourself a nigger." A few of them composed new words to a popular Milwaukee polka. The words spread, and soon most of the youths were singing, "Eee-yi-eee-yi-eee-yi-oh; Father Groppi's got to go." In future months, the song would be sung with those same words at wedding receptions on the south side. It became apparent during the march that the issue, as far as the spectators were concerned, was Father Groppi himself. All along the march route, spectators strained to see him, pointed him out to others, and spat their vilest epithets at him personally, "Nigger lover" was one of the milder ones. Another was, "Why don't you go to confession? You white nigger bastard!" Adjectives derived from four letter words were common.[103]

The march ended with the arrest of 16 white hecklers.

The events of August 28 prompted Maier to urge citizens to observe a voluntary curfew during subsequent marches and to view the marchers and by implication the open housing issue as an "unworthy cause." The following evening a second march again drew 200 Youth Council participants and from 6,000 to 8,000 white counter-demonstrators, again by police estimate, who waited for the marchers to enter Milwaukee's south side. The mood of the white crowd was even more hostile toward the marchers than the night before.[104] Police had to use tear gas twice and fire volleys of shots into the air to break up counter-demonstrating whites who attacked marchers and police alike. Twelve police officers and dozens of march participants were injured by thrown bottles, cans, firecrackers, rocks and eggs. The evening's violence finally ended when the marchers returned to the demonstration starting point to find Freedom House, a place of residence to some and headquarters for all Youth Council members, burned to the ground.

The next morning Maier sought to preclude a repetition of these events by issuing a proclamation banning night marches and demonstrations. The ban prohibited for 30 days "marches, parades, demonstrations or other similar activites. . .upon all public highways, sidewalks, streets, alleys, parks and all other public ways and public grounds within the city of Milwaukee between the hours of 4 p.m. and 9 a.m."[105] Undaunted, the Youth Council continued to demonstrate and march. After three nights, in which, respectively, 58, 137 and 15 demonstrators were arrested, Maier withdrew the emergency proclamation.

Issue Deflection

The Youth Council marches in late August captured local, state-wide and national attention. As they continued, the news media and citizens became less concerned about the competing programs offered by the mayor and governor, and increasingly troubled about how Maier would handle the marches and demonstrations. Prior concern about which executive had built the better case was replaced by fear of renewed violence. Frequent demands were made to call out the National Guard to protect marchers and to satisfy Youth Council demands by placing an open housing ordinance before the city council. Maier did neither. Demands were made to silence Father Groppi and to prohibit the Youth Council from continuing demonstrations and rallies. Silencing Groppi was clearly beyond the mayor's authority and ending demonstrations not only violated constitutional guarantees of assembly, but had proved ineffective the first time Maier tried it.

Maier had previously captured the initiative with his 39-point program and had created the impression that Knowles had refused to act decisively. With the advent and continuation of Youth Council demonstrations, however, blacks and whites engaged in open conflict on Milwaukee streets and the mayor's recommendations began to lose visibility. Attention focused once again on the mayor's office, as the media and citizens petitioned him for measures to ease community tensions and preclude renewed violence. The impact on Maier's post-riot strategy was described by James C. Newcomb, the mayor's chief administrative assistant:

> With the 39-point program we had Knowles over a barrel. We demanded to get a hearing during a special session for the bills that we had prepared under the 39-point program for consideration by the state legislature. We met with the Republican leadership and they promised consideration of the bills. We had them on the run. Then, on August 28th, Groppi marched on the south side. All that we had going for us was gone. The mayor said: "I feel like the Austrian platform builder hit by a revival meeting—it's all gone." What Groppi did by marching on the south side was to take the state government off the hook. It took Knowles and the Republicans off the hook we had them on. We had public attention on Mayor Maier versus Governor Knowles. Groppi took the focus off that.[106]

418

The "revival meeting" that hit the "Austrian platform builder" proved to be no passing and easily dismissed phase of black protest. Youth Council members marched through city streets for an incredible 240 consecutive days, and the size of the contingents increased from 200 in late August to a peak of over 2,000 by mid-September. By September, the Youth Council protest marches had turned to demands that Maier change his intransigent stand on issues affecting black residents in Milwaukee, only one of which concerned open housing. Indicative of this transformation, Youth Council members marched on the mayor's office in early September and occupied it for over five hours. During the sit-in, furniture was defaced, file cabinets overturned, chairs slashed and other destruction occurred. By this time, Maier was the object of the demonstrators' antagonism as much as the open housing issue.

These developments in Milwaukee were not lost on state officials. The Republican-controlled state government capitalized on the consequences of these events by ignoring Maier's insistent call for a special legislative session. Later Maier presented all of the relevant measures from the 39 points to a regular session of the state legislature. Nine of the 14 proposals were drafted in bill form for introduction at the beginning of the regular session on October 17, 1967. The cost of the nine bills was established at $134 million. The mayor's testimony on behalf of the bills pictured their passage as necessary for the continued life of Milwaukee itself: "If you fail to give these programs consideration, within the next 10 years you will be the proud recipients of a charter which will be returned to the state."[107] The urgency of his message had little impact; only one of the nine bills passed. It authorized the innocuous merger of the redevelopment and public housing authorities in Milwaukee. Although the city's legislative package had in large part failed, a forum had been recreated to show the intransigence of state Republican officials. The case built by Maier prior to Youth Council demonstrations had been partially re-established.

Governor Knowles's administration vacillated on how to meet the mayor's renewed challenge. Rhetoric initially substituted for substantive programs. For example, in reviewing programs proposed for Milwaukee's Inner Core, Knowles reiterated his previous stand: "Job opportunities and an economic base for these people are what is required. We have to get back to first principles. These people have got to realize that they have got to work."[108] Subsequently a series of concrete proposals were developed for Milwaukee intended to minimize Maier's critique. On August 1, 1967, a new state agency, the Department of Local Affairs, came into existence under a comprehensive state government reorganization plan, but its mission remained in doubt during the early months of its existence.

After the city administration challenge developed, the agency opened field offices in Milwaukee's Inner Core with three tasks: to help residents obtain jobs, to administer special pilot programs and to provide information about other state-run programs. Personnel in the field office made a point of excluding the city administration from any participation in its programs because of Maier's alleged inability to communicate with Inner Core blacks. One field office representative commented: "The state has decided that if it is going to get anywhere, it is going to have to by-pass Henry Maier."[109] In characteristic language, Maier charged that "the state has done nothing—zero" for Milwaukee's Inner Core problems "except hire Negro porkchoppers" to serve state political figures like his old nemesis, Commissioner Joseph Fagan.[110]

The partisan and jurisdictional divisions over who was to blame for not addressing conditions in Milwaukee had been re-established and continued over the ensuing months. The 39-point program was repeatedly delayed and finally blocked by the stalemate between officials from city and state jurisdictions of different partisan affiliations. While frustrating the 39-point program, the stalemate did not prove entirely injurious to the agendas of the executives from the two jurisdictions and may have facilitated the political objectives of both. Knowles did launch several state programs for the Inner Core independent of the city administration and, as described in chapter 9, Maier obtained several programs that he had long sought. Simultaneous with these minimal substantive program developments, each executive could and did rhetorically accuse the other of failing to assert leadership.

State Interests and the Little Kerner Commission

While the partisan division between city and state dominated Milwaukee's post-riot politics, the Little Kerner Commission conducted deliberations and issued recommendations that reinforced the position adopted by Knowles and other Republicans. It sought to place some responsibility for responding to the disorder on Maier's administration. It did so, as shown in chapter 8, by pointing to shortcomings in

420

Milwaukee's city administration and by calling for reforms at the municipal level.

Only two bills sponsored by the Little Kerner Commission were passed by the Wisconsin state legislature. Both reinforced the Republican agenda in opposition to the Democratic agenda of Mayor Maier. The alliance of the Little Kerner Commission with state Republican interests can be seen in the two educational areas where it achieved some success. The first successful bill gave increased power to the State Superintendent of Public Instruction to investigate cases of discrimination in teacher assignments in public schools. The second redefined state law pertaining to compulsory school attendance for underprivileged children.

Both education-policy changes coincided with and amplified policies being pursued by the Knowles administration. To bypass the city administration, the state administration made sizeable commitments to improving Inner Core schools. The mayor's office had relatively little control over the expenditure of state aids to Milwaukee's school system. Governor Knowles introduced and his administration guided a special $4.75 million appropriation through the Republican-controlled legislature for educational services to Milwaukee's Inner Core students from low-income families. The special appropriation provided dramatic evidence, so Republican partisans argued, of Knowles' concern for conditions in Milwaukee's black community. The state totally excluded Maier's administration from the program by creating a 15-member citizen advisory council drawn from Inner Core residents to review and decide on proposals for expenditure of the appropriated funds. The citizen advisory council embarrassed Maier by funding a project administered by the Youth Council—whose daily marches against him were in progress—to provide special educational services to black parolees. The policies pursued by the Knowles administration were thus augmented by the two bills the Little Kerner Commission sponsored and saw enacted in the legislature.

In the partisan division between city and state that dominated the post-riot implementation period, some minimal reforms were enacted as a direct consequence of the previously prevailing partisan conflict. Nearly half of the 39 points which were implemented received favorable action within the primary jurisdiction—the city of Milwaukee. The minimal reforms adopted by the city provided superficial confirmation of Maier's claim, much like Addonizio's in Newark, that his administration was doing all that it could and the real failure to respond rested with the state. The Little Kerner Commission's failure to obtain favorable action at the municipal level is similarly understandable, as is its success in enacting two education reforms through the Republican-controlled state legislature. These two policy measures coincided with the Knowles administration's efforts to establish the credibility of its claim that the state had committed sizeable resources to upgrading educational services in Milwaukee. Thus the minimal success of the 39-point program and the Little Kerner Commission's recommendations resulted from the same partisan division and resulting stalemate between city and state executives that accounts for the failure to implement reform measures proposed by city and state riot inquiries.

The Political Significance of Riot Commissions

This discussion provides initial answers to questions raised in introducing the last two chapters: what political impact do the recommendations of riot inquiries have? On the basis of the frequency of their implementation, as shown in chapter 9, it may be tempting to conclude that reforms proposed by riot inquiries have little or no impact on the political system. But this is not our view. In our three cities, reform measures developed by riot inquiries occupied a central place in leaders' responses to the 1967 riots.

The acceptance or rejection of riot inquiry recommendations appears to depend on prevailing characteristics of the political system, of which the investigations are a part. Controversies surrounding the adoption or rejection of recommendations developed as extensions of divisions within the political system predating the 1967 racial violence in each city. The evolution of riot inquiry recommendations into extensions of previous political divisions starts with the recruitment of representatives of selected interests to serve on the study panels. It continues with the anticipation by riot inquiries of the needs of appointing executives and the shared values of executives and panel members. It concludes when chief executives advance or retard the implementation of recommendations in accord with their own political needs antedating the outbreak of the riots.

To conclude that the effort to implement riot inquiry recommendations involves an extension of previous divisions over issues does not mean that study panels have no independent impact on the political system. Riot inquiries renew and reinforce public visibility for the issues they deem important. The recommendations influence the executive agendas and give visibility to issues that otherwise might not achieve such prominence. Although the study panels had little independent impact in seeing reform measures carried out, they did raise the salience of various issues.

The significance of decentralization and federalism in the American political process is observable in the outcomes of riot inquiry recommendations. Riot commissions at the subnational level characteristically direct the majority of their recommendations at governmental jurisdictions other than the one in which they are originally appointed. The Governor's Commission, with the state of New Jersey as its primary jurisdiction, thus issued more recommendations directed toward Newark and other local governments than it did toward the state. Milwaukee's 39-point program sought state and suburban reform to a greater extent than municipal change. Riot commission recommendations are most likely to be implemented where the targeted jurisdiction is the one in which it is appointed. In part this may be explained by the congruence of views between appointing executives and the structure within which recommendations were developed.

In the conflict between Addonizio and Hughes, between Cavanagh and an entrenched bureaucracy, and between the mayor of Milwaukee, his black constituents and the Wisconsin Republicans, post-riot recommendations are aspects of continuing political struggles. At the local level, the urgency of racial crisis was transformed to politics as usual.

NOTES, CHAPTER 10

1. Governor's Select Commission, *Report for Action* (Trenton: State of New Jersey, February 1968), p. 20. The shortcomings are discussed on pp. 2-100.

2. Newark *News*, 16 February 1968.

3. New York *Times*, 14 February 1967.

4. Newark *News*, 11 February 1968. In the same statement the mayor did offer important reservations on the riot commission process in general:

I would like to warn of one danger I see developing in reports such as this and in the mass media's general interpretation of things. Newark, it seems, has been cast in the role of handy scapegoat—the terrible place where terrible people did everything wrong. That kind of simpleminded explanation helps most people avoid facing the real truth about the depth and dimension of the problems everywhere in American life.

5. Ibid., 15 February 1968.

6. Governor's Select Commission, *Report for Action*, p. 164.

7. New York *Times*, 19 February 1968.

8. Newark *News*, 19 February 1968.

9. Ibid., 29 February 1968.

10. This excerpt from the Schiff report is quoted in New York *Times*, 28 April 1968.

11. The president of the Newark Patrolmen's Benevolent Association assailed the plan: "It may well turn out that Newark policemen will be protecting the volunteers. Crime can only be effectively combated by a professional police force professionally trained and professionally paid. More attention should be paid to reinforcing the wages and the facilities of Newark's regular police force and not have energies dissipated on an ineffective voluntary corps" (Newark *News*, 9 October 1968).

12. Fraternal associations among Newark policemen, as they are in most large, Northeastern cities, are numerous and based on ethnic ties. In Newark, Italian policemen join the "Columbian Association," Jewish officers have the "Shomrin Society," Irish officers the "Emerald Society" and German officers the "Steuben Association." Black officers were prevented from becoming members of any existing ethnic associations and thus formed the "Black Shield."

13. While the "Black Shield" remained silent on specific race issues confronting the police department during its formative months, it did announce that in the future public stands would be taken. The president of Black Shield indicated: "The Negro people constantly say to us that every group speaks out except the Negro police officers. We can no longer remain silent and refuse to speak. Our wives and our children want to be proud of us and not hang their heads in shame because we remain silent in the face of criticism" (Newark *News*, 17 February 1968).

14. In announcing the Black Shield's intention not to honor the strike, the president of the group explained: "We will neither speed up nor slow down. We will issue no more and no less traffic summonses. Neither will we take part in any organized sick-call program which would deny any citizen full service from this department. We deplore these actions on the part of men who take an oath to protect these same citizens" (Newark *News*, 24 October 1968).

15. Newark *News*, 20 February 1968.

16. The city administration's consolidation of control over the poverty program is given detailed consideration in David J. Olson, "Politicians, Professionals, and the Poor: A Medical and Dental College Locates in a Ghetto," (Paper presented to the symposium of New York

Academy of Medicine on Decision Making and Control in Health Care, New York City, July 1970) pp. 57-62. The observations in the following paragraphs on the medical school are drawn from the more intensive analysis of the medical school controversy reported there.

17. See Ibid. for this assessment.

18. Governor's Select Commission, *Report For Action*, pp. 20, 162.

19. The four grand jury presentments resulted in the indictment and conviction of only one person, a low-ranking police officer. This particular desk officer was convicted for failure to properly enter an arrest in police records.

20. Governor's Select Commission, *Report For Action*, p. 20.

21. Newark *News*, 16 April 1968.

22. Ibid.

23. Newark *News*, 17 April 1968.

24. Ibid.

25. Newark *News*, 26 July 1968.

26. Decision quoted in Newark *News*, 8 November 1968.

27. The presentment, in part, stated:

It is evident that there has been a breakdown in the enforcement of gambling laws; that the bureau responsible for the enforcement of these laws has neglected its duty; that the director [Spina] is aware of the dereliction of duty and has been negligent because he did not take positive action to see to it that the gambling laws were enforced by the bureau responsible for such enforcement. There continued to be a lack of vigor on the part of those in the Newark Police Department charged with enforcing the gambling law and this lack of vigor still extends from the top of the department to the bottom. These findings are not to be taken lightly!

Quoted in Newark *News*, 10 January 1969.

28. Ibid.

29. New York *Times*, 11 December 1969.

30. For an indication of DeCavalcante's central importance in the gambling network, see the verbatim conversations taped from his office as compiled in Henry A. Zeiger, *Sam the Plumber* (New York: Signet, 1970).

31. New York *Times*, 17 December 1969. For indictments the federal grand jury relied heavily upon information provided by an Organized Crime Strike Force from the U.S. Department of Justice, the first of its kind in the nation to combine federal, state, and local law enforcement operations. Significantly, the local input came from information left over from Prosecutor Lordi's investigation. State

cooperation came only after Governor-elect William T. Cahill assured Justice Department officials that his yet-to-be-appointed state attorney general would not interfere with gambling arrests.

32. Besides Mayor Addonizio the public officials indicted were: City Councilman Frank Addonizio, a distant cousin of the mayor; City Councilmen Calvin D. West and Irvine I. Turner, both moderate Democrats and the only blacks on the City Council; Municipal Judge Anthony Builiano, a former city councilman who was immediately suspended from court duty by the chief justice of the New Jersey Supreme Court; Secretary to the Municipal Utilities Authority James Callaghan, a former city councilman; former City Councilman Lee Bernstein; former Corporation Counsels Philip Gordon and Norman N. Schiff; and Executive Director of the Municipal Utilities Authority Anthony LaMorte, formerly Director of the Newark Public Works Department.

33. Governor's Select Commission, *Report for Action*, p. 141.

34. Grand jury presentment quoted in Newark *News*, 24 April 1968. For a book-length treatment of the failures of this grand jury, see Ron Porambo, *No Cause for Indictment: An Autopsy of Newark* (New York: Holt, Rinehart, and Winston, 1971).

35. Newark *News*, 24 April 1968.

36. Ibid.

37. Porambo summarizes this grand jury's work:

Despite the words of hundreds of eyewitnesses, formal deposition, complaints, bloodstains, spent bullets, and hospital records, not *one charge* against Newark police, National Guard, or State Police was conclusive enough—black people were told—to warrant even an admission of guilt, much less punishment. Many police had carried their own personal weapons, making ballistic reports uncheckable. Units or officers who might have been involved in specific incidents couldn't be identified, it was claimed. Out of hundreds of incidents in one of the most brutal domestic occupations in the nation's history, *not one* could be substantiated. "I don't know what I can tell the people if legal redress is unavailable," Oliver Lofton said.

(See Porambo, *No Cause for Indictment*, p. 29.)

38. Considerable importance was attached to Gibbon's statement because at the time he was president of the New Jersey State Bar Association.

39. Newark *News*, 24 April 1968.

40. Albert Black, chairman of Newark's Human Rights Commission, collected and submitted accounts of fourteen specific incidents of police misconduct to state authorities in August of 1967. Black claimed

that "every single one of them is valid. . .they have to admit their men were wrong. . .it's clear cut" (Newark *News*, 7 January 1968).

41. Governor's Select Commission, *Report for Action*, pp. 140-43.

42. Newark *News*, 16 February 1968.

43. Newark *News*, 7 January 1968. Kelly's preliminary report drew the following attack from Albert Black, chairman of Newark's Human Relations Commission: "Kelly's statement is an affront and an insult to the intelligence of the citizens of the City of Newark. It is an attempt to whitewash and push under a rug the tragic events that involved many of your state police actions towards Newark citizens" (Newark *News*, 11 January 1968).

44. Illustrative of the general nature of commission recommendations aimed at the state of New Jersey are the following: "The State Office of Consumer Protection, and especially its consumer education activities, should be strengthened," and, "The Division of Civil Rights must take a more aggressive posture, and act on its own initiative to seek out and correct racial discrimination in industry and labor," and, "The State Legislature should grant reasonable budget requests of the Department of Community Affairs for rent supplements, demonstration grants, and code enforcement training programs" (Governor's Select Commission, *Report for Action*, pp. 172, 170, 169).

45. Ibid.

46. Newark *News*, 14 February 1968. The letter elaborated: "As to the first recommendation that the state administer the Newark school system—utilizing state funds as a new resource. . .I heartily endorse such a step as an honest beginning in regionalizing our school system and distributing the special costs of education which we face on a much broader scale" (ibid.).

47. New York *Times*, 15 February 1968.

48. The governor's office not only released the ratio of favorable and unfavorable letters, but it also disclosed the content of letters that attacked the commission in anti-Semitic and antiblack terms. For a sampling of the letters, see Newark *News*, 23 February 1968.

49. Newark *News*, 18 February 1968. The mayor used the same phrasing the next day to justify his proposal to nominate the chairman of the Governor's Commission to a civilian review board if one were created. See footnote 8 above.

50. "A Moral Recommitment for New Jersey: Special Message of Richard J. Hughes to the Legislature" (mimeo., Trenton, New Jersey; Governor's Office; dated 25 April 1968), p. 1.

51. The literature quoted is entitled, "Majority Response Rally: In Support of the Findings of the N.J. Commission for the Study of Civil Disorders" (mimeo., distributed at the rally; n.d.; copies in the authors' files), p. 1.

52. Newark *News*, 28 May 1968.

53. Although it is beyond the scope of this study, the 1967 Newark riot unquestionably had very significant electoral consequences, not the least of which was the increasing political mobilization of blacks leading up to the 1970 election.

54. For an excellent analysis of Cavanagh as a reform mayor and a description of the extent of reform in the Detroit Bureaucracy, see J. David Greenstone and Paul E. Peterson, *Race and Authority in Urban Politics* (New York Basic Books, 1973), ch. 7. In essential agreement with this observation and others about Detroit politics that follow in the text are: J. David Greenstone, *Labor in American Politics* (New York: Knopf, 1969), particularly ch. 4; Edward C. Banfield, *Big City Politics* (New York: Random House, 1965), especially ch. 3; and Samuel J. Eldersveld, *Political Parties: A Behavioral Analysis* (Chicago: Rand McNally, 1964). The history of early reform in Detroit is chronicled in Melvin G. Holl, *Reform in Detroit: Hazen S. Pingree and Urban Politics* (New York: Oxford, 1969).

55. Cavanagh began to publicly discuss problems of bureaucratic compliance with mayoral directives at this time and continued to do so throughout his second term. One year later, for example, he said:

Even in this dream world of computers and simulation, however, a mayor will be faced with much the same problem he is faced with today—and that is, how does he assure that his policies are being implemented. In a government such as we have in Detroit, many of the jobs are filled by civil service, including some of those who are the heads of major departments. Thus protected, they can be—and sometimes are—reluctant to implement policies of the Mayor's Office. In order to effect change in such a department, we have found that we must intervene directly and in great detail through the use of staff members in the Mayor's Office. However, since the Mayor's staff is normally extremely small, the number of problems that they can handle is minimal.

See "Remarks by the Honorable Jerome P. Cavanagh, Mayor of Detroit, at the Summer Study on Urban Policy," (mimeo., Berkeley, Calif.: University of California, 15 August 1968), p. 4.

56. The only substantial control exercised over the Civil Service Commission is by the common council through the budgetary process. But even the council refrains from directly intervening in commission affairs. In part this is due to the nonpartisan elections in Detroit that have made parties there among the weakest in the nation in local elections, and the at-large election of councilmen has tended to restrain them from looking after "ward-based" constituency concerns.

57. Political reform in Detroit is extensive: elections are nonpartisan in fact as well as in name and are held the year following presidential elections; the nine councilmen are elected at-large; the form of government is strong mayor-council; and, as a consequence of these reformed structures, formal organizations play a relatively unimportant role in local elections.

58. For a discussion of this tactic by the mayor, see Allan Rosenbaum, "Participation, Programs, and Politics—The Federal Impact on the Metropolis" (paper delivered at the sixty-sixth annual meeting of the American Political Science Association, Los Angeles, California, 8-12 September 1970).

59. The Development Team introduced its *Report* by saying:

When the Mayor formed the Development Team, his desire was to reassure the citizens of Detroit that what appeared to be the lowest ebb in the city's history could become its finest hour. His intention was that change born of the conflict would bring the government closer to all the members of the community in a new urban coalition to lead the way for other communities in need of change.

See Mayor's Development Team, *Report to Mayor Jerome P. Cavanagh* (Detroit, Michigan: City of Detroit, October 1967), pp. 9, 10.

60. It said:

With these things in mind, the Development Team set about to do what it could to indicate new directions to be taken and bold approaches to be made by the City in making the most of its potential to respond to its citizens' needs. Recommendations for the reorganization of some city government activities are contained within the report as are proposed redirections of departments and suggestions for other revitalizing moves. (Ibid. p. 10)

61. Collectively these agencies submitted over 175 pages of reactions to the *Report*, ranging in length from one to 43 pages.

62. Merit recruitment into the bureaucracy based upon passage of civil service exams reinforced city agencies' personnel "lag" behind the current population composition of the city.

63. See footnote 60 above for the degree to which the Development Team adhered to the mayor's agenda.

64. Cavanagh's reliance on persuasion provided part of the logic for placing experienced city-agency hands on the Development Team in the first place. He did convince them of the necessity for agency consolidation, but not the departments whose autonomy was in question.

65. Cavanagh had just experienced an alteration in a program he highly valued. Greenstone and Peterson show how Detroit's reformed bureaucracy, because of its reform characteristics, significantly detracted from the degree of participation in the community action program there, contrary to the strong and consistent urging of Cavanagh. See Greenstone and Peterson, *Race and Authority in Urban Politics*, ch. 7.

66. For a discussion of similar bureaucratic behavior in New York City, see Wallace S. Sayre and Herbert Kaufman, *Governing New York City* (New York: Norton, 1960), particularly pp. 251-64, 402-407.

67. Letter from secretary and chief examiner, Civil Service Commission, to Mayor Jerome P. Cavanagh, dated 22 November 1967, p. 10. This letter, along with those cited below, was made available to the authors by James L. Trainor, Jr., an administrative assistant to Mayor Cavanagh. These letters and supporting materials constitute an invaluable source for the present study and permission to use them is gratefully acknowledged. The original letters are in the mayor's office in Detroit, Michigan.

68. Letter from director, Office of Civil Defense, to Mayor Jerome P. Cavanagh, dated 27 November 1967, p. 1.

69. Ibid., pp. 1, 2.

70. Letter from director, City Plan Commission, to Mayor Jerome P. Cavanagh, dated 22 November 1967, p. 8.

71. The City Plan Commission's reanalysis led it to reject the Development Team's recommendation for consolidating housing, renewal, and planning activities. Its interpretation of the information reads:

The only city which has an overall agency which combines planning, renewal, and housing is Milwaukee. It appears that the Team's proposal was patterned almost completely after that of Milwaukee's and even incorporated whole phrases in their description of the nature of the proposed organization and the manner of its functioning. Contrary to the Team's assertion "the single agency is the most efficient and effective means of organization for a city the size of Detroit," in the article accompanying their response to the Team's letter, Milwaukee's development agency director himself states that he recommends this type of organization for small- and medium-sized cities only, not for major cities the size of Detroit. In addition, the director of Milwaukee's development agency admits that the present combined organization is cumbersome in its functioning, and confusing administrative relationships are inherent in the present Milwaukee organizational structure. This is evidenced by the continuing unsuccessful efforts to revise the structure since 1961 when it was established. (Ibid.)

430

72. Letter from director-secretary, Detroit Housing Commission, to Mayor Jerome P. Cavanagh, dated 22 November 1967, p. 2.

73. The Housing Commission concluded:

Although we realize that our comments are heavily negative, we are cognizant of the difficulties faced by the MDT in preparing the report in the time allocated. If the pressure of time had been less, perhaps some of the MDT recommendations could have been modified in terms of the innumerable social, financial, and political "facts of life" which we, as a long-standing operating department encounter daily. (Ibid., p. 11)

74. Letter from commissioner, Department of Buildings and Safety Engineering, to Mayor Jerome P. Cavanagh, dated 27 November 1967, p. 2. The same department included a defense of its plumbing bureau, which reads:

We are at a loss to understand what is meant by "noticeable gaps in inspection" because we are of the opinion that our plumbing inspection operation is one of the best and most thorough in the state. Since the policy of the Department has always been compliance rather than penalty, some violations do remain open without abatement or court prosecution for extended periods of time. Experience has proven that court prosecution only leads to the payment of fines rather than correction of the defect and it is frequently true that the money spent in fines might be better applied to the correction. (Ibid., p. 4)

The department's response poses a frequently encountered dilemma for riot commissions generally: often enough thesre is simply no agreement among professionals as to the most effective policy. Here as elsewhere in this section, we do not propose to weigh the merits of proposed reforms so much as examine the sources of successful agency resistance.

75. Letter from Director, City Plan Commission, to Mayor Jerome P. Cavanagh, dated 22 November 1967, p. 7.

76. Its claim reads:

In terms of the results obtained, while the Team does not make reference to this consideration, we believe that Detroit's renewal program has been remarkably productive and successful and that this program has, on any objective evaluation, placed Detroit among the very forefront of the major cities of the nation. We believe also that renewal in the future will require, more than ever, effective pre-planning and community relations work since projects will be small and scattered. (Ibid., p. 8)

To support its claim about national recognition, the City Plan Commission cited a survey conducted in 1961 by the Institute for Research and Social Sciences at the University of North Carolina that placed Detroit first among all major cities of the nation in terms of comprehensive planning and development programs. Second, it cited a 1964 study by the American Institute of Planners that judged Detroit to have the most effective comprehensive planning program among all cities above 500,000 population. Third, the City Plan Commission's defense of its past performance noted that in 1965 the American Institute of Architects awarded Detroit the first national citation for excellence in community architecture and urban design resulting from planning activities. The City Plan Commission finally cited studies, reports, and recommendations by the Public Administration Service in Chicago, the Institute of Public Administration in New York, the Urban Renewal Study in Baltimore, and the Citizens Research Council of Michigan to support its opposition to consolidation of planning functions under a superagency also dealing with public housing, urban renewal, and other physical development agencies.

77. Letter from executive chief of the Detroit Fire Department, to Mayor Jerome P. Cavanagh, dated 22 November 1967, p. 2.

78. See letter from deputy commissioner, Department of Health, to Mayor Jerome P. Cavanagh, dated 21 November 1967, pp. 2, 3.

79. See letter from secretary and chief examiner, Civil Service Commission, to Mayor Jerome P. Cavanagh, dated 22 November 1967, p. 3.

80. The department concluded: "In summary, we estimate that at a cost of $7,500,000.00, these goals will be achieved." See letter from general superintendent, Public Lighting Commission, to Mayor Jerome P. Cavanagh, dated 22 November 1967, p. 2.

81. Letter from secretary and chief examiner, Civil Service Commission, to Mayor Jerome P. Cavanagh, dated 22 November 1967, p. 2.

82. Letter from director, Mayor's Committee for Industrial and Commercial Development, to Mayor Jerome P. Cavanagh, dated 27 November 1967, p. 2.

83. Letter from deputy commissioner, Department of Health, to Mayor Jerome P. Cavanagh, dated 21 November 1967, p. 1.

84. Letter from Board of Assessors to Mayor Jerome P. Cavanagh, dated 20 November 1967, p. 12.

85. Letter from director, Department of Streets and Traffic, to Mayor Jerome P. Cavanagh, dated 21 November 1967, p. 1.

86. Letter from commissioner, Department of Building and Safety Engineering, to Mayor Jerome P. Cavanagh, dated 27 November 1967, p. 1.

87. James L. Trainor, Jr., quoted in Detroit *Free Press*, 26 January 1969.

88. Richard Strichartz quoted in ibid.

89. Letter to one of the authors from Bernard W. Klein, controller of the City of Detroit, dated 16 June 1969.

90. Corresponding to this observation was the pattern of city agencies' intensity of opposition to Development Team reform proposals. Those agencies which the mayor's office had least control over and which possessed the greatest degree of autonomy, independence, and resources were also the agencies most hostile to the recommendations. Agencies with less autonomy, independence, and resources were less hostile to the reform proposals, although they too opposed the recommendations. This pattern may also explain why the police and fire departments, which possessed significant resources, independence, and autonomy, were specifically exempted from review by the Development Team and few structural reforms were aimed in their direction.

91. The text of Fagan's letter read: "The bearer named below is one of several working closely with the state industrial commission to preserve order and prevent trouble. Please give them every consideration and your cooperation" (Milwaukee *Sentinel*, 4 August 1967).

92. Mayor Maier went on to say that Fagan had "pitted his superior judgment against the administration in Milwaukee." Moreover, he called the letter a "reward" for Fagan's "chosen friends." See Milwaukee *Journal*, 3 August 1967.

93. Quoted in Milwaukee *Journal*, 1 August 1967.

94. Milwaukee *Sentinel*, 7 August 1967.

95. The partisan division over calling a special legislative session began when the Republican Speaker of the State Assembly declared himself "absolutely and definitely opposed to a special session at this time" (ibid., 4 August 1967). The state assembly's Republican majority leader accused Milwaukee's mayor of using the violence as a pretext for gaining his long-sought objectives: "I'm sorry that he [Maier] feels that as a result of this [rioting] Milwaukee will get more of the pot. The request for a special session tends to dignify the rioting and holding one would lead to the conclusion that this [riots] helps" (ibid.).

Predictably, Democratic state legislators from Milwaukee defended Maier's proposal and criticized the governor for inaction. The Democratic minority leader, representing Milwaukee's south side, commented: "I don't believe that Governor Knowles is going to do anything to unbalance his so-called balanced budget. He is more concerned about that than any of the city's problems" (ibid., 7 August 1967).

96. Milwaukee *Journal*, 11 August 1967.

97. Ibid., 12 August 1967.

98. Ibid., 16 August 1967.

99. Ibid., 18 August 1967.

100. *Urban Problems and State Action* (mimeo., Office of the Governor, State of Wisconsin; dated 25 August 1967).

101. Ibid., p. 14.

102. Milwaukee *Journal*, 27 August 1967. On the same occasion, Fagan commented on the governor's 30-point program: "There's no doubt about it—we want to get into the city of Milwaukee. We don't just want to get in as a political party, the Republican party. We are interested in getting in there to try our ideas toward solving some of the problems that obviously exist there" (ibid.).

103. Frank A. Aukofer, *City With a Chance* (Milwaukee, Wisconsin: Bruce, 1968), p. 112.

104. Aukofer gives this account of the crowd's behavior:

> This time, the hoodlums were organized and waiting. Several hundred of them gathered at Crazy Jim's used car lot. Rock 'n' roll music blared from loudspeakers. A grotesque effigy of Father Groppi, with swastikas painted on it, swung by its neck from a rope. There also was a crude, six foot tall caricature of the priest painted on a board. Several youths held up a Confederate flag, while others waved signs saying, "Groppi—Black God," "Trained Nigger," and "Work Don't March." (Ibid., p. 114)

105. Milwaukee *Journal*, 30 August 1967.

106. Newcomb's account was merely a restatement of the mayor's own public position: "After the riot, we were proceeding on a 39-point 'Little Marshall plan' but suddenly we found ourselves in the position of an Austrian carpenter trying to build a platform in the middle of a revival meeting" (Milwaukee *Journal*, 19 September 1967).

107. Milwaukee *Sentinel*, 15 September 1967.

108. Milwaukee *Journal*, 12 September 1967.

109. Milwaukee *Sentinel*, 22 September 1967.

110. Ibid., 25 September 1967. The mayor also contended that: "State funds are being used to employ people for agitation against this administration" (ibid., 23 September 1967).

IV
CONCLUSION

11

The "Processing" of Racial Crisis in America

Few studies of American politics adequately prepare us for analyzing periods of crisis. On the contrary, most studies focus on observably dominant power relations and "normal" political patterns displaying extraordinary stability. Most research on national institutions concentrates on the bargaining between major participants, the constraints of office, and the requirements of role.[1] Conflicts are said to be resolved through negotiation, bargaining, and eventual compromise. Consensual models of the political system have been developed that place primary stress on the harmony among institutions, brokerage politics, and cooperative elite relations.[2] However diverse they may be in other respects, studies of major aspects of American political life tend to describe a pragmatic politics where change, if it occurs at all, is gradual and incremental.

Yet this is clearly not enough. To comprehend adequately any political system one must focus not only on "normal" political behavior but also on periods of mass insurgency when the system's ability to respond to stress is tested and the manner in which it does so becomes observable. Exclusive concentration on routine politics yields characterizations of the political system that mask enduring conflicts and contradictions that become more readily appreciable when the usual restraints on the expression of demands break down.[3] The civil

435

turmoil of the 1960s provides us with an opportunity to examine these significant but rarely studied dimensions of American politics.

The issue has practical as well as theoretical relevance. If rapid and significant change is unlikely in "normal" periods, what are the prospects in times of domestic crisis? There is some basis for concluding that major shifts in the allocation of resources can occur in periods when external threats are widely perceived and vigorously acted upon by elites. For example, a war economy was quickly mobilized during the presidency of Franklin Roosevelt and the extraordinary development of foreign aid as a Cold War strategy occurred during the Truman administration. These examples of priority shifts under perceived external threat have been instructive to those who seek domestic change; witness the reorientation of federal aid to education and science in the name of national defense after the Soviet Union's Sputnik triumph.[4]

With these exceptions, which were all responses to external pressures, we have few examples of rapid change in policy priorities during the twentieth century.[5] Yet a reasonably rapid and significant shift in priorities has been the major objective of all organizations of minority groups in America and their nonminority allies. This goal has been incompatible with the usual patterns of American politics that inhibit pressures for change in domestic policy. The eruption of massive civil disorder in the 1960s presented the possibility that a sufficiently grave stimulus could break the confines of incremental change and permit more rapid progress.[6] This study has been devoted in part to examining this hypothesis and its implications.

After a decade of agitation over legal barriers to black equality, the United States confronted in the mid-1960s what many at the time believed to be the greatest domestic crisis since the Civil War.[7] The riots of the mid-1960s, culminating in the summer of 1967, posed a threat to white America on many levels. They threatened domestic tranquility; large sections of many cities were burned and looted; unending and possibly escalating violent urban conflict seemed likely. A large minority of Americans appeared implacably hostile to the white majority and seemed prepared to express that hostility in the near and distant future. The riots posed a material threat. Ghetto homes were burned and destroyed and business and other normal economic activities were suspended, while further destruction to white businesses and white residential areas seemed likely. Enormous physical and psychological costs and an endlessly mobilized, "garrison" state loomed in the future.

The riots forced white liberals to confront the fact that social welfare programs dating back to the New Deal were not enough to deflect the active expression of black grievances. The riots threatened white racial conservatives, whose worst fears were undoubtedly confirmed by the violence. Perhaps most significantly, the riots jeopardized the social contract of slow racial accommodation to which most Americans, including blacks, had seemed to consent and without which the future of interracial relations could no longer be considered predictable. Waiting in the wings was the ominous white backlash to black progress.

Intermittent collective racial violence, sometimes massive, has characterized American history in the twentieth century. Race-related riots have occasionally disturbed the smooth functioning of economic and social relations, particularly in the sixties when black-initiated actions against white-owned property and the police replaced the white-initiated, people-focused violence of earlier generations. Throughout this century, *the typical political response of elites to such events has been to create riot commissions or other official investigations.*

This final chapter examines the contributions made by these riot response patterns to the maintenance and stability of the political system, and to the potential for significant changes in the arrangements of politics and the outcomes of policy. We turn shortly to assessing how the study of elite responses to riots illuminates important questions about different perspectives on American politics. The dominant pluralist perspective provides limited but important insights into the ideological foundations of elite manipulation of crisis. An alternative perspective focusing on conflict between dominant and subordinate groups provides a structure for understanding elite activities contributing to depoliticizing the riots and returning the political system to a status quo where previously dominant groups continue to prevail— through reducing the sense of crisis and minimizing the impact of crisis. Throughout our discussion riot commissions are viewed as the institutional embodiment of elite management in the processing of riot-induced crises. Although our discussion focuses on the defusing of the crisis attending civil disorders, our analysis may be generally applicable whenever crisis threatens to disrupt the stability under which dominant groups prosper and find security in prevailing political relations.

Riot Commissions and Perspectives on
American Politics

The study of elite responses to riots illuminates important questions in analyzing perspectives on American politics. The familiar pluralist perspective provides limited but important insights into the ideological foundations of elite manipulation of crisis and the functioning of dominant political institutions. But pluralism, as we shall argue shortly, is descriptive of only one mode of political intercourse. Perspectives focusing on other modes of conflict regulation must be developed in order to adequately comprehend American political life, at least where the sustained subordination of racial minorities is concerned.

The dominant popular and scholarly perspectives on American politics assert that politics consists of bargaining among legitimate groups, all of which have access to political institutions and processes. In these views, often summarized or labeled as the "pluralist" perspective, political influence is said to be dispersed at the top, at least to the extent that it is shared among a plurality of elites.[8] At the bottom, all legitimate groups are said to receive at least some response when they articulate grievances. Furthermore, it is maintained that there is sufficient consensus about the importance of respecting the "rules of the game" that more powerful groups, and potential majorities, are constrained in their exercise of power. The pluralist perspective maintains further that the system is one of adjustment and compromise, where excesses are held to a minimum by widespread respect for the just claims of all organized groups. All groups are not considered equal or equally powerful. But in the American political system it is thought that the process of bargaining and inclusion is more valued than are the benefits and costs of conducting politics to the exclusive advantage of the more powerful. The pluralist conception of American politics is not the child of any single approach or school of inquiry but has been supported and reinforced by a wide range of approaches.

The pluralist perspective is consistent with popular impressions of how the political process works.[9] It is consonant with conventional wisdom that the political process is an arena of alliances and bargaining among contending parties, that likely policy outcomes are those that call for marginal changes in existing programs, and that the height of political wisdom is appreciation of the "possible." Moreover, the pluralist perspective has ideological dimensions. In focusing on openness, balance, and moderation, pluralism is a powerful statement of

438

how many think the system *ought* to work. Thus, to establish institutions that embody pluralist virtues is to resonate with popular views of fairness and civic values.

As we argue in greater detail below, riot commissions give the appearance of being preeminently pluralistic. To the extent that they appear open, representative of dominant groups and exhibit other pluralist features, mass publics respond positively to the creation of riot commissions because the commissions seem to exhibit qualities that are generally approved in American society. Riot commissions thus appear to be consistent with fundamental public attitudes toward governmental institutions.

Although institutions may appear to be pluralist, they may not, in fact, contribute to the wide dispersal of influence or the openness of the political system. Nor is the pluralist analysis of American politics necessarily an appropriate perspective from which to understand the functioning of riot commissions. Thus we have the irony that riot commissions may be preeminent expressions of the pluralist impulse, at the same time that they provide an excellent vantage from which to view some of the major weaknesses of pluralist analysis.

In the 1960s, stirred by the arousal and mobilization of previously quiescent minority groups, the pluralist perspective came under attack for inadequately describing various relationships between elites and nonelites.[10] It ignores the tricky question of which groups are "legitimate" and thus fall within the descriptive potential of this way of thinking. Moreover, the political resources of relatively powerless groups are so few and unstable when compared to those of elite groups that it may be inappropriate to conclude that all groups have access to political institutions. And to say that such groups have access begs the question of whether they have any chance of success. Relatively powerless groups may be able to force elites to respond to them, but the response may be punitive or symbolic rather than ameliorative and substantive. Furthermore, the agenda of politics may be structured in ways favorable to elites, thereby excluding from consideration issues of greatest concern to less powerful groups. Pluralist theory is able to accommodate the notion of conflict, but it does conceive conflict as relatively limited, significantly muted by citizens' multiple allegiances, and posits characteristic and conceptually limited ways in which conflict may be resolved.[11]

Nonetheless, despite its defects, the pluralist framework continues to serve as a guide for thinking about politics, in part because it remains compelling for *certain aspects* of the American political process. This is particularly true in respect to the bargaining processes that some have mistakenly thought to comprise the whole of American politics (for example, interest-group lobbying over legislation, administrative bargaining practices, or bloc vote calculations in presidential campaign tactics). Pluralism also remains compelling in the absence of a viable and well-articulated alternative conceptualization.

Although the pluralist model, as we have noted, accommodates some dimensions of the riot commission process, it does not seem to account persuasively for significant aspects of riot commission politics. Pluralism posits the inclusion of all legitimate groups in the society, but relatively powerless and excluded groups experience difficulty in gaining entry to the political process. Pluralism highlights the potential of included groups to have an impact *of some kind* on the policy process, but policy changes resulting from the efforts of relatively powerless groups tend to be minimal, at best. Pluralism emphasizes the ability of all groups to be heard, but political leaders and elites in general are better able to give direction to the kinds of messages that are placed into public controversies. Pluralism sees a process of bargaining through mutual concessions, but dominant groups often structure the implicit bargaining process so as to minimize concessions.

Unless we are forever to patch together the pluralist quilt, we require alternative perspectives for analyzing significant political questions falling outside this dominant framework. With other analysts whose work is self-consciously outside the pluralist framework (rather than once more criticizing it)[12] we reject understanding American political stability as the successful purchasing of mass loyalty by more or less including all legitimate groups in the processes and rewards of politics. Rather, the system may be understood by examining groups relatively lacking in political and economic resources as perpetually in heuristic conflict with more dominant groups. This conflict is not always manifest because relatively powerless groups may be socialized to accept the current distribution of resources, recognize the futility of insurgency, or be too disorganized to act effectively. Or they may make conflict manifest but be undermined when they attempt to organize, or be repelled with minimal concessions when they are able to mount a challenge. At times they may come to be included in the constellation of dominant groups, but then only on terms that do not threaten existing relationships. Such a perspective enables us to make better sense of the developments we have elaborated in this book than does

440

the pluralist orientation, specifically, the manner in which elites regularly deny claimant groups, minimize concessions to them, and structure political activity so as to restore the status quo.

However, we may continue to profit from the insights of pluralist theory while recognizing its limitations by distinguishing between different modes of conflict. Ralf Dahrendorf proposes two modes of conflict. The first, *regulated conflict* (suggestive of pluralist group competition) is characterized by appreciation by all parties of the justice of others' claims, the presence of organized interest groups, and agreement on the "rules of the game." The second, *unregulated conflict* (of which racial violence is illustrative), is characterized by efforts to destroy one's opponents, by the presence of unorganized interests, and by lack of norms of procedure or limits of claims.[13]

Where the pluralist perspective directs attention to the generation of policy concessions even when they are minimal, we direct attention to the lack or minimal nature of change, even when some concessions have been forthcoming. Where politicians' behavior in policy development after riots seems confused, ineffectual, and futile, we direct attention to the ways in which post-riot elite behavior consistently focuses on conflict regulation favoring the status quo.

Obviously the same events permit different conclusions and analyses depending on the perspective. The pluralist perspective is most appropriate for analyzing the exchange of influence among established groups or the distribution of political and material rewards when all contending parties accept prevailing patterns of authority and distribution. But the more unequal the contestants, or the more some groups challenge prevailing authority relationships, the more appropriate a conflict perspective becomes for understanding ensuing political activity. That this is so will hardly surprise social analysts who recognize the similarity between racial conflict in the United States and the structure of ethnic or racial-group conflict in many other societies. It is probably a peculiar general failing of American social science that it is necessary to advance arguments for a conflict approach.[14]

In this approach, the analyst focuses on strategies elites employ to maintain the status quo. A pluralist perspective may focus on order maintenance, recruitment, bargaining, and integration in the study of racial politics. These categories reflect the unstated assumption that these processes contribute to the long-term inclusion of racial groups into the dominant majority. A conflict theorist, by contrast, might label the same phenomena as suppression, cooperation, accommo-

441

dation, and assimilation, focusing instead on the processes by which the subordination of racial groups is sustained and reinforced.

Were the 1967 civil disorders political?[15] Were they directed toward changing patterns of income distribution or the structures by which power, authority, status, and material resources are allocated? The question goes to the heart of the importance of the riots as expressions of black grievances, and, thus, as "demands" upon the political system. Most analysts have tried to answer this question by studying rioters' motivations. The generally higher economic status of rioters compared to nonrioters provides some grounds (for others see ch. 1) for concluding that riot participants had higher stakes in community life, and a better capacity to control resources necessary for political action. But even so, the post-hoc re-creation of motivation during civil disorders is extremely difficult.

However, the analysis of the political content of civil disorders is not exhausted by the study of the social backgrounds and attitudes of riot participants. Thus, we need to know how the riots were perceived and responded to. Whether actions are "political" depends partly on how others understand the actions, and partly on the extent to which the actions are thought to require a political response.

As we have argued in chapter 1, political messages cannot be sent effectively unless channels are open and the receivers of such messages are prepared to "hear" their political content. In the world of bargaining the deaf and the lame are plausibly protected from the shrillest cries and excused from the implementation of vigorous action. These considerations in turn are affected by the analytical perspective through which political events are understood. The sympathy of recent riot commissions for black aspirations might lead many to think that black demands were provided expression and received a hearing in authoritative circles. The disinterest of two presidents and various local officials might be attributed to the political "realities" that politicians in pluralist systems are always weighing. This sort of analysis is blind to important differences in the intensity of demand-making, is unable to account for the imbalance between political activity and substantive outcomes, and neglects the *pattern* of dealing with minority demands that we have charted along one particular dimension at great length in this study.

442

Depoliticizing the Riots

Two associated general processes appear to minimize the perception of the disorders as political and to reduce their potential political impact. One set of responses to the riots reduces the sense of urgency with which they are perceived among mass publics. A related set facilitates restoration of previously prevailing political relationships.

Phenomenological implications are inherent in both areas. Reducing the sense of urgency surrounding mass concerns about riots lowers their priority for political action and makes room for other issue concerns. Lacking urgency and displaced by more usual policy issues, the riots are dismissed as of little account, or pronounced ended and become historical curiosities to be chronicled and examined, having failed to penetrate political arenas. Perceiving their lack of impact, society "reads back" meaning to the original riot events. Like the successful candidate for office who is considered clever and a good politician, while the loser, perhaps equally talented, is considered wanting and unable to organize successfully, civil disorders may ultimately be evaluated by whether they were followed by major policy concessions. The meaning of actions taken by subordinate groups, both to themselves and to outsiders, comes to be understood in terms of the reaction of dominant groups. In many ways this is what black militants like Stokely Carmichael meant when they repeatedly urged blacks not to permit whites to define them and their actions. These processes ultimately form the basis for our conclusion that riot commission politics and the disposition of their recommendations cumulatively help to reestablish elite control and a status quo expressive of dominant political patterns.

Reducing the Sense of Crisis

Simplistic denials of a crisis amidst civil disorder usually fail to satisfy the concerns of citizens. Citizens seek answers to questions about the violence and demand responsive action in its wake. The magnitude of racial crisis and its political significance have been effectively diminished by elites after the violence ends, however, through at least four interrelated processes: stressing localized dimensions of the problem, deflecting citizens' immediate concerns through short- and long-range assurances, lowering riot visibility and challenging the legitimacy of riot participants.

Official descriptions of civil disorders commonly discount their gravity and significance for the society as a whole by stressing their local nature. Analyses focusing on city characteristics and prescriptions calling for local solutions imply that riots are the product of isolated malfunctions within deviant and exceptional municipalities rather than system related and generalized throughout the nation. Official rhetoric contributes to this decentrist theme; initially, surprise is expressed at the location of riots and later attention is directed to unique community characteristics thought to precipitate violence. The rather narrow vision of most riot commissions concerning which questions to investigate reinforces the tendency to emphasize local problems. In this respect riot inquiries may reflect the general tendency in the United States to stress decentralized solutions to problems, particularly where racial inequalities are concerned. Such solutions historically have carried with them prescriptions for local autonomy and national inaction on social problems.

A second process of crisis reduction deflects citizen concerns by providing visible evidence that law enforcement agencies are capable of coping with immediate threats to order and giving assurances that remedial steps will be taken in the future. Throughout the twentieth century elites have attempted to negate the urgency of the moment by mobilizing police forces and promising that appropriate actions will be forthcoming. In the long run this may be achieved by providing symbolic reassurances that real grievances eventually will be addressed. As we have suggested throughout this book, the creation of riot commissions and their subsequent activities are a preeminent expression of this tendency in the United States. The fanfare with which commissions are launched, the questions specified for investigation in their charges, the authority seemingly granted to them by appointing executives, and the high status of individuals named as members hold out the promise of a thorough and objective report at some future date on the nature of the problem and appropriate solutions. Riot commission deliberations and other associated activities give further assurances that events are under control and that the problems causing racial violence are being investigated with an eye toward providing solutions.

One important reason appointment of riot commissions frequently meets at best with general popular approval and at worst with resigned acceptance is that these bodies are quintessentially expressive of the pluralist impulse in America. Commissions promise to seek out all shades of opinion in their investigations and to develop recommendations built upon a consensus of the diverse—if dominant—groups

444

represented on these bodies. They appear to reflect the Madisonian virtues of providing politically dominant minorities with vetoes over the preferences of minorities or even majorities less intensely affected by policy in the area of concern. They ultimately promise to channel diffuse and volatile expressions of discontent into manageable forms. Political demands are removed from expression at the street level and returned to more familiar bargaining and deliberative forums. Riot commissions are ostensibly open to the testimony of all "legitimate" interests, although they themselves define who is or is not a legitimate witness. Political demands can then be processed by authoritative political institutions that already incorporate prevailing power relationships.

The pluralistic merits of the commission also commend it to executives who need to respond to crisis events but for various reasons short-circuit the appointment of full-fledged commissions. In order to give the impression that they have consulted all legitimate parties, they appoint bodies to search widely for evidence and viewpoints to represent or reflect dominant interests, and to present a consensual document for consideration. That most local commissions or their equivalents focus a significant number of their recommendations on jurisdictions other than the ones to which they report confirms the pluralist conviction that power is scattered and diffuse, and that no single authority (perhaps itself dominated by a single interest) dominates political affairs.

Perhaps most important, riot commissions reflect the pluralist observation that political activity that is not directed toward governmental authorities or representational structures is illegitimate and hence not, in fact, political. Even when commissions in the sixties were sympathetic to black aspirations, they specifically condemned the behavior of the rioters that brought attention to their needs. Beyond condemning violence in general, American political elites reject rioters as political actors. This is partly a deliberate effort to discredit them and downgrade the significance of their actions. Certainly the rioters, by their actions and by definition, reject accepted standards of political behavior. And they are clearly not an *organized* interest that might be expected to take its place in the pluralist congress seeking appropriate bargaining and concessions. Because the rioters are not an organized interest and their behavior is directed toward fundamental changes, they are regarded as illegitimate within the political system. Yet it is conceivable that they might have been recognized as a politically relevant group that did not bargain at the conference table but instead waited to see how the rest of society responded to what they felt were their just claims. Radical movements are rarely initially legitimate to leaders of the governments they seek to reconstruct. Yet they may come to gain legitimacy in time. Significantly, members of the Kerner Commission sought to legitimate established black organizations and their leaders, whose loss of credibility among the black masses was regarded as a major threat to the prevailing system of race relations. Also they denounced the antisystem street behavior of rioters in terms aimed at discrediting them.

Elites also provide short-term assurances of their capacity to contain and suppress violence. Rioters are not only condemned, but threats are made to increase the cost of rioting beyond tolerable limits to the rioters. Public officials and the inquiries established after riots commend improved police and National Guard training and increased armaments for the forces of control. By stressing official capacities to cope with riot threats and by promising more forceful suppression and recommending increased manpower and weaponry, officials reduce one dimension of the anxiety surrounding riots by responding to calls to restore and maintain order more effectively.

Third, a predictable diminishing level of interest in collective violence on the part of the media helps reduce the sense of crisis by lowering its visibility. The media initially tend to feature sensational and dramatic accounts when reporting threatening events like street rioting. Then, with passage of time, an opposite pattern is observable where the same kind of events receive episodic and more muted coverage. Although they do not control this tendency directly or entirely, political elites periodically contribute to it. Thus when the Kerner Commission urged greater circumspection in the media's coverage of riots, it contributed to more subdued reporting of riot events. In the post-Kerner Commission years, civil authorities and the media adopted guidelines and technical changes to insure "calm, accurate" reporting in times of crisis. Newspapers have moved away from "the front-page buildup, complete with splashy pictures and boxscores of the latest 'riot' news."[16] Municipal authorities have become more circumspect in reporting violence and have shown restraint in predicting future disorders.[17]

Media influence on reducing perceptions of crises may be illustrated by their role in covering riots in the late 1960s. A widespread belief arose following the Kerner Commission's work that the number of riots diminished in the years after 1967. According to the Lemberg Center for the Study of Violence, however, the number of riots actually increased through 1969. In 1967 the Center reported 257 race-related civil disorders, while in 1968 it recorded 724 riots and in 1969, 835 riots.[18] The Justice Department reported more civil disturbances in 1970 than in 1969 and almost as many in the peak quarter of 1971 as in the peak quarters of the two previous years.[19] Although "large cities, with their huge numbers of poor blacks, still suffered from racial conflict" in 1969,[20] the fact that racial violence tended to occur in smaller and medium-sized cities meant those cities receiving substantial media attention were no longer the focal point of riots. A riot in Los Angeles is more likely to receive media attention than a riot of equal proportions in Pasadena. In addition, many disorders were associated with public schools and prisons, thus appearing to have an institutionally specific focus, which may also have contributed to the public perception that riots had diminished. The disorders were also more spread out over the year, so that the "long-hot summer" was somewhat cooler but replaced by a considerably warmer riot "year."[21] More even riot distribution over the calendar year reinforced tendencies to reduce public visibility of the violence because the media tended to underplay events whose newsworthy qualities partially derived from their seasonal concentration.

The observation that civil disorders have declined in recent years in most instances rests on newspaper reports that, in fact, tend to undercount the frequency of civil disorders. Newspapers generally give less space and sometimes no space at all to events they would have covered fully a few years ago because of their perception that coverage might contribute to inflaming the disorders, the Kerner Commission maintained. Civil disorders are also less newsworthy than they were. What is news is what is new, and as the coverage of civil disorders diminishes, so too does public awareness of them.[22]

By the mid-1970s the question "what happened to the 1960s-style riots?" had become a familiar query among scholars and citizens alike. Perhaps a partial answer is provided by focusing on "what happened to the *media coverage* of the 1960s-style riots?" The riots continued much longer than the media record would acknowledge, outliving the attention of the media and hence recognition by the wider society. In this sense understanding what happened to the riots is perhaps less germane than understanding the process that first resulted in sensational coverage, and then led to the minimal chronicling of their occurrence. Reducing the sense of crisis by withdrawing recognition from the events originally creating the crisis is not limited to the media, as those officials who urge policies of "benign neglect" fully appreciate.

The establishment of socially accepted "facts" is affected by the availability of data, however accurate or inaccurate. Political elites recognize the relationship between *reports* of violence and the extent to which violence is perceived to be a public problem. Developments in official data collection in areas of social policy unrelated to violence bear this out. The elimination of the category of *poverty* in favor of the term *low-income* and the Nixon administration's decision to cease collecting data on "underemployment" and on ghetto unemployment all represented efforts to diminish the potential for monitoring progress in these areas and to reduce the potential of organized groups to mobilize around them.[23] Manipulating definitions of crimes and methods of criminal justice data collection also enable political leaders to achieve the image of success (for example, lower crime "rates") without affecting actual behavior patterns.[24]

Challenges to the legitimacy of participants in civil disorders provides a fourth means of reducing the sense of crisis. Calling rioters "conspirators" or "riffraff" contributes to the view that the social fabric is being picked at by troublemakers and others who have not earned a place in a society of equals. Denying the legitimacy of rioters' acts reduces the extent to which riots are perceived as related to real grievances and as strategies designed to gain redress. It is interesting that these attributions are made of participants from subordinate social groups regardless of whether they initiate or are victims of the violence. When race-related violence breaks out, white leaders consistently exaggerate the atrocities committed by blacks, the amount of property damage, the existence of snipers, the extent of predetermination of events, and the degree of outside manipulation of black groups.[25]

The discreditation of insurgent groups is not a peculiarly "American" phenomenon. We may hypothesize that political elites in most political systems generally try to dismiss collective violence as the work of the riffraff, criminal elements, conspirators, or irreconcilable small minorities with minimal systematic importance. Outbreaks of aggressive protest and violence from below consistently elicit official denunciation from above by those whose authority is to various degrees challenged. For example, responsibility for the 1968 student riots in Poland, which lasted for about seven days, was variously attributed by Polish authorities to "utterly irresponsible" political elements, "a conspiracy group linked with Zionist centers," and "Zionist, liberal intellectuals and discredited Stalinists."[26] Similarly, official Polish explanations of the widespread rioting in December 1970, initiated this time by the Gdansk shipyard workers, focused on "hooligans and inciting elements" and on "unpredictable adventurers recruited among the outcasts of society."[27] An official inquiry established to determine the causes and origins of the violence in Northern Ireland attributed it to "hooligans" on both the Catholic and Protestant sides.[28] The work of Eric Hobsbawm and George Rude suggests historical continuities for these observations. In their account of the destruction of newly introduced farm machinery by British agricultural laborers in the first half of the nineteenth century, they note the extraordinary extent to which myths circulated attributing the uprising to a conspiracy of the French, the Irish, the Papists, foreign government agents, or radicals and revolutionaries in general.[29]

Of course, any given political event may indeed have been caused by riffraff or conspirators. Three observations may be made in response to this possibility. First, political elites systematically attribute illegitimacy to the origins of collective violence.[30] Thus when Portuguese police fire into an unruly crowd of 5,000, or injure 80 and arrest 200 after a demonstration, elite Lisbon sources ignore the fertile climate prompting the actions of the crowd and instead blame communist agents for organizing the demonstrations. When Greek farmers demand higher wheat prices, the ensuing rioting is laid at the communists' door.[31]

Second, even when events are indeed caused by conspirators, attributing them exclusively to conspirators diminishes the extent to which mass publics perceive that there may be popular support for disorders. Yet even conspirators require sympathy from the crowd, as the Kerner Commission investigators confirmed in the case of Cambridge, Maryland, where blacks by and large *rejected* the inflammatory rhetoric of H. Rap Brown. And regardless of whether or not conspirators contribute to disorders, it is the instigators whose identities and ideological preferences are recorded, not those of the crowds with which they must resonate. The result is that popular sympathy is eliminated from accounts of events, and thus the political importance that might accompany expressions of widespread discontent with the regime is minimized.[32]

Third, elites who would tend to deny that political factors account for collective violence at home are often ready to attribute collective violence to political factors when it occurs elsewhere. The communist press has regularly explained black disorders in America as resulting from discriminatory political, economic, and social conditions.[33] Similarly, the American press regularly explains domestic violence in socialist countries in terms of felt grievances and unmet political demands. The above-mentioned Polish student riots in 1968, for example, were editorially explained by the New York *Times* as expressive of demands for civil liberties, less Russian influence in foreign policy, and greater economic prosperity and security.[34] The *Times* labeled the larger-scale violence in Poland two years later as testimony "to the discontent of a misgoverned nation and the bankruptcy of a politico-economic system."[35] We may hypothesize that elites generally tend to dismiss riotous behavior as apolitical, illegitimate, and criminal when it occurs domestically, but praise it as political, legitimate, and socially useful when it occurs in societies whose values they oppose. This relationship appears to be pronounced valid when and where domestic attitudes toward violence from below are easily manipulated by elite characterization.

Minimizing the Impact of Crisis

Delay and the establishment of institutions that permit leaders to provide symbolic rewards and the appearance of responsiveness without delivering are among the structural supports minimizing the impact of crisis.

Delay minimizes the impact of crisis by changing the conditions under which leadership must respond. Crisis is characterized, perhaps defined, by uncertainty, threat, and anxiety. The endurance and potential of contending parties is untested and their objectives may be undeclared. In such situations the risks to leadership are high; there are more unknown factors to enter into a decision than under more normal and routine circumstances. Delay permits leaders to wait until after the actual threat has diminished and public attention has crested.[36]

Delay also permits leaders to await the fading of weak or spasmodic organizations and movements that cannot sustain themselves. And subordinate groups, which lack the organizational resources to sustain long-term influence, are particularly likely to be adversely affected by delay. When threat is a component of the crisis, as it is in riots, delayed response from public officials is all the more adverse to riot groups because the credibility of the threat understandably comes into question as time passes. The mere announcement and appointment of riot commissions lends the appearance of meaningful action and relieves officials from momentary pressures for decisive leadership. Mandating putative black grievances to study, with the implicit promise to act upon findings later, allows public officials to postpone action until such time as the commission reports. By then the demands on officials will have changed, conforming more closely to normal pressures and facilitating incremental responses or no response at all.

The complex policy process characteristic of American politics delays action without making it appear that any individual is responsible. It is the "system" that must be negotiated. The Constitutional separation of governing institutions among executive, judicial, and legislative branches and the marble cake of federalism where policies are comprised of federal, state, and local components also provide cushions, since so many public officials justly claim that they are not totally responsible for any particular social condition or policy area. For example, both riot commissions and public officials tend to identify the pressing needs of the country as requiring changes in the policy agendas of institutional branches of government or jurisdictions *other* than those over which they preside.

These dynamics represent inversions of functions the federal system was presumably designed to accomplish. The framers of the Constitution sought to establish safety from an aroused majority by complex Constitutional arrangements, but these have simultaneous consequences for the minorities for whom vigorous action might depend upon a sense of urgency. Those rare moments when crisis conditions make the country open to mobilization for change more easily fade if responsibility cannot be fixed and public officials cannot be held accountable.

Institutional arrangements facilitating inaction, lack of responsibility, and nonaccountability are settings for action or inaction; actual behavior within such settings suggests additional explanations for the low impact of crises. Political rhetoric and symbolic actions that may gratify psychologically but fail to provide substantive changes are also a characteristic reaction to crisis. Rhetoric of firmness and sensitivity takes the place of actual firmness and sensitivity. Appointment of high-status commissions to study problems, speeches approving efforts of moderate leaders, and selection of representatives from minority groups to high-status positions are a few of the more common symbolic gestures. The appointment of riot commissions generally provides symbolic reassurances to mass publics grown anxious over racial conflict. The systematic appointment of commissions or official boards of inquiry during periods of racial crisis—or for that matter nearly whenever threats to established arrangements appear to elude institutional resolution—suggests the symbolic significance of these bodies above and beyond the advisory roles that they are manifestly charged with performing.

The establishment of commissions of inquiry, advisory boards, secret task forces, and the like may be viewed in part as providing advice and intelligence to political executives and in part as rewards to various constituencies for whom public officials are not yet prepared to provide substantive rewards. Symbolic recognition may be secured through the appointment of representatives of constituencies to advisory bodies. Or committing to study the subject in which a constituency is vitally interested may provide symbolic rewards. These rewards are not given gratuitously, but form an implicit bargain. Public officials reward constituencies with the status *and expected influence* accruing from such appointments or the promise that issues of concern will be addressed, expecting supportive responses from those constituencies.[37] But these implicit bargains are regularly and systematically violated by public officials who are free to ignore or oppose the suggestions of their advisory bodies without suffering any penalties of office. Yet it is the nature of the implicit bargain that the public in varying degrees expects the forthcoming advice to be taken seriously.

It may be reasonably argued that chief executives should not be required to take the advice they seek. Indeed, if they were so required, it would not be advice any longer.[38] Different arguments seem more compelling, however, when this observation is measured against the frequency with which commissions are established, and the regularity with which their advice is thrust aside if it fails to coincide with executives' preferences or agendas. Chief executives find value in the potential inherent in establishing boards of inquiry for dispensing reassurances to concerned constituencies. These rewards are effective only because they involve implicit exchanges of status and potential for influence. Public officials later turn away from the advice of these boards with apparent impunity and only marginal injury to their subsequent ability to strike similar relationships in the future.

Moreover, one may argue that chief executives have not repudiated the implicit bargain—if the fundamental promise is to restore order and diminish the threat implicit in the violence. The "benign" receipt of riot commission recommendations by the executive and the "neglect" in implementing them is unimportant if one takes passage of the crisis itself as fulfillment of the pledge. Through such bargaining the status quo is preserved. These observations modestly suggest the potential significance of crisis periods for producing responses to the demands of subordinate groups, as well as the superior capacity of chief executives to deflect pressures for change.

It is in the relationship of public officials, and particularly of political executives, to the advisory bodies they create that appearances of responsiveness without delivery and deflection of demands most noticeably minimizes the impact of crisis. Public officials confront at least minimal requirements to mollify all contending parties. For aggrieved groups this means implicitly promising to examine the preconditions for violence and working to affect change. The imperative for recognized representatives of the subordinate population (politicians, community leaders, and others who may have had nothing to do with the rioting) is to focus on immediate, concrete concessions while manipulating threats to reinvoke violent conflict, without at the same time going so far as to increase the impulse of others to suppress the rioters and the communities from which they come. However, the superior capacity of public officials to deflect pressures for change is illustrated by the ease with which riot commissions may be appointed, deflating pressures for concrete actions. Having established public bodies to provide recommendations for official action, chief executives may praise the commission for its efforts without again referring to its recommendations; may assign its recommendations to another government agency or task force for study; may identify strongly with insignificant aspects of the group's work, supporting those reforms proposed for other political jurisdictions or those that cost less to implement; or may simply ignore or reject outright the reform proposals.

Advisory commissions are launched with the full rhetorical support of chief executives, but they report some months later in a political context where they have lost whatever authoritative support they may once have enjoyed. Other study groups emerge, employing many of the same symbols of legitimacy used by official commissions. Without executive support, the ability of official commissions to see their recommendations implemented is severely reduced.

Although there is little evidence that riot commissions are directly controlled by public officials—and therefore overtly engage in "whitewashing" the executive—in important respects commissions do accept the needs of the executive as their own. They accept the need to

453

reassure anxious publics and dispense symbolic rewards of status and potential influence to representatives of various executive constituencies on whom they may be dependent for assistance. Commissions anticipate an executive's political needs by tailoring recommendations in recognition of the executive's importance in securing adoption of recommendations. Through the internal dynamics of commission representation and deliberations, specific criticisms of significant interests are often minimized because of the deference shown to commissioners who represent those interests. Finally, commissions frequently focus a significant portion of their recommendations for change on jurisdictions other than the one in which they have been asked to operate or on branches of government antagonistic to the executive who created them.

Chief executives thus appoint commissions or study groups in which they have confidence, surrounding them with symbols of objective inquiry, and endowing them with implicit assurances that they will receive the most serious attention. Their designees, in all conscientiousness, act pragmatically to maximize their impact, and executives use portions of the commissions' work to advance their previous goals and political fortunes. Sometimes politicians are quick to acknowledge that a crisis exists; other times they are reluctant to provide groups even minimal symbolic recognition. But rarely if ever do they act as if new trails should be blazed or alliances forged. Except for peacekeeping and immediate reconstruction, politics as usual prevails; the forces originally precipitating the overt conflict cannot sustain themselves and dissipate or are suppressed.

Nor do selective implementation or the more usual nonimplementation of recommendations affect only our assessment of the effectiveness of riots. The implementation of commission recommendations may affect citizens' evaluation of their own behavior during riots, their future support for such behavior, or their ideas concerning the effectiveness of mass action. If there is little policy impact, rioting will not appear efficacious. At the crudest level, this is the goal of political leaders whose initial reactions to civil disorders were to maintain that there would be "no rewards for rioters." This was a prophecy they were in a position to fulfill, although not before a diversion in which they alleged an interest in the objective recommendations of impartial commissions they would create and pledge to assist. When commissions transform concerns stimulated by rioting into partisan debates and continuations of prior political conflicts, the public may also get the message that policy priorities have not changed.

These developments have significance for the political meaning of demands. When decisions are postponed and minimal policy changes result, the conclusion is easily drawn that the original demands were, literally, not significant. This conclusion is enhanced when, for whatever reasons, the apparent tactic—rioting—is not repeated or, if repeated, fails for various reasons to capture media attention. Delay also fosters this impression, since delay increases the probability that sustained political activity will not be evident when recommendations are announced. Yet, in a system widely regarded by its citizens as pluralist, only sustained and organized pressures are granted legitimacy. Citizens who normally require enduring structures to represent their interests and are unable to organize around sympathetic reports or recommendations retain the lack of credibility characteristic of their pre-riot images.

How are we to know the political content of civil disorders when public officials or their designees reduce blacks' claims of injustice to self-interested squabbles over appropriate jurisdictional responsibility, problematic concerns for governmental organization, or misguided and paltry philanthropy? How could implicit statements of grievances be taken as such when elites are paralyzed by conflicting claims of civil servants concerned that black demands will affect their roles and status? How ultimately can society view outbursts as political when blacks' claims are—paradoxically—recognized as just but uncalled for, and then—paradoxically again—considered of little account by the public institutions responsible for distributing the values and perquisites of society? The process of crisis reduction diminishes the system's capacity for change and the sense that there is a need for change.

The study of riots and their political impacts thus ultimately illuminates both the responses to riots and the extent to which those events are viewed as requiring responses. Riot commission politics is part of the process by which the United States purchases system stability at the expense of blacks and through explicit and implicit mechanisms that substantially insulate the system from their political influence. The explicit mechanisms are familiar. Blacks have struggled to secure full status as American citizens despite the implacable hostility of political and economic institutions. Only in the most recent years have these institutions become at times supportive of black needs and aspirations.

The implicit mechanisms are less obvious. Formal political institutions are only one way citizens can influence political life. For affluent citizens or the corporations many of them direct, money can purchase influence outside the law. For others, demonstrations can gain attention when petitions fail. The fewer a group's resources, the more it is likely to rely on a combination of legitimate and quasi-legitimate activities to secure political ends. Elite capacities to diminish or injure the effectiveness of a group's access to legitimate political channels thus becomes a critical advantage in the contest over scarce resources. Prior to World War II, black claims of injury in racial conflict went ignored or, if investigated, were usually dismissed as unworthy by the groups commissioned to investigate their claims. In the more recent period nonviolent protest activities were condemned as illegal, then coopted and accommodated as the remaining legal bastions of segregation were assaulted and dismantled. But for the most part, the institutional foundations of discrimination and inequality remained impenetrable.

The level and content of demands on a political system cannot be measured or assessed without appreciating the volume and the range of frequencies that the system can receive. The politics of riots and riot commissions (the preeminent response to riots) suggest that to a significant extent American politics "processes" crisis-bred political demands so as to erase or filter out their political content. The riots of 1967, potentially the most vigorous statement of discontent, were sufficiently *processed* by the groups and individuals established to deal with them that the political pressures they might otherwise have induced were vitiated.

On criteria of severity, frequency, and duration, the 1960s black riots represented levels of threat and challenge to governing elites and to the institutions they presided over unprecedented in this century, save possibly for the Great Depression of the 1930s. Governing elites yielded significant gains during the Depression for working-class Americans, including formal rights to recognition, bargaining and organizing, and the development of employment and income-security programs. No comparable or even faintly similar concessions were forthcoming in the 1960s during the riot-induced crisis. Accounting for the *manner* in which elites accomplished the depoliticization of rioters' demands, the reduction in the sense of urgency so pervasive during and immediately following the riots, and ultimately the minimization of the riots' political impact, requires examination of the central institutions elites relied upon when explicitly responding to the riots.

456

Advisory commissions of investigation provided the institutional formats for elite responses to the riots, and helped restore for race relations in the 1970s patterns of dominance and subordination between whites and blacks prevailing prior to the rioting. The regular appointment of commissions—significantly in virtually all cases where riots occurred throughout this century—signal elite recognition of the inadequacies of political institutions to cope with the magnitude of the crisis. Implicit in creating riot commissions is public officials' awareness that conventional executive, legislative, judicial, and bureaucratic structures are inadequate and perhaps irrelevant to the management of the crisis. In contrast, the attractiveness of riot commissions rests upon their ability to provide rapid and visible response; dramatic appearances of meaningful, thorough, and objective inquiry into unknown dimensions of the problem at hand; widespread assurances to deeply divided and aroused groups; and the promise of action some time distant from the immediate period of turmoil. These are all qualities of political processes distinctly lacking in the pluralist world of bargaining, negotiation, deliberation, and concession leading to incremental adjustments. The commission device succeeds where usual political institutions are found lacking.

How does a political system remain stable in the face of persisting social inequality without resorting to terror and large-scale suppression? For "normal" times one would explain this stability by focusing on factors that lead some citizens to participate politically and to feel supportive of the political system, that limit participation or otherwise induce withdrawal from or disinterest in participation on the part of others, and that, in general, successfully mediate conflicts among dominant political groups and their supporters. We would look as well to generalized beliefs (in the potential for individual upward mobility, racism, and anticommunism, for example) that contribute to support for the status quo. These factors have been discussed extensively elsewhere.

The American political system, however, even in "normal" times, pulses with discontent. Indeed, the high degree of conflict among well-represented interests has led some observers to conclude that the United States has been politically successful because the conflicts normally dealt with apparently have been resolved to the general support of most of the population. This analysis neglects consideration of the extent to which fundamental issues tend to be suppressed, and neglects the terms on which they are often resolved.

457

What happens when this discontent exceeds proportions that can be guided by forces normally resulting in consent or acquiescence, and in reasonably peaceful conflict regulation? The study of elite response to riots fills a critical gap by drawing attention to conflict regulation in crisis, hence, helping to explain the persistence of American political stability, and hence, the persistence of structural inequality.

This is not to say that virtually any crisis at all can be manipulated or made insignificant by elite action. The ghetto riots clearly reflected a profound but *sectoral* crisis. It juxtaposed the intensely felt claims of a significant minority and its supporters to the indifference or opposition of the majority. The sectoral nature of the crisis becomes particularly clear in recommendations aimed at developing equal employment opportunities, reversing the process of ghettoization, and achieving integrated education, which remain issues invoking passionate conflict. Although the black position in America suggests the most profound challenges to American democratic and pluralistic claims, the crisis of the riots clearly did not mass a majority of the population in support of a change in the status quo. Nor were the perhaps well-intended but unfocused efforts of some public officials and some riot commissions to develop sympathy for the black situation sufficient to overcome the institutional supports of American racial policies or mass public attitudes with which these policies resonate.

A political system incapable of perceiving and acknowledging political messages from a passionate minority deprives itself of those demands that, if not accorded legitimacy in the political process, inevitably find expression in other ways. The attitudes of black Americans, for example, have changed significantly in the early 1970s, tending to be much more supportive than before of militant political leaders and activities, and exhibiting heightened alienation from conventional political forms and institutions.[39] In practice, black politics has increasingly focused in the 1970s on gaining electoral office. This is a development profoundly welcomed by sophisticated supporters of the American political system, who recognize in it the potential for treating black demands in conventional institutional ways, and diverting or discrediting radical demands for dramatic changes in priorities and the distribution of power and income. White attitudes have also become increasingly polarized in recent years.[40] This is suggested by the attractiveness of "law and order" and "crime in the streets" as rallying symbols for white politicians, and the decline of white liberal support for civil rights groups and civil rights policies in general. There is every reason to think that the riots and the manner in which they were processed provided the catalyst for these developments.

These attitudinal changes are a legacy of the riots not entirely subject to control by political elites. Yet even here we may note that heightened political polarization and alienation, however potentially destabilizing in the long run, have had few immediate consequences for institutional and political change. On the surface the institutional status quo prevails, although the attitudinal base beneath the surface may be shifting and slipping considerably. Institutional forms remain resistant to change, despite repeated crises reflecting declining support for those same institutions.

The internal, structural contradiction in American race relations highlighted by this study is the unresolved tension between increased black expectations and demands and the institutional tendency to subvert perception of those demands and minimize responses to them. In every phase of the black protest movement since 1960 (and before), tactics used to compel the attention of the white majority have been condemned as dangerous and irresponsible, and inappropriate to a (pluralist) political system characterized by its beneficiaries as exhibiting openness and accessibility to all. In this sense the American political system itself contributes substantially to black separatist impulses, and to the general cynicism toward American institutions characteristic of many black and white Americans. The remaining question is whether, having reclaimed a degree of system stability, the United States will be able to accommodate black grievances following conventional political patterns, or whether the strains left unresolved by the processing of racial crisis will result in the generation of even more profound strains and future crises that may be more difficult to mediate.

NOTES, CHAPTER 11

1. To name only a few leading examples we mention: Richard E. Neustadt, *Presidential Power*, rev. ed. (New York: John Wiley, 1968); Richard F. Fenno, Jr., *The Power of the Purse: Appropriations Politics in Congress* (Boston: Little, Brown, 1966); Walter F. Murphy, *Elements of Judicial Strategy* (Chicago: University of Chicago Press, 1964); and Aaron Wildavsky, *The Politics of the Budgetary Process* (Boston: Little, Brown, 1964).

2. For examples see: Anthony Downs, *An Economic Theory of Democracy* (New York: Harper and Row, 1957); David B. Truman, *The Governmental Process* (New York: A. Knopf, 1951); and Robert A. Dahl, *Democracy in the United States: Promise and Performance*, second ed. (Chicago: Rand McNally, 1972).

3. For discussion of this general observation in the specific context of electoral politics see Walter Dean Burnham, "Theory and Voting Research," *American Political Science Review* 68 (September 1974): 1,002-1,023.

4. Witness, too, the appeals to a domestic Marshall Plan by Urban League Director Whitney Young and others as a way of evoking the image of successful mobilization in external affairs for relief at home. It may be instructive that in the absence of a perceived external threat, this appeal failed. For accounts of the impact Sputnik had on increasing federal aid to education and science through the enactment of the National Defense Education Act in 1958 see Lawrence J. R. Herson, "Government and Education," in *Functions and Policies of American Government*, second ed., J. W. Peltason and James M. Burns (Englewood Cliffs, N.J.: Prentice-Hall, 1962), p. 332; and Eugene Eidenberg and Roy D. Morey, *An Act of Congress* (New York: W. W. Norton, 1969), pp. 16-17.

5. Robert Dahl concludes that the expansion of welfare measures, government intervention in the economy, and the "steps toward the ultimate political, economic, and social liberation of blacks" represent, on the contrary, significant changes in domestic policy in this century. (Robert Dahl, *Democracy in the United States*, p. 295.) With the exception of the dismantling of the legal basis of segregation, however, these changes were observable only over a generation. We prefer a somewhat shorter time frame in assessing the incidence of rapid change in social policy. For an excellent discussion of the study of political change, and a critique of Dahl's lack of precision in determining the existence of change in an earlier study, see Kenneth M. Dolbeare, "Political Change in the United States," in *Power and Change in the United States*, ed. Kenneth M. Dolbeare (New York: John Wiley, 1969), ch. 7.

6. For a similar assessment of the magnitude of the crisis created by the 1960s riots see Robert Dahl, *Democracy in the United States*, p. 361.

7. Ibid. For explicit statements to this same effect by national officials see: Congressional Quarterly, "Special Report: Urban Problems and Civil Disorder," *Congressional Quarterly Weekly Report*, no. 36 (8 September 1967): 1,714, 1,751-55.

8. The comments that follow combine the threads of various

pluralist writers. An excellent bibliography on the subject may be found in *The Search for Community Power*, ed. Willis D. Hawley and Frederick M. Wirt (Englewood Cliffs, N.J.: Prentice-Hall, 1968), pp. 367-79.

9. See, for example, William H. Form and Joan Rytina, "Ideological Beliefs on the Distribution of Power in the United States," *American Sociological Review* 34 (1969): 19-31.

10. The following are only a few of the many recent attacks on the descriptive adequacy of the pluralist perspective: Peter Bachrach and Morton Baratz, "The Two Faces of Power," *American Political Science Review* 56 (December 1962): 947-52; Matthew A. Crenson, *The Un-Politics of Air Pollution* (Baltimore, Md.: Johns Hopkins, 1971); Richard F. Hamilton, *Class and Politics in the United States* (New York: John Wiley, 1972), pp. 34-46; Michael Lipsky, "Protest as a Political Resource," *American Political Science Review* 62 (December 1968): 1,144-58; Michael Parenti, "Power and Pluralism: A View from the Bottom," *Journal of Politics* 32 (1970): 501-530; Edward C. Hayes, *Power Structure and Urban Policy* (New York: McGraw-Hill, 1972).

11. For an explicit discussion of conflict resolution from a pluralist perspective see Robert Dahl, *Democracy in the United States*, ch. 21 and 23.

12. We make particular reference to: Allen D. Grimshaw, ed., *Racial Violence in the United States* (Chicago: Aldine, 1969); William A. Gamson, *Power and Discontent* (Homewood, Illinois: Dorsey, 1968); and W. A. Gamson, "Stable Unrepresentation in American Society," *American Behavioral Scientist* (Nov.-Dec. 1968): 15-21; Ira Katznelson, *Black Men, White Cities* (London: Oxford, 1973); Lewis Killian and Charles Grigg, *Racial Crisis in America* (Englewood Cliffs, N.J.: Prentice-Hall, 1965); and William J. Wilson, *Power, Racism, and Privilege* (New York: Macmillan, 1973).

13. Ralf Dahrendorf, *Class and Class Conflict in Industrial Society* (Stanford, Calif.: Stanford University Press, 1959), pp. 225 ff.

14. For an exception and a discussion of the application of conflict theory to societies characterized by racial or ethnic cleavages, see Katznelson, *Black Men, White Cities*.

15. For a discussion of the term *political* see ch. 1, n. 3, and accompanying text.

16. Terry Ann Knopf, "Media Myths on Violence," *Columbia Journalism Review* 9, no. 1 (Spring 1970): 18.

17. Ibid., pp. 17-18.

18. Jane A. Baskin, Joyce K. Hartweg, Ralph G. Lewis, and Lester W. McCullough, Jr., *Race Related Civil Disorders: 1967-69* (Waltham, Mass.: Brandeis University Press, 1971), p. 3.

19. U.S. Bureau of the Census, *Statistical Abstracts of the United States: 1972*, 93rd ed. (Washington, D.C.: U.S. Government Printing Office, 1972), p. 33.

20. "Racial Violence: New Trends Since King's Death," *Congressional Quarterly* (1970), p. 63.

21. Ibid., pp. 63-66. See *Brandeis University Gazette*, 10 February 1972, reporting on the publication of the Lemberg Center's study, "The Long, Hot Summer?" in *Justice* (February 1972).

22. Various factors make newspaper reports undependable guides to what actually happened. Low advertising lines can reduce the number of news pages, a key reporter may be assigned elsewhere on a day when a disturbance occurs, or news considered more important can crowd an event out of the papers. If there were a *constant* bias, newspapers might indicate yearly *trends* even though the actual numbers might be undercounts. Yet even this assumption cannot be made easily, since there is probably no subject matter in recent years about which one could make such an assumption with *less* validity than about reporting on black affairs generally and civil disorders specifically.

23. See Eugene Keller, "Politicizing Statistics," *Dissent* (Spring 1973), pp. 142-45; see also Philip M. Hauser, "Statistics and Politics," *American Statistician* 27, no. 2 (April 1973): 68-71.

24. In a quasi-experimental time-series study of crime in Washington, D.C., David Seidman and Michael Couzens show how the District of Columbia police underreported the value of stolen property so that it would not show up in reports of felonies. Their study concluded: "The political importance of crime has apparently caused pressures, subtle or otherwise, to be felt by those who record crime, pressures which have led to the downgrading of crimes." See David Seidman and Michael Couzens, "Crime, Crime Statistics, and the Great American Anti-Crime Crusade: Police Misreporting of Crime and Political Pressures" (paper presented at the Annual Meeting of the American Political Science Association, Washington, D.C., 1972).

25. See Murray Edelman, *Politics as Symbolic Action* (Chicago: Markham, 1971), pp. 109-113.

26. Foreign Broadcast Information Service Daily Report (F.B.I. S.D.R.), 12 March 1968, SS5, 25 March 1968, SS2; New York *Times*, 18 March 1968, p. 11. We are grateful to Richard Danner for collecting many of the data in these paragraphs.

27. New York *Times*, 16 December 1970, p. 7; F.B.I.S.D.R., 29 December 1970, G5.

28. New York *Times*, 7 April 1968. This is not to say that underlying causes remain unarticulated if the violence is longlasting. This surely was the case in the United States following the riots of

1967, as it was with the Scarman report on Northern Ireland. On the Northern Ireland case see Richard Rose, *Governing Without Consent* (Boston: Beacon, 1971).

29. Eric Hobsbawm and George Rude, *Captain Swing* (New York: Pantheon, 1963), pp. 215-16. Cited in Edelman, *Politics as Symbolic Action*, pp. 109-110. See also Claud Cockburn, "Troublemaking," in *The Incompatibles: Trade Union Militancy and the Consensus*, ed. Robin Blackburn and Alexander Cockburn (Middlesex, England: Penguin, 1967), pp. 113-30.

30. Appreciation of this is enhanced by Murray Edelman's discussion of the function of such myths in these circumstances. See Edelman, *Politics as Symbolic Action*, pp. 109-13.

31. On Portugal: New York *Times*, 2 February 1962, 22 April 1962, and 3 May 1962. On Greece: New York *Times*, 11-12 July 1966.

32. The scapegoating of "Communist Sympathizers," and more recently, "radical students," in the United States is perhaps well enough known so that additional commentary is not required.

33. See, for example, F.B.I.S.D.R. for 26-28 July 1967. An example of these attributions was provided in *Pravda* following the Newark riot in 1967:

> The fact that the U.S. Government has sent in the regular army for the armed suppression of its own country's citizens who are demanding their elementary rights has exposed with new cogency the misanthropic visage of racism, has shown once again the true complexion of America's "democracy."

(Translation from: "The Current Digest of the Soviet Press," 19, no. 30 [16 August 1967]: 6).

34. New York *Times*, 15 March 1968.

35. New York *Times*, 20 December 1970.

36. See Anthony Downs, "Up and Down with Ecology—The Issue-Attention Cycle," *The Public Interest*, no. 28 (Summer 1972), pp. 38-50.

37. For a full discussion of the premises underlying the assumption that leaders' actions may be conceived as implicit bargains see Sidney Waldman, *Foundations of Political Action: An Exchange Theory of Politics* (Boston: Little, Brown, 1972).

38. See Thomas R. Wolanin, "Presidential Advisory Commissions, 1945-1968" (Ph.D. dis., Department of Government, Harvard University, 1971); and Martha Derthick, "On Commissionship—Presidential Variety," *Public Policy* 19, no. 4 (Fall 1971): 623-38.

39. On the polarization of attitudes among racial groups see Joel D.

Aberbach and Jack L. Walker, *Race in the City* (Boston: Little, Brown, 1973); and Jack Citrin, Herbert McClosky, J. Merrill Shanks, and Paul M. Sniderman, "Personal and Political Sources of Political Alienation" (paper delivered at the 1973 American Political Science Association convention, New Orleans: 4-9 September 1973). For analysis of increasing alienation along racial lines see Arthur H. Miller, "Political Issues and Trust in Government: 1964-1970," *American Political Science Review* 68, no. 3 (September 1974): 951-72.

40. See Angus Campbell, *White Attitudes Toward Black People* (Ann Arbor, Mich.: Institute for Social Research, 1971).

Index

Index